THE ROUTLEDGE HANDBOOK OF FRENCH POLITICS AND CULTURE

The Routledge Handbook of French Politics and Culture provides a detailed survey of the highly differentiated field of research on French politics, society and culture across the social sciences and humanities.

The handbook includes contributions from the most eminent authors in their respective fields who bring their authority to bear on the task of outlining the current state-of-the art research in French Studies across disciplinary boundaries. As such, it represents an innovative as well as an authoritative survey of the field, representing an opportunity for a critical examination of the contrasts and the continuities in methodological and disciplinary orientations in a single volume.

The Routledge Handbook of French Politics and Culture will be essential reading and an authoritative reference for scholars, students, researchers and practitioners involved in, and actively concerned about, research on French politics, society and culture.

Marion Demossier is Professor of French and European Studies at the University of Southampton, UK, where she holds a Chair in Social Anthropology.

David Lees is Senior Teaching Fellow in French Studies at the University of Warwick, UK.

Aurélien Mondon is Senior Lecturer in Politics at the University of Bath, UK.

Nina Parish is Professor in French and Francophone Studies at the University of Stirling, UK.

ROUTLEDGE INTERNATIONAL HANDBOOKS

For more information about this series, please visit: www.routledge.com/Routledge-International-Handbooks/book-series/RIHAND

THE ROUTLEDGE HANDBOOK OF FRENCH POLITICS AND CULTURE

*Edited by Marion Demossier, David Lees,
Aurélien Mondon and Nina Parish*

Routledge
Taylor & Francis Group

LONDON AND NEW YORK

'Any scholar of modern and contemporary France must confront the question of whether the country is, or has ever been, exceptional in relation to the rest of the global North. This rich and diverse collection of essays on French politics and culture is a very welcome and timely update on that perennial question. It provides illuminating overviews and detailed case studies on themes such as the 2017 elections, official and counter-narratives of the banlieue and Jewish culture and popular music, written by many of the leading experts in French studies. It is essential reading for anyone wanting to understand French society today.'

Jan Windebank, University of Sheffield, UK

First published 2020 by Routledge

2 Park Square, Milton Park, Abingdon, Oxon OX14 4RN
605 Third Avenue, New York, NY 10017

Routledge is an imprint of the Taylor & Francis Group, an informa business

First issued in paperback 2021

Publisher's Note

The publisher has gone to great lengths to ensure the quality of this reprint but points out that some imperfections in the original copies may be apparent.

British Library Cataloguing in Publication Data
A catalogue record for this book is available from the British Library

Library of Congress Cataloging-in-Publication Data
A catalog record for this book has been requested

ISBN: 978-1-138-10175-3 (hbk)
ISBN: 978-1-03-217650-5 (pbk)
DOI: 10.4324/9781315656717

Typeset in Bembo
by Apex CoVantage, LLC

CONTENTS

TABLES

FIGURES

CONTRIBUTORS

Gill Allwood is Professor of Gender and Politics at Nottingham Trent University. She is the author of a number of books on gender and politics in France, including *French Feminisms: Gender and Violence in Contemporary Theory* (1998); *Women and Politics in France 1958–2000* (with Khursheed Wadia, 2000); *Gender and Policy in France* (also with Khursheed Wadia, 2009) and *Refugee Women in Britain and France* (also with Khursheed Wadia, 2010). Since 2011, Gill has been the editor of *Modern and Contemporary France*.

Marion Demossier is Professor of French and European Studies at the University of Southampton, where she holds a Chair in Social Anthropology. She has previously taught French and European politics and society at the University of Bath. She holds a PhD in Social Anthropology from the EHESS in Paris. She has published more than 20 scholarly articles in leading academic journals in Britain, France and the United States. She has recently completed her third monograph on the anthropology of wine and terroir: *Burgundy, a Global Anthropology of Place and Taste* (Berghahn 2018).

Benoît Dillet is Teaching Fellow in French Studies at the University of Bath. He is currently writing a monograph entitled *The Right to Problems* and has previously published work on contemporary arts and politics, including *The Political Space of Art: The Dardenne Brothers, Arundhati Roy, Ai Weiwei and Burial* (2016) and has co-edited two books, *The Edinburgh Companion to Poststructuralism* (2013) and *Technologiques: La Pharmacie de Bernard Stiegler* (2013).

Jocelyn Evans is Professor of Politics at the University of Leeds. He has published widely on voting behaviour, particularly in France and other European countries, and on parties of the radical right, and has written over 50 articles on various aspects of electoral behaviour. He is the co-author, with Gilles Ivaldi, of books on the 2012 and 2017 French presidential elections.

Abdellali Hajjat is Assistant Professor of Political Science at the Université de Paris-Ouest Nanterre. He has published on questions of race and citizenship in French law, urban uprisings and political mobilisation by postcolonial immigrants in France. Recent publications include *The Boundaries of "National Identity": The Injunction to Assimilate in Metropolitan and Colonial France*

(2012), *The March for Equality and against Racism* (2013) and the co-edited *Political History of Postcolonial Immigration, France 1920–2005* (2008).

Christina Horvath is a specialist in contemporary French literature and in particular of the urban novel genre. Senior Lecturer at the University of Bath, she lectures broadly on French society and culture, as well as on contemporary French and Francophone writing. Author of the monograph *Le roman urbain: un genre de la surmodernité*, organiser of a series of conferences and workshops on the banlieue and the postcolonial city and co-founder of 'Banlieue Network,' she is currently working on a book addressing contemporary literary representations of the French banlieue.

Rebecca Infield is a PhD candidate in French Studies at the University of Warwick. Her PhD research focuses on theatre censorship during the time of decolonisation in both France and Britain. Rebecca is drawing on archival materials to examine how censors and audiences reacted to the theme of decolonisation when it was depicted in theatres during the 1950s and 1960s. Rebecca has previously worked as a *lectrice* at the Université de Poitiers.

Shirley Jordan is Professor of French Studies at Newcastle University. Shirley's research interests include twentieth- and twenty-first-century French and Francophone literature and visual culture, especially new women's writing in French, feminisms, life writing and photography. Shirley is the author of books on the art criticism of Francis Ponge, on new women's writing in French and on the work of Goncourt-prize-winning author Marie NDiaye (2017).

Raymond Kuhn is Emeritus Professor of Politics at Queen Mary University of London. He has published several prominent works on the media and political communication in France and in the UK, including *The Media in France* (1995), *The Media in Contemporary France* (2011) and *Politics and the Media in Britain* (2007 and 2011). Raymond was previously the editor of *Modern and Contemporary France* between 2004 and 2006.

David Lees is Senior Teaching Fellow in French Studies at the University of Warwick, where he teaches and researches political campaigns, communications and propaganda in modern and contemporary France. He is the co-editor, with Lindsey Dodd, of *Everyday Life in Vichy France: Confronting the Challenges of Wartime, 1939–1945* (2018) and has also published work on the centre and far right in France. David is working with Brian Sudlow on an edited collection around 'teaching and learning the Occupation of France' and with Chris Reynolds towards a new edition of the textbook *Contemporary France*.

Benjamin Leruth is an Assistant Professor in Public Administration at the Institute for Governance and Policy Analysis, University of Canberra, specialising in comparative European politics and public policy. Prior to joining the Institute for Governance & Policy Analysis, he worked as a Research Associate at the University of Kent and as a Teaching Fellow in French and European Politics at the University of Bath. He also held a visiting fellowship at the ARENA Centre for European Studies (University of Oslo). He holds a PhD in Politics from the University of Edinburgh, an LLM in European Law from the University of Kent and a BA in Political Science from the University of Namur. He is the co-author and co-editor of various books, such as *Differentiated Integration in the European Union* (Routledge, 2015), *Euroscepticism as a Transnational and pan-European Phenomenon* (Routledge, 2017), *After Austerity* (2017) and *The Routledge Handbook of Euroscepticism* (Routledge, 2018).

Mehammed Mack is Associate Professor of French Studies at Smith College, USA. Mehammed's research focuses on contemporary immigration to France, gender and sexuality, diversity in the banlieues, and the relation between culture and politics. His larger teaching and research interests include Franco-Arab cultures, travel literature, the development of French Islam and media studies. Recent publications include *Sexagon: Muslims, France and the Sexualisation of National Culture* (2017).

Margaret A. Majumdar is Emeritus Professor of Francophone Studies at the University of Portsmouth. Margaret has published extensively on French political philosophy, including the work of Louis Althusser and Jean-Paul Sartre, and the wider French-speaking world in the postcolonial context, with a particular emphasis on Franco-Maghrebian relations. She is presently working on a critical examination of the concept of progress in its various philosophical, political, economic and cultural facets, including the uses and abuses to which it is subjected in the current economic and political context.

Tom Martin is Associate Lecturer in French at Lancaster University. He has published on anti-racist movements in France, including the work of SOS Racisme, and on left-wing populism. Tom is a regular book reviewer for *Modern and Contemporary France* and has also worked on questions of national identity.

Marwan Mohammed is a Sociologist and Director of Research at the CNRS, Paris. He also works at the Centre Maurice Halbwachs and the École Normale Supérieure. His research focuses on, amongst other themes, the working-class youth; non-conventional forms of politicisation and the usage of ethnicities. He has published widely on Islamophobia in France. Recent publications include, with Abdellali Hajjat, *Islamophobie: comment les élites françaises fabriquent le problème musulman* (2013) and with Julien Talpin, *Communautarisme* (2018).

Aurélien Mondon is a Senior Lecturer in politics at the University of Bath. His research focuses predominantly on the impact of racism and populism on liberal democracies and the mainstreaming of far right politics through elite discourse. His first book, *The Mainstreaming of the Extreme Right in France and Australia: A Populist Hegemony?*, was published in 2013 and he recently co-edited *After Charlie Hebdo: Terror, Racism and Free Speech* published with Zed. His forthcoming book *Populism and Reactionary Democracy: How Racism and the Far Right Became Mainstream*, co-written with Aaron Winter, will be published with Verso in early 2020.

Anne Muxel is Director of Research in Political Sciences at the CEVIPOF institute (CNRS/Sciences Po). Her work can be broken down into three principal fields: the socialisation of politics amongst the youth; electoral participation and analysis of voting patterns and the study of the politicisation of individuals, especially in terms of private exchanges. Anne has also published on aspects of individual and collective memories. Her recent work includes *Politics in Private. Love and Convictions in the French Political Consciousness* (2014).

Nina Parish is a Professor in French and Francophone Studies in Literature and Languages at the University of Stirling. She works on representations of the migrant experience, difficult history and multilingualism within the museum space. She was part of the EU-funded Horizon 2020 UNREST team working on innovative memory practices in sites of trauma including war museums and mass graves (www.unrest.eu). She is also an expert on the interaction between text and image in the field of modern and contemporary French Studies. She has published widely on this subject, in particular, on the poet and visual artist, Henri Michaux.

Philippe Poirrier is Professor of Contemporary History at the Université de Bourgogne and Vice-President of the History Committee of the French Ministry of Culture and Communication. His work focuses in particular on the history of cultural policies in twentieth-century Europe. Recent publications include *Les Politiques Culturelles en France* (2002) and he has edited *Quelle politique pour la culture? Florilège des débats (1955–2014)* (2014).

Nicolas Renahy is Director of Research in the Department of Social Sciences in INRA (the National Institute of Agronomic Research). Nicolas is a member of the editorial committee of the journal *Politix* and has published widely on a wide variety of issues including working-class involvement in rural spaces and the history of social sciences. Recent publications include *Les Gars du Coin* (2010) and the co-authored *Sociologie des classes populaires contemporaines* (2015).

Chris Reynolds is Associate Professor in French and European Studies at Nottingham Trent University where he is French subject leader. He is the author of two monographs, *Memories of May 68. France's Convenient Consensus* (2011) and *Sous les pavés . . . The Troubles in Northern Ireland, France and the European Collective Memory of 1968* (2014), and has authored numerous articles and chapters on the events of 1968 in France and Europe. Chris is also reviews editor for the journal *Modern and Contemporary France*.

Eleanor Rowley is a doctoral candidate at the Department of Politics, Languages and International Studies at the University of Bath, where she is exploring the visitor experience at First World War museums. She is interested in heritage education practices, and the ways in which young people interpret cultural memory messages during school field trips to museums and heritage sites. She also contributed to empirical work on museums and memory to the Horizon 2020-funded project 'Unsettling Remembering and Social Cohesion in Transnational Europe (UNREST).'

Chris Tinker is Professor of French in the Department of Languages and Intercultural Studies (LINCS) at Heriot-Watt University, Edinburgh. His research interests are in Media and Popular Music in France and Britain (1960s–), particularly issues relating to gender, generation/ageing, nostalgia and charity. He is author of *Georges Brassens and Jacques Brel: Personal and Social Narratives in Post-war Chanson* (2005) and *Mixed Messages: Youth Magazine Discourse and Sociocultural Shifts in Salut les copains (1962–1976)* (2010), and has co-edited special issues of *Modern and Contemporary France* on Representing Paris (with Alison Fell, 2000), on Youth Cultures in the Fifth Republic (with Wendy Michallat, 2007) and on Media, Memory and Nostalgia (with Hugh Dauncey, 2015).

Fabien Truong is a sociologist and lecturer at the University of Paris 8. His research focuses on urban marginalisation, youth, education, social mobility, juvenile delinquency and religiosity. He has published *Des capuches et des hommes. Trajectoires de 'jeunes de banlieue'* (Paris: Buchet-Chastel, 2013), for which he received the Ecrit Social prize in 2014, *Jeunesses françaises. Bac +5 made in banlieue* (La Découverte, Paris 2015) and *Radicalized Loyalties. Becoming Muslim in the West* (Polity Press, 2018). He co-edits the 'L'envers des faits' series at La Découverte and has co-directed with Mathieu Vadepied the documentary film *Les défricheurs* (2019).

Rebekah Vince is Teaching Fellow in French Studies at the University of Durham, having previously taught at the University of Warwick, where she completed her PhD in 2018. Rebekah's doctoral research explored Francophone North African texts which deal with the Israeli–Palestinian conflict, underpinned by the traumatic legacies of genocide and colonialism. Rebekah has previously been a visiting scholar at the University of Ghent (Belgium) as part of the Cultural Memory Studies Initiative, directed by Stef Craps. Rebekah sits on the Advisory Board of the Memory Studies Association and the Executive Committee of the Society for Francophone Postcolonial Studies.

ACKNOWLEDGEMENTS

The editing process of this handbook has been both pleasurable and arduous. The 2017 presidential and legislative elections led to many changes in the political and cultural landscape in France, as we note in the introduction, and this led to many chapters requiring rewriting to reflect these changes. We could not have completed this book without the generous help of our contributors, who have graciously and patiently updated their chapters over the past few years. We are immensely grateful for their time and dedication. They are too many to thank by name here, but we hope that they are happy with the final version of this book. We are indebted to the team at Routledge, Andrew Taylor and Sophie Iddamalgoda, for their patience and for bearing with us during the editing process. We thank them for their support. We also extend our warm thanks to the translators of some of the chapters from the French, Steven Wonnacott, Katy Brown and Georgia Corps.

We are very grateful to the two anonymous readers who provided feedback on our proposal and on the outline of the handbook. We also thank colleagues in the French Studies communities in the UK, US and Australia for their encouragement and support.

Finally, we dedicate this book to our friends and family. We thank them for their love, friendship and kindness.

The Editors, April 2019

ABBREVIATIONS

ACCT	Agence de coopération culturelle et technique
ANRU	Agence Nationale pour la Rénovation Urbaine
CFDT	Conféderation française démocratique du travail
CGT	Conféderation Générale du Travail
CSA	Conseil Supérieur de l'Audiovisuel
EM	En Marche!
FAC	Fonds d'Aide à la Coopération
FN	Front National
FNSEA	Fédération nationale des syndicats d'exploitants agricoles
LFI	La France Insoumise
LO	Lutte Ouvrière
LR	Les Républicains
LREM	La République en Marche!
MIR	Mouvement des Indigènes de la République
MNA	Mouvement National Républicain
MODEM	Mouvement Démocrate
MRG	Mouvement Radical de Gauche
NPA	Nouveau Parti Anticapitaliste
OIF	Organisation Internationale de la Francophonie
ORTF	Office de Radiodiffusion Télévision Française
PACS	Pacte civil de solidarité
PCF	Parti Communiste Français
PS	Parti Socialiste
QP	Quartiers Prioritaires
RPF	Rassemblement du Peuple Français
RN	Rassemblement National
SFIO	Section Française de l'Internationale Ouvrière
SGI	Secrétariat Général à l'Information
SPCJ	Service de Protection de la Communauté Juive
UDI	Union des Démocrates et des Indépendants
UDF	Union pour la Démocratie Française

UMP	Union pour une Majorité Présidentielle (2002)/Union pour un Mouvement Populaire (2002–2014)
UNR	Union pour la Nouvelle République
UPR	Union Républicain Populaire
ZUS	Zones Urbaines Sensibles

GLOSSARY OF KEY TERMS

Cohabitation   The power-sharing between the executive and legislative branches of government which took place most notably during the presidency of François Mitterrand (1981–1995) and the first term of that of Jacques Chirac (1995–2002).

Quinquennat   The five-year term of presidential and legislative branches of government in France.

Septennat   The seven-year term of the presidential branch of government in France, in force between 1958 and 2002.

INTRODUCTION

French politics and culture in the Macron era

Marion Demossier, David Lees, Aurélien Mondon
and Nina Parish

France has often been labelled as exceptional. In many ways, the contemporary French political and cultural landscape remains exceptional. The era of president Emmanuel Macron has, to date, witnessed a swathe of political innovations, not least the development of a brand-new political party, while a mass protest movement has brought the country to a standstill in late 2018 and early 2019. As the manuscript of this book is submitted, the *gilets jaunes* – yellow vests – movement continues to mobilise, most notably in the Paris region, against the perceived aloofness of the incumbent president.

When this book was first envisaged, in 2015, Macron was a comparatively little-known minister of economics to then-president François Hollande and it appeared very likely that one of the major parties on either the centre left or centre right would yield Hollande's successor. Yet Macron positioned himself as an outsider to sweep to victory in the 2017 French presidential elections, forming in the process a movement which became a brand-new political party, La République En Marche! (LREM), which in turn secured a huge majority in the French National Assembly. Only in France, one might well argue, would a rank outsider, with no backing from any pre-existing political party, take executive office in such a convincing way. Only in France, one might add, would a mass movement – sometimes violent, sometimes peaceful – coalesce around opposition to increases in fuel duty and signal support through the donning of the yellow fluorescent jackets compulsory for all occupants of vehicles in France, before shifting to an all-encompassing protest movement. Even the way that the French have responded to the *gilets jaunes* protest, including through the formation of local citizens' assemblies, in an echo of the aftermath of the Great Revolution of 1789, is palpably French.

In many ways, this book is focused precisely on the question of the particularities of French politics and culture when compared with those of other contemporary developed countries. Many of the chapters in this book demonstrate the continuity of this French exceptionalism, while others argue that France is in many ways simply reflecting global and European phenomena. Indeed for all of its history of revolt and rebellion, and the open wounds of the *gilets jaunes*, the French political system has stood firm under Macron. When compared to ongoing events in the United Kingdom around Brexit, France perhaps appears more stable, and therefore less exceptional, than has been the tradition, and arguably has become the bedrock of European centrism.

1

We have sought to explore how politics and culture function at a variety of levels in contemporary France, from rural affairs through to Islamophobia, and from the mass media through to museum policy. Nonetheless, while the chapters in this book capture many facets of French cultural and political life, managing to stay abreast of a frequently changing, fast-shifting cultural and political landscape since the presidential and legislative elections of 2017 has been a near-impossible feat. As editors, we have long tried the patience of our publishers in seeking to provide as well-updated a version of events as possible, but in the end, we have drawn the line in spring 2019. No doubt the pace of change will continue to overtake some of what is written in these pages: as both the Macron phenomenon and the *gilets jaunes*, which few predicted, attest. We acknowledge that there are some areas of French politics and culture which are absent from this book but wherever possible we have sought to offer a range of perspectives on some, but by no means all, aspects of modern French politics and culture. Many of the chapters were first written in 2015, long before the rise of Macron. Some have required relatively little change since their first inception; others have required rewriting to attempt to reflect some of the exceptional developments of the last two years, not least the development of the LREM party and the demise of the centre left Parti Socialiste (Socialist Party) and to a lesser extent the diminution of the centre right party, Les Républicains. There is indeed virtually no aspect of contemporary France that has not been in some way affected by Macron's presidency, from foreign affairs to political communications and the handling – and arguably control – of the media. Likewise, Macron has overseen some major commemorations and events, not least the centenary of the Armistice of the Great War in November 2018, which in turn had repercussions for cultural and museum policy.

This book is a timely snapshot into France in 2019. At this stage, two years into the Macron presidency, it is possible to discern some of the tendencies of the current administration, which reflects the combination of exceptionalism and 'normalisation,' continuity and change, that has dominated French politics and culture in the twentieth and early twenty-first centuries. In its exploration of these tensions, the book addresses the French political and cultural landscape across four major sections. The first sets out the functioning of the contemporary French political system; the second explores the question of 'identification and belonging' – what is it to be French and how France has dealt with questions of immigration, integration, racism and anti-racism; the third examines spaces of political and cultural contestation, not least the role of 'la rue,' the street, in shaping the French political and cultural landscape; while the fourth section looks at issues around mediating memories and cultures. Many of the chapters in the book take a multidisciplinary perspective. While each chapter seeks to examine a specific aspect of modern and contemporary France, their authors draw on a variety of disciplines, from sociological approaches through to queer theory and cultural policy. The book brings together scholars from a range of career stages and across international borders, from institutions in the UK, France, the US and Australia. In the same way, while much of the focus in the book is firmly on metropolitan France, there is coverage of French relations with the rest of the world and on France in the international and European arenas. The book therefore combines a variety of approaches and disciplines to examine both modern and contemporary French politics *and* French culture.

Part I Politics in modern and contemporary France

The book begins with an examination of the contemporary political system in France in the first substantive section. Aurélien Mondon examines the case studies of the 2017 presidential and legislative elections and explores the question of the future of the Republic following the election of Macron and the victory of his LREM party. Mondon argues that the failings of the presidential system in France were laid bare by the composition of the two candidates in the second round of the presidential elections. For Mondon, neither Emmanuel Macron nor Marine Le Pen really possessed the support of the majority of the French electorate; rather, both candidates reached this stage of the electoral process through the failure of other candidates, especially on the centre right and centre left, and because of tactical voting by part of the electorate. Mondon argues that Marine Le Pen's electoral performance was expected, given the mainstream media's discourse around her attempts to cleanse the image of the Front National, and that Le Pen could have fared much worse had she faced either the centre right François Fillon or the far left Jean-Luc Mélenchon in the second round. As Mondon notes, the over-personalisation of the French presidential system meant that the legislative elections were met with little enthusiasm from the electorate, while Macron skilfully navigated the legislative system to ensure a significant majority in the National Assembly. Mondon's chapter is followed by an exploration of the party political system in France by Jocelyn Evans, who examines the threat to the *bipartiste* – two-party – system posed by Macron's new political party. Having seen French politics dominated by the traditional parties of the centre left and centre right, with intermittent inroads by parties of the extremes – variously the Front National (now the Rassemblement National) on the far right and the Parti Communiste Français (PCF), the Nouveau Parti Anticaptaliste (NPA) and La France Insoumise (LFI) on the far left – the rise of the LREM is, according to Evans, the greatest-ever disturbance to the traditional party structures of the current Fifth Republic. Evans notes that political parties have historically played second fiddle to the heavily personalised presidential system, largely because of de Gaulle's inherent mistrust in political parties, and argues that all parties have come under increasing strain because of financial and other commitments, which in turn has led to financial irregularities and political turmoil for some of the more established parties. Into this context came LREM: the first major centrist party of the Fifth Republic. While Evans argues that the long-term impact of LREM is uncertain, Macron's movement has injected fresh impetus into the party political system in France. Benajmin Leruth then examines the history of Gaullism in modern France, from de Gaulle to the present day. Margaret A. Majumdar follows this exploration of domestic French politics with an examination of recent developments in French foreign policy towards Africa. Majumdar argues succinctly that, for all the narrative around the 'outsider' status of Macron, current policy would suggest a continuity of the (largely Gaullist) status quo in foreign affairs, not least through the ongoing importance attributed to the concept of *la Francophonie*. Majumdar traces the development of French policy towards Africa through the process of decolonisation, including the bloody war of Independence in Algeria (1954–1962), then the Gaullist presidency, through to the present day. Despite recent rhetoric by François Hollande aimed at quashing the continuity of *Françafrique* – the process in which France developed a paternalistic view of its former colonies and sought to exploit natural resources for economic and political gain – some parts of this policy appear destined to continue under Macron, who has nonetheless sought to develop better relations with Algeria, including during his comments before and after his election around crimes against humanity committed by French forces against Algerians. Finally, Gill Allwood provides a lucid analysis of the role of gender in contemporary French politics, beginning by tracing the development of women's voting patterns and participation in the political process since 1945 – the first legislative elections where women were able to vote and to stand as candidates – and arguing that the female electorate is clearly not homogenous. Most recently this has been evidenced by a greater proportion of women voting for Marine Le Pen as leader of the now Rassemblement National, shifting from a historic reluctance to vote for the far right by female voters. Allwood then analyses the role played by the *parité* reforms in recent French history aimed at numerical equality between men and women, arguing that these reforms have had relatively modest success on a national level. While there may have been a record number of women entering the National Assembly in 2017, Allwood argues that the percentage of deputies who are female remains below the 50% minimum required by law, and women are still being selected for seats which are harder to win. Moreover, the women who are elected to representative positions at various levels of government in France, from the local through to the national, tend to come from the same sociocultural elite as their male colleagues. As Allwood concludes, the way in which the state deems religious faith and ethnicity to be irrelevant to the role of the political representative has hindered efforts to ensure the political sphere is truly reflective of society as a whole.

Part II Identification and belonging

The second part explores in more depth a number of key contemporary social issues in France, and particularly tensions with certain groups and communities created by unfulfilled promises of the French Republic, but also by its mythologising. French universalist ideals, under the devise of *Liberté, Egalité, Fraternité* have become part and parcel of the political hegemony in France. This has been so entrenched that to this day it remains illegal to collect data on ethnic and religious background amongst other characteristics: being French is all one needs to be. More recently, François Hollande proposed to remove the word 'race' from the constitution (BFMTV 2012). This was eventually signed off by Emmanuel Macron in 2018 (Les Échos 2018). Yet French supposed universalism and the proclaimed ignorance of race through the simple removal of the word is very much based in the denial of the country's colonial past and its systemically discriminatory present. The five chapters in Part II provide readers with an overview of key issues which demonstrate that France still has a long way to go to fulfil its universal ideals, and often demonstrate that these can in fact often be counterproductive, as their naturalisation makes it almost impossible to contest the current unequal state of things.

In his chapter, Abdellali Hajjat provides an in-depth overview of the politics of migration in France and its impact on various communities as the French state failed to live up to its ideals and responsibility and instead has often used migrant communities as scapegoats in times of crisis. In recent years, Hajjat argues powerfully that the process of integration 'has become an injunction to conform to majority norms, a way to produce racial difference against Muslims and to question their fundamental human rights as the right to education and the right to work.' These shortcomings are further developed in Marwan Mohammed's chapter on Islamophobia where he traces the history of the concept and its development in French politics. Mohammed deconstructs the process of racialisation suffered by Muslim communities or those seen as such, and laments the current state of play in France and the internalisation of an 'incapacity to envisage a shared future and a common imagination that include the Muslim population of France.' Racialisation is also at the core of Marion Demossier's chapter which focuses on the Roma and provides another insight in the way the French state has constructed 'others' through its public discourse and policies. Demossier argues that a complex and multilevel process of re-nationalisation and securitisation has taken place, which has led to a rise in racist discourse and hate crimes against groups which are defined as non-territorial. Just as Muslims in Mohammed's chapter, the Roma here encapsulate this new politics of racialisation and the double standards commonly applied and entrenched in the land of *Liberté, Egalité, Fraternité*. With Anne Muxel's chapter, we turn to another often-overlooked community in French politics: young people. In her chapter, Muxel develops a detailed picture of young people's relationship with politics in France today. While abstention remains predominant in this category of the population and continues to grow, Muxel highlights that, as in other European countries, young people are not depoliticised but rather they prioritise other forms of political engagement: 'the politicisation of young people today is less normative, more expressive and freer from institutional and organisational norms.' Finally, Tom Martin's chapter provides us with an analysis of the responses to entrenched discriminations and racism. In particular, he explores the ways in which the anti-racism struggle has evolved, adapted, succeeded and failed through two case studies: the mainstream SOS Racisme and the radical, postcolonial Mouvement des Indigènes de la République. While Martin's chapter provides leads to combat racism, it also demonstrates, as do the other chapters, that France and its universalist ideals enshrined uncritically in its national myth by all politicians not only do not live up to scrutiny but may be an impediment to a real assessment of its shortcomings and way to address deep issues of inequality and exclusion.

Part III Spaces of political and cultural contestation

The third part includes discussion of both symbolic and physical spaces in contemporary France. Some of these spaces are notoriously French in their composition and use 'la rue,' whereas others have been marginalised and stigmatised (the 'banlieue'), neglected (rural areas) or quite simply not considered worthy of discussion and therefore ignored (the young, the elderly). The analysis of these spaces contributes to a richer and deeper understanding of what it means to be French today and what it means to live in France today and reveals much more difference and diversity than any traditional universalist Republican discourse would have us believe. These spaces allow us to reconsider many of the myths constructed around French identity and encourage us to make space for representations and realities which have hitherto not made it into official discourse, cultural representations or external perspectives on France. This section also includes examination of cases where these spaces are becoming more limited because of increasingly conservative attitudes to, for example, gender equality and how outlets for these ideas can be found in the cultural sphere.

The section opens, perhaps unsurprisingly, with a consideration of how la rue is perceived and commonly used by the French as a space where they can express their dissatisfaction. It is a commonplace that the French will not hesitate to take to the streets to protest; the current *gilets jaunes* movement is yet another manifestation of this use of space, marked in particular by their choice to divert from traditional well-trodden protest routes in Paris. Chris Reynolds' chapter examines the importance of the phenomenon of la rue in France by studying a number of recent protests and highlighting their Frenchness in relation to particular structural considerations as well as the weight of history and memory-making processes.

This use of la rue to protest generally takes places in the centre of cities, the traditional locus of much symbolic and cultural capital. The next three chapters in this section take us to the peripheries of these cities, the 'banlieue,' made notorious in the French imaginary space and elsewhere through Matthieu Kassovitz's cult film, *La Haine*, amongst others. In Chapter 12, Christina Horvath deconstructs the banlieue myth through an evaluation of official representations of the banlieues and counter-narratives. She demonstrates how, since the 1980s, the banlieues have been turned into France's major social problem by biased political and media representations and urban policies promoting a territorial approach to ethnic and socio-economic inequalities. She focuses on the rise of the banlieue myth and examines the suburbs' progressive decline in public imagery. She looks at the major public debates which have been shaping the banlieues' image in recent years and she explores how a range of counter-narratives have been developed by residents and artists in response to the myth of the ghetto. Her analysis of these different components of the banlieue present a much more diverse space socially, demographically, architecturally and culturally than homogenous official representations allow.

Fabien Truong's consideration of 'banlieue youth' in Chapter 13 continues this exploration of marginalised and stigmatised spaces and identities. The findings from his ethnographic fieldwork make us reconsider stereotypical images of banlieue youth and encourage attitudes towards young people growing up in these areas which include nuance and ambivalence. Moving away from conventional academic frames of belonging and roots, Truong is interested in how teenagers from the working-class banlieue make their way in the world and find their place, moving through space and time. In Chapter 14, Mehammed Mack reveals another complexity of banlieue spaces and identities by introducing the study of rhetoric about fashion and beauty. He argues that certain activists, whose mission it is to advocate for sexual and ethnic minorities in France's multi-ethnic suburbs, such as Malek Boutih, stigmatise locals' efforts to conceive of their own beauty and self-worth, because it would resemble communitarian pride too closely. Using a discourse analysis and cultural studies approach, he examines what appears to be harmless rhetoric about fashion and beauty to come to worrying conclusions about the perceived lack of worth of banlieue and Arab life trajectories. In broader terms, Mack's contribution indicates a pattern by which anti-discrimination activists who aim to combat social alienation and segregation in the banlieue actually do just the opposite, through a complex process of othering with regard to fashion, style and self-worth.

Another peripheral area of France, in relation to the time and space afforded it, is its countryside. This is surprising when we consider just how much of France is made up of rural areas, but less so when we realise that the vast majority of French people live in towns and cities and their suburbs. Nicolas Renahy's research on rural areas contributes to a revived interest in rural studies and examines the political and cultural situation of these spaces, in particular in relation to education and access to leisure and cultural activities. This chapter shows how social, political and cultural interactions have been transformed in these spaces. Recent generations growing up, living in and also moving to these areas have had to face starkly different realities and challenges to previous generations. One of these challenges is an ageing population, and the gendered realities of this experience is one facet explored in the final chapter in this section by Shirley Jordan on women's experimental writing in French at the beginning of the twenty-first century. The others are mothering, sexual violence and eating disorders, and Jordan demonstrates how these embodied experiences are finding new expression in women's writing; a necessary innovation, as the space for them in the public sphere, rather than growing, is becoming increasingly limited. Jordan, therefore, examines gender through the lens of crisis and a growing conservatism with regard to women's role and 'place' in society and equality more broadly in France.

Part IV Mediating memories and cultures

In this final part, contributors have chosen to focus on specific windows which illustrate the increasing mediation of memories and cultures in France as well as their fragmentation over the last three decades. Discussing a broad range of themes, including museums, cultural policy, intellectuals, the media, Jewish culture and popular music, our authors demonstrate how their respective fields have become highly politicised and global, while retaining a distinct French flavour. They also illustrate the difficult challenge faced by the French state and its citizens as the traditional certainties provided by Jacobin centralism and republicanism begin to crumble. The contemporary public sphere is increasingly characterised by complex processes of mediation between different agenda, groups and individuals and the growing presence of new communication tools and technologies. As a result, the mediation of memories and cultures has transformed France, leaving the nation grappling with its past, present and future.

In Chapter 17, entitled 'Remembering the First World War in France: The Historical de la Grand Guerre and Thiepval Museum,' Nina Parish and Eleanor Rowley remind us of how central to the field of memory studies the First World War remains. The generation who experienced 1914–1918 has passed away and yet its remembering constitutes a collective historical lesson to be preserved and transmitted. The centenary of the First World War constitutes a key point in the memory of the conflict as biological and family links to the event begin to fade. Large sums of public funds have been pledged by the French and the British governments to a range of commemorative events, underlining the political capital they hope to recoup. Flows of tourists from both sides of the Channel visit these sites religiously during a stopover when rushing to their holiday destinations. The present moment of First World War commemoration enables critical examination of heritage practices, where popular and formal as well as national and transnational conceptions of the past encounter each other. Both the *Historial de la Grande Guerre* and the Thiepval Museum offer different platforms to articulate the past, present and future for a range of institutional and social actors. They also face challenges as new forms of tourism emerge in the twenty-first century.

The twentieth century saw French participation in two world wars; occupation by, and collaboration with, Nazi Germany; a bloody war of decolonisation in Algeria; and the events of May 1968. While the French appear to have a predilection for engagement in political violence, France also has a strong history of engaging in cultural warfare through propaganda. In his chapter, aptly titled 'Waging the War of Words: Propaganda and the Mass Media in Modern France, 1939–2017,' David Lees scrutinises the role of propaganda in modern France. Poorly equipped and under-experienced in the art of propaganda before World War I, the French state has since gained a deserved reputation for monitoring and directing the content of the media. In short, Lees provides a thorough overview of the way in which propaganda has been utilised by the French authorities to support their own war efforts, whether waged against an external or internal enemy. Arguing for continuity in terms of how the French state exercises control over its mass media, Lees points out the non-state power, and especially the role of the far left, in bypassing state regulations.

Yet if wars constitute a point of remembrance and serve as a point of connection to the past, present and future through imagined and fictional narratives, France has traditionally relied on culture and cultural policies to ensure political stability. Philippe Poirrier, in Chapter 19 'Cultural Policy: A Weakened Exception? (1959–2016),' reviews the failed attempts to bridge the gaps between state development and social well-being. The last two decades have seen some significant trends develop, affecting all public cultural policies: the professionalisation of those involved in the worlds of art and culture, the modernisation of management and the autonomy of cultural establishments, the partnership and contract agreements between the state and local authorities, and the use of private sponsorship. In a context marked both by globalisation and the growing territorialisation of state policies, the French public has felt increasingly disillusioned by the attempt to democratise culture and education.

One example of the particular configuration of this gap and its expression through the prism of nostalgia is illustrated by the field of popular music discussed by Chris Tinker. Tinker argues that recent press and television coverage of the 1980s RTL Party 80 nostalgia tour, cinematic representations in the spin-off 2012 film *Stars 80* and associated press reviews identify nostalgia as an intense, emotional, joyous and festive experience. In his view, the combination of 'simple' and more 'reflexive' forms of popular music offer an escape from the current financial crisis and provide an attempt to reconnect with one's youth. Moreover nostalgia works as a force for social and generational cohesion. A good example was recently provided by the death of Johnny Hallyday, who came to embody *Les Trente Glorieuses*, the 30-year post-war boom, remembered fondly by French baby boomers. Yet beyond joy, social cohesion and happiness, nostalgia acted as a brake on social change threatening to impede French economic development.

Johnny Hallyday was the personification of a celebrity culture that has gone hand in hand with the changes affecting the political sphere. The mediatisation and personalisation of presidential elections reflects many of the challenges identified when studying public opinion. Raymond Kuhn, in Chapter 21, examines the media in contemporary France and its contribution to presidential election campaigns. He argues how certain key aspects of France's hybrid media system, in which 'old' and 'new' elements fulfil different but mutually complementary functions, helps to create a hybrid public sphere. Kuhn demonstrates how this hybrid media environment conditions the way in which presidential elections are now fought. During these campaigns the media are powerful political communication tools and audiences continue to filter messages, often unconsciously; they engage in a selective process of exposure, perception and retention, influenced by pre-existing partisan attitudes.

Benoît Dillet, in a chapter entitled 'The Multiple Deaths of the Intellectual in France,' argues that despite a tendency to think of French intellectuals as moral legislators, their contribution to public debate has been limited. Dillet proposes a new role based on that of the US model, namely, whistleblowers and thought-leaders. Whistleblowing is in its nascent state and it is less the persona (as whistleblower) than the practice (whistleblowing) that matters, hence the role of anonymous groups and identities. The practice of the whistleblowers establishing new relationships with journalists (especially with the International Consortium of Investigative Journalists [ICIJ]) is perhaps one of the most creative strategies that has taken place in developing a new public discourse and counter-power. The second form of intellectual power that has developed very recently is the rise of thought-leaders against public intellectuals.

In the final chapter, Rebekah Vince and Rebecca Infield discuss Jewish culture in twenty-first-century France. Their chapter situates France's diverse Jewish community, the largest in Europe, in relation to Holocaust memory, exile from North Africa, the Israeli–Palestinian conflict, anti-Semitism and cultural (co-)production. The chapter begins by historically contextualising contemporary anti-Semitism and goes onto explore recent cultural representations, including Jewish–Muslim artistic collaborations. Contemporary anti-Semitism in France is driven by three main motivations which sometimes overlap, namely, radical Islam, the Israeli-Palestinian conflict and old anti-Semitic stereotypes. Education and cultural production (particularly collaborative, that is, through Jewish–Muslim cooperation) are particularly important in combating the conflation between Jews and Zionists, and in expressing solidarity between Jews and Muslims, who are both victims of racism in France albeit in the differing forms of anti-Semitism and Islamophobia.

References

BFMTV. 2012. Holllande veut supprimer la mention de la race dans la constitution française. Available at: www.bfmtv.com/politique/hollande-veut-supprimer-la-mention-de-race-dans-la-constitution-fran caise-208043.html [Accessed: 11.04.2019].

Les Échos. 2018. L'Assemblée supprime à l'unanimité le mot race de la constitution. Available at: www. lesechos.fr/politique-societe/politique/0301969747005-lassemblee-supprime-a-lunanimite-le-mot-race-de-la-constitution-2191849.php [Accessed: 11.04.2019].

PART I

Politics in modern and contemporary France

1

FROM DESPAIR, TO HOPE, TO LIMBO

The French elections and the future of the Republic

Aurélien Mondon

Few thought that the 2017 presidential elections would be particularly interesting or surprising. While the potential accession of Marine Le Pen to the second round was discussed as reminiscent to the 2002 shock when her father beat Parti Socialiste (PS) candidate Lionel Jospin in the first round, the situation was rather different. What was a surprise to many in 2002, was expected by most in 2017: the far right would make it to the second round.

In fact, a year before the election, it seemed that very little needed to be decided. Had Hollande and Juppé/Sarkozy been selected as the champions of the centre left and right as planned, Marine Le Pen would have found herself in a perfect position to reap the benefits of decades of disappointment. Since 2012, the media, commentators and politicians appeared to have uncritically accepted that Le Pen would reach the second round and what remained to be decided was who she would face. As Hollande's ratings went from bad to worse, it became obvious that she would be facing the candidate of Les Républicains (LR), whoever they might have been. Le Pen had received 17.9% and almost 6.5 million votes in 2012, a record for the party, and had since won the 2014 European elections (thanks in part to a huge level of abstention) and broke another record in the 2015 regional elections where the party received 6.8 million votes, but failed to win any single region. As is usually the case in France, the electoral system prevented the Front National (FN) from winning in the second round, as the PS decided to withdraw in favour of the centre right where there was a risk. Yet, as abstention was predicted to be as high if not higher than in 2002, it seemed unavoidable that with a reserve of more than two million votes compared to her father's best, Marine Le Pen had a clear path to the second round. Ten days before the first round, a poll conducted by Ipsos Steria (2017a) for *Le Monde* highlighted that only 66% of respondents were certain to vote.

For a party with only two members of parliament elected in 2012, the FN, and Marine Le Pen in particular, received a disproportionate amount of coverage between the two presidential elections. While most of the coverage far right parties tend to receive is negative, various studies have shown that there is no such thing as bad publicity and being in the media ensures that the party's message is heard (see for example Dézé in Crépon et al. 2015). Jean-Marie Le Pen was famous for exploiting such publicity in periods of electoral calm when the party was no longer in the limelight by uttering deeply racist comments, most famously about the Holocaust. Since she took power in 2011, Marine Le Pen has no longer had to rely on crudely racist comments to receive media coverage. While she does make use of polemical statements such as comparing Muslim prayers to an 'occupation' or her more recent comments on the *Vel d'hiv* round-ups of 1942,[1] she has been treated in a much more amenable manner by the mainstream press (see Alduy in Crépon et al. 2015), at least until the second-round debate. It seems as though the change of leadership and a veneer of moderation in its discourse sufficed to convince much of the media that the FN was a changed party, even though Marine Le Pen decided to keep the name of the party and retain many of the ideas present in previous programmes. While most academics warned that the change is for the most part discursive and superficial (Crépon et al. 2015; Alduy and Wahnich 2015), the mainstream media and commentators took Le Pen at her word that the FN had changed, ignoring that the normalisation process started in the 1980s/90s and had been progressive and superficial.

Everything seemed therefore set for a remake of the 2002 election, bar the shock. Were she to face Hollande on the centre left and Juppé/Sarkozy on the centre right, Le Pen would have been in an incredibly comfortable situation to progress to the second round. Compared to other parties, hers seemed to be gaining steam, and united in its approach. In a climate of deep political distrust and faced with former leading figures of the 'establishment' considered responsible for the past 20 years of failed French politics, her status as an outsider, someone who had no share of responsibility in the current situation, made her a natural favourite. This was reinforced by her portrayal in much of the elite discourse as the sole alternative to politics as usual, despite the party's mixed appeal (Mondon 2015). A tribute to the lack of political imagination in the political elite in France, very few took seriously the possibility of other outsiders emerging despite growing discontentment with the hegemony.

En Marche or enough?

The first signs that the 2017 election would not take place as planned came from the mainstream parties' nominations.

François Hollande's dismal approval ratings throughout his mandate had made clear early on that he would be in a difficult position in the first round, and yet it was long expected that he would run (Lees 2016). It was in fact the first time in the Fifth Republic that a healthy outgoing president did not compete for a further mandate. When François Mitterrand retired in 1995, he was already suffering from the cancer that would take his life a year later. Similarly, when Chirac passed on the baton in 2007, his health was deteriorating. Hollande's decision not to run for a second mandate came very late and as such, it came as both a surprise and relief to most Socialists. This was the first shock in the campaign, as primaries would decide who would be the PS candidate, giving the left a remote chance it would not have had under Hollande. Manuel Valls stood as Hollande's heir; his legacy as minister of the interior and prime minister meant that his prospects would have remained rather poor in the first round. It was therefore not surprising that Socialist supporters chose a candidate removed from the Hollande presidency: Benoît Hamon, probably the most radical candidate on offer in the primaries, defeated Valls with more than 58% of the vote in January 2017 (Haute Autorité des Primaires Citoyennes 2017).

In November 2016, the Républicains' primaries had already demonstrated that the obvious status quo was under threat. It had been widely anticipated that the first primaries organised on the right would crown either Chirac's former prime minister and centre right candidate Alain Juppé or the former president and hard-liner Nicolas Sarkozy. Yet late in the campaign, François Fillon, Sarkozy's former prime minister and an unknown quantity to most due to his rather dull and technocratic persona, began rising in the polls thanks to his promise to break away from politics as usual. He won in the first round decisively, dealing yet another blow to Sarkozy's ego after his defeat to Hollande in 2012, and the second round proved a formality as the gap between Fillon and Juppé in the first round was simply too wide (Haute Autorité de primaire ouverte de la droite et du centre 2016). Right-wing voters had chosen their champion and Fillon was given a clear mandate to push through his mix of radical traditional moralism and neo-liberal austerity economics (for more detail on Fillon's campaign, see Lees 2017).

The defeat of centrist candidates to more radical alternatives created a gap which Emmanuel Macron, a former banker and former minister of the economy under Hollande, managed to occupy successfully. Macron's fresh face, his polished communication strategy, his age, the fact that he was not a career politician and had never been elected all played in his favour. Throughout the campaign, he managed to retain this centrist position unscathed, appealing to both the centre left and right, despite receiving the support of politicians from the PS, LR and the centrist Mouvement Démocrate (MODEM) party. Even Valls' support, which was clearly not welcome by Macron, did not seem to damage his image.

When Hamon was selected in the PS primaries, it was expected, as early polls suggested (Ipsos Steria 2017a) that he would soon swallow Mélenchon's electorate and become the lead left-wing candidate. However, the former Socialist senator turned rogue in 2008 had already proven a convincing and resilient candidate in 2012 when he received 11.10% of the vote (with polls giving him up to 14%, suggesting that his final result may have been potentially reduced by a last-minute *vote utile* for Hollande). This time, the candidate of La France Insoumise (Untamed France; LFI) declared his candidacy early, taking his Communist allies by surprise and forcing them to lend their support before they could see who would be running for the PS. Throughout his campaign, Mélenchon demonstrated the strength of his support and his oratory skills, drawing huge crowds in large events, both live and through holograms. Despite such clear support on the ground, opinion polls did not suggest until the last days of the campaign that he could indeed garner enough support to reach the second round.

On the 23rd April, results were far closer than polls had predicted and only a few thousand votes separated the top four candidates (Table 1.1).

The results of the first round were widely viewed as representing the end of bipartisanship in France, as well as the end of the left/right divide in place of a national/global one. However, such conclusions drawn in the heat of the moment do not hold close scrutiny. A more careful breakdown of the first-round results, beyond the two 'winners' points to change, but not the sort of change which has been widely accepted since, in an almost dogmatic manner.

Macron began to lead the polls in late March (Huffpost Pollster 2017), disproving the many who had mocked his candidature early on. Valls in particular had insisted that Macron lacked the necessary experience and represented a 'populisme light' with no future (France Info 2016). Surveys proved accurate and Macron won the first round, although not as comfortably as predicted. Perhaps more troubling was the composition of his electorate and their degree of support for Macron and his politics. Early post-election polls suggested that voters who turned to Macron did so without much enthusiasm for either him or his programme. According to a Harris Interactive (2017) poll, only 52% of respondents who declared to have voted for Macron did so because of ideological proximity (*vote d'adhésion*), while 27% considered it a utilitarian choice (*vote utile*) and 16% because they had no other choice (*vote par défaut*). A key myth built around the now youngest French president of the Fifth Republic appeared to be smashed as Macron was not the candidate of the young and energetic, despite his carefully choreographed appearances. Instead, his electorate suggests that he is very much that of the old status quo, drawing most of his support from the 35+ age group, while the young turned predominantly to Mélenchon, Marine Le Pen and abstention (Harris Interactive 2017).

Table 1.1 Results for the first round of the 2017 presidential election.

Candidates	Vote	% registered vote	% vote
Emmanuel MACRON – *En Marche*	8,656,346	18.19	24.01
Marine LE PEN – *Front National*	7,678,491	16.14	21.30
François FILLON – *Les Républicains*	7,212,995	15.16	20.01
Jean-Luc MÉLENCHON – *La France Insoumise*	7,059,951	14.84	19.58
Benoît HAMON – *Parti Socialiste*	2,291,288	4.82	6.36
Nicolas DUPONT-AIGNAN – *Debout La France*	1,695,000	3.56	4.70
Jean LASSALLE – *Résistons!*	435,301	0.91	1.21
Philippe POUTOU – *Nouveau Parti anticapitaliste*	394,505	0.83	1.09
François ASSELINEAU – *Union populaire républicaine*	332,547	0.70	0.92
Nathalie ARTHAUD - *Lutte ouvrière*	232,384	0.49	0.64
Jacques CHEMINADE – *Solidarité et progrès*	65,586	0.14	0.18

	Total	% registered vote	% vote
Registered voters	47,582,183		
Abstention	10,578,455	22.23	
Votes	37,003,728	77.77	
Blank ballots	659,997	1.39	1.78
Void	289,337	0.61	0.78
Counted	36,054,394	75.77	97.43

Pyrrhic victory for the FN

While still a shock, the reaction to Marine Le Pen's accession to the second round was much more tame and resigned than had been the case in 2002, and did not lead to mass demonstrations. When Jean-Marie Le Pen beat Lionel Jospin in the first round to face off against Jacques Chirac, a panicked reaction took hold of France when Le Pen's face appeared on screens: the new face of fascism was at the gates of power, or so it seemed. However, something crucial was lost in the mainstream apocalyptic narrative: Le Pen's vote had in fact been stagnating since 1988 when he first reached around 4.5 million votes (Figure 1.1).

If Le Pen had reached the second round, it was not because the FN was on an irresistible rise, or because it was 'asking the right questions,' but because other parties had failed. Therefore, what should have made the headlines in 2002 was that the vote for the three main parties had totally collapsed, to the point where their combined share of the vote almost equalled that of an unprecedented level of abstention. The other element which made the news that year was that PS candidate Lionel Jospin's defeat was to be blamed on the fragmentation of the vote on the left. While former socialist sovereignist Jean-Pierre Chevènement took a share of Jospin's vote, the radical left with the Communist party and perhaps more surprisingly the two Trotskyist candidates, Olivier Besancenot of the Communist Revolutionary League (now New Anticapitalist Party – Nouveau Parti Anticapitaliste/NPA) and Arlette Laguillier of the Workers' Struggle (Lutte Ouvrière/LO), both managed impressive results at the expense of the obvious candidate on the left. In this respect, the situation was not too dissimilar to 2017: the vote expressed a clear exasperation with the status quo after years of cohabitation and assimilation when president Jacques Chirac was forced to nominate Jospin as prime minister after losing the 1997 legislative election.

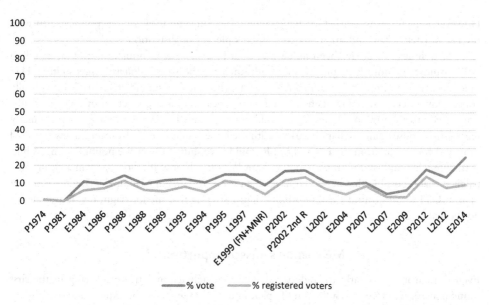

Figure 1.1 Evolution of the vote of the Front National (FN) at presidential elections in France since its inception in 1972.

Under 2017's circumstances, it is thus not particularly surprising to see the FN's candidate progress to the second round, particularly as the strategy of *dédiabolisation*, which was accelerated under Marine Le Pen's leadership and widely accepted and publicised by the media, allowed the party to broaden its electoral base. However, while Le Pen succeeded in her bid to reach the second round and broke a new record for the party in terms of vote, this was not the victory she had anticipated and could understandably have planned for mere months before the election. Her campaign for the first round was lacklustre and tensions had already appeared within the FN as to how far the process of normalisation should go (France Info 2017). Le Pen was also mostly absent from the headlines, and in a campaign which soon focused on economic issues, she failed to impose her agenda based on immigration and strong responses to terrorism. This was partly due to the tone of the campaign, but also to her own focus on economic issues as an attempt to broaden her base. This was a clear failure, as she not only appeared far from convincing but also went against what her electorate usually responds to, whether they are from a working-class background or more traditionally right-wing social classes: immigration (Mayer in Crépon et al. 2015).

Qualifying to the second round had thus been the bare minimum for the party; with polls suggesting that she would win the first round comfortably for most of the year leading up to the election, it is safe to assume that anything but a victory would have been considered a defeat within the party. In November 2016, an Ifop-Fiducial (2016) poll suggested that Le Pen could even get up to 30% of the vote. However, an important caveat to the theories about the rise of the FN or Le Pen's successful detoxification of the party is that such polls relied on a very high abstention rate, which seemed likely early in the campaign as candidates from mainstream parties appeared less than popular and the alternatives failed to gain traction. While the second round would see her defeated by a weakening but still large enough Front Républicain, it would have positioned her ideally to claim in the next five years that *she* was the largest party in France.

However, her prospects seemed to change when the campaign took a more political turn with the rise of Mélenchon and his ability to bring people out of abstention.

In fact, things could have been much worse for Le Pen – the nomination of François Fillon as LR candidate could have proven the death knell for the party's *dédiabolisation* strategy. Had Fillon not been embroiled in a number of corruption scandals (Durand et al. 2017), his radically conservative social views and agenda could have appealed to a large section of the FN's traditional electorate whose social views are at odds with the new leadership of the party, particularly regarding homosexuality (Chapuis 2016). With the close results of the first round, a few hundred thousand votes away from the FN and to LR could have shifted the entire political scene. While, as the French would say, 'with ifs, you could put Paris in a bottle,' if Fillon had run a clean campaign, it is also possible that he would have taken some votes from Macron, leaving the prospect of an LR/FI second round a real possibility, demonstrating that the left/right divide was clearly not buried in 2017.

Mélenchon's missed opportunity?

Even though it is too early to understand whether Mélenchon's strong showing in the first round is anything more than a flash in the pan, a number of leads can be explored to explain the momentum the FI candidate gained towards the end of the first-round campaign, and why he failed to reach the second. First, the Socialist primaries demonstrated that a left-wing alternative is all but a marginal demand in France. Valls' mix of Sarkozyist macho securitisation and Hollandist economic centrism proved appealing to only a third of those most invested in the party, the remaining votes going for the most part to the *frondeurs* (rebels) Montebourg, Peillon and Hamon (Haute Autorité des Primaires Citoyennes 2017). The desire for more radical politics on the left has most likely developed following the reaction of many prominent socialist politicians who left Hamon for Macron, demonstrating both their opportunism and economically liberal politics. While this weakened Hamon who seemed unable to affirm his candidature, it reinforced Mélenchon who had been running a tight ship. The legislative elections confirmed the trend as the PS appeared unable to turn the tide and overcome its divisions. Valls, who was elected as a PS candidate, left the Socialist group soon after the election to join LREM (Le Figaro 2017a).

Going back to the presidential elections, the second debate with all 11 candidates on the 4th April was another turning point. While Mélenchon had emerged positively from the first debate between the five main candidates, the second one and its aftermath gave space for left-wing politics to enter centre stage. More antagonistic politics, away from the consensual approach the electorate had become used to and bored with, took place on that night, and one only needs to look at the mainstream media's reaction to know that something went wrong for the proponents of the status quo (Perrotin 2017). The two Trotskyist candidates Philippe Poutou (NPA) and Nathalie Arthaud (LO) proved particularly convincing in the debate. First, they did not restrain their attacks against Le Pen and Fillon, the two candidates crawling under a number of corruption charges, breaking what seemed to be some sort of taboo for Macron, Mélenchon and Hamon, who had mostly skirted the topic during the first debate. They also demonstrated that, contrary to what had been a common narrative in the mainstream media (Mondon 2017), the defenders of the working class and the poor should not be sought on the far right but on the left. This limiting narrative pitting the far right as the 'working class' party is of course not limited to the FN and similar incomplete pictures have been drawn in the US and the UK to explain the support of Trump, United Kingdom Independence Party (UKIP) and even Brexit (see Mondon 2017; Mondon and Winter 2019). While this may be partly true with regard to vote, such conclusions usually ignore abstention, which is particularly high among the working class, and thus crucial to take into account when making generalisations about the behaviour of this particular section of society. To put it simply, if 33% of manual workers vote for a particular party, but 65% abstain, then that particular party receives the vote of only one in ten manual workers. While both statements '33% of the working-class vote goes to the far right' and '1 out of 10 workers vote for the far right' are correct, they have a significantly different impact on the reader/voter, and the fact that the first one is always preferred in elite discourse is telling of the low esteem in which the elite holds the working class and lower classes in general.

It is exactly this disconnect between voters and the disillusioned that Arthaud and Poutou exposed in a debate watched by more than six million viewers on the night. It is therefore not surprising that some of the key interventions made by Poutou went viral, not only in France but far beyond its borders. Poutou busted the myth of the FN as the working-class party by showing that the far right party was not only the enemy of the people but also very much part of the system, leaving Le Pen literally speechless. While his comments resonated across France and beyond, the right-wing media demonstrated that class remains a reality, attacking Poutou, a factory worker, for his choice of clothes, his posture and his language. Needless to say that this proved fruitless and even counterproductive. While Poutou did not perform any better than expected at the polls (1.09% of the vote), the main beneficiary of this return of class in the political debate was Mélenchon, whose strategy was vindicated. While the FN remained the party which appealed to most working class voters (not including abstainers), LFI gained ground within this category of voters, finishing second and considerably weakening the FN's assumed hold on this symbolic category of the population. More strikingly, polls suggest that Mélenchon managed to win over most young people, another category of voters which had been predicted to turn *en masse* to the FN in 2017 (Ipsos Steria 2017b), again ignoring that abstention is rampant within this section of the population. However, while Mélenchon managed to bring people out of abstention, the record number of 'blank votes' proved that he was not the alternative sought by many, pointing to the necessity of more radical debates (Dagorn 2017).

The rise of Mélenchon in the polls led to reactions beyond the right, and were at times stronger than those against the FN, demonstrating the unease of mainstream politicians and media with the rise of a left-wing alternative. Hollande (in De Royer 2017), who had promised not to get involved in the campaign, characterised the rise of Mélenchon as a 'fad' and warned of 'the perils of simplifications and falsifications': for Hollande, 'the campaign smell[ed] bad.' The leader of the Confédération française démocratique du travail (CFDT) (in 20 Minutes 2017), one of France's major unions, warned about Mélenchon's 'rather totalitarian' vision. The reaction of the media was also striking, and far more negative than that to Marine Le Pen, who had been touted as a contender for months. Le Figaro (2017b) went furthest, denouncing the 'devastating project' of 'Maximilien Ilitch Mélenchon.' Four articles and three pages (including a front page) were dedicated to Mélenchon's 'social big bang from another era.' *The Financial Times* (Stothard and Khan 2017) warned that the financial sectors had begun to react to that possibility, in a manner similar to that used during the EU referendum campaign in the UK.

Victories for Le Pen and Macron?

As expected, the second round was a mere formality for Macron (Table 1.2). However, as the election took place soon after Brexit and the Trump upset, the media was prone to panic and, particularly on the international scene, many began musing about a potential fascist victory in France. This was despite the fact that it would have taken a real political earthquake for Le Pen to win. In 2007 and 2012, Le Pen would have needed more than 18 million votes to win the election; her current record is 7.7 million. While her supporters tend to be loyal, her vote base

Table 1.2 Results for the second round of the 2017 presidential election.

Candidates	Vote	% registered vote	% vote
Emmanuel MACRON – *En Marche*	20,743,128	43.61	66.10
Marine LE PEN – *Front National*	10,638,475	22.36	33.90

	Total	% registered vote	% vote
Registered voters	47,568,693		
Abstention	12,101,366	25.44	
Votes	35,467,327	74.56	
Blank ballots	3,021,499	6.35	8.52
Void	1,064,225	2.24	3.00
Counted	31,381,603	65.97	88.48

tends to be more restricted, and in line with other surveys, a Kantar Sofres (2017) poll suggested in March 2017 that 58% of respondents consider the party as a threat to democracy. Considering that Les Républicains and the PS called to vote for Macron, and that Mélenchon's supporters were more likely either to abstain or to turn to the En Marche leader, it was mathematically obvious that Le Pen faced certain defeat in the second round. Contrary to Trump who was the Republican candidate and Brexit, which was backed by many mainstream political actors, Le Pen and her party remained anchored in the far right, both through their policies and their perception by the electorate. Therefore, what mattered was how well she would lose and whether she would be able to break the glass ceiling decisively.

However, a dreadful second-round campaign punctuated by a debate in which an angry Le Pen demonstrated that she remained the candidate of the far right (Magnaudeix and Turchi 2017), led her to be defeated by a wider margin than expected. Le Pen received 33.9% and less than 11 million votes, which, while a new record for the party, was clearly below anticipated, leading to a number of complaints by prominent FN *cadres* regarding the strategy (Faye and Mestre 2017). The new crisis within the FN became clear when Marion Maréchal-Le Pen, Marine's niece, Jean-Marie's granddaughter and one of the most popular FN politicians, particularly with hard-liners, decided to quit politics weeks before the legislative elections. This was a blow for the FN and the strategy of *dédiabolisation*. A further blow took place in the legislatives where – despite increasing its number of parliamentarians from two to eight – the party performed rather poorly. The number of votes the FN received in 2017 was in fact similar to previous years. Adding further to the division within the party, Florian Philippot and his brother were both defeated, weakening their position and strategy further.

Conclusions: where to now?

Throughout its history, the FN has been used as a convenient scarecrow, making the consensual neo-liberal politics of the centre right and left acceptable in the face of an exaggerated fascist threat. Of course, the rise of the FN is extremely concerning and its impact on mainstream politics and the day-to-day lives of many people in France is clear and alarming (Mondon and Winter 2017). However, the party itself is not at the gates of power, and more importantly, its

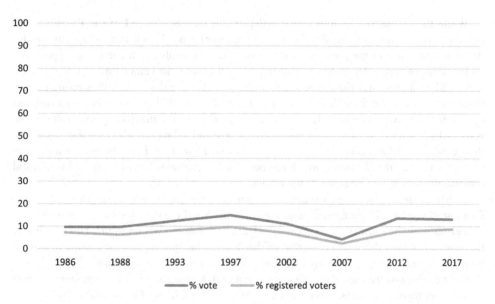

Figure 1.2 Evolution of the vote of the Front National (FN) at legislative elections in France since its inception in 1972.

normalisation has been a two-way process where the party itself modernised its image and discourse but could only achieve its transformation by being accepted by the mainstream media and politicians (Mondon 2013). For the past few years, the hype around the so-called project of *dédiabolisation* has allowed the diversion of attention from broader discontentment and distrust of the current hegemony (Glynos and Mondon 2016). Mainstream politicians and media risked little in promoting the former fascist party, as it is near impossible to imagine that Le Pen could increase her vote share enough to win the second round.

Macron and his new La République en Marche (LREM) party navigated the legislative elections expertly and secured an overwhelming majority in the National Assembly. However, here again, Macron's victory was not so much a plebiscite as a failure of other parties to ignite the campaign. In fact, these elections represented a record in terms of abstention, making Macron's mandate much weaker in terms of vote than would have seemed at first sight.

While Macron is the second best-elected president of the Fifth Republic behind Chirac, and the one with the largest majority, it is unlikely his mandate will be a stable one. His lack of popular ideological support expressed both in terms of vote and opinion polls is likely to lead to resistance when his government attempts to push through radical reforms in terms of work rights and pensions for example – the *gilets jaunes* movement attests to the scale of the discontent at Macron's perceived aloofness and the radicalism of his proposed reforms. This could lead to further disillusionment, as he was elected on a platform promising change. Should Macron fail to tackle key issues within French society such as high unemployment and the growing deficit, the FN could find itself in an ideal position in 2022 to create a new upset. However, this would necessitate that the party overcome its divisions and manage to hold its uneasy ideological stretch between its traditional electorate and its new-found but limited popularity in some working-class areas. It appears increasingly likely that the party will be forced to decide between pursuing its so-called social turn or attempting to replace the traditional right which will struggle to regain stability following the pre- and post-election infighting.

While the legislative elections confirmed that this may be the end of the PS as a major political force, Mélenchon failed to become *the* alternative on the left and to capitalise on his strong performance in the presidential election. While his result and his ability to appeal to a wide variety of voters demonstrated that there is still appetite in France for left-wing politics, it would be a mistake for the left to see this outcome as more than it is. Still, a strong performance on a radical platform demonstrated that the left/right divide has not yet been replaced by a global/national antagonism. It was the campaign debates and the space given to alternative voices which revived the interest of the French people and led to a much lower abstention rate than expected. Debates and disagreements shifted the focus away from the toxic nationalism promoted by the Front National, which had been lazily borrowed by mainstream politicians and opportunistically hyped by much of the media.

In 2017, France seemed at a turning point, with the two parties who have governed France for most of the Fifth Republic suffering terrible blows. Yet the system is such that only the two candidates with the most votes are allowed to battle it out in the second round. This meant that the voice of 60% of the voters (plus that of the 20% of the population who abstained) was no longer democratically relevant. This voice must either be voided in abstention or blank ballots or given to the least-worst candidate. After the first round, Macron and Le Pen represented overall only 34% of registered voters. This is even more striking considering 45% of Macron's electorate appears to have voted tactically in the first round. In this overly personalised system, the legislative campaign appeared dull and failed to grab the attention of the public, despite much more being at stake. Therefore, if anything, what 2017 has shown us is that it is high time to rethink this plebiscitary system should we wish to see more democratic and optimistic politics become commonplace in France.

Note

1 The *Rafle du Vel d'hiv* was the most notorious round-up of Jewish people during the Vichy regime and German Occupation of France in World War II and took place on 16 and 17 July 1942. In total, 12,884 Jewish men, women and children were taken to the Vélodrome d'hiver in Paris where they were held in insanitary conditions for up to five days, before deportation to transit camps in the Loiret region and thence to the Nazi death camps. See Chapter 23 by Infield and Vince in this volume.

References

20 Minutes. 2017. Présidentielle: Le patron de la CFDT Laurent Berger alerte contre la "vision assez totalitaire" de Mélenchon. In *20 Minutes*, 13 April. Available at: www.20minutes.fr/elections/2049295-20170413-presidentielle-patron-cfdt-laurent-berger-alerte-contre-vision-assez-totalitaire-melenchon [Accessed: 08.11.2017].

Alduy, C. and S. Wahnich. 2015. *Marine Le Pen prise aux mots: Décryptage du nouveau discours frontiste*. Paris: Seuil.

Chapuis, N. 2016. Primaire de la droite: les multiples ressorts du vote Fillon. In *Le Monde*, 21 Novem- ber. Available at: www.lemonde.fr/election-presidentielle-2017/article/2016/11/21/primaire-de-la-droite-les-multiples-ressorts-du-vote-fillon_5034830_4854003.html [Accessed: 08.11.2017].

Crépon, S., A. Dézé and N. Mayer. (Eds.). 2015. *Les faux-semblants du Front National: Sociologie d'un parti politique*. Paris: Sciences Po Les Presses.

Dagorn, G. 2017. Votes blancs et nuls, abstention: les résultats du second tour s'ils étaient pris en compte. In *Le Monde*, 8 May. Available at: www.lemonde.fr/les-decodeurs/article/2017/05/08/et-si-les-resultats-de-la-presidentielle-avaient-pris-en-compte-le-vote-blanc-ou-l-abstention_5124412_4355770.html [Accessed: 08.11.2017].

De Royer, S. 2017. François Hollande sort de son silence: "Cette campagne sent mauvais." In *Le Monde*, 12 April. Available at: www.lemonde.fr/election-presidentielle-2017/article/2017/04/12/a-dix-jours-du-premier-tour-hollande-sort-de-son-silence_5109768_4854003.html [Accessed: 08.11.2017].

Durand, A-A., A. Pouchard, M. Delrue and P. Sztajnkrycer. 2017. Tout comprendre aux affaires Fillon. In *Le Monde*, 12 April. Available at: www.lemonde.fr/les-decodeurs/article/2017/04/12/tout-comprendre-aux-affaires-fillon_5110215_4355770.html [Accessed: 08.11.2017].

Faye, O. and A. Mestre. 2017. Marine Le Pen fait face à des critiques internes. In *Le Monde*, 8 May. Available at: www.lemonde.fr/election-presidentielle-2017/article/2017/05/08/marine-le-pen-fait-face-a-des-critiques-internes_5124062_4854003.html [Accessed: 08.11.2017].

France Info. 2016. Valls accuse Macron de représenter 'une forme de populisme light.' In *France Info*, 2 October. Available at: www.francetvinfo.fr/politique/manuel-valls/video-valls-accuse-macron-de-representer-une-forme-de-populisme-light_1852513.html [Accessed: 08.11.2017].

France Info. 2017. Tensions au Front national. In *France Info*, 3 April. Available at: www.francetvinfo.fr/economie/retraite/reforme-des-retraites/tensions-au-front-national_2128483.html [Accessed: 08.11.2017].

Glynos, J. and A. Mondon. 2016. The political logic of populist hype: the case of right wing populism's 'meteoric rise' and its relation to the status quo. Populismus Working Paper, Vol. 4. Thessaloniki: Populismus.

Harris Interactive. 2017. Le 1er tour de l'élection présidentielle 2017: Composition des différents électorats, motivations et éléments de structuration du vote. In *Harris Interactive*. Opinion poll conducted for *M6*. Available at: http://harris-interactive.fr/wp-content/uploads/sites/6/2017/04/Rapport-Harris-Sondage-Jour-du-Vote-1er-tour-de-lelection-presidentielle-M6.pdf [Accessed: 08.11.2017].

Haute Autorité de primaire ouverte de la droite et du centre. 2016. Décision du 23 novembre 2016 de la Haute Autorité de la primaire portant proclamation des résultats du 1er tour, arrêtant la liste des deux candidats habilités à se présenter pour le 2nd tour. In *La primaire ouverte de la droite et du centre*. Available at: www.primaire2016.org/ [Accessed: 11.11.2017].

Haute Autorité des Primaires Citoyennes. 2017. Communiqué de la Haute Autorité des Primaires Citoyennes – 25 janvier 2017 – Les Primaires citoyennes de la Gauche – 22 et 29 janvier 2017. In *Les Primaires citoyennes de la Gauche*, 25 January. Available at: www.lesprimairescitoyennes.fr/la-haute-autorite-des-primaires/ [Accessed: 17.11.2017].

Huffpost Pollster. 2017. Poll chart: French presidential election. In *Huffington Post*. Available at: http://elections.huffingtonpost.com/pollster/france-presidential-election-round-1 [Accessed: 08.11.2017].

Ifop-Fiducial. 2016. Les intentions de vote à l'élection présidentielle de 2017 après l'annonce de candidature d'E. Macron. In *Ifop-Fiducial*. Opinion poll conducted for *Sur Radio* and *Lyon Capitale*. Available at: www.ifop.com/media/poll/3562-1-study_file.pdf [Accessed: 08.11.2017].

Ipsos Steria. 2017a. Le rapport de forces and l'état d'esprit des Français à 10 jours du 1er tour de l'élection présidentielle. In *Ipsos Steria*. Opinion poll conducted for *Le Monde*. Available at: www.ipsos.fr/sites/default/files/doc_associe/enquete_presidentielle_ipsos_le_monde.pdf [Accessed: 08.11.2017].

Ipsos Steria. 2017b. 1er tour présidentielle 2017: sociologie de l'électorat. In *Ipsos Steria*. Available at: www.ipsos.fr/decrypter-societe/2017-04-23-1er-tour-presidentielle-2017-sociologie-l-electorat [Accessed: 08.11.2017].

Kantar Sofres-one point. 2017. Baromètre 2017 d'image du Front National. In *Kantar Sofres-one point*. Opinion poll conducted for *Le Monde* and *Franceinfo*. Available at: http://fr.kantar.com/opinion-publique/politique/2017/barometre-2017-d-image-du-front-national/ [Accessed: 08.11.2017].

Le Figaro. 2017a. À l'Assemblée, Valls siègera comme député apparenté au groupe La République en marche. In *Le Figaro*, 27 June. Available at: www.lefigaro.fr/flash-actu/2017/06/27/97001-20170627FILWWW00068-l-assemblee-manuel-valls-siegera-comme-depute-apparente-au-groupe-la-republique-en-marche.php [Accessed: 08.11.2017].

Le Figaro. 2017b. Jean-Luc Mélenchon, un projet dévastateur pour la France. In *Le Figaro*, 12 April. Available at: www.lefigaro.fr/elections/presidentielles/2017/04/11/35003-20170411ARTFIG00330-jean-luc-melenchon-un-projet-devastateur-pour-la-france.php [Accessed: 08.11.2017].

Lees, D. 2016. Where did it all go wrong? François Hollande flops out of the presidential race. In *The Conversation*, 2 December. Available at: https://theconversation.com/where-did-it-all-go-wrong-francois-hollande-flops-out-of-presidential-race-69806 [Accessed: 08.11.2017].

Lees, D. 2017. A controversial campaign: François Fillon and the decline of the centre-right in the 2017 presidential elections. In *Modern and Contemporary France*, 25:4, 391–402.

Magnaudeix, M. and M. Turchi. 2017. Marine Le Pen "trumpise" le débat du second tour. In *Médiapart*, 4 May. Available at: www.mediapart.fr/journal/france/040517/marine-le-pen-trumpise-le-debat-du-second-tour [Accessed: 08.11.2017].

Mondon, A. 2013. *A populist hegemony? The mainstreaming of the extreme right in France and Australia*. London: Ashgate.

Mondon, A. 2015. Populism, the people and the illusion of democracy – the Front National and UKIP in a comparative context. In *French Politics*, 13:2, 141–156.

Mondon, A. 2017. Limiting democratic horizons to a nationalist reaction: populism, the radical right and the working class. *Javnost/The Public: Journal of the European Institute for Communication and Culture*, 24:3, 355–374.

Mondon, A. and A. Winter. 2017. Articulations of Islamophobia: from the extreme to the mainstream? In *Ethnic and Racial Studies*, 40:13, 2151–2179.

Mondon, A. and A. Winter. 2019. Whiteness, populism and the racialisation of the working-class in the UK and the US. In *Identities: Global Studies in Culture and Power*, forthcoming.

Perrotin, D. 2017. Philippe Poutou jugé "indigne" par les éditorialistes de BFMTV. In *Buzzfeed*, 5 April. www.buzzfeed.com/davidperrotin/philippe-poutou-juge-indigne-par-les-editorialistes-de-bfmtv?utm_term=.puAyYodd5p#.nm8vQVzznp [Accessed: 08.11.2017].

Stothard, M. and M. Khan. 2017. Investors sell off French debt as leftwinger surges in polls. In *The Financial Times*, 11 April. Available at: www.ft.com/content/dc62e780-1e9c-11e7-b7d3-163f5a7f229c?mhq5j=e1 [Accessed: 08.11.2017].

2

POLITICAL PARTIES IN MODERN AND CONTEMPORARY FRANCE

Jocelyn Evans

In democratic regimes, political parties are traditionally regarded as the vehicles of mass representation. In parliamentary regimes, parties are the main touchstones for voters to identify their political tendency. Even in presidential regimes, individual candidates will generally be backed by a political party, providing broadly aligned ideological and programmatic positions, as well as material support. In France, however, much of its post-war political history has been characterised by active attempts to weaken political parties, and perceptions of parties acting in ways that weakened themselves. Very little focus on political parties has suggested growth or success as competitive organisations. The reasons for this have been diverse, and related not just to the actions of party leaders and members but also to the institutional framework, to social and economic change, and to political events. Yet, if one is looking for a proof of political parties' strength as units of political aggregation, the French case to date is equally one which stands out, with parties still fundamental to electoral politics and legislative representation, despite the numerous challenges.

Across time, organisations held largely responsible by the Fifth Republic's founder, Charles de Gaulle, for the collapse of the previous regime, and consequently side-lined in the constitution and its founding statutes, have inevitably re-established themselves in French political life, playing different roles as national federations, mass movements and elite power bases, according to the demands of different vote-, policy- and office-seeking contexts. One of the reasons for parties' staying power in French politics has been their relative flexibility, both in terms of their role and powers, and in their organisational reinvention. From a period of the mass parties of the Communists and the Gaullists constituting the anti-system components of the Fourth Republic party system, political parties of the moderate left and right, and subsequently the far right, coalesced either in the formation of single umbrella coalitions, and subsequently single parties, from multiple small constituents (e.g. the Union pour la Démocratie Française, UDF) or in the establishment of a hegemonic bloc party absorbing smaller groups and clubs, for example the Parti Socialiste (PS) in the 1970s or the Union pour une Majorité Présidentielle/Union pour un Mouvement Populaire (UMP) in the 2000s.

And indeed, the Fifth Republic marks the maturing of French political parties and the establishment of a relatively stable period of representative politics in the 1970s and 1980s, in terms of labels and ideological positioning. This chapter will examine how this ideal-type of moderate multipartism lasted less than a decade, challenged by the rise of the Front National (FN), introducing radicalising dynamics to the right of the political spectrum, as well as increasingly challenging the left in many of its bastions. It will consider how the political centre was regarded as politically unviable in an institutional system based upon a majoritarian logic – even if that logic is now distorted by radical parties on the left and right, as well as by a new challenger, in the shape of La République en Marche! (LREM), the movement formed to back Emmanuel Macron's successful presidential campaign in 2017.

Since the 2000s, and the establishment of the UMP, the French party ideal-type has become progressively more oriented around parties as support units for presidential hopefuls and, further disempowered by the *quinquennat* electoral calendar putting legislative elections and govern-mental formation secondary to the presidential race, increasingly distanced party elites from the grass roots. Party hierarchies which in the 1960s and 1970s often dragged local and regional fed-erations into line are once again witnessing a dislocation between national and local structures, with a concomitant rise in local party autonomy.

But LREM's ancillary role as a 'virtual' party formed by free online membership, and lending its label to a politically diverse group of legislative candidates forming a presidential majority in the National Assembly, disrupts not just the socially encapsulating role of political parties but also the broader political landscape. Straddling the left–right divide, if sustainable in the longer term, ostensibly overwhelms the two-bloc logic of the Fifth Republic party system, so dominant to date. As the latest in a sequence of challenges to the bipolar system, which this chapter considers, other parties' attempts to retain a capacity for mobilisation and channelling of electoral support, as well acting as ideological loci, will remain crucial to understanding their role in France today.

Developments in political parties

The presidentialisation of national parties

The classic account of French political parties under the Fifth Republic seems to presage their failure, or at least marginalisation, from the constitutional underpinnings and initial embedding of the regime. Conscious of the role of multiple parties of varying sizes in the fragmentation and instability of the Fourth Republic, and in particular the inability of these actors to provide strong leadership when faced with the Algerian crisis, Charles de Gaulle ensured that the successor Republic would minimise the role of parties, restoring sovereign oversight and the exercise of executive power in key domains to ensure clear, effective governance, as well as a broader com-mitment to France's significance on the world stage. Some 55 years later, the student of French politics cannot help but note the ever-present political parties whose influence remains strong and, in some cases, potentially pathologically so.

Yet, this durability of parties has been complemented by a recent period, under Nicolas Sarkozy, which has been described as one of 'hyper-presidentialism' (Hayward 2013). Indeed, throughout the Fifth Republic, presidential power has been both exercised through and ham-pered by parties. The history of political competition and the periodicisation of the regime has been based upon the dynamics of the political parties, to as great an extent as the terms of office of its seven previous presidents. At the extreme, one might argue that reforms such as the inver-sion of the electoral calendar in 2001 after 2000's referendum on the *quinquennat*, to place the legislative elections after the presidential race, demonstrate the need for institutional support in ensuring primacy of the Elysée over the Bourbon Palace.

Constitutional domains aside, the extent to which even de Gaulle's ability to rise above par-tisan politics via '[a] public display of monarchical aloofness' have been exaggerated (Cole 2013: 57). Where presidents have been 'above' parties, this is where they have chosen to keep these organisations at arm's length, often to distance themselves from the negative products of their own programmatic interventions – Giscard d'Estaing and the UDF in the late 1970s, Mitterrand and the PS in the mid-1980s. Most recently, Emmanuel Macron's pronouncement that he would play a 'Jupiterian' role as president strongly echoes the Gaullian notion of being 'above' politics (Gaffney 2010; Hanley 2017). In conjunction with periods of cohabitation, this has strengthened parties of the (presidential) opposition, and therefore government, in counter-balancing presidential primacy, but with an inferior popular mandate.

The institutional framework of the Fifth Republic in the long term pulled parties towards a balanced two-bloc system, if not a two-party system (Grunberg and Haegel 2007), where informal coalitions of parties in the first round should cooperate where necessary in a two-bloc run-off. Constitutionally required for the presidential ballot, a similar pattern is largely assumed for a 'normal' legislative ballot, but that tendency has been disrupted most notably and consistently by the FN's 'nuisance power' (*pouvoir de nuisance*) in three-way run-offs (*triangulaires*), and most recently from the centre, where LREM has bridged between a stricken Socialist Party and the moderate wing of Les Républicains (LR) to form an informal cooperative coalition. Emerging from a Fourth Republic whose two principal anti-system parties – the Parti Communiste Français (PCF) and the Gaullist Rassemblement du Peuple Français (RPF), subsequently the Union pour la Nouvelle République (UNR) – were also the two largest mass parties (Bartolini 1984), dominance of the Right bloc by the UNR's litany of successors ensured governing monopoly until the early 1980s when facing a still anti-systemic PCF and a more moderate but factionalised SFIO (Section Française de l'Internationale Ouvrière) and its satellites. Cooperation, if not unity on the left, the incorporation of left-wing political clubs in the new PS and a nationalised leadership above its historic factions (Cole 1989) were a necessary condition of the left's eventual victory in 1981.

One fundamental dynamic identifiable in party system theory and confirmed empirically by the Fifth Republic had been the eradication of the political centre as a pole in party politics. From the centrist coalitions among radical, social and Christian democrats of the Fourth Republic, the centre had become a location which a number of parties have tried to claim, but which was almost inevitably overridden by the two-bloc logic of the two-round run-off system. In the contemporary period, parties still attempt to locate themselves 'away' from LR and PS in a notional centre, including the Union des Démocrates et des Indépendants (UDI) and Mouvement Démocrate (MODEM). Yet the national electoral position of these parties had tended to the right, even if support for a particular coalition or presidential candidate of the right inevitably split the party. There had been exceptions – Michel Rocard included centrist Ministers from the UDF in his government in 1988, bolstering the Socialist-Mouvement Radical de Gauche (MRG) minority with the Union du Centre in the National Assembly (Dompnier 2012). In 2007, the Socialist presidential candidate, Ségolène Royal, promised to work with the centre if she were elected (she was not). Famously, MODEM leader François Bayrou's decision to vote for the Socialist candidate, François Hollande, in the 2012 presidential race, cost him the ire of the UMP and indirectly contributed to the loss of his own Pau constituency. Overall, such flexibility à la German Free Democratic Party (FDP) had been short-lived and inevitably regress the centre to the right-wing partner role.

Only under a set of unique circumstances – the internal division and collapse of the Socialist Party on the left, and the hamstringing of the expected right-wing presidential victor by corruption allegations – was the centre able to become a viable location for a successful electoral campaign in 2017, allowing Emmanuel Macron and subsequently LREM to mobilise voters of both the centre left and centre right with a mixed social liberal programme that appealed to both camps, and in particular garnered support against a strong far right FN party and presidential candidate with a programme diametrically opposed to his progressive agenda.

It is too early to say whether this renaissance of the centre represents a temporary realignment or a longer-lived realignment. However, the famous *quadrille bipolaire* still represents for many the natural or normal state of the French party system, with four parties in two blocs – specifically, the PCF and PS on the left, UDF and RPR on the right in the late 1970s and early 1980s. Part of the attraction is undoubtedly that, from a party system perspective, the evolution from the 1950s to the 1970s represents an archetypical shift from a case of polarised to moderate pluralism, ostensibly through a change in institutional structures (Sartori 1976). The multiparty-friendly first round, encouraging small parties to contest seats (Elgie 2005: 123) is accompanied by a need for cooperation in identifying second-round partners and acceptable recommendations for vote transfers.

Yet, the presidentialising force which pushed the factionalism of the SFIO and its left-wing satellites to unify as a single party entity, albeit still heavily factionalised, in the 1960s, has paradoxically also encouraged the formation of small, *notable*-led parties often claiming ideological distinctiveness, but as often defined by personality. Again, the case of Emmanuel Macron's LREM demonstrates the potential strength such small, elite-oriented movements can garner in a very short space of time. Whilst the hegemonic parties of left and right have tried to open primary elections to all parties and voters of their bloc, these attempts to coalesce before the election have largely been rejected, thereby fragmenting political supply, and lowering the bar for smaller cadre parties. Conversely, as well as parties with significant legislative representation standing away from such aggregations, candidates such as Nicolas Dupont-Aignan or Philippe de Villiers have used small political parties as platforms for profile-raising presidential campaigns which nonetheless have never come near 5% of the vote.

Parties can arguably be seen to have been weakened more in situations where presidents have assumed the role of executive leader on policy. The stranglehold of a presidential programme dominates, at least in the short term, any programmatic autonomy a governing party may enjoy. Since 2012, the series of social liberal U-turns in the Socialist executive's economic policy, particularly with the appointment of the then-technocratic minister of the economy, Emmanuel Macron, met with significant resistance from party members and notables, including former minister of industry Arnaud Montebourg and former first secretary Martine Aubry, and a range of *frondeurs* – dissident deputies and other party elites angered by the move away from anti-austerity measures. In the past, whilst the executive influence of the party in the short term may have been weak, the internal fractures such dissent causes have been more likely to be deleterious for individuals and politicians than for the party (and certainly for the notion of party) itself. The abandoning of the PS in 2017 by the majority of its *notables*, after the presidential and legislative election cataclysm, and its apparent lack of political future, at least in the short to medium term, is therefore even more striking.

Nonetheless, the reform to a five-year presidential term, and the locking of the electoral calendar to ensure legislative elections follow presidentials, has meant that the elections focused on parties and the party-oriented legislature have become little more than a confirmatory plebiscite of the presidential race, gifting a working majority to the incumbent (Dupoirier and Sauger 2010). Parties have become selection machines and power bases – strong in that respect, if weakened in their impact on policy and government.

The localisation of parties

The presidentialising dynamic of the Fifth Republic was countered by the localising dynamic of the succession of decentralisation reforms from the late 1970s to the early 1990s (Knapp and Le Galès 1993). In a multi-level governance structure transferring significant powers to the municipal and particularly regional levels, politicians with strong power-bases in larger cities could effectively develop partisan support networks distinct from the national elite. The incumbent in a large town hall, including a Paris as distinct from the national seats of government as any other big city, can assert themselves both locally and nationally through funding and infrastructure unreliant on national coffers. In passing, it is worth noting that paradoxically this decentralisation does not seem to have empowered regional identity politics (with the partial and recent exceptions in metropolitan France of Corsica (De La Calle and Fazi 2010) and Brittany (Cole 2006: 49)) – as Pasquier surmises, the governance regions do not generally correspond with the historical regions of identity (2015: 55–56). Whether the regional reforms of 2016 and the adoption of culturally and historically resonant names – Occitanie, Nouvelle-Aquitaine, for example – for these new agglomerations results in a growth of regionalist politics remains to be seen.

The key position where politicians can build their power base locally, largely beyond the reach of national executives, is through mayors and presidents of regional councils. Particularly for the former, national party apparatuses are limited in their ability to influence, let alone remove, an incumbent (John and Cole 1999: 105). The cost to the incumbent, except for politicians with high national profiles or in the largest conurbations, is potentially a restriction on their political life beyond the borders of this fiefdom (Borraz and John 2004: 118). For those in the largest metropolises, or regional power, the resources and influence open to them can pave the way to significant national positions – for instance, Gérard Collomb, Lyon's Socialist mayor whose dissident support for Emmanuel Macron, rather than his own party's candidate, in the early stages of his campaign secured the high-profile post of minister of the interior in the Philippe government of 2017.

The dual logic of presidentialisation and local implantation follows the notion of party adaptation (Katz and Mair 1995, 2002) but has applied increasingly as a 'composite construct' to parties across multiple governance and electoral levels simultaneously (Bardi et al. 2015). Across different regions and municipalities, the shape and nature of party cooperation differs heavily from the national level, with relatively rare instances of top-down intervention from national HQs, for example the 1998 expulsion of three regional presidents for securing election with FN councillor support. Nonetheless, local politicians feel empowered to ignore national party directives at odds with their perception or interests, whether these are met with penalties, and certainly if they are met with indifference or impotence. During François Hollande's incumbency, three notable instances of 'local insurrection' illustrated the separation between national and local. In the 2012 legislatives, Olivier Falorni stood as a dissident Socialist and refused to stand down against the official candidate, Ségolène Royal. Jean-Pierre Masseret, senator and leader of the Socialist lists in Alsace-Champagne-Ardenne-Lorraine, refused to stand down in the 2015 regional elections as part of the *front républicain* against the FN, as ordered by Jean-Christophe Cambadelis, first secretary of the PS. Finally, in his regional campaign in Brittany, the Socialist defence minister Jean-Yves Le Drian removed his party's symbol from his campaign literature, to distance his local campaign from an unpopular incumbent[1] – a distance which increased upon his nomination to the post of foreign minister in the 2017 Philippe government.

Contemporary French parties in crisis?

The decline of political parties, in France and elsewhere, has been heralded in the party literature for many years, as these organisations seemingly struggle to survive internal factional divides, financial vulnerability and mass disenchantment among their support bases. The challenges discussed next indeed represent significant issues to party organisation and functions, but their response illustrates to date their endurance and capacity to adapt.

Party membership

Political party membership in France is among the lowest, proportionate to the population size, in Europe (Van Biezen et al. 2012: 28). Historically, the post-war period began with reported membership of almost 2.5 million across just the two mass Gaullist and Communist parties. Nonetheless, two distinct trends are visible. Despite having lost almost a million members since the late 1970s, halving the membership size, the period from the 1990s to 2009 actually saw an increase of around 200,000 members – far from replacing the lost cohorts of the 1970s, but still at odds with the prevailing trend in most other European countries in the last 20 years (Van Biezen et al. 2012: 32–24, tables). Trends of secular dealignment, and the fracturing of the traditional, socially encapsulated mass society of trades unions and church organisations, visible in the voter–party relationship are magnified in the subset of activists. The decline of the PCF contributed markedly to this fall, although estimates vary just how much (Bell and Criddle 1989: 518). Similarly, Gaullist party membership fell heavily after the early 1980s (Knapp 2004: 355). The more recent upturn has been ascribed to a range of factors, from mobilisation among moderates on the back of Jean-Marie Le Pen's 2002 presidential run-off (Billordo 2003: 141) to the formation of the UMP in 2002. However, since 2010, the best evidence suggests another decline in membership for both the Socialists and the UMP/LR. Only the FN, now the Rassemblement National (RN), appears to have increased its membership.[2]

Modern political activism has also moved away from the card-carrying member stereotype towards a greater selectivity on issues and style of participation. Movements such as the Front de Gauche on the left, or Christine Boutin's Parti Chrétien-Démocrate have succeeded in mobilising individuals in collective action on specific social and economic issues. The so-called *Manif' pour Tous* ('Demonstration for All'), against the Taubira laws on same-sex marriage, and the *mouvement social* against the El Khomri employment bill, led by unions and supported by radical left parties, took policy opposition away from the mainstream opposition, to give a direct protest voice and opportunity to be involved in politics in non-traditional ways. Through social media, in particular, the citizen can become mobilised and politically active periodically, rather than committing wholesale (and often passively) to a party machine and its programme.

Despite the decline in numbers of party members, and their anachronistic position in contemporary political activism, they have seen their position in many parties strengthened through becoming the selectorate for party leaders and presidential candidates. Whilst the 2017 presidential primaries saw both the PS and LR open up candidacies to other parties, and voting to potentially the entire electorate, the election of relatively radical candidates less suited to a moderate centrist position in a presidential race illustrates the strength ideologically hardline core support can exercise, whether or not this is electorally viable. In line with the perceived convergence on *bipartisme* highlighted earlier, the logic of the two-ballot presidential system and the need to identify a candidate to unify the left or the right led to a presidentialisation of parties and their organisations, and for both the UMP and PS, the adoption of internal primaries (Ivaldi 2007). This democratisation of internal party life nonetheless may weaken parties where members' selection does not mirror broader perceptions in the electorate. In the lead-up to the Republicans' presidential candidate selection in 2016, for example, support for Alain Juppé over François Fillon amongst the general electorate was at distinct odds with greater support among the membership for the latter. Such disparities can reinforce the sense of disconnect between parties and their electorates.

Party–voter disconnect

In keeping with the cartel party theory (Katz and Mair 1995), France's political parties have moved away from their mass support, becoming groups of professionalised political elites focused on maintaining power and disconnected from civil society (Knapp 2004). The clear social delineations associated with class and religious party support have been replaced by a more complex set of sociological drivers (Evans and Mayer 2005) which motivate vote indirectly through issues and attitudes, rather than mobilising directly, and certainly have far less purchase on party activism. Parties mobilise and socialise less (Haegel 2005: 28).

That institutional distance is reflected in a similarly large confidence gap. In opinion polling, French parties regularly poll the worst of all political institutions (see Table 2.1). Even after the financial crisis and the Kerviel affair, French voters have greater confidence in banks than they do in any of the political institutions. Individual councillors fair slightly better, but most noticeably mayors are the only group to enjoy majority support.[3] There is of course a world of difference between the mayor of a large urban agglomeration, with strong partisan support, and that of a small rural commune, whose figurehead status from patronage, personal interaction and strong 'friends-and-neighbours' support is more akin to an administrative pillar than a political notable.

The decline of the mass linkage to parties is also visible in the simple decline in turnout at French legislative elections (see Figure 2.1). After the reinstigation of the two-ballot majoritarian system in 1988, abstention has climbed steadily since 1993 in the first round, and since 1997 has moved from just over a quarter to almost one-half of the electorate in the second round – well over twice that of a presidential election. Undoubtedly, the reform of the electoral calendar has turned the legislative elections into two further plebiscitary rounds of the presidential race, political parties' campaigns having less impact in most constituencies. But the low esteem in which parties are held has also clearly reduced the willingness of French voters to turn out in support of the very organisations backing the presidential candidates of a month earlier.

Party financing

The little institutional attention paid to French parties under the Fifth Republic instigated a system which treated them as associations with little capacity to garner donations or claim

Table 2.1 Percentage support for politicians and institutions in France, 2014–2016.

	Confidence in institution (%)		
	2016	2015	2014
Mayors	63	66	63
Departmental councillors	39	39	35
Regional councillors	37	39	37
Banks	*36*	*41*	*35*
Unions	34	35	31
EU	27	35	31
National Assembly	27	31	28
Senate	27	30	27
Media	28	27	23
Deputies	21	26	23
Political parties	**8**	**9**	**8**

Source: Ipsos/Sopra Steria, *Fractures Françaises 2016*.

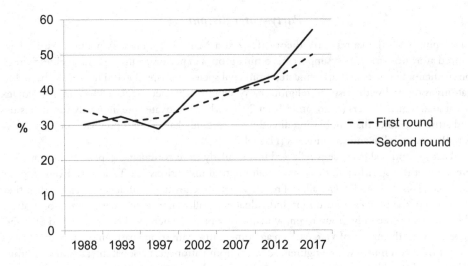

Figure 2.1 Abstention rates as percentage at legislative elections in France, 1988–2017.
Source: www.tns-sofres.com/publications/abstentions.

significant membership fees, a position made increasingly untenable by the rising cost of campaign finance (Evans 2003: 81). As well as under-the-table donations, an informal network of patronage among service providers, diversion of funds from local to party support, and a more formalised top-slicing of party official salaries offset the absence of other funding sources. Yet, a growing number of electoral levels, from three at the beginning of the Fifth Republic to six by the proportional representation reform of the legislative elections in 1986, and larger party apparatuses placed additional pressure on party coffers, which had to resort to increasingly dubious means. The party financing reform laws in the 1990s, in the wake of an increasing number of scandals and a slew of failed attempts to regularise funding in the 1970s and 1980s (Clift and Fisher 2004: 682), extended state funding to vote share in electoral results, consequently tying funds to performance, and established ceilings to expenditure.

The establishment of these rules, against decades of custom and practice at all levels of governance which had 'oiled the wheels' of administration, and their constant amendment to allow and disallow varying types of funding perversely led French parties to be secretively transparent. By the 2012 presidential elections and after, allegations of campaign funding from Colonel Gaddaffi to Nicolas Sarkozy and loans from Russian banks to the FN, admitted by the party treasurer after police raids on the party headquarters, continued to beleaguer political parties within and outside campaigns. In 2017, François Fillon's campaign was effectively blocked by allegations of fraudulent payments to his wife as a parliamentary assistant for a job that she never carried out. Scrutiny has equally been present at the local level, and not just from the media but also the FN: illicit party financing of the PS in the Nord Pas-de-Calais region formed part of Marine Le Pen's campaign for her seat in the 2012 legislatives.[4] Le Pen's use of this tool was notably more timid in the 2017 presidential campaign, amid allegations that her own party had misused European Parliament funds for unrelated political activities in France.

For those prosecuted for corruption, the effects are often short-term – a point that Emmanuel Macron underlined in his campaign for a 'moralisation of political life,' including a commitment to removing the suspension of sentences for shorter prison terms. The opinion poll frontrunner for Les Républicains' presidential nominee, mayor of Bordeaux Alain Juppé, returned within a decade after a suspended prison sentence and ban on holding public office in 2004. During his short-term leadership of LR as its presidential candidate, François Fillon inherited a party which in 2012 lost a third of its state funding after its presidential electoral defeat;[5] had lost its party chairman, Jean-François Copé, for suspicion of links to the 'Bygmalion' invoices scandal that already involved Sarkozy; and had only just started to pay off large debts that had threatened its financial viability in 2015.[6] In the aftermath of the 2017 elections, both MODEM and the FN saw formal investigations into their possible misuse of European parliamentary assistants for domestic party political work. For political parties as presidential vehicles with primaries as well as the national election itself, there is no sign that such financial pressures will abate. The media coverage of scandals derived from the attempts to solicit funding will continue to tarnish reputations in the public eye, even where illegality is not venal.

Party relevance in a globalised system

One of parties' principal functions, whatever its organisational shape, power-structure or personalisation, has been to generate and modify programmatic position, or more broadly put, ideology. Typologisation of parties conceives different roles for this content, with a growing emphasis in more modern types, such as the cartel party, on competence and efficiency of government over sectoral representation characteristic of mass parties (Katz and Mair 1995: 18). Part of this evolution has been driven not just by power-seeking factors endogenous to political systems but also by a broader socio-economic and geopolitical context which limits the programmatic tools that are effective in modern polities. Whatever the programmatic vehicle bringing parties to power, the constraints of European Union regulation, the demands of international trade and economic competition, as well as the burden of welfare state and other inertial government spending, and shocks such as the sovereign debt crisis in 2012, severely limit the choice of policy alternatives that can be implemented, and their effectiveness (Evans and Ivaldi 2013: 92; Grossman and Sauger 2017).

In many ways, this has returned internal party debate to the status of coffee house discussion associated with the cadre politics of the nation-building process. While political alternatives espoused by significant tranches of the party membership may hold elites to ransom within their party, the capacity to deliver such policies is severely curtailed. In periods of strong presidential control of the executive, such as under Sarkozy between 2007 and 2012, other social issues, for example security and national identity (Perrineau 2009), can be used as a campaign policy, and subsequently to try to offset failings in economic terms. Party dissent on this was thus muted. Where presidential and governmental control of the party is weak, such as in the subsequent presidency of François Hollande, factional rebellion on austerity and social liberalism of the government agenda by the Socialist *frondeurs*, whilst unlikely to result in a policy U-turn or even a shift in the party programme, weakens the executive. Party power is thus strong, but only in undermining its own leadership.

Parties against parties

The principal challenge to parties of government in France has come from other party actors. It is perhaps unsurprising that the aforementioned issues dealt – direct activism, voter dissatisfaction, corruption, government straitjacket – have found their focus through radical parties of the left and the right. Since its decline as a mass party, the PCF in the 2000s has positioned itself alongside the shifting array of Trotskyist and other radical left parties such as Lutte Ouvrière and the Nouveau Parti Anticapitaliste, and more recently cooperated with Jean-Luc Mélenchon's Parti de Gauche in the Front de gauche, now la France Insoumise. The use of social media, mass meetings, street demonstrations and a strong presence in *mouvements sociaux*, such as those organised against the El-Khomri employment law in 2016, characterise a more populist face to the radical left than intellectualised and apparatchik-dominated discourse of the PCF of the 1970s and 1980s. In the personalised vehicle of the Front de gauche, at its apogee in the 2012 presidential elections, Mélenchon characterised in some ways a very traditional attitude towards parties, in trying to appeal beyond the boundaries of a partisan organisation, to mobilise a social network of young, disenchanted voters – or, more accurately for many, abstainers (Evans and Ivaldi 2013: 55). The appeal of this movement was programmatic in its rejection of the perceived social liberal agenda of the PS, and more generally the EU, and promoting instead a set of anti-austerity measures. Through its universalist appeal, it mobilised just as strongly against Marine Le Pen and the FN. Indeed, Mélenchon's campaign against Le Pen the FN seemed in many ways a separate battle from that between the moderate left and right. In 2017, the key effect of Mélenchon's presence was to eat into the left-wing support of the Socialist candidate, Benoît Hamon.

It would be difficult to overstate the perceived role of the FN in the crisis of parties and more broadly of politics and representation in France since the 1980s. Within the French system, the FN has always been treated as *sui generis*, with a set of social, political and competitive dynamics placing it apart from 'mainstream' parties, or indeed radical parties of the left. Debate over the true extent of its difference (Andersen and Evans 2003, 2005; Grunberg and Schweisguth 2003) has not detracted from the party's undoubted capacity to provide a 'winning formula' (Kitschelt 1995) of social and attitudinal appeals to disaffected, dislocated voters in increasingly broader territories of French electoral geography. Indeed, from an electoral low point in the early 2000s, after the internal party schism with Bruno Mégret's Mouvement National Républicain and Jean-Marie Le Pen's futile attempt to emulate his 2002 success in 2007, the party's renewed success since Marine Le Pen's assumption of its presidency in 2011 has pushed the party to higher shares of the vote not just by strategic targeting of its strongholds in the Nord Pas-de-Calais and Provence-Alpes-Côte d'Azur regions but also with stronger shares of the vote in areas previously 'immune' to the FN's appeal (Perrineau 2014: 47–48). If there is a new territorial aspect now to the FN's support, it is perhaps the peri-urban location of many FN voters which is most striking (Gombin 2015).

In the success of the FN, the viability of parties as strong political actors is evident. In challenging the hegemony of the 'UMPS,' as the FN previously styled the main parties of government, it has managed to mobilise grass roots support, and build a multi-level infrastructure which had eluded it for many years. Its challenge on an increasingly equal footing to the mainstream may itself 'normalise' the party as a competitor in the French system, if not in its programmatic appeals, which remain radical, despite attempts at cleansing the image of the party. To date, this normalisation has not occurred. Despite Marine Le Pen's success in reaching the second round of the 2017 presidential elections, her subsequently disappointing (to her supporters) performance in the second round, epitomised by a failed performance in the presidential debate against Emmanuel Macron (Evans and Ivaldi 2018: 115–118), saw a mobilisation of left and right moderates in the front républicain (Republican front) against her candidacy. While not as convincing as Jacques Chirac's victory over her father in 2002, the 32-point differential still illustrated the continued unacceptability of the FN for many.

Conclusions

The role of political parties under the Fifth Republic was initially defined as weak in the regime's constitution and the intentions of its principal founder. However, the structural role which political parties play in the mobilisation of support and resources, even in an intensely presidentialised system, inevitably bring the parties into the foreground of any election, and of the entire legislative and governance edifice. Attempts to suppress parties institutionally to avoid the side-effects of fragmentation, minority coalitions and personalised politics simply alter the rules of the game for parties, rather than eradicating them.

In France in 2017, the effects of parties responding to their environment produces effects as deleterious to themselves and to their leaders as in any other period. The period since 1978 and the *quadrille bipolaire* had seen what some authors have referred to as *hyper-alternance* (Evans and Ivaldi 2002) – the alternation of governmental power between left and right at every election, with the exception of the 2002 and 2007 Raffarin and Fillon governments. The inability of political parties to identify a successful programmatic offer to satisfy voter demand resulted in a series of one-term executives.

Parties remain influential but often in a way that undermines the parties themselves and to the effectiveness of government, and even to democracy. In 2016, a president and prime minister both had alarmingly low opinion polls ratings prey to factions supported by grass roots disenchantment, and forming a group of *frondeurs* in many ways as opposed ideologically to the executive as the official opposition. *Notables* such as former first secretary Martine Aubry, now with a strong personal power base as mayor of Lille, similarly openly criticised the Socialist president from within the party. While party unity would not save an unpopular executive in the subsequent presidential and legislative elections, empowered dissent from within certainly exacerbates the difficulties. Indeed, the parlous performance of Hamon for the Socialists, and the mobilisation of support from a number of Socialists for the Macron presidency, pose a challenge as significant as any that the PS has faced in its history. On the other side of the political spectrum, Jean-Marie Le Pen's attempts to regain a position of influence, if not outright control, in the FN, having ceded the presidency to his daughter in 2011, similarly points to an organisation which is deemed worth fighting for.

As across many European democracies, the relevance of French parties is increasingly challenged in their unrepresentativeness of the broader electorate. Organisationally, they may act as power bases for presidential candidates, but the composition and views of the membership may be at odds with that of their voters. From a competitive perspective, when memberships make suboptimal choices of leaders and candidates, the disconnect between voters and parties – either in lower engagement and turnout, or through changing allegiances, potentially to radical alternatives – becomes greater. The presidentialisation of the system means that a party of whatever ideological positioning and initial size can return a majority if the individual at its helm occupies the Elysée. Perhaps the greatest evidence of this has been the recent landslide majority for LREM. In many ways, it is too soon to analyse this movement *qua* political party, given that it has 'only' contested – and won – one election. In that sense, it tells us more about the institutional incentives and subservient role to the president.

As a party against parties, covered in the previous section, it is also not yet possible to say how LREM will compete in the longer term, however great its initial success. But it is highly unlikely that LREM will remain a docile legislative foundation to its president's programme. As its deputies and members, many of whom have never held office (Evans and Ivaldi 2017) learn the political system, and it becomes an established party actor within the French political system, the same characteristics and behaviours of other political parties seem certain to emerge. Whether it is able to remain, first, cohesive and, second, centrist in its political positioning will depend upon the executive's ability to provide the incentives for this to occur. Should it not remain cohesive, the most likely split will be across the political centre, with the remergence of a left–right division. However, the very success of LREM in bridging this divide demonstrates the viability of a political centre in the absence of strong poles of mobilisation in the traditional blocs. In systemic terms, then, the stable alternation between two moderate blocs characterised as the French party system's 'normal' state may well be consigned to history.

Notes

1 See www.lefigaro.fr/elections/regionales-2015/2015/10/30/35002-20151030ARTFIG00098-regio nales-en-bretagne-le-drian-fait-disparaitre-le-ps-de-son-materiel-de-campagne.php [Accessed: 26.05. 2016].
2 See www.lemonde.fr/les-decodeurs/article/2015/09/22/des-republicains-au-ps-la-desertion-des-mil itants_4766932_4355770.html [Accessed: 09.05.2016].
3 The other organisations to enjoy majority support (not shown in the table) are SMEs (82% in 2016), the army (81%), the police (79%) and schools (75%). The political sphere in France with only few exceptions holds a special place for mistrust.
4 See '2012: Marine Le Pen fait "des affaires" son cheval de bataille,' in *Le Parisien*, 14 December 2011. www.leparisien.fr/election-presidentielle-2012/candidats/2012-marine-le-pen-fait-des-affaires-son-cheval-de-bataille-14–12–2011–1768398.php [Accessed: 16.05.2016].
5 See 'L'UMP amputée d'un tiers de son financement,' in *Le Monde*, 19 June 2012. www.lemonde.fr/politique/article/2012/06/19/l-ump-perd-50-de-son-financement-public_1720639_823448.html [Accessed: 16.05.2016].
6 See especially 'Financièrement, Les Républicains vont mieux (que l'UMP),' in *Europe 1*, 2 September 2015. www.europe1.fr/politique/financierement-les-republicains-vont-mieux-que-lump-2508749 [Accessed: 16.05.2016].

References

Andersen, R. and J. Evans. 2003. Values, cleavages and party choice in France, 1988–1995. In *French Politics*, 1:1, 83–114.
Andersen, R. and J. Evans. 2005. The stability of French political space, 1988–2002. In *French Politics*, 3:3, 282–301.
Bardi, L., E. Calossi and E. Pizzimenti. 2015. Party modelling and changes in party organization. Paper presented at ECPR General Conference, Montreal, 26–29 August.
Bartolini, S. 1984. Institutional constraints and party competition in the *French party system*. In West European Politics, 7:4, 103–127.
Bell, D. and B. Criddle. 1989. The decline of the French Communist Party. In *British Journal of Political Science*, 19:4, 515–536.
Borraz, O. and P. John. 2004. The transformation of urban political leadership in Western Europe. In *International Journal of Urban and Regional Research*, 28:1, 107–120.
Clift, B. and Fisher, J. 2004. Comparative party finance reform: the cases of France and Britain. In *Party Politics*, 10:6, 677–699.
Cole, A. 1989. Factionalism, the French socialist party and the Fifth Republic: an explanation of intra-party divisions. In *European Journal of Political Research*, 17:1, 77–94.
Cole, A. 2006. Decentralization in France: central steering, capacity building and identity construction. In *French Politics*, 4:1, 31–57.
Cole, A. 2013. Sarkozy's political leadership and the institutions of the Fifth Republic. In G. Raymond (Ed.), *The Sarkozy Presidency: Breaking the Mould?* Basingstoke: Palgrave Macmillan, 56–78.
de la Calle, L. and A. Fazi. 2010. Making Nationalists out of Frenchmen? Substate nationalism in Corsica. In *Nationalism and Ethnic Politics*, 16:3–4, 397–419.
Dompnier, N. 2012. Les Centres à l'Assemblée nationale face aux logiques de bipolarisation. In *Revue Politique et Parlementaire*, 1063:64, 160–166.
Dupoirier, E. and N. Sauger. 2010. Four rounds in a row: the impact of presidential election outcomes on legislative elections in France. In *French Politics*, 8:1, 21–41.
Elgie, R. 2005. France: stacking the deck. In M. Gallagher and P. Mitchell (Eds.), *The Politics of Electoral Systems*. Oxford: Oxford University Press, 119–136.
Evans, J. 2003. Political corruption in France. In M. Bull and J. Newell (Eds.), *Corruption in Contemporary Politics*. Basingstoke: Palgrave Macmillan, 79–92.

Evans, J. and G. Ivaldi. 2002. Quand la crise du consensus profite à l'extrême droite. In *Le Figaro*, 18 May, 14.

Evans, J. and G. Ivaldi. 2013. *The 2012 French Presidential Elections: The Inevitable Alternation*. Basingstoke: Palgrave Macmillan.

Evans, J. and G. Ivaldi. 2017. An atypical 'honeymoon' election? Contextual and strategic opportunities in the 2017 French legislative race. In *French Politics*, 15:3, 322–339.

Evans, J. and G. Ivaldi. 2018. *The 2017 French Presidential Elections: A Political Reformation?* London: Palgrave Macmillan.

Evans, J. and N. Mayer. 2005. Electorates, new cleavages and social structures. In A. Cole, P. Le Galès and J. Levy (Eds.), *Development in French Politics*, 3rd edition. Basingstoke: Palgrave Macmillan, 35–53.

Gaffney, J. 2010. *Political Leadership in France: From Charles de Gaulle to Nicolas Sarkozy*. London: Palgrave Macmillan.

Gombin, J. 2015. Le changement dans la continuité: Géographies électorales du Front national depuis 1992. In S. Crépon, A. Dézé and N. Mayer (Eds.), *Les faux-semblants du Front national. Sociologie d'un parti politique*. Paris: Presses de Sciences Po.

Grossman, E. and N. Sauger. 2017. *Pourquoi Détestons-nous autant nos politiques?* Paris: Sciences Po Les Presses.

Grunberg, G. and F. Haegel. 2007. *La France vers le bipartisme? La présidentialisation du PS et de l'UMP*. Paris: Presses de Sciences Po.

Grunberg, G. and E. Schweisguth. 2003. French political space: two, three or four blocs? In *French Politics*, 1:3, 331–347.

Haegel, F. 2005. Parties and organizations. In A. Cole, P. Le Galès and J. Levy (Eds.), *Development in French Politics*, 3rd edition. Basingstoke: Palgrave Macmillan, 18–34.

Hanley, D. 2017. Left and Centre-Left in France – endgame or renewal? In *Parliamentary Affairs*. doi: 10.1093/pa/gsx042.

Hayward, J. 2013. 'Hyper-presidentialism' and the Fifth Republic state imperative. In D. Bell and J. Gaffney (Eds.), *The President of the French Fifth Republic*. Basingstoke: Palgrave Macmillan, 44–57.

Ivaldi, G. 2007. Presidential strategies, models of leadership and the development of parties in a candidate-centred polity: the 2007 UMP and PS Presidential nomination campaigns. In *French Politics*, 5:3, 253–277.

John, P. and A. Cole. 1999. Political leadership in the new urban governance: Britain and France compared. In *Local Government Studies*, 25:4, 98–115.

Katz, R. and P. Mair. 1995. Changing models of party organisation and party democracy: the emergence of the cartel party. In *Party Politics*, 1:1, 5–28.

Katz, R. and P. Mair. 2002. The ascendancy of the party in public office: party organizational change in twentieth-century democracies. In R. Gunther, J. R. Montero and J. J. Linz (Eds.), *Political Parties: Old Concepts and New Challenges*. Oxford: Oxford University Press, 113–135.

Kitschelt, H. 1995. *The Radical Right in Western Europe: A Comparative Analysis*. Ann Arbor, MI: University of Michigan Press.

Knapp, A. 2004. *Parties and the Party System in France: A Disconnected Democracy*. Basingstoke: Palgrave Macmillan.

Knapp, A. and P. Le Galès. 1993. Top-down to bottom-up? Centre-periphery relations and power structures in France's Gaullist party. In *West European Politics*, 16:3, 271–294.

Pasquier, R. 2015. *Regional Governance and Power in France: The Dynamics of Political Space*. London: Palgrave Macmillan.

Perrineau, P. 2009. La "défidélisation" des électeurs de Jean-Marie le Pen. In B. Cautrès and A. Muxel (Eds.), *Comment les électeurs font-ils leur choix?* Paris: Presses de Sciences-Po, 201–220.

Perrineau, P. 2014. *La France au Front. Essai sur l'avenir du FN*. Paris: Fayard.

Sartori, G. 1976. *Parties and Party Systems: A Framework for Analysis*, Vol. 1. Cambridge: Cambridge University Press.

van Biezen, I., P. Mair and T. Poguntke. 2012. Going, going, . . . gone? The decline of party membership in contemporary Europe. In *European Journal of Political Research*, 51:1, 24–56.

3

GAULLISM AS A DOCTRINE AND POLITICAL MOVEMENT

Benjamin Leruth

Throughout its history, the French political landscape has been shaped and influenced by prominent personalities. In the likes of other major political leaders across the world, Charles de Gaulle's legacy was materialised by the creation of a long-standing political movement representing key tenets advocated during his presidency. De Gaulle's influence in French history is still being referenced and used as an example of French *grandeur* by contemporary political leaders on all sides of the political spectrum.

The notion of Gaullism is often used by academics and practitioners to refer to de Gaulle's influence beyond the Appeal of 18 June. However, the Gaullist literature is marked by strong disciplinary divisions, which is exacerbated by the absence of a commonly accepted definition. Political scientists tend to focus on its impact on institutions (such as political parties, governments and leadership issues) and election results (e.g. Charlot 1970; Pickles 1972; Hoffmann and Hoffmann 1974). Historians such as Berstein (2001), Mahan (2002) or Watson (2001) have paid particular attention to events that happened under de Gaulle's presidency, the evolution of Gaullism throughout the 1960s and its legacy beyond de Gaulle's death. Sociologists would adopt different approaches, such as analysing the role of de Gaulle as a charismatic leader (e.g. Waldman et al. 1990) or the impact of Gaullism on the emergence of new social movements (e.g. Singer 2002). Relatively new notions such as neo-Gaullism or Sarkozysm add to such complexity.

This contribution offers a brief review of the existing literature and argues that Gaullism is best studied in two different ways: as a political doctrine and as a political movement. In the following section, a definition of Gaullism based on the existing literature is put forward; such definition attempts to reconcile diverging views over the nature of the concept. It is argued that Gaullism should not be considered as a true political ideology but rather as a French political doctrine which also had impacts beyond the national context. The third section then focuses on Gaullism as a political movement and highlights the divisions that have occurred within Gaullist parties over the past three decades regarding the issue of European integration. Following the 2012 and 2017 presidential and legislative elections defeats, the fourth and final section assesses whether the Gaullist movement (or even the Gaullist doctrine) is currently facing a crisis. It concludes that despite the semantic confusion surrounding this notion and internal divisions within the different Gaullist-inspired movements, Gaullism is one of the most successful national doctrines, and beyond its historical appeal, it is likely to continue shaping contemporary French politics.

Gaullism as a doctrine

While the notion of Gaullism has been widely used in the rich literature on French politics and society, it has been interpreted in different ways by scholars, journalists and practitioners. Most existing studies refer to Gaullism to categorise French foreign policy under de Gaulle's presidency and his legacy, especially emphasising the importance of strong nation states and national sovereignty (see e.g. Morse 1973; Kolodziej 1974; Cerny 1980; Gordon 1993). Others, such as Williams and Harrison (1961), categorised Gaullism as a (then) modern form of moderate conservatism. Pickles (1972) argued that Gaullists were never concerned with ideological principles. Yet, Gaullism should not be categorised as 'ideological emptiness' (Hoffmann and Hoffmann 1974: 217). Some scholars have argued the legacy of Gaullism is solely the result of de Gaulle's authority and is a modern form of Bonapartism (Rémond 1982). According to Watson (2003: 255) who argued that such view is an oversimplification, historians should give more credit to Gaullists as they realised that 'Gaullism could not survive on the basis of de Gaulle's prestige alone and gave it a doctrine and method of action which ensured its survival after the General's departure from office in 1969.' The fact that the notion of Gaullism itself still prevails nearly 50 years since de Gaulle's death would support such stance.

Accordingly, much of the academic debate on Gaullism focuses on whether it should be categorised as a political ideology or as a doctrine. There is a fine line between these two notions. Based on the work of Crick (2005: 156), a political doctrine should be interpreted as 'a coherently related set of proposals for the conciliation of differing social interests in a desirable manner,' while an ideology is an ideal-type, a broad set of ideas and principles which 'cannot be taken up and set down by politicians as a weapon' (Crick 2005: 37). Yet, two questions need to be answered in order to determine what Gaullism effectively *is*.

Firstly, what principles does Gaullism consist of? Knapp (1994: 4–6) distinguished four key tenets. The first one is the *independence of France*, with a categoric refusal to submit France and French policy to the authority of supranational organizations. The second one is the *authority of the State*, according to which a strongly centralised state and its institutions constitute the ultimate source of power and imply the presence of a strong core executive often considered as 'dirigiste.' The third one is the *unity of the French people*, referring to de Gaulle's willingness to 'rally the French beyond the confines of political parties,' beyond right and left ideologies (a claim which is nowadays used by most contemporary French leaders). The fourth and final tenet highlighted by Knapp is the *leadership of de Gaulle*, perceived as a charismatic leader who is the founder of a new relationship between the State and its citizens. These four tenets are further illustrated by the following statement from the Gaullist party manifesto in 1965:

> What, essentially, is Gaullism composed of? Of the combination of national sentiment and the French humanist tradition, of the desire for progress and the conviction that it would not be possible without a strong state, nor would it be desirable unless it were to serve mankind. [. . .] Gaullism, the modern form of patriotism and democracy, is, in its essence, the affirmation that a certain idea of France has always shaped our destiny.
> *(Union pour la Nouvelle République, cited and*
> *translated in Cerny 1980: 25)*

Furthermore, the relevance of cultural politics as a tool to improve France's prestige in the world (as illustrated by the creation of a French ministry of culture under de Gaulle's presidency) is often referenced as a fifth feature of Gaullism (see e.g. Kritzman 2006).

Secondly, if Gaullism is built around the *grandeur* of de Gaulle in a particular national context, does it have any significance beyond the French borders? Berstein (2001: 308), who argued that Gaullism is 'neither a doctrine nor a political ideology,' provides some elements of response:

> [i]t appears unfair to liken Gaullists to national leaders such as Amintore Fanfani in Italy who are determined to advanced the parochial interests of their countries in the international community, for none has exceeded de Gaulle himself in promoting the conditions designed to accomplish his objectives or in understanding the consequences of those objectives. Gaullism appears to be a peculiarly French phenomenon, without doubt the quintessential French political phenomenon of the twentieth century.

However, this statement needs to be nuanced, as Gaullism was often referenced by other European leaders and often had an influence over elite positions on foreign policy issues. In the context of European integration (which is further developed in a following section), Gaullists joined forces with other intergovernmentalist movements from countries such as Italy to form a relatively influent pan-European force in the European Parliament from 1965 onwards. This pan-European group, the European Progressive Democrats, committed to promote a Gaullist vision of Europe which emphasised national sovereignty, though it initially remained French centred. A subsequent neo-Gaullist pan-European movement founded in 1995, the Union for Europe, abandoned a French-centric vision and campaigned for a European Union of nation states as a response to the ratification of the Maastricht Treaty (Leruth 2017; see also below). As such, some key principles of Gaullism were advocated beyond the French context at the transnational and pan-European levels.

As such, while scholars agreed over a series of key policies and tenets Gaullism stands for, there is very little consensus over what Gaullism effectively is. Some will argue that it is very close to an ideology. Others will say that it is nothing but a French vision of modern conservatism. Despite the lack of a widely accepted definition, Gaullism is best understood as a French political doctrine favouring a strong, centralised and sovereign state which unites its citizenry, as advocated by Charles de Gaulle during his presidency. Unlike Thatcherism, it is not driven by grounded economic principles, as the stance advocated by Gaullist parties fluctuated between economic conservatism and liberalism depending on the political context.

Gaullism as a political movement

From the Union pour la Nouvelle République to Les Républicains

Over the past 50 years, the Gaullist movement has generally been represented by one 'mainstream' political party. Between 1959 and 2018, five major centre right Gaullist parties were formed: the Union pour la Nouvelle République, which co-existed with the smaller, left-wing Gaullist Union Démocratique du Travail; the Union des Démocrates pour la (Cinquième) République; the Rassemblement pour la République; Union pour la Majorité Présidentielle/Union pour un Mouvement Populaire; and Les Républicains since 2015. As of 2018, a total of four presidents and 12 prime ministers came from the Gaullist movement (see Table 3.1).

Under de Gaulle's presidency, the Gaullist movement was driven by the key principles highlighted in the preceding section: a strong, united and *dirigiste* state, combined with a commitment to improve French prestige around the world. The societal transformation of France from the mid-1960s onwards suggested that the Gaullist movement failed to respond to key demands and concerns from the French society. Workers became increasingly concerned over the lack

Table 3.1 List of major Gaullist parties, presidents and prime ministers, 1959–2018.

Party	President	Prime minister
Union pour la Nouvelle République (1959–1967)	Charles de Gaulle (1959–1969)[1]	Michel Debré (1959–1962)
		Georges Pompidou (1962–1968)
Union Démocratique du Travail (1959–1967)		
Union des Démocrates pour la (Cinquième) République (1967–1976)		Maurice Couve de Murville (1968–1969)
	Georges Pompidou (1969–1974)[2]	Jacques Chaban-Delmas (1969–1972)
		Pierre Messmer (1972–1974)
		Jacques Chirac (1974–1976)[3]
Rassemblement pour la République (1976–2002)		Jacques Chirac (1986–1988)[4]
		Édouard Balladur (1993–1995)[5]
	Jacques Chirac (1995–2007)	Alain Juppé (1995–1997)
Union pour la Majorité Présidentielle/Union pour un Mouvement Populaire (2002–2015)		Jean-Pierre Raffarin (2002–2005)
		Dominique de Villepin (2005–2007)
	Nicolas Sarkozy (2007–2012)	François Fillon (2007–2012)
Les Républicains (since 2015)		*Édouard Philippe (2017)[6]*

Notes:
1 Following Charles de Gaulle's resignation, centrist (non-Gaullist) Alain Poher became president ad interim between 28 April and 20 June 1969.
2 Following Georges Pompidou's death, Alain Poher became president ad interim from 2 April to 27 May 1974.
3 Under Valéry Giscard d'Estaing's presidency.
4 Under François Mitterrand's presidency (cohabitation).
5 Under François Mitterrand's presidency (cohabitation).
6 Under Emmanuel Macron's presidency. Édouard Philippe effectively left Les Républicains in 2018 and never effectively represented the party as prime minister.

of commitment to get them involved in industry management, and the education system was in urgent need of further reforms which were not conducted by the government. The student strikes and revolts of May 1968 marked the beginning of the end of de Gaulle's presidential era. As hypothesised by Kritzman (2006: 54), the May 1968 events may have been 'the consequences of de Gaulle's sacrifice of domestic issues at the expense of an international politics based on the idea of grandeur.' He would eventually resign in 1969, following the outcome of the referendum on decentralisation and reform of the Senate.

The idea and interpretation of Gaullism as a political movement has evolved since de Gaulle's presidency. The main Gaullist parties have undergone major ideological shifts, juggling between conservatism and liberalism as ideal-types. Most of these changes took place following disappointing election results, thus suggesting that change is driven by voters rather than by changes in the movement's leadership (Demker 1997). Since de Gaulle's death in 1970, several competing categorisations have emerged. Touchard (1978) identified different versions of Gaullism: the Gaullism of de Gaulle (as a political leader), the Gaullism of influential Gaullist personalities (such as Malraux, Mauriac, Debré and Georges Pompidou), the Gaullism of political movements (i.e. parties) and the Gaullism of the nation (see also Watson 2001).

Knapp and Wright (2006: 226) listed five movements which materialised from the 1970s onwards:

1   *Gaullisme de Résistance*: movement loyal above all to 'the man of 18 June 1940,' i.e. the General who played a major role during the Second World War;
2   *Gaullisme de Gauche* (or left-wing Gaullism): movement focusing on the social dimension of Gaullism, often linked to social democracy (first advocated by the Union Démocratique du Travail);
3   *Gaullisme pompidolien*: movement loyal to the legacy of Georges Pompidou, emphasising the need for France to adapt to an increasingly competitive world while preserving social peace;
4   *Gaullisme chiraquien de première génération*: movement loyal to the original populist argument advocated by Jacques Chirac in the late 1970s, characterised by a fierce opposition to European integration and the free-market;
5   And the *Gaullisme chiraquien de deuxième génération*: movement loyal to the aggressive profree-market and pro-European rhetoric advocated by Chirac from the mid-1980s onwards.

Other concepts have been used to categorise political transformations over the past decades. The notion of 'neo-Gaullism' is often used in the existing literature to describe the ideological transformations that have occurred within the Gaullist movement under Jacques Chirac's leadership. More recently, the concept of Sarkozysm was coined as a potential successor to the traditional idea of Gaullism. Marlière (2009) linked Sarkozy with the more 'populist' atmosphere of Gaullism embracing its right-wing traditions and attempting to be perceived as a 'man of the people' despite being committed to implement neo-liberal policies before the Great Recession. One might argue that these new 'types' of posthumous Gaullism are the product of political contexts (see Watson 2001 for a thorough historical analysis).

Gaullism and European integration

Besides some ideological shifts which tended to occur following elections setbacks, the movement also suffered from a series of minor and major internal divisions. These divisions were managed differently throughout the history of the Gaullist movement, with some leaders favouring the creation of cluster movements within the party (e.g. Sarkozy), and others imposing their own approach which would ultimately lead to its fragmentation into smaller groups (e.g. Chirac). Splinter movements arose especially from the early 1990s onwards, and the Gaullist legacy was always disputed among themselves. While internal conflicts over a wide range of socio-economic issues took place over the past 50 years (most recently over welfare policy reforms such as pensions, unemployment benefits and access to services for migrants), the issue of European integration is a recurring theme which has been fuelling such divisions.

Scholars of European studies (especially in the field of Euroscepticism) have often struggled with Gaullists' attitudes towards European integration. Even though the first aforementioned key principle of Gaullism as an ideology emphasises the reluctance to submit to supranational authority, it would be too simplistic to categorise it as Eurosceptic. During de Gaulle's presidency, the key principle advocated by the movement was a European Community that serves the interests of nation states as demonstrated by the president's approach to the Common Agricultural Policy (Leruth and Startin 2017). Throughout the early 1960s, France opposed a series of proposals put forward or favoured by the other five member states, such as increasing the powers of the European Parliament and opposing the United Kingdom's first application for Community membership in 1963. This led to the 'empty chair crisis' of 1965–66 during which de Gaulle opposed Qualified Majority Voting as well as a supranational approach to the Common Agricultural Policy.[1] Yet, de Gaulle's position on European integration can hardly be identified as a form of Euroscepticism: instead, the empty chair crisis demonstrated his commitment to promoting an intergovernmentalist vision of Europe mostly based on trade between nations, with weak supranational institutions and decision-making power.

The post-Gaullian era was marked by strong internal divisions and uncertainties over the issue of European integration. The election of the pro-European, centre right and Christian Democrat Valéry Giscard d'Estaing as president in 1974 fuelled such divisions within the movement. Giscard d'Estaing tended to favour a federalist vision of European integration, which was opposed by the Gaullist movement. Its leader, Jacques Chirac, resigned as prime minister in 1976, notably because of disagreements with the president over the introduction of European Parliament elections from 1979 onwards. In 1978, Chirac's "Appel de Cochin" reflected Charles de Gaulle's vision of Europe, by emphasising an opposition to supranationalism and the need for greater French influence at the international level (Chirac 1978).

This was followed by a major U-turn in 1983, due to the conversion of the majority of the Gaullist movement's elites to economic liberalism. The Gaullist movement then moved towards a more modern, pro-European approach by advocating further supranational economic, monetary and defence cooperation. Internal divisions resurfaced in the early 1990s with the referendum regarding the ratification of the Maastricht Treaty, which paved the way for the development of a political union. While the majority of the party's elite was in favour of the Treaty, some senior members (led by Philippe Séguin and Charles Pasqua) campaigned against its ratification, claiming that Maastricht would pave the way for a federal Europe, which goes against the principle of nationalism as advocated by de Gaulle (Shields 1996). As many grass roots members shared such concerns, then Party Chairman Alain Juppé (1992: 1) felt unable to give a voting guideline: '[t]he Gaullist movement has decided to accept its differences in opinion. We could have chosen, like some others, to impose a party line on our supporters but we preferred to play a more open game based on transparency and truth.'

The referendum, which took place on 20 September 1992, was approved by 50.8% of voters with a turnout of 71.1%. Following the ratification and the pro-European stance advocated under Chirac's leadership, four Gaullist splinter parties were formed throughout the 1990s: the small 'Rassemblement pour la France,' founded by Nicolas Stoquer in 1992; Philippe de Villiers' 'Mouvement pour la France,' founded in 1994 following the success of the 'Majorité pour l'Autre Europe' list in the European elections; Charles Pasqua's Rassemblement pour la France et l'indépendance de l'Europe, founded in 1999 to unite *souverainistes* defectors from the Rassemblement pour la République; and Debout la République (nowadays called Debout la France), an openly Eurosceptic movement founded by 2012 and 2017 presidential candidate Nicolas Dupont-Aignan. Under Jacques Chirac's presidency, the Gaullist movement opted for a rather unified, pro-European stance and supported proposals to deepen and widen the European integration process. The foundation of the Union pour la Majorité Présidentielle in 2002 as a merger of the Rassemblement pour la République and non-Gaullist, pro-European centrist parties, strengthened the pro-European message within the centre right. Such stance was further advocated under Nicolas Sarkozy's leadership, though he ended his presidency by vowing to reform the 'broken' Schengen agreements in case of re-election in 2012 (Leruth and Startin 2017).

While the main Gaullist party was able to unify its stance on European integration following the creation of Euro-Populist splinter parties throughout the 1990s, internal divisions started to arise again following Nicolas Sarkozy's defeat in the 2012 presidential election against François Hollande. Such divisions were first accommodated through the formal institutionalisation of *courants* (movements) within the party. These included La Droite Sociale, led by current party leader Laurent Wauquiez, which advocated France's withdrawal of Schengen to the creation of a hard EU core consisting of the six founding member states within the Union (Leruth and Startin 2017). However, following Sarkozy's comeback as party leader in 2014 and the rebranding of the Union pour la Majorité Présidentielle as Les Républicains in 2015, these courants became dormant. Divisions over the issue of European integration re-emerged during the 2016 primary elections, which aimed at designating Les Républicain's candidate for the 2017 presidential elections. The most striking divisions occurred between the two main contestants, Nicolas Sarkozy and Alain Juppé; the former advocated less European integration and strong reforms, while the latter favoured further developments at the supranational level especially in the areas of security and defence. This primary election was unexpectedly won by former prime minister François Fillon, who attempted to find a compromise between both visions during the 2017 presidential campaign, which was heavily dominated by this issue following the Brexit vote.

In sum, the Gaullist movement's position over European integration fluctuated over time. As noted by Startin (2005: 65), '[t]he Gaullist movement's ability or inability to react to EU wide developments in an increasingly globalised world has become fundamental to its future direction.' Leruth and Startin (2017: 155–156) suggested that three distinct (and at times conflicting) stances were adopted by Gaullist political elites: Euro-Federalism, which advocates further transfers of political competences from the national to the supranational level without necessarily favouring the idea of a 'United States of Europe'; Euro-Pragmatism, which is defined as 'contingent support for the European Union combined with a certain reluctance towards the principles of closer integration'; and Euro-Populism, which can be interpreted as a form of 'soft' Euroscepticism under which political elites portray the European Union as the 'corrupt elite' acting against the sovereign state.

Conclusions. After 2017, is Gaullism in crisis?

The study of Gaullism requires scholars to make a distinction between Gaullism as a political doctrine and as a political movement. As a doctrine, it is best defined as a set of policy principles favouring a strong, centralised state and a united society. As a political movement, it has been represented by one 'mainstream' political party and (especially since the 1990s) smaller splinter parties, mostly located on the centre right of the traditional left–right spectrum. These parties have adopted socio-economic policies which fluctuated between modern conservatism and economic liberalism over the past six decades. Tensions over the future of European integration are common within the Gaullist movement, and these were amplified in the 1990s following the ratification of the Maastricht Treaty. Yet, the key components of Gaullism identified by Knapp (i.e. a strong, independent state, the unity of the French people, and referenced to the leadership style of de Gaulle) remained prominent in each of these parties.

Charles de Gaulle's legacy is uncontestably still prominent in French politics, even beyond mainstream Gaullist parties. During most election campaigns, candidates from all sides of the political spectrum refer to his legacy, with many attempting to appear as his 'true successor.' In the context of the 2017 presidential elections for instance, de Gaulle's legacy was used by prominent candidates such as François Fillon, Benoît Hamon, Marine Le Pen, Emmanuel Macron and even Jean-Luc Mélenchon (see e.g. Le Parisien 2017).

Following the defeat of François Fillon in the first round of the French presidential election held on 23 April 2017, the Gaullist movement entered yet another period of crisis. Les

Républicains are currently sitting in opposition after having lost 93 of its 229 seats in the 2017 legislative elections due to the emergence of La République En Marche! The future of the movement became increasingly complex with the nomination of former Républicain deputy Edouard Philippe as prime minister by Emmanuel Macron in an attempt to build a cross-party coalition and break with the traditional partisan mould. If the parliament is not dissolved before the end of the current term (in 2022), the Gaullist movement will sit in opposition for at least ten years and possibly break the record set between 1976 and 1986 (see Table 3.1). The results of the (low-key) French Senate elections held on 24 September 2017 were welcomed with a sigh of relief within the party, as it managed to extend its majority by gaining a total of 146 seats. The new leader of the movement, Laurent Wauquiez, was formally elected on 10 December 2017.

At the time of writing, it is too early to determine the long-term impact of Emmanuel Macron's victory on the Gaullist movement. However, in the first months of 2018, it looked like Les Républicains were contemplating the idea of an alliance with the Front National, thus suggesting that the Gaullist movement would move further to the right on issues such as immigration. As the main party sitting in opposition, Les Républicains initially struggled to oppose key socio-economic policies put forward by the Philippe government. The pro-European vision of Macron and his government could invigorate internal divisions over this issue within the Gaullist movement; advocates of a Euro-Populist stance could become more prominent within the party's structure, especially in the context of the European elections of 2019.

Yet, it would be exaggerated to say that the idea of Gaullism is facing a major crisis which could ultimately lead to its demise. The history of the Gaullist movement is marked not only by strong periods of electoral success but also by periods of crises marked by internal divisions, the creation of splinter parties and various failed attempts to modernise the party. The 2012 and subsequent 2017 election results are part of such cycle. In the past, the Gaullist movement has adapted its programme following election results; the most recent election defeats are no exception to the rule. Furthermore, given the salience of the issue of European integration and as most presidential candidates referred to de Gaulle during the election campaign, Gaullism as a political doctrine will keep on playing a major role in French politics.

Note

1 The 'empty chair crisis' was more of an attempt to weaken France's growing influence within the European Community rather than being the product of France's dissatisfaction over the way European integration was moving forward, as argued by Piers Ludlow (1999).

References

Berstein, S. 2001. Gaullism. In J. Krieger (Ed.), *The Oxford Companion to Politics of the World*, 2nd edition. Oxford: Oxford University Press, 307–308.

Cerny, P. G. 1980. *The Politics of Grandeur: Ideological Aspects of de Gaulle's Foreign Policy*. Cambridge: Cambridge University Press.

Charlot, J. 1970. *The Gaullist Phenomenon: The Gaullist Movement in the Fifth Republic*. New York: Praeger.

Chirac, J. 1978. *Discours pour la France à l'heure du choix*. Paris: Stock.

Crick, B. 2005. *In Defence of Politics*, 5th edition. London: Continuum.

Demker, M. 1997. Changing party ideology: Gaullist parties facing voters, leaders and competitors. In *Party Politics*, 3:3, 407–426.

Gordon, P. H. 1993. *A Certain Idea of France: French Security Policy and the Gaullist Legacy*. Princeton, NJ: Princeton University Press.

Hoffmann, S. and I. Hoffmann. 1974. De Gaulle as a political artist: the will to grandeur. In S. Hoffmann (Ed.), *Decline or Renewal? France since the 1930s*. New York: Viking Press, 202–253.

Juppé, A. 1992. Le Traité de Maastricht. In *Lettre de la Nation*. Paris: Rassemblement pour la République.

Knapp, A. 1994. *Gaullism since de Gaulle*. Aldershot: Dartmouth Publishing.

Knapp, A. and V. Wright. 2006. *The Government and Politics of France*. London: Routledge.

Kolodziej, E. A. 1974. *French International Policy under de Gaulle and Pompidou: The Politics of Grandeur*. Ithaca, NY: Cornell University Press.

Kritzman, L. D. 2006. Gaullism. In B. J. Reilly (Ed.), *The Columbia History of Twentieth-century French Thought*. New York: Columbia University Press, 51–54.

Le Parisien. 2017. Présidentielle: ils votent tous de Gaulle! Available at: www.leparisien.fr/elections/presidentielle/presidentielle-ils-votent-tous-de-gaulle-07-05-2017-6923634.php [Accessed: 21.02.2018].

Leruth, B. 2017. Is 'Eurorealism the new 'Euroscepticism?' Modern conservatism, the European conservatives and reformists and European integration. In J. FitzGibbon, B. Leruth and N. Startin (Eds.), *Euroscepticism as a Transnational and Pan-European Phenomenon: The Emergence of a New Sphere of Opposition*. London: Routledge, 46–62.

Leruth, B. and N. Startin. 2017. Between Euro-federalism, Euro-pragmatism and Euro-populism: the Gaullist movement divided over Europe. In *Modern and Contemporary France*, 25:2, 153–169.

Mahan, E. R. 2002. *Kennedy, De Gaulle, and Western Europe*. Basingstoke: Palgrave Macmillan.

Marlière, P. 2009. Sarkozysm as an ideological theme park: Nicolas Sarkozy and right-wing political thought. In *Modern and Contemporary France*, 17:4, 375–390.

Morse, E. 1973. *Foreign Policy and Interdependence in Gaullist France*. Princeton, NJ: Princeton University Press.

Pickles, D. 1972. *The Government and Politics of France*, Vol. 1: Institutions and Parties. London: Methuen.

Piers Ludlow, N. 1999. Challenging French leadership in Europe: Germany, Italy, the Netherlands and the outbreak of the empty chair crisis of 1965–1966. In *Contemporary European History*, 8:2, 231–248.

Rémond, R. 1982. *Les Droites en France*. Paris: Aubier.

Shields, J. G. 1996. The French Gaullists. In J. Gaffney (Ed.), *Political Parties and the European Union*. London: Routledge, 86–109.

Singer, D. 2002. *Prelude to Revolution: France in May 1968*. Cambridge, MA: South End Press.

Startin, N. 2005. Maastricht, Amsterdam and beyond: the troubled evolution of the French right. In H. Drake (Ed.), *French Relations with the European Union*. Abingdon: Routledge.

Touchard, J. 1978. *Le Gaullisme 1940–1969*. Paris: Seuil.

Waldman, D. A., B. M. Bass and F. J. Yammarino. 1990. Adding to contingent-reward behavior: the augmenting effect of charismatic leadership. In *Group and Organization Management*, 15:4, 381–394.

Watson, J. 2001. *The internal dynamics of Gaullism*. PhD thesis. Oxford: Trinity College, University of Oxford.

Watson, J. 2003. The internal dynamics of Gaullism, 1958–69. In N. Atkin and F. Tallett (Eds.), *The Right in France: From Revolution to Le Pen*. London: I.B. Tauris, 245–261.

Williams, P. and M. Harrison. 1961. *De Gaulle's Republic*. London: Longmans.

4

FRANCE AND THE WORLD

The African dimension

Margaret A. Majumdar[1]

Central to France's self-image as a nation state is *rayonnement* – the projection of French power overseas. This notion, which predates the Revolution, is rooted in the idea that the country is the harbinger of a civilisation that has universal value and that it therefore has a right, indeed a duty, to share this greatness (*grandeur*) with the rest of the world. In the post-war period this was expressed notably by president Charles de Gaulle, who put this idea at the very centre of his foreign policy. Following decolonisation and the loss of empire in the early 1960s, the policy had four pillars: the development of an independent nuclear deterrent, the defence of France's permanent seat on the UN Security Council, positioning France alongside Germany at the heart of the European construction project and the maintenance of a sphere of influence in Africa. This chapter will focus on the fourth of these pillars. It will show how Africa became *the* privileged arena for the projection of French power overseas after 1960 and how it has retained this position in the post–Cold War period. It will explore the economic, political, military, diplomatic and cultural dimensions of the French presence in Africa and analyse how and why these have evolved under the Fifth Republic.

A brief history of the French colonial empire in Africa and the decolonisation process

Initially, France's presence in Africa is explained and defined by the imperial and colonial encounter. From small beginnings through trading posts in the seventeenth century, primarily in West Africa, tied closely to French Atlantic operations and the slave economy, the French African colonial empire was to develop to such an extent that it could be perceived as a rival to the British colonial presence on the continent by the end of the nineteenth century. After the loss of most of its earlier overseas territories as a result of wars with Britain in the New World and in India, most notably the Seven Years' War, which ended in 1763, it was the invasion and conquest of the North African territory of Algeria, beginning in 1830, that gave the impetus for a second spurt of imperialist activity on the part of France. This was then to develop significantly into a third major phase from the 1870s onwards under the Third Republic, largely through the massive expansion of territory held in West and Central Africa, with a presence in the Horn of Africa in the East with Djibouti and French Somaliland, and on Madagascar and other island territories off the East African coast (Aldrich 1996; Conklin et al. 2015; Cooper 2014; Ferro 1994).

In spite of its defeat at the hands of the Nazis and the resulting occupation of its metropolitan territory, France managed to come out of World War II with its colonial empire largely intact. Indeed, the colonies and large numbers of colonial troops had played an important role in the war (as they had in World War I). This does not mean that France, and particularly its wartime leader, Charles de Gaulle, did not understand the need for change. It became clear that old-style colonial relations could not continue if France was to retain its position in Africa. Although its colonial supremacy was soon to be challenged by growing anti-colonial nationalist movements, most notably in North Africa, Madagascar and Indochina, the need for reform of the French empire was already apparent by the end of the war. Indeed, it had already been encapsulated in 1944 at the Conference called by de Gaulle in Brazzaville, administrative capital of the AEF (French Equatorial Africa), in the Brazzaville Declaration, which set an agenda for social and economic reform as well as constitutional change to enable greater political participation by Africans. At the same time, de Gaulle also made it clear that the French were committed to maintaining their presence in Africa.

Thus, there were changes. The empire was renamed the French Union (*Union française*) in the new constitutional settlement after the Liberation culminating in the establishment of the Fourth Republic. It foresaw a more federal structure for the new greater France, implying a higher degree of autonomy for the territories, as well as the aim of forming the colonial subjects into citizens of this newly defined union, with the political participation that entailed. This was not seen as the first stage towards independence and self-rule, as much as the provision of a firmer – because it was fairer – foundation for the continuation of the French presence in Africa. The Tunisian and Moroccan independences of 1956 were also very much intended to reincorporate existing powers under new guises (Ikeda 2015).

These attempts to make France's role in Africa more palatable to Africans themselves were reinforced by a number of developments on the wider international stage. The increasing strength of anti-colonial and nationalist movements across Africa and Asia was reflected in the Bandung Conference of 1955, which brought together 29 African and Asian countries and was to lead to the foundation of the Non-Aligned Movement. This followed close on the defeat of the French army at the hands of the Vietnamese independence fighters at Dien Bien Phu in 1954. Another was the emergence of the US as a burgeoning superpower, with a widely proclaimed policy of anti-colonialism, as a result of its own history no doubt, but also its sense that the European colonial powers needed to be brought down to size, as indeed they were in the Suez debacle of 1956.

However, it took the bloody Algerian War of Independence of 1954–1962 and the subsequent political crisis which brought down the French Fourth Republic in 1958 to make the end of empire in Africa inevitable. The speed at which the end of the empire occurred could be considered surprising. The French presence in Africa had, after all, provided the clout behind France's claims to remain a great power in the post-war period and thus entitled to a permanent seat on the Security Council of the United Nations. Moreover, it was during the time of the Fourth Republic that new ideas were emerging and being pursued to support the necessity of the preservation of the connection with Africa. This was the case for the hugely influential notion of Eurafrica (Hansen and Jonsson 2014), which revived earlier pre-war visions of a strategic union of Europe and Africa to provide European industry with the raw materials it needed and make a powerful competitive bloc in the face of other pan-continental groupings in the Americas and Asia. As it was propounded at this time by François Mitterrand and others, it provided a remedy to the perceived decline and weakness of Europe, through the synergies provided by the riches and vitality of Africa.

However, notwithstanding the support for Eurafrica and other newly rejigged forms of colonial or neo-colonial relations, decolonisation in West and Central Africa came speedily. It was achieved in mainly peaceful fashion via the 1958 referendum on the proposed changes to transform the French Union into the French Community, offering autonomy to the various colonies. This referendum resulted in agreement by all the territories involved with the sole exception of French Guinea, which opted for immediate independence. Within a few years, however, most of the African countries moved rapidly to full independence and the French Community became defunct. Independence in Djibouti followed rather later in 1977.

The decolonisation of Algeria was anything but peaceful. It was marked by violent guerrilla warfare and brutal counter-insurgency measures, including severe judicial repression and the widespread use of torture. Among the factors that singled Algeria out were the presence of a large population of European settlers in the territory who were almost uniformly hostile to Algerian independence and its unique status amongst the French colonies in Africa, as a result of being incorporated into France as part of the national territory in the nineteenth century, beginning with the creation in the northern part of the country of the three *départements* of Alger, Oran and Constantine in 1848 (Elkins and Pedersen 2005: 226). The bitterness of the struggle, leading to the mass flight of most Europeans to France and other countries, remains a factor in Franco-Algerian relations to this day, although the economic, cultural, political and indeed military ties that now exist also form part of this configuration.

French influence in Africa following decolonisation

Elsewhere in Africa, political independence did not mean the end of the French presence and influence. As we have seen, the maintenance of a sphere of influence in Africa for France was one of the key pillars of de Gaulle's foreign policy. How this was achieved was quite specific to France.

Whereas Britain contrived to incorporate most of its former colonies, with a few notable exceptions, into the formalised institutional framework of the Commonwealth, de Gaulle's short-lived Franco-African Community failed to create similar lasting formal ties (Rouvez et al. 1994: 217–218). Continued British influence was based on retaining historical links and remnants of tutelary power relations, notably through the overarching role of British judicial institutions in some cases and the role of the British monarch, with a number of countries even retaining the Queen as head of state. France, however, adopted a quite different strategy, which encompassed several approaches.

In the immediate aftermath of decolonisation, bilateral ties with the newly independent African countries were preferred. These were sealed in a number of agreements for military, defence, technical and cultural cooperation. Close relations with African leaders and elites were fostered and nurtured at a personal level in most cases, with a stress on the common culture and language linking them to France, but also on economic, technical and, above all, military support for the new regimes. The importance of these ties to France was reflected in the way in which the relations were managed. African affairs were very much the domain of the president of the French Republic himself and thus formed part of his reserved powers, not subject to scrutiny from other political bodies, such as the parliament, nor within the control of the foreign ministry. These questions were dealt with at the Elysée, the French presidential palace, through a special cell operating under Jacques Foccart as chief advisor on Africa and director of sometimes covert operations. This cell managed the networks that were set up to serve the French national interest, while also ensuring the loyalty of the African elites through a system of rewards and mutual self-interest. The fact that Foccart maintained this position over many years, from 1960 to 1974, under the presidencies of de Gaulle and Pompidou and then again under Jacques Chirac from 1986 until his death in 1997, with advisory roles in the interim, is indicative of his huge influence, of the personal nature of the networks established and the continuity of the policy.

While much of this networking took place behind the scenes, there was also a public face to the Franco-African relationship, which took the form of high-profile meetings and visits by and to African leaders, and particularly the Franco-African summits, initiated after a suggestion by Niger's Hamani Diori in 1973. Apart from any discussions of policy, these were designed first and foremost to reinforce the sense of belonging to a family, whose members were united by the influence and prestige of France, and thus help to maintain these nations within the French orbit.

As we shall see, these endeavours on the part of France were not opposed by other powers. During the time of the Cold War, the US in particular did not perceive Africa as strategically important and was happy to allow France to maintain its privileged sphere of influence in West and Central Africa (Chafer 2014). Indeed, the maintenance of French influence in Africa was seen as a valuable bulwark against the competing influence of the Soviet bloc and the potential spread of communism in the former colonies. This tacit support could thus even extend to more overt acceptance of the need for French intervention, not least in its military form. Indeed, the presence of French troops and military facilities in a number of African countries often made France the first port of call in a crisis.

The economic, military and diplomatic dimensions of the French presence in Africa

Throughout the Cold War, France maintained what Alden has called 'the viability of the long-nurtured Franco-African security system' (Alden 1996: 20). The Cold War chessboard offered economic and political opportunities, not least through arms trade, but it also placed a burden on French defence missions. In line with bilateral defence agreements that had been in force since independence, France has intervened militarily in Africa more than 30 times since decolonisation, most recently in Mali, Chad, Central African Republic, Somalia and Ivory Coast. This amounts to an average of one intervention every year between 1960 and 1990 (Chafer 2014; Lellouche and Moisi 1979). In addition, France remains a major supplier of military equipment, including aircraft and armaments, to African countries. It also maintains military bases in a number of countries, including Gabon, Senegal and Djibouti, and a large presence of permanently stationed troops which number 10,000 or more (Chafer 2014).

Along with the military and diplomatic ties that have played such a vital part in Franco–African relations, the economic and financial dimension has had an equally important role, through the various networks linking France and the African continent. These networks encompassed the many French companies, some of them state controlled or with strong links to the state, which have extensive economic, financial and commercial interests in Africa, such as France Telecom, Compagnie Générale des Eaux, Bouygues, Bolloré, Eiffage, amongst others. At the end of 2015, 14 French multinationals figured among the top companies with interests in Africa, including Total, Castel, Orange, Lafarge, Vinci, Bouygues and Technip (Piot 2017).

Amongst the most powerful companies operating in Africa, the oil conglomerates have had a particularly important role. The one-time state-owned French giant, Elf-Aquitaine (later to become Total-Fina-Elf and then Total) has been crucial in this regard and, along with other oil multinationals, has been subject to criticism on economic, financial and environmental grounds, as well as involvement in local politics, military conflicts and corruption. While these erupted in legal proceedings in 2003 and led to a severe crisis in relations with the ruling regime in Congo–Brazzaville, it was largely through the existence of the close personal networks that problems were resolved and no lasting damage was done to Franco–African relations.

Increasingly, as in the case of Elf-Aquitaine, French companies have become transformed into multinational concerns. Moreover, their economic relations have not just been with Francophone Africa. Many have widespread interests in the so-called Anglophone countries too. For instance, the car manufacturer Peugeot has had a significant present in South Africa and the former Rhodesia, now Zimbabwe.

Nonetheless, economic relations between France and Francophone Africa have benefited from a number of special conditions. Importantly, the economic and financial ties were reinforced through the maintenance of the 'franc zone,' which entailed the pegging of the African countries' currency to the French franc and required them to keep most of their foreign currency reserves with the Bank of France (Chafer 2014).

Also significant to the ongoing French influence has been the policy of 'cooperation,' instituted by de Gaulle in the wake of decolonisation and designed to reinforce the ties between Francophone Africa and France, whilst making a contribution to economic, social and cultural development of the newly independent countries (Mesli 2013). Development aid and programmes associated with 'cooperation' policy have certainly reinforced the economic and financial ties with France's former African colonies which have received by far the greatest share of French development aid. The greatest influence has been in the education sector, with France sending a significant number of teachers at all levels to Africa, as well as contributing to education infrastructure. From 1959 to 1967, for instance, the fund set up to channel French development aid, the Fonds d'Aide à la Coopération (FAC), devoted more than 38% of its budget to higher education, 27% to secondary education, 13% to primary education and only 7.4% to the technical and vocational sector (Mesli 2013). Moreover, the very presence of young French '*coopérants*' in a variety of sectors has served to strengthen and propagate French cultural influence in many African countries (Bossuat 2003).

France's cultural policy in Africa and the role of *la Francophonie*

Thus, important as these concrete economic, financial and commercial factors have been for France and its African partners, along with the political and military interactions, they do not by any means tell the whole story of how and why France has managed to maintain a power base across the African continent. To fully understand the factors which have supported and boosted French power in Africa, we have to give the cultural dimension its full due. Indeed, much of France's influence derives from what is sometimes called 'soft' power, in contrast to hard financial, political and military clout. This 'soft' power derives from the prestige attached to France, not just, or even primarily, because of its role as a wealthy European power, but because of what it stands for in the history of political ideas of liberty and modernity, its role as perceived champion of the 'Third World' and its position at the forefront of a universal culture not designed solely for the French people of France but for enlightened citizens of the world wherever they might be.

This image of France as a beacon of humanist republicanism, promoting liberty, equality and fraternity, along with a doctrine of universal human rights, has proved surprisingly resilient into the twenty-first century. This is in spite of the uses and abuses of these ideas in the service of the French Empire through a colonial ideology that rationalised France's imperial enterprise through various forms of the *mission civilisatrice*, the civilising mission to bring the benighted peoples of the world, and especially those in Africa, to progressive enlightenment in the bosom of France.

Although the actual propagation of the French language and culture to Africans prior to decolonisation was by and large limited to a fairly small elite who pursued their studies in France, there is no denying that under the Fifth Republic, the French state has used various means at its disposal to carry through its cultural policy, inspired by the deeply rooted ideal of *rayonnement*. This does not just extend to language-teaching programmes but also to a broader notion of 'cultural cooperation.' In this, the role of the relatively small francophone elite in 'cascading' their cultural values to the rest of the African populations is worth noting, making them sometimes better advocates of French culture than the French themselves. Even long after Independence, high economic and social status are often linked to how conversant one is with the French language and culture, largely as a result of education.

What is remarkable is the extent to which many members of the African elite have themselves subscribed to this view of the exceptionalism of the French language and culture. Indeed, we can situate the origins of the development of what has come to be known as *la Francophonie* in an intellectual movement springing from the aims and ideals of some of the leaders of the newly independent African countries. These were individuals such as Léopold Sedar Senghor of Senegal, Habib Bourguiba of Tunisia and Hamani Diori of Niger, who linked up with some non-African figures such as Norodom Sihanouk of Cambodia, to propose a new form of relations following the end of empire. These would no longer be based on colonial relations of domination but on a concept of community which would embrace and bring together all those members of the francophone family, defined in the first instance as all those who had the French language in common and who thereby shared a common culture and values. These were specifically the values of enlightened republicanism as propounded by the France of the universal rights of man.

The initial impetus for this movement was the publication in 1962 of a number of articles by the aforementioned politicians and intellectuals in the review *Esprit*. It then developed along the lines of cultural and technical cooperation through the offices of the ACCT (Agence de coopération culturelle et technique). It was, however, many years before the movement assumed any concrete political reality. It was François Mitterrand who realised its potential and inaugurated the first Francophone summits when he became president. It has undergone many subsequent changes, mainly in the direction of strengthening its institutions and giving them a permanent basis, staffing and leadership in the form of the Organisation Internationale de la Francophonie (International Francophone Organisation, OIF). While there have also been significant shifts in the ideological emphasis of *Francophonie*, particularly with the inclusion of many countries as members whose claim to be 'Francophone' in the true linguistic sense could be seen as quite tenuous, the idealistic discourse portraying France and French culture as a beacon of progressive values remains largely intact.

Within this organisation and the francophone family, African countries play a very important role, making up 32 out of the total number of 59 full members of the organisation (www. francophonie.org 2017). Moreover, the African presence in *Francophonie* is not just represented by the former French colonies and protectorates; it also includes former Belgian colonies such as Democratic Republic of Congo, Rwanda and Burundi, as well as some former territories of the British Empire, such as Ghana which is an associate member. Indeed, some countries, such as Cameroon, Rwanda, Mauritius and the Seychelles, belong both to the OIF and to the British Commonwealth.

This, along with other factors such as the increased membership of Eastern European countries, has entailed the relaxation of the French language criterion for membership of the OIF.

However, it nonetheless remains the case that the future of the French language is closely bound up with its development in Africa. Given that France is the only country where French is the sole language (Toft and Verstraete-Hansen 2009), the claims of French to remain an important world language rest very substantially on the presence of over 96 million French speakers in Africa,[2] a figure that is projected to increase substantially in the coming years.

One former French colony, and a very important one at that, has so far refused to join, although at various moments it seems to have toyed with the idea. This is Algeria, for whom the memory of the colonial period and the bitter struggle of the War of Liberation remains vivid and appears at times to constitute a stumbling block to the recasting of Franco–Algerian relations in a more normalised diplomatic form. There have been various attempts to put the past to rest and several diplomatic initiatives, such as the recent visit of the Algerian minister of *moudjahidine* to Paris in January 2016, to discuss the problematic issues that continue to sour these relations: notably, the question of the restitution of the archives from the colonial period; the ongoing lack of information about the 'disparus,' still unaccounted for many years after the end of the war; and, finally, the question of compensation for those whose health has been affected by the nuclear tests which France carried out in the Sahara in the early 1960s. These ongoing difficulties form a counterpart to the general prestige from which France benefits on the African continent. However, they should not be exaggerated, as there is in fact a close relationship between the French and Algerian regimes and a developing degree of cooperation, not just on economic relations but also on defence and security concerns.

From *Françafrique* to twenty-first-century engagement

The continuation of colonial relations in new forms that characterises *Françafrique* has been increasingly challenged not just by Africans but also by the ruling French political class. Originally, this term was used in a positive fashion to stress the closeness of the ties which bound together France and Africa. It was the Ivoirian leader Félix Houphuouët-Boigny who was credited with its invention to express the 'special relationship' that he wanted to maintain between African countries and France (Chafer 2014: 514–518).

However, while it appeared to provide mutual benefits for the ruling elites in both France and African countries, its blatant shortcomings and shady dealings made it more and more discredited and threatened to tarnish France's reputation on the world stage. This critique was encapsulated in the work of François-Xavier Verschave and others who laid bare the operations and nefarious practices covered by the term (Verschave 1998). Even more than this, it became clear that the tightly knit networks of *Françafrique* no longer corresponded to the real economic and political dynamics on the African continent and became an impediment to the development of French influence where it mattered.

On the one hand, the economic interests of France could no longer be linked solely, or even mainly linked, to its former African colonies. The most dynamic economic development was increasingly to be found in countries which had been linked to the British Empire, such as the burgeoning economic powerhouses of South Africa, Nigeria and now, increasingly, Angola. Thus one of the ways in which France reframed its relationship with Africa was to extend the scope of its involvement beyond its previous colonial and postcolonial sphere of influence, often referred to as the *pré carré*, to encompass relations with Anglophone countries. This did not just involve economic and commercial relations with these countries, through trade in essential commodities and raw materials, the growth of investment and military sales, important as these all were. It also involved the development of new political ties through the inclusion of these countries in the Franco–African summits, for instance in 2013 all African countries except Zimbabwe were represented at the summit in Paris, along with a number of international organisations (Elysée Summit 2013). This is in line with the development since the 1990s which has seen the accession of non-francophone countries, in the strict sense, to membership of the International Francophone Organisation and participation in the Francophone biannual summits. The development of cooperation between France and other players on the African continent, such as the UK and the European Union, also ensured that more multilateral ways of operating, particularly but not only within the military and security fields, became more common. The 1998 Franco–British summit held in Saint-Malo was instrumental in instigating a new phase in Franco–British cooperation on security issues in Africa (Chafer 2014; Chafer and Cumming 2010). This tendency was further boosted by a new emphasis by France on supporting multilateral cooperation between the African countries themselves, through the African Union and also regional groupings such as ECOWAS (Economic Community of West African States) and others to further political and economic cooperation, through the establishment of joint military forces to tackle security threats and the greater prominence of the role of the African Union. Increasingly, France has come to see its role as providing support in terms of logistics and training, rather than taking the lead in operations.

The colonial and postcolonial relations which had operated under the cover of the menace of Cold War power politics became more and more redundant in the new world order, following the fall of the Berlin Wall in 1989. The collapse of the Soviet Union was to have a profound effect on the geopolitical balance of forces between the different powers in their relations to Africa. Whereas France had been more or less given free rein by the other major world powers to intervene in Africa, particularly in its own *chasse gardée*, to preserve what were perceived to be Western interests, this position became more and more untenable towards the end of the twentieth century. Increasingly, the interventions, whether economic, military or diplomatic, came to be seen as failures. Not only had they failed to bring about any substantial economic development, but they had also failed to ensure lasting political stability or even to keep the peace.

The crunch came in 1994 with the drastic move to devalue the CFA franc by 50%, accompanied by the failure of UN peacekeepers to prevent the genocide in Rwanda. There has been much polemical debate concerning the role of France, its support for the Habyarimana regime and its alleged complicity in this murderous set of events (Collombat and Servenay 2014; Prunier 1998). This was to cause a serious dent in France's reputation and ultimately lead to calls for 'African solutions to African problems,' with the African Union (previously the Organisation for African Unity) and various other regional groupings becoming aware of the need to take more responsibility for the maintenance of peace and security.

Moreover, the failure of most African countries to effectively transform their economies and societies to combat poverty and underdevelopment was recognised and taken on board by the movement to establish the United Nations Millennium Development Goals in 2000 and the associated attempts to forge new partnerships under the aegis of NEPAD (New Partnership for Africa's Development), set up in 2001 to ensure that the African countries could pursue their own paths to development, and adopted by the African Union in 2002.

Increasingly, French policy has sought to make France part of multilateral endeavours, rather than taking on individual responsibility in its traditional sphere of influence. This was reflected in a greater desire to work with the EU on African matters, and particularly with countries such as the UK, where common interests were identified. Other European countries have been less enthusiastic in their support for what is perceived as the French agenda in Africa. In principle, it also entailed the strategic goal of transferring responsibility for security and peacekeeping to the African countries themselves. Needless to say, this is still a work in progress, as evidenced by recent operations in Mali, for instance.

It is notable that all recent French presidents have made a point of announcing their intention to break with *Françafrique*, or 'France à fric' as some would have it. As early as the 1980s, François Mitterrand was promising to end the practices of *Françafrique*. He was followed in this by subsequent presidents, most notably Nicolas Sarkozy and François Hollande. This stated intention has not, however, been carried out in practice. As part of Sarkozy's first visit to Africa, he made a point of meeting Omar Bongo of Gabon, one of the key figures of *Françafrique*. When Sarkozy's minister for cooperation and Francophonie Jean-Marie Bockel criticised the declared policy on *Françafrique*, he was removed from his post in 2008, apparently following pressure by some African leaders, such as Omar Bongo and the Congolese president Denis Sassou-Nguessou. Perhaps the most significant indication of Sarkozy's entrenchment in outdated views of France's relations with Africa was his speech to students in Dakar in 2007, where he expounded a vision of an Africa stuck in the past, outside of history and slow to make the transition to modernity (Sarkozy 2007).

Unlike Sarkozy, François Hollande made no promises to reform Franco–African relations prior to his election. Once elected, he did, however, declare his intentions to change fundamentally the relationship (Chafer 2014: 521). In spite of continued rear-guard action by those who wanted to preserve things the way they were, it was increasingly seen that France and its African partners would have to move with the times, conduct their relationship more in line with the predominant modes of operating in the present global economy and, as a subsidiary concern but an important one nonetheless, clean up their act and refurbish their public image which was threatening the moral prestige of France. When Hollande made his own Dakar speech on 12 October 2012, the tone and the content were in marked contrast to those of Sarkozy.

It was not long into his presidency, however, that François Hollande made the decision to intervene militarily in Mali through Operation Serval in 2013. Although this was seen by many as a reversion to the old ways of doing business in Africa, others have argued that this cannot be seen as a simple resumption of the old *Françafrique* model. For one thing, Mali has not traditionally considered itself part of *Françafrique* and with no major economic interests in the country, Mali has not played a great part in French policy and indeed relations with France have often not been as good as they might have been (Chafer 2014). Nonetheless faced with an imminent threat to the Mali government, and the lack of any alternative force in the region capable of taking the rebels on, France felt it had no alternative but to intervene. It later replaced this intervention with the much bigger Operation Barkhane, which it has pursued with five African countries from the region, Mauritania, Mali, Niger, Burkina Faso and Chad, collectively known as the G5 Sahel (Chafer 2016a). France responded similarly to the UN secretary-general Ban Ki-moon's request for French military intervention in the Central African Republic in late 2013. These interventions are seen as the fulfilment of France's international commitments and its view of its role in securing the security of this part of the world. Increasingly, security has become the major focus of French African policy, as demonstrated by the holding of the African security summit in Paris in December 2013.

France's policy towards Africa is also determined by the perceived need to develop economic ties through new economic partnerships which will extend beyond the old *pré carré*. This is in a context of the decline of France's share in the African market, which has been estimated to have reduced by 50% in the last ten years. While some sectors are buoyant, with important markets for French logistics, services, telecoms and infrastructure companies, overall French market share in Africa has dropped from 7.73% of exports and 9.08% of imports in 1960 to just 2.82% of exports and 2.05% of imports in 2011 (Melly and Darracq 2013). This is in the context of an estimated increase of the Chinese market share from less than 2% in 1990 to 16% in 2011.

The election of Emmanuel Macron to the French presidency on 7 May 2017 was viewed positively in many African countries, both francophone and non-francophone. The Nigerian *Daily Trust*, for instance, claimed on 10 May 2017 to 'look forward to better relations with France under its youthful, centrist new president.'[3] However, Macron's victory is unlikely to lead to major changes in French African policy, although there may be some superficial differences. The inclusion of African musicians, Ivory Coast's Magic System, in his victory speech ceremony at the Louvre is indicative of this change of style and has been described as a 'nod to Africa' by the BBC's Lamine Konkobo (Konkobo 2017).

Macron's discourse certainly promises change, although the issue of French policy in Africa did not figure largely in his campaign. He has said he will increase French aid to Africa, in which promise he joins a long line of predecessors. He has also expressed his view that it is for African countries to decide whether to keep the CFA franc or not. Like his recent predecessors, he also has spoken of bringing an end to *Françafrique*. However, he has clearly gone further in his pronouncements. Prior to the election, his visit to Algeria had provoked controversy in some quarters when he used the occasion to condemn French colonialism and, in particular, the crimes against humanity committed in its name during the Algerian War[4] (*El Watan* 2017). His open approach to the positive benefits of immigration have also demarcated him from the policies which had been the hallmark of his rival for the presidency, Marine Le Pen.

While it is far too early to make an assessment of Macron's probable impact in the area of Franco–African policies and relations, it remains to be seen whether there will be continuity or rupture in French military involvement in matters of African security. However, it is interesting that his first visit to Africa as president was to visit French troops in Mali, where he pledged to continue French military support, while insisting that other European countries should play a greater part (Daldorph 2017). His appointment of his predecessor's defence minister, Jean-Yves Le Drian, as minister of Europe and foreign affairs also points to a desire for continuity in African policy. It also seems unlikely that, given his position on the EU, he would challenge the overall direction of European policies that affect Africa directly in other ways.

Conclusions: current challenges to French influence in Africa

There is no doubt that France still retains immense influence in Africa on the economic, political, cultural, military and diplomatic fronts (Chafer and Keese 2013). It is clear that it is not ready to abandon its role as one of the major peacekeepers in Africa, given that security on its southern flank is perceived as a major concern. However, this is not perceived as a practical matter alone and the relationship is still largely underpinned by the notion of *rayonnement*, which still plays an important role in determining broader French policy. It is also worth mentioning that French influence in Africa is consolidated by the presence of a large population of those of African origin in France itself, either permanently settled, some several generations down the line, or transient visitors who come to France to study or work for a while.

France's influence in Africa is, however, increasingly challenged by the growing presence of other powers which turn to Africa for raw materials, for agricultural land, for financial investment opportunities and so on. These include not just the traditional Western powers, such as the US and the UK, but the newly burgeoning powerhouses of the global economy. Most notable amongst these is China, but increasingly followed by India and Turkey.

We are now faced with the question, what future does the 'special relationship' between France and Africa have? It seems clear that Africa will remain important to France, not just as a source of raw materials, economic outlets and financial investment opportunities, nor even as an increasingly important strategic element of its defence strategy, as set out in the 2013 French Defence White Paper, which emphasised the need for multilateralism, Africanisation and the maintenance of France's capacity to intervene alone if necessary (Chafer 2016b). Whilst the inability of most African countries to get involved in military operations, together with the reluctance of other EU powers and the US to put boots on the ground in Africa, places France in a severe political predicament and challenges its military resources; its acknowledged responsibility and role in Africa also act as an important support for its claims to a place at the global top table.

The question that remains is whether France will remain important to Africa. Given the multiple choices that most African countries now have when it comes to selecting their economic partners and political allies, what does France still have to offer? Given its relative economic and political decline, will the 'soft power' it projects to the world through its prestige and political reputation suffice for it to maintain its position in what some French policymakers see as its African backyard? Given the decisive role played by African elites in the relationship with France, it is as yet unclear what role the consolidation of democratic institutions (or their unravelling) will play in redefining this role.

Notes

1 I would like to acknowledge the valuable input of other members of the University of Portsmouth's Francophone Africa research cluster.
2 See in particular 2017. www.ascleiden.nl/Library/Webdossiers/Francophonie.aspx [Accessed: 30.03. 2017].
3 See http://allafrica.com/stories/201705100881.html [Accessed: 11.05.2017].
4 See for example *El Watan*, 29 March 2017.

References

Alden, C. 1996. From policy autonomy to policy integration: the evolution of France's role in Africa. In C. Alden and J-P. Dalloz (Eds.), *Paris, Pretoria and the African Continent*. Basingstoke: Macmillan.
Aldrich, R. 1996. *Greater France: A History of French Overseas Expansion*. Basingstoke: Palgrave Macmillan.
Bossuat, G. 2003. French development aid and co-operation under de Gaulle. In *Contemporary European History*, 12:4, 431–456.
Chafer, T. 2014. Hollande and Africa policy. In *Modern and Contemporary France*, 22:4, 513–531.
Chafer, T. 2016a. France in Mali: towards a new Africa strategy? In *International Journal of Francophone Studies*, 19:2, 119–141.
Chafer, T. 2016b. The French military in Africa: successes, challenges ahead? In *Rethinking Francophone Africa* blog. Available at: http://francophone.port.ac.uk/?p=1051 [Accessed: 21.04.2016].
Chafer, T. and A. Keese. (Eds.). 2013. *Francophone Africa at Fifty*. Manchester and New York: Manchester University Press.
Chafer, T. and G. Cumming. 2010. Beyond Fashoda: Anglo-French security cooperation in Africa since Saint-Malo. In *International Affairs*, 86:5, 1129–1147.
Collombat, B. and D. Servenay. 2014. *'Au nom de la France': Guerres secrètes au Rwanda*. Paris: La Découverte.
Conklin, A. L., S. Fishman and R. Zaretsky. 2015. *France and Its Empire since 1870*, 2nd edition. New York: Oxford University Press.
Cooper, F. 2014. *Africa in the World: Capitalism, Empire, Nation-State*. Cambridge, MA and London: Harvard University Press.
Daldorph, B. 2017. Macron pledges to be tough on terrorism during Mali visit. 23 May. Available at: http://en.rfi.fr/africa/20170519-macron-pledges-be-tough-terrorism-during-mali-visit [Accessed: 23.05.2017].
Elkins, C. and S. Pedersen. 2005. *Settler Colonialism in the Twentieth Century: Projects, Practices, Legacies*. New York: Routledge.
Elysée summit for peace and security. 2013. Available at: www.ambafrance-ng.org/Elysee-Summit-for-Peace-and [Accessed: 16.02.2016].

Ferro, M. 1994. *Histoire des colonisations. Des conquêtes aux indépendances, XIIIe-XXe siècles*. Paris: Seuil.

Hansen, P. and S. Jonsson. 2014. *Eurafrica: The Untold History of European Integration and Colonialism*. London: Bloomsbury.

Hollande, F. 2012. Available at: www.elysee.fr/declarations/article/discours-de-m-le-president-de-la-republique-devant-l-assemblee-nationale-de-la-republique-du-senegal/ [Accessed: 11.02.2016].

Ikeda, R. 2015. *The Imperialism of French Decolonisation: French Policy and the Anglo-American Response in Tunisia and Morocco*. Basingstoke: Palgrave Macmillan.

Konkobo, L. 2017. French election: what Emmanuel Macron's win means for Africa. Available at: www.bbc.co.uk/news/world-africa-39843396 [Accessed: 11.05.2017].

Lellouche, P. and D. Moisi. 1979. French policy in Africa: a lonely battle against destabilization. In *International Security*, 3:4, 108–133.

Melly, P. and V. Darracq. 2013. A new way to engage? French policy in Africa from Sarkozy to Hollande. Chatham House Paper, 2013:1. Available at: www.chathamhouse.org/sites/files/chathamhouse/public/Research/Africa/0513pp_franceafrica.pdf [Accessed: 27.04.2016].

Mesli, S. 2013. French co-opération in the field of education (1960–1980): a story of disillusionment. In T. Chafer and A. Keese (Eds.), *Francophone Africa at Fifty*. Manchester and New York: Manchester University Press, 120–134.

Piot, O. 2017. Les entreprises françaises défiées dans leur pré carré. In *Le Monde diplomatique*, April, 22–23.

Prunier, G. 1998. *The Rwanda Crisis: History of a Genocide*, 3rd edition. New York: Columbia University Press.

Rouvez, A., M. Coco and J-P. Paddack. 1994. *Disconsolate Empires: French, British and Belgian Military Involvement with Post-Colonial Subsaharan Africa*. Lanham, New York, and London: University Press of America.

Sarkozy, N. 2007. Available at: http://www.lemonde.fr/afrique/article/2007/11/09/le-discours-de-dakar_976786_3212.html [Accessed: 11.02.2016].

Smith, S. 2010. *Voyage en postcolonie. Le Nouveau Monde franco-africain*. Paris: Grasset.

Toft, L. and L. Verstraete-Hansen. (Eds.). 2009. *Une Francophonie plurielle. Langues, idées, cultures en mouvement*. Copenhagen: Museum Tusculanum Press.

Verschave, F-X. 1998. *La Françafrique: le plus long scandale de la République*. Paris: Stock.

5

GENDER AND POLITICS IN MODERN AND CONTEMPORARY FRANCE

Gill Allwood

All legislation passed in France since the introduction of universal suffrage in 1944 has been made by a parliament comprised of at least 61% men, and until 2017, more than 73% men. Men have decided whether women can have an abortion, whether rape and marital rape are criminal offences, and what clothing women are allowed to wear in public spaces. They have decided what will be taxed and how the budget will be spent. They have made decisions on foreign policy, defence, transport and agriculture, and, until 1945, women were unable to vote and therefore did not even have a say in which men would make these decisions. Gender and politics scholars argue that this matters, although they do not all agree on why it matters. For some, women's presence in sites of decision making matters because they believe that women have different needs and interests (whether this is based on the fact that they are women or that, as women, they have different social experiences), and that these needs and interests are best represented by women politicians. For others, it is less clear that women have a discrete set of needs and interests which are unaffected by class, ethnicity, religion, sexuality and other vectors of inequality. Nevertheless, most agree that there is no justification for the exclusion of women from political decision making on equal terms with men. Women are now better educated than men (Insee 2017: 114), and are present in the same professions as the men who make up the political elite, even if the glass ceiling prevents them from access to the top echelons of occupational hierarchies. There is no evidence that women lack the competence to occupy high political office or that they are uninterested in doing so. Women are active in local and community politics and in other forms of civic engagement. They may mobilise as feminists, as anti-feminists, or as activists who are motivated by issues other than gender. Women have been active in trade unionism, anti-racism and environmentalism, for example. Gender and politics scholars seek to explain why there is a persistent under-representation of women in mainstream political institutions, particularly the higher you ascend the pyramid of power. Many are also interested in asking *which* women are present. They argue that adding white middle-class women from a narrow sociopolitical and educational background to a male political elite with the same characteristics does not make representative democracy much more representative. Others concentrate on the relation between gender and policy, asking what underlying gendered assumptions influence policymaking and what gendered impact policies have. This chapter reflects these areas of enquiry. It focuses first on women's political participation, from voting behaviour to political office. It then examines the relation between gender and policy, asking how gender issues arrive on the policy agenda; which actors play an important role in promoting and defining them; and what impact the outcomes have on women, men and gender equality.

Political participation – voting behaviour

French women won the right to vote and to stand for election in 1944, nearly 100 years after men (1848). Women constitute 51.6% of the population and 52.6% of the electorate (Haut Conseil à l'Egalité entre les Femmes et les Hommes 2016: 31). How they vote matters to political scientists, and also to political parties and politicians seeking election. In the 2002 presidential election, for example, if only women had voted, Jean-Marie Le Pen would not have made it to the second round. If only men had voted, he would have won the first round (Sineau 2007: 353).

In 1955, two important studies of women's political participation appeared: Mattei Dogan and Jacques Narbonne's (Dogan and Narbonne 1955) *Les Françaises face à la politique* and Maurice Duverger's (Duverger 1955) *La participation des femmes à la vie politique*. Dogan and Narbonne took as a starting point the late arrival of women in a political system created by men, and asked how successfully they had integrated themselves into it. Did their political behaviour differ from that of men and to what extent? And did these differences vary according to the social and economic status of the women concerned, or were they based purely on sex? They found that women voted less than men and attributed it to their lower levels of political interest and access to information. They also found that nine out of ten women voted like their husbands, claiming that this was because they were subordinate to them and bowed to their superior knowledge. Finally, they found that women voted more to the right than men, although they attributed this to factors other than gender itself, notably age and occupational status.

The second important contribution to the study of women's political participation which appeared in 1955 was Maurice Duverger's report synthesising the results of four national surveys, sponsored by UNESCO and conducted in West Germany, France, Norway and Yugoslavia between 1952 and 1953. In terms of voting turnout and electoral choice, Duverger observed that women's participation did not differ substantially from that of men. He conceded that they abstained more than men, voted to the right and more often for Christian parties, but stated that these differences were very slight. Moreover, they could often be explained by factors other than sex, for example, age.

Until the early 1990s, research by political scientists Mariette Sineau and Janine Mossuz-Lavau, which formed almost the entire corpus of work on women's political participation in France, showed that women's political behaviour was evolving and would soon 'catch up' with that of men. Later, Mossuz-Lavau (Mossuz-Lavau 1997) began to argue that women's vote was no longer 'catching up' with that of men, but was developing an autonomy of its own. She divides women's political behaviour since 1945 into three phases, during the course of which women gradually came to vote as much as men, then as much for the left as men, and later, more so. The female electorate is not, however, homogenous. It is differentiated by age, education and occupational status (Sineau 2007: 354), and these divisions have an effect on electoral preference. In the 2007 presidential elections, Sineau found very similar voting preferences between men and women, and very comparable motivations for these choices. Like men, women's choice of candidate was based on concerns about unemployment (39%), the cost of living (25%) and social inequalities (23% women and 22% men) (Sineau 2007: 356). Sineau identifies a 'gender generation gap' where young men vote less for the left than young women, and older women vote more for the right than older men. However, older women did not vote for Jean-Marie Le Pen. Sineau argues that this is because of the conflict between his politics and their Catholic values. Young women, who are less Catholic, voted for Jean-Marie Le Pen in equal numbers with young men (Sineau 2007: 357). Women's reluctance to vote for the far right is now disappearing under Marine Le Pen's Front National leadership (Mayer 2013). Nonna Mayer offers three explanations for this. The first relates to occupational segregation. Men are more often blue collar workers, the occupational group with the lowest level of education, income and status, and the most exposed to precariousness and unemployment, where Le Pen votes are more frequent. However, women are over-represented in the growing unskilled service proletariat, which has been hit hard by the economic crisis (Mayer 2013: 173). The second relates to religion. Prior to 2006, religion had no impact on anti-immigrant opinions. Since 2006, however, Catholics have been more anti-immigrant than non-Catholics (Mayer 2013: 174). Thirdly, Marine Le Pen presents a softer image than her father, appears to condemn anti-Semitism, and promises more public services, thus appealing to women voters.

Political participation – political office

Globally, women are under-represented in elected institutions. Only two countries (Rwanda and Bolivia) have attained or exceeded 50% representation of women (IPU Women in National Parliaments 1 June 2017), and 146 countries out of the 193 listed by the IPU have parliaments containing more than 70% men. The average in Europe is 73.4% men and in the world 76.6% men.

The first elections (1945) in which women stood as candidates resulted in a National Assembly with 33 women out of a total of 586 (5.6%). It was assumed that women would gradually acquire confidence and experience, and their numbers would increase. However, 50 years later, in 1995, women still made up only 6.1% (35/577) of the National Assembly (Allwood and Wadia 2000: 149). This, combined with concerns about the crisis of representative democracy, led to a search for explanations for the persistently low representation of women, and to a campaign for change.

Early explanations for women's under-representation in sites of decision making focused on their presumed shortcomings in comparison with men. It was assumed that they were less interested in politics, less knowledgeable, and lacked the skills and experience necessary for political office. Later research challenged these arguments, claiming instead that some electoral systems are less favourable to the renewal of the political elite than others, and that the political parties, which act as gatekeepers to political office, exclude women – and other newcomers – through their candidate selection procedures. It found that institutional culture also acts as an obstacle to women's political participation, as does the public/private split and the construction of the idea of the universal citizen, which hides the exclusion of women (Allwood and Wadia 2000: 132–134).

From the late 1970s and throughout the 1980s women politicians, feminists and alternative left and ecology parties made various attempts to increase women's political representation. They argued that measures had to be introduced which would either remove the obstacles that stood between women and political office, or enable women to overcome them. Initially the demands were for quotas for women within party hierarchies and on candidate lists. However, quotas were widely criticised for running counter to Republican universalism and for dividing the nation into categories. By the 1990s, the efforts of campaigners and the opportunism of politicians made the media-friendly notion of 'parity' (numerical equality between men and women) a subject for public debate. In contrast to quotas, parity was supported by a broad spectrum of politicians, all main parties, European organisations, some feminists and intellectuals, and a large majority of public opinion (Allwood 1995).

In the context of concern over the crisis of democracy (low voter turnout, low levels of trust in political institutions), politicians on the left and the right were quick to embrace the idea of parity. The introduction of women into the political elite is claimed by some to be a way of bridging the gap between the people and an increasingly distant elite. Nuanced debates about how this connected to representative democracy were side-lined, and a mainstream politically acceptable version of parity was enshrined in the law in 2000 (see Table 5.1). This version was brought fully into line with Republican universalism. There could be no suggestion that the state would distinguish between citizens. Instead, it was argued that humanity is universally gendered and that representative bodies should reflect this (Scott 2005). Sexual difference (fixed and unchanging) was distinguished from other differences which, on the grounds of universalism, continue to be denied public and political relevance (Allwood and Wadia 2000: 210).

Many studies have been conducted on the impact of the parity law (Achin and Lévêque 2014; Bousquet et al. 2017; Haut Conseil à l'Egalité entre les Femmes et les Hommes 2016; Murray 2012). They have found that parity has had most success in elected bodies where it has been compulsory and where the electoral system has been most favourable. It has been most effective in municipal council elections in districts of over 3,500 inhabitants, where parity is now almost attained. These elections are run under a proportional representation system with mixed member party lists and strict alternation of male and female candidates. The law of 17 May 2013 has extended this to communes of more than 1,000 inhabitants, which previously used a first past the post system, unfavourable to the election of women candidates. Since this change, the proportion of women elected in communes of 1,000+ has increased to 48.2% (Haut Conseil à l'Egalité entre les Femmes et les Hommes 2016: 23). No parity measures apply to communes of fewer than 1,000 inhabitants, and women remain under-represented in them.

Candidates in first place on party lists, the chairs of executive bodies (presidents of regional, departmental and intercommunal assemblies and mayors), communes of fewer than 1,000 inhabitants, and national assemblies are not constrained by strict parity measures, and have not achieved parity (Haut Conseil à l'Egalité entre les Femmes et les Hommes 2016: 24). As a result of the law of May 2013, female departmental councillors represent half of the assemblies and the executive (13.8% in 2011, 50.1% in 2015). But men are 90.1% of the presidents of departmental councils and 83.3% of presidents of regional councils (Bousquet et al. 2017: 8).

The National Assembly has been resistant. The proportion of women in the National Assembly has never exceeded the current 38.7% (see Table 5.2) and did not exceed 20% until 2012.

The parity laws require parties only to select an equal number of candidates, not to achieve equality of outcome. The smaller parties on the left and far left (les Verts, Lutte Ouvrière, Ligue Communiste Révolutionnaire), followed by the mainstream left (Socialist Party and Communist Party), have been more proactive in advancing the goal of parity than the parties of the right and far right. In 2012, only two parties achieved parity in their parliamentary delegation – the Greens, as a result of long-term commitments, and the FN because of their dependence on State funding (Murray 2013: 200). The main parties prefer to pay the fines, despite the increased loss of funding that this entails following reforms introduced in 2007, and first applied in 2012 (Murray 2013: 198). The 2014 law for equality between women and men doubles the financial penalties for parties which do not present equal numbers of women and men (Haut Conseil à l'Egalité entre les Femmes et les Hommes 2017b).

A record number of women were elected to the National Assembly in June 2017. Of the 577 elected members, 223 are women (up from 155). With 38.7% women in the lower house, France moves from 64th place to 17th in the world rankings of female parliamentary representation and to 6th place in Europe (Interparliamentary Union 2017). This is less than the percentage of women candidates selected, showing that they are still more likely to be placed in constituencies which are difficult to win. The 42.4% women candidates selected is also still short of the 50% required by the law (Haut Conseil à l'Egalité entre les Femmes et les Hommes

Table 5.1 The parity laws.

Constitutional reform, 8 July 1999. Revision of articles 3 and 4 of the Constitution of 1958. The
following text is added to article 3: 'the law favours equal access for men and women to electoral
mandates and elected office.' Article 4 states that 'the parties and political groups contribute to the
implementation of this principle.'

The first parity law of 6 June 2000 requires political parties to select an equal number of women and
men in elections in which lists of candidates are presented. Strict alternation of male and female
candidates applies in single-round elections: European and senatorial. In two-round elections (regional
and municipal – in the case of communes with more than 3,500 inhabitants), there must be an equal
number of women and men candidates in every group of six candidates. Parity is not compulsory in
legislative elections. It is encouraged through financial incentives.

Law of 10 July 2000 – a list system is introduced for the indirect election to the Senate in departments
electing at least three senators (previously five).

Law of 11 April 2003 – reform of the electoral system for regional and European elections. Introduction
of strict alternation of men and women on candidate lists.

Law of 20 July 2003 – reform of the electoral system for senatorial elections. The list system and
proportional representation introduced for departments electing at least four senators (rather than three).
Single-candidate elections with no legal obligations for parity apply to half of the seats in the Senate.

Law of 31 January 2007 – introduction of strict alternation of women and men on electoral lists for
municipal elections (3,500+ inhabitants) and introduction of requirement for parity in regional and
municipal (3,500+ inhabitants) executive posts. Increase in the financial penalty applied to parties
which do not respect parity in their candidate selection.

Constitutional reform of 23 July 2008. Article 1 of the constitution is modified to read: 'The law favours
the equal access of women and men to electoral mandates and elected office as well as to positions of
professional and social responsibility.'

Law of 27 January 2011 – introduces a gradually increasing quota of women on the executive boards of
large private companies.

Law of 12 March 2012 – introduction by 2018 of a 40% quota for the appointment of women to top
management positions in public sector organisations.

Law of 17 May 2013 – reform of the system for electing councillors. Communes of more than 1,000
inhabitants (previously 3,500+) elect their municipal council by list election, respecting alternation
of male and female candidates. General councils are renamed departmental councils, and are now
elected by a binominal majority vote (two candidates, one man and one woman, on the same ticket).
Departmental executives are also required to respect parity.

Law of 22 July 2013 – parity in higher education and research through alternation of women and men in
electoral lists and appointments to institutional governance bodies.

Law of 2 August 2013 – reform of senatorial elections. List elections again apply in departments electing
at least three senators. These make up 73% of the seats. Senators are elected indirectly by an electoral
college, made up of local representatives. These delegates are now elected on the basis of lists which
comprise alternating candidates of each sex.

Law of 14 February 2014 – the law extends rules limiting the number of offices held at any one time. It
is no longer legal to combine the following mandates:

national or European parliamentary seat with a local executive office (president or vice-president of a
regional, departmental or intercommunal council, mayor or deputy mayor);

parliamentary seat with more than one local mandate (regional, departmental or municipal council);

More than two local mandates/executive functions.

Law of 4 August 2014 – the law for equality between women and men has a section on implementing
parity. It doubles the financial penalties for parties which do not respect parity in national elections.
It extends the implementation of the equal representation of women and men in public institutions,
private companies and sports federations.

Source: Haut Conseil à l'Egalité entre les Femmes et les Hommes 2016.

Table 5.2 Percentage of women candidates selected and women elected to the National Assembly.

Year	Percentage of women candidates	Percentage of women elected
1958	2.3	1.3
1962	2.4	1.7
1967	2.9	1.9
1968	3.3	1.7
1973	6.6	1.7
1978	16.3	4
1981	13.1	5.5
1986	25.1	5.8
1988	11.9	5.6
1993	19.5	5.9
1997	23.2	10.8
2002	39.3	12.1
2007	41.6	18.5
2012	40	26.9
2017	42.4	38.7

Source: Observatoire des inégalités (2017a).

2017b). The increase in 2017 was due to the doubling of the financial penalties for parties which do not respect parity, the declared commitment to parity by Macron's winning party, and the restrictions on the number of positions that can be held at the same time (*cumul des mandats*). The practice of holding more than one political office at the same time acts as an obstacle to the renewal of the political elite and to the increase in the proportion of women. The Haut Conseil à l'Egalité entre les Femmes et les Hommes found in its 2013 study that 80% of members of parliament who held another mandate were men (Haut Conseil à l'Egalité entre les Femmes et les Hommes 2017b). The law of 22 January 2014 (in force since July 2016) strengthened the limitations introduced in 2000. It is no longer legal to combine:

- National or European Parliament and a local executive office (president or vice-president of regional, departmental or intercommunal council, mayor or deputy mayor);
- Parliament and several local mandates – only one local and one national;
- Several local mandates and local executive functions (Haut Conseil à l'Egalité entre les Femmes et les Hommes 2016: 28).

The parity laws have had a positive effect on the proportion of women in elected office, although this has been very gradual in the case of the parliament. Where the laws have not been stringent, executive posts have also remained in the hands of men. Since 1958, for example, not one of the 15 presidents of the National Assembly has been a woman (Haut Conseil à l'Egalité entre les Femmes et les Hommes 2017a: 1). Within the National Assembly, there is a gendered division of responsibility, with men concentrated in the most powerful parliamentary commit-tees. In the National Assembly in May 2014, women represented 26.1% of deputies. They were over-represented on the committees for social affairs (47.9%) and education and cultural affairs (40%), but not on the committees for finance (13.9%), foreign affairs (16.1%) or defence (21.1%) (Achin and Lévêque 2014: 126).

Women have been more present in government than in parliament in France, rising from 14% in 1981, 27.9% in 1995 (although this quickly dropped to 12.1% with Juppé's first reshuffle),

34.4% in 2007, and 47–50% throughout Hollande's presidency (2012–17). In 2017, Emmanuel Macron's government had equal numbers of men and women (11 of each), although men held all of the important portfolios. In France, the government is appointed rather than being drawn from parliament. Appointing women has therefore been an opportunity for male presidents and prime ministers to demonstrate their equality credentials, especially in the early days of new governments when media interest is high.

There are few vocal opponents of the principle that women and men should be equally present in decision making, and the parity laws have made some progress towards achieving this. Parity has also had some symbolic success, as can be seen in the spread of the idea of parity to other areas of public and commercial life, including public administration and corporate boards. However, parity does not ask which women are included and excluded, and it does not challenge the poor representation of particular social groups. The dominant conception of representative democracy in France is one which sees the elected representative as mandated to represent the will of the nation as a whole, rather than to reflect society in all its diversity. The sex, age and ethnicity of the representative have no relevance in public life, and all citizens are equal. While egalitarian in principle, this can, in practice, deny the existence of inequalities, including the exclusion from political life of women and ethnic minorities, amongst others. Elected bodies have acquired more women but remain exclusive to a social elite, older and white (Achin 2012: 51–52). In 2017, 2.8% of deputies in the National Assembly were manual workers or unskilled service sector workers, whereas these categories make up half of the working population (Observatoire des inégalités 2017b: 1). On the rare occasions when ethnic minorities are elected, they are often women. Murray (Murray 2016) suggests that the appointment of ethnic minority women to government can satisfy gender and ethnic diversity agendas while causing minimal disruption to the white male majority.

By focusing on the insertion of a female elite into political institutions, parity risks missing the question of what difference this would make to all women. We need to ask which women are present in elected bodies and whose interests they represent. Gender inequality must be discussed in the context of other inequalities, including class, ethnicity and religion. Scholars such as Eléonore Lépinard (Lépinard 2013) and Leah Bassel and Akwugo Emejulu (Bassel and Emejulu 2010) have begun to examine the way that these inequalities intersect. Others have focused on groups of women who are particularly marginalised from mainstream political activity, such as refugee women (Allwood and Wadia 2010) and Muslim women (Joly and Wadia 2017), exposing not only the obstacles that exclude them but also the diverse forms of activism and civic engagement in which they participate.

Gender and policy

Gender and politics scholars have been interested in how women's and feminist movements push issues onto the political agenda and frame them in a particular way. They have shown, for example, how feminists fought to place abortion on the political agenda, to have rape defined in law, and to engage policymakers in the struggle against domestic violence (Allwood and Wadia 2009). They have studied the relation between activists and feminist actors within state institutions to establish which factors are most likely to produce policy that favours gender equality. Republican universalism has provided a backdrop against which all of this plays out (Bassel and Emejulu 2010; Lépinard 2013; Lépinard and Mazur 2009). Positive gender equality outcomes are more likely when there is a 'strategic partnership' (Halsaa 1998), or 'velvet triangle' (Woodward 2003), of women in elected office, women's/feminist movements, and women's policy agencies, working together on a specific issue (Mazur 2002: 4). Factors which favour state feminism include the presence in power of left-wing parties when there are links between these parties and the women's movements; coherence within the movement around their demands; and high agenda status within the movement for the issue in question. When these conditions are not present, women's policy agencies with feminist leaders can still intervene effectively. In the absence of effective women's policy agencies and a left-wing government, it is still possible for strong movements to have some impact.

France has a long history of women's policy machinery, which has played a role in much policymaking explicitly concerning women. There has been some kind of government department responsible for women's issues or women's rights since 1974, when Giscard d'Estaing appointed Françoise Giroud as junior minister for women. In 1981, Mitterrand created a ministry for women's rights under Yvette Roudy. The status and title of the department and of the individual responsible for it have changed, as has its funding and potential influence on decision making. The government department has at its service the administrative Service des Droits des Femmes which has a central office in Paris and a network of offices throughout the country. Two parliamentary delegations were created in 1999 in order to advise parliament on issues relating to women's rights and to ensure the implementation of laws in the area. In addition, there was the Observatoire de la Parité, created in 1995 and responsible for commissioning, undertaking and publishing research on women's status; studying gender inequalities and obstacles to political, social and economic equality; and advising the government. In 2013, it was replaced by the Haut Conseil à l'Egalité entre les femmes et les hommes (HCE).

In 2012, France regained a full Ministry for Women's Rights. The minister, Najat Vallaud-Belkacem, introduced a number of policies, including the 2014 law on equality between women and men, which was an attempt to ensure that gender equality cuts through all areas of policy, rather than being seen as a discrete policy issue. Her actions were not without their critics, and in 2013 large numbers protested against same-sex marriage and gender equality education in schools. The ministry was downgraded in 2014 in the second Valls government, when women's rights were moved to Affaires sociales et de la santé, under Marisol Touraine, and Pascale Bois-tard was appointed head of a secrétariat d'Etat chargé des droits des femmes. In 2017, there is no Ministry for Women's Rights, but a junior minister, Marlène Schiappa, who reports to the prime minister.

The study of gender and policy in France has focused to a large extent on the relation between gender and the welfare state, and, in particular, on family, employment and reconciliation (or work-life balance) policy. Studies of the welfare state have demonstrated that it rests on a series of assumptions about the sexual division of labour. Social policy has reinforced the division between the public and the private, associated with production and reproduction, and with men and women. Work on care and on family policy illustrates this. The presumed gender neutrality of public policy is brought into question by scholars such as Jacquot and Mazur (Jacquot and Mazur 2010: 463). Gender and policy scholars are interested in policy which is obviously gendered, for example, abortion and maternity leave, but also in the gendered effects of ostensibly gender-neutral policy, such as transport and taxation. They ask how issues arrive on the policy agenda, and how these issues are framed as gendered or gender neutral. They ask what role social movements and other non-state actors, including feminists and women's advocacy networks, play in this process, who is included in and excluded from policy formulation and implementation, and whether the outcomes affect women and men differently. There is a growing interest in implementation, as can be seen in the cross-national comparative research programme, Gender Equality Policy in Practice (Mazur 2017).

Conclusions

Public, political and academic debates about gender and politics have been dominated since the early 1990s by the issue of parity. The principle of women's participation in political, economic and social decision making has caught on, and practice has followed in some areas, including the election of local councils. The women who participate in mainstream institutional politics come from a small sociocultural elite (as do their male colleagues), and parity has not addressed broader questions of democratic representation. Part of the reason for this is the strength of Republican universalism, which denies the relevance of difference in the public and political sphere. The new generations of multicultural, anti-racist feminisms described by Achin et al. (2017) could offer a challenge to the forms of state feminism which have dominated debates since the 1990s.

References

Achin, C. 2012. Au-delà de la parité. In *Mouvements*, 69:1, 49–54. doi: 10.3917/mouv.069.0049.

Achin, C., V. Albenga, A. Andro, I. Jami, S. Ouardi, J. Rennes and S. Zappi. 2017. Paysage féministe après la bataille. In *Mouvements*, 89:1, 69–77. doi: 10.3917/mouv.089.0069.

Achin, C. and S. Lévêque. 2014. La parité sous contrôle. Égalité des sexes et clôture du champ politique. In *Actes de la recherche en sciences sociales*, 204:4, 118–137. doi: 10.3917/arss.204.0118.

Allwood, G. 1995. The campaign for parity in political institutions in France. In D. Knight and J. Still (Eds.), *Women and Representation*. Nottingham: WIF Publications, 7–20.

Allwood, G. and K. Wadia. 2000. *Women and Politics in France*. London and New York: Routledge.

Allwood, G. and K. Wadia. 2009. *Gender and Policy in France*. Basingstoke: Palgrave Macmillan.

Allwood, G. and K. Wadia. 2010. *Refugee Women in Britain and France*. Manchester: Manchester University Press.

Bassel, L. and A. Emejulu. 2010. Struggles for institutional space in France and the United Kingdom: intersectionality and the politics of policy. In *Politics and Gender*, 6:4, 517–544. doi: 10.1017/S1743923X10000358.

Bousquet, D., R. Sénac, M-P. Badre and M. Berthy. 2017. *Quel partage du pouvoir entre les femmes et les hommes élu.e.s au niveau local?* Paris: Haut Conseil à l'Egalité entre les Femmes et les Hommes.

Dogan, M. and J. Narbonne. 1955. *Les Françaises face à la politique*. Paris: Armand Collin.

Duverger, M. 1955. *La participation des femmes à la vie politique*. Paris: UNESCO.

Halsaa, B. 1998. A strategic partnership for women's policies in Norway. In G. L. Nijeholt, V. Vergas and S. Wieringa (Eds.), *Women's Movements and Public Policy in Europe, Latin America and the Caribbean*. New York and London: Garland, 167–189.

Haut Conseil à l'Egalité entre les Femmes et les Hommes. 2016. *Guide de la parité*. Paris.

Haut Conseil à l'Egalité entre les Femmes et les Hommes. 2017a. Contraintes renforcées et volontarisme affiché: une progression sans précédent des femmes à l'Assemblée. Available at: www.haut-conseil-egalite.gouv.fr/parite/actualites/article/contraintes-renforcees-et [Accessed: 10.07.2017].

Haut Conseil à l'Egalité entre les Femmes et les Hommes. 2017b. Parité des candidatures aux élections législatives de 2017: une quasi-stagnation en dépit du renforcement des contraintes légales. Paris: Haut Conseil à l'Egalité entre les Femmes et les Hommes. Available at: www.haut-conseil-egalite.gouv.fr/parite/actualites/article/parite-des-candidatures-aux [Accessed: 10.07.2017].

Insee. 2017. *Femmes et hommes, l'égalité en question*. Paris: Institut national de la statistique et des études économiques. Available at: www.insee.fr [Accessed: 10.07.2017].

Interparliamentary Union. 2017. Women in national parliaments. Situation as of 1 June 2017. Available at: www.ipu.org/wmn-e/classif.htm [Accessed: 10.07.2017].

Jacquot, S. and A. G. Mazur. 2010. Politiques publiques et genre. In *Dictionnaire des politiques publiques*, 4th edition. Paris: Presses de Sciences Po (P.F.N.S.P.), 460–469.

Joly, D. and K. Wadia. 2017. *Muslim Women and Power: Political and Civic Engagement in West European Societies*. London: Palgrave Macmillan. doi: 10.1057/978-1-137-48062-0.

Lépinard, E. 2013. For women only? Gender quotas and intersectionality in France. In *Politics and Gender*, 9, 276–298.

Lépinard, E. and A. G. Mazur. 2009. Republican universalism faces the feminist challenge: the continuing struggle for gender equality. In S. Brouard, A. Mazur and A. M. Appleton (Eds.), *The French Fifth Republic at Fifty: Beyond Stereotypes*. Basingstoke and New York: Palgrave Macmillan, 247–266.

Mayer, N. 2013. From Jean-Marie to Marine Le Pen: electoral change on the far right. In *Parliamentary Affairs*, 66:1, 160–178.

Mazur, A. G. 2002. *Theorizing Feminist Policy*. Oxford: Oxford University Press.

Mazur, A. G. 2017. Toward the systematic study of feminist policy in practice: an essential first step. In *Journal of Women, Politics and Policy*, 38:1, 64–83. doi: 10.1080/1554477X.2016.1198210.

Mossuz-Lavau, J. 1997. L'évolution du vote des femmes. In *Pouvoirs*, 82, 35–44.

Murray, R. 2012. Parity in France: a "dual track" solution to women's under-representation. In *West European Politics*, 35:2, 343–361.

Murray, R. 2013. Towards parity democracy? Gender in the 2012 French legislative elections. In *Parliamentary Affairs*, 66:1, 197–212.

Murray, R. 2016. The political representation of ethnic minority women in France. In *Parliamentary Affairs*, 69, 586–602. doi: 10.1093/pa/gsv064.

Observatoire des inégalités. 2017a. Forte progression de la représentation des femmes à l'Assemblée. Available at: www.inegalites.fr/spip.php?article59 [Accessed: 19.06.2017].

Observatoire des inégalités. 2017b. L'Assemblée ne compte quasiment plus de représentants des milieux populaires. Available at: www.inegalites.fr/spip.php?page=articleandid_article=166andid_rubrique=138andid_groupe=12andid_mot=92 [Accessed: 12.06.2017].

Scott, J. 2005. *Parité: Sexual Equality and the Crisis of French Universalism*. Chicago: University of Chicago Press.

Sineau, M. 2007. Effets de genre, effets de génération ? Le vote hommes/femmes à l'élection présidentielle 2007. In *Revue française de science politique*, 57:3–4, 353–369. doi: 10.3917/rfsp.573.0353.

Woodward, A. 2003. Building velvet triangles: gender and informal governance. In T. Christiansen and S. Piattoni (Eds.), *Informal Governance in the European Union*. Cheltenham: Edward Elgar, 76–93.

PART II

Identification and belonging

6

THE POLITICS OF MIGRATION

Abdellali Hajjat

In the late nineteenth and early twentieth centuries, France was one of the main immigration countries in the world: by the 1930s the proportion of foreigners on its territory exceeded that of the United States. This surge in migration was essentially initiated by French businesses, and reflected both economic and demographic needs (labour necessary for an industrial revolution combined with low fertility rates and mass slaughter from world wars). It was not until the First World War that the French state articulated a genuine migration policy, endowed with legal tools (laws, circulars, decrees) and a specialised bureaucracy. The main instruments of control and surveillance of foreigners, sometimes denounced as human rights violations, were invented in the exceptional circumstances of the war, but the exception rapidly became the rule: most tools, such as the identity card for foreigners and the deprivation of nationality, were renewed after the war and are still today founding elements of the migration policy. Thus, the history of French migration policy is structured by a tension between the protection of human rights accorded to foreigners and refugees on the one hand, and on the other, the establishment of a state monopoly of movement inside the territory (Torpey 2000). The latest example has been the welcoming of Syrian refugees in 2015. While asylum is supposed to be an inalienable right for refugees and both a moral and legal obligation of the French state as a signatory of the 1951 Geneva Convention, this right has been severely hampered by inhospitable government practices denounced by human rights organisations. It is this tension between human rights and restrictive policy that is analysed in this chapter, exploring the different dimensions of the politics of migration.

Firstly, this chapter will focus on the evolutions of state regulation of the non-national population (foreigners and refugees). It will distinguish different fields of governmental action that regulate the population arriving from European countries and former colonies, in terms of migration, asylum, internment, deportation and citizenship policies. Migration policy deals with the entry and residence of foreigners. Throughout the twentieth century, it largely served the interests of businesses, to the detriment of the unions, although in the early 1970s the immigration service adopted the idea of 'managed migration' and succeeded in convincing political and economic elites to 'suspend' immigration. The tightening of migration policy affected all categories of foreigners (workers, family members and students, amongst others), which resulted in the increased casualisation of the alien status and triggered mobilisations in defence of foreigners (movement of the undocumented migrants/*mouvement des sans papiers*). While international treaties frame asylum policy, national discretion is important in defining the criteria. The

69

French implementation of the Geneva Convention reveals a severe hardening towards the recognition of refugee status, especially for applicants from Africa and the Middle East. Migration policy finally includes the policy of internment and deportation of undocumented migrants and foreigners convicted of crimes or offences (principle of 'double-peine'). This dimension often moves centre stage in the public debate because of the desire for most political actors to portray themselves as 'tough' against 'illegal' immigration. The citizenship policy was marked by a relative openness in the 1980s, including the ending of past discrimination affecting naturalised people, but since the 1990s we have observed a hardening stance, which has undermined *jus soli* (1993–1998) and the liberal naturalisation policy (with refusal rates above 50% since 2011).

This chapter will then turn to the interaction between immigrant mobilisations and the transformations of the 'integration' policy. It will analyse the institutions' discourse and concrete policy that aims at tackling inequalities and discriminations against immigrants. From the 1970s to the 1980s, many governmental reports have recognised the state's 'accountability' to guarantee the conditions of immigrants' integration into society. The state is accountable for guaranteeing immigrants their basic needs (including housing and work), but, in this framework, immigration was considered to be a temporary phenomenon. Nonetheless, after the 1983 March for Equality and Against Racism, it became clear that the 'myth of the return' had vanished when the children of first-generation migrants proclaimed their will to stay. Thus, as most migrants are coming from former colonies and are therefore racialised, the migrant issue is articulated through both social and racial issues. The 'migrant problem' shifted to the 'black' and/or 'Muslim problem.' Since the first Islamic headscarf controversy in 1989, a conceptual inversion has occurred whereby the responsibility to 'make efforts' to integrate has been put firmly on the shoulders of immigrants and their children. 'Integration' has become a state injunction that informs all aspects of the relations between the state and racial minorities.

State regulation of migration

Migration policy

The earliest forms of regulation of migration flows were government decrees and laws passed in the late nineteenth century. The influx was massive and initiated, without state intervention, by private companies with the number of foreigners increasing from 655,000 foreigners in 1876 (1.7% of the total population) to 1,127,000 in 1886 (3% of the total population). But Republican governments maintained some degree of control by forcing the newly installed foreigners to be registered at the prefecture (January 1887) and a year later with their local mayor (decree of 2 October 1888).

This decree was confirmed by the 8 August 1893 law (Residence of Foreigners and the Protection of National Labour), which inaugurated a distinction between legal and illegal immigration (Noiriel 2007). These decrees and laws introduced an *a posteriori* administrative control of foreigners, who had to declare themselves to the authorities only after arriving in the country. The state maintained a role in the migration of foreign workers, which was considered to be too secondary by a nebula of reformers, composed of experts in demography, employers' associations, labour unions and senior officials (Larbiou 2003). All converged on the idea that the state should play an increased role in the management of migratory flows, but each according to a specific logic: demographers adopted a logic of population (a quantitative and 'qualitative' selection of foreigners); employers and unions a logic of workforce (lower costs for some, and protection of French workers for others); and for senior officials of the interior ministry the logic of law and order (control and surveillance of foreigners). In fact, at the end of the nineteenth century Republican governments had not implemented the control upon immigration flows essentially for ideological reasons: the principle of non-state intervention in the labour market and the free movement of foreigners were constitutive of human rights according to the liberal thinking of the time.

However, these ideological locks were shattered during the First World War. This exceptional context favoured state control over migration policy, since the war economy required a foreign and colonial workforce, given that hundreds of thousands of French men had gone to the battlefront. Under the Ministry of War's remit, are thus created the Service of Foreign Work-force (1915), the Service of the Organization of Colonial Workers (1916) and then the Inter-ministerial Commission for the Workforce. This is a crucial moment in the institutionalisation of theoretical frameworks and practices developed by the reformers, which allowed for the arrival of 450,000 foreign and 225,000 colonial workers. The effectiveness of the migration policy owed much to the implementation of the ID card for foreigners. By 1912, the 'anthropometric card' was already in use and enabled the control and monitoring of 'nomad' populations, both foreign and French (About and Denis 2010). Founded in 1917 by decree, a foreigner's identity card used unprecedented visual identification techniques (photo, distinctive signs and card-based coloration of the economic sector) to track the foreigner and settle him/her in a geographic area and specific economic sector according to the needs of the industrial and agricultural economy.

Thus, the instrument of control of foreigners was significantly strengthened during the war, and the exception became the rule, as the identity card for foreigners was not abandoned and the registration of foreigners in the 1930s was extended to children. On the eve of the Sec-ond World War, the migration administration gathered seven million individual files. Although the private companies, through the General Society of Immigration (1924), had the power to welcome new foreigners without the state's authorisation, the state signed international trea-ties with Italy, Poland and other European neighbours and could use the ID cards to regulate migratory flows by fixing various criteria for the initial application or the renewal (income, health, housing and tax). But international events of the interwar period (Italian Fascism, Ger-man Nazism, Spanish Civil War, anti-Semitic pogroms in Eastern Europe, the 1929 economic crisis) and the rise of far right movements in France favoured an unprecedented tightening of migration policy. The aim was to protect the national labour market (law of 1932), to imprison illegal immigrants and deport 'undesirable' ones (unemployed, peddlers, domestics, prostitutes, the mentally disturbed). All these measures and forms of police pressure led to mass deportations (500,000 between 1930 and 1936) and created an extremely efficient bureaucracy which would play a dramatic role under the Vichy regime.

There is a vibrant academic debate on the continuities and ruptures between the Third Republic and Vichy (Paxton 2001). For some, Vichy was not France, and is a departure from the Republican tradition (Weil 2005). For others, the Vichy regime inherited from the Third Republic administrative practices of monitoring and control of foreigners (Noiriel 1999), which made possible the persecution of Jews and resistance fighters. In reality, Vichy only systema-tised the existing surveillance practices on the population, making it even more effective and extending it to French citizens through the creation of a national identity card, in the context of a desire for both total control and collaboration with the Nazi extermination project of the 'undesirable' (including most notably Jews, Gypsies). For example, it is not the Vichy regime that created the systematic identification of Jews, but the Third Republic through the Decree Law of 2 May 1938, which instructed German and Austrian refugees to notify the police if they were 'of Jewish origin.' However, foreigners were 'treated' differently according to whether they lived in the Occupied Zone (North) or the 'Free' Zone (South). In the Occupied Zone, the regime wanted to tackle unemployment by implementing quotas on foreigners by profession, but the

Nazi occupiers reacted negatively since the measure applied to their allied countries' nationals (Italians, former Austrians). In the 'Free' Zone, foreigners were treated differently according to their nationality. Allied states' nationals, above all Italians, were privileged since they could easily renew their ID cards. For others, the regime was restrictive, especially through the creation of 'groups of workers' (forced labour camps peopled by foreigners, refugees and demobilised soldiers) and Requisitions for Compulsory Labour Service (Service du Travail Obligatoire, 1943).

After the Second World War, most of the bureaucratic tools were maintained (cards, files and similar records). Only the national identity card for French citizens was discarded after the Liberation (but restored in the 1970s). Between 1945 and 1974, the migration policy was defined by the Ordinance of 2 November 1945, which was devised by the interim government without debate in parliament (Spire 2005). A heated debate was held within the High Committee on Population over the selection criteria. Some wished to impose a 'hierarchy of quality' based on ethnic criteria, invented by the expert demographer Georges Mauco, while others rejected any notion of distinction and ranking between foreigners. In the end, the ordinance made no distinction between nationalities, even though administrative practices remained tainted by discrimination. For 30 years, the migration policy was implemented by the National Office for Immigration (ONI), which alone could issue three types of residence permits: 'temporary' (covering arrival, duration and renewal stages at the discretion of the prefecture), 'regular' (attribution of the residency at the discretion of the prefecture, after police investigation, medical conditions and income details) and 'privileged' (valid for ten years and automatically renewed). In other words, the stability of foreigners increased as they were able to extend their stay in France. The need for labour to rebuild the country prompted a new influx of foreigners, mainly from Europe but also the 'postcolonial' Maghreb and African regions, to the extent that the state left the selection process to private companies. The state's action was primarily to regularise *a posteriori* foreigners who had arrived through employers' initiatives: the share of foreigners regularised *a posteriori* increased, compared to those registered by the ONI (23% in 1949, 50.3% in 1957 and 82% in 1968).

The relative openness of borders during the 'Thirty Glorious Years' era was followed by a period of closed doors that started in the 1960s. Contrary to common perception, the French administration adjusted to the idea of controlling migration flows long before the 1973 oil crisis. Indeed, the independence of former colonies radically transformed migration policy. The Evian agreements between France and Algeria guaranteed freedom of movement between the two countries, but only the Algerians actually benefited as the French exited Algeria in droves. France then sought to regulate the entry of Algerians multiplying restrictive measures such as the introduction of a 'certificate of residence,' the first electronic database and the deportation of 'false tourists.' Finally, a new agreement was negotiated in 1967 which resulted in the co-management of migratory flows with the Algerian National Workforce Office. But the French prohibitive regulations were extended to other nationalities by restricting the possibilities for *a posteriori* regularisation: the 'Marcellin-Fontanet circular' of February 1972 made it very difficult to obtain a residence permit, which was now conditional on the obtaining of a work permit (and therefore an employment contract) and 'decent housing.' Overnight, thousands of legal foreign workers became illegal, triggering the new undocumented migrants' movement in December 1972, made famous by hunger strikes and church occupations throughout France (Siméant 1998). This circular became the prelude to an even greater dramatic hardening: the suspension of workers and family migration introduced on 3 July 1974.

This historic decision of the Chirac government is often explained by the economic crisis of 1973. In fact, the economic factor was only secondary in the minds of senior officials responsible for immigration, such as André Postel-Vinay, who had managed to convince the government and large companies usually supportive of the constant influx of cheaper paid workers (Laurens 2009). The suspension of immigration was in reality motivated by a number of concerns: the supposed demographic imbalance with Third World countries; the risk of a possible 'new' May 1968, only this time with the support of a mass of foreign workers; the need to dramatically deter new entrants; and, finally, by financial reasons, since public companies provided housing to foreigners. While the suspension of workers' migration was never challenged by the successive left-wing and right-wing governments, the suspension of family migration was called into question. Indeed, human rights organisations challenged the order in court, and the Council of State ruled in their favour in 1975 in a decision which for the first time guaranteed foreigners the 'right to family life' (Lochak 1985).

The year 1974 thus inaugurated a long period of increasingly hostile migration policies for non-EU nationals while, due to the signing of the EU treaties (Rome in 1956, Schengen in 1985), European community nationals benefited from freedom of movement and settlement. Thus, the public debate on immigration focused on Africans who were accused of not being 'assimilated' as well as 'culturally different.' The ascension to power of the Socialist Party in 1981 marked a break from the restrictive policy of the previous government with the regularisation of thousands of undocumented foreigners, the suspension of the 'double penalty' (foreigners both convicted and deported) and the increased accessibility of the 'privileged' resident card (Law of 1984). However, the stabilisation of foreigners arriving in the country went hand in hand with the fight against 'illegal' immigration, which revealed an ideological convergence of the left and the right on immigration policy. Indeed, the rise of the Front National (FN) hardened the stance of the left-wing government, which believed according to its prime minister Laurent Fabius in 1984, that the FN had bad solutions to the right questions. All parties and governments thus shared the idea of an 'immigration problem' and the migration policy became a key election issue. To the extent that neo-liberal ideology had been adopted equally by both the right and the left (from 1983), migration policy was one of the few areas of public action where they tried to distinguish themselves from one another. This explains why the number of immigration laws significantly increased – around 20 between 1974 and 2015. It culminated in 2010 in the creation of the Ministry of Immigration and National Identity, the title of which sparked an uproar as it implied that immigration was a threat to 'national identity.' Migration policy has been characterised by a tightening of conditions for granting and renewal of residence permits, a generalisation of detention centres, increased deportations (between 25,000 and 30,000 per year since 2007) and, overall, deteriorating living conditions of foreigners.

Asylum policy

The asylum policy is marked by the tension between two different conceptions of asylum (Valluy 2009): on the one hand a universalist conception, which enshrines freedom of movement and a wide-scale protection of refugees, and on the other a derogatory conception where the principle of national sovereignty limits the freedom of movement of refugees and gives significant powers to the state to provide, or not, refugee status. The principle of asylum law in the modern sense is inspired by Enlightenment philosophy and appears in Article 120 of the Constitution of 1793 (although it was never implemented). Until the adoption of the 1946 Constitution, the welcoming of refugees was at the discretion of governments. From 1930 to 1939, between 200,000 and 300,000 Jews arrived from Germany, Austria and other countries under Nazi influence. In 1936, hundreds of thousands of Spanish refugees crossed the Pyrenees to escape Franco's fascism. While left-wing parties and community organisations welcomed them warmly, Republican governments barred their access to certain professions (doctors, lawyers and dentists in particular, led by their interest groups) and the administration reacted with similar hostility, since many of the Jews were considered as 'unassimilable' and described as 'bogus refugees.' In 1934, undocumented and unemployed German Jews were deported to Germany. Spanish refugees were also regarded with mistrust and forbidden to live in the north of the Loire river and in the Paris region (1934) and, from 1938, the state took the unprecedented step of building internment camps in the South. It was not until the Decree of 2 May 1938 that refugee status was recognised officially, but asylum applications were overwhelmingly rejected and a new legal category appeared in January 1939, the 'un-deportable deported,' imprisoned in 'special detention centres.'

After a long absence in constitutional texts since the French Revolution, the right for asylum reappeared in the preamble to the 1946 Constitution. The trauma of the Second World War and the disastrous fate of Jewish refugees led to the 1948 Universal Declaration of Human Rights (UDHR), which proclaimed the founding principle of the modern asylum law: freedom of movement to seek asylum in another country. But the UDHR was only declarative. The signing of the Geneva Convention in 1951 eventually provided a legally binding framework on refugees. Although officially international, the Convention was primarily European, since it applied only to European refugees, until the signing of the New York Protocol in 1967. According to that Eurocentric convention shaped by the Cold War, the aim was not to welcome refugees *en masse*, but rather to show the virtues of the 'free' capitalist world in inviting dissidents from communist countries. Thus, the definition of refugee was narrowly individualistic, as the applicant must prove an individual and specific persecution against them to receive protection. The issue of freedom of movement was almost completely unaddressed by the Convention and reduced to a simple request for states to make their land accessible to people fleeing persecution. The agreement forbade states to sanction refugee status applicants for unauthorised residence, prohibited in principle the deportation to dangerous borders, and extended 'favourable treatment' to refugees for the right to stay and work. Nonetheless, the bureaucratic practices of the French administration – French Office for the Protection of Refugees and Stateless Persons (OFPRA) established in 1952 – often has contradicted international commitments.

Indeed, administrative practices have varied widely depending on the period and, especially, according to the legitimacy of the exile (Spire 2005; Valluy 2009). Between 1956 and 1960, Hungarian refugees, among them many intellectuals fleeing the invasion of Soviet tanks, had secured refugee status, financial aid, housing, a residence permit and a work permit with relative ease, whereas the Yugoslav refugees, mostly workers, faced work restrictions because the Ministry of Labour wanted to protect the national labour market, while French diplomats doubted the veracity of the persecution. Between 1951 and the early 1970s, the number of asylum applications remained low, the vast majority were accepted (85% of applications were accepted in 1973) and applicants were predominantly European: 98% of refugees recognised by the OFPRA between 1951 and 1972 were Spanish, Russian, Armenian, Polish, Hungarian. From the early 1970s, broadening the Convention's scope to include the Third World (New York Protocol of 1967, ratified in 1971), asylum policy hardened because the Ministries of Interior and Labour refused an influx of asylum applications from Africans. Thus, the refusal rate has steadily increased until today: approximately 5% in 1973, 50% in 1984, 85% in 1990, 95% in 2003. However, there are substantial differences in refusal rates according to nationality. From 1972, the refusal rate has been almost 100% for non-Europeans compared to 15% for Europeans. The only non-European refugees enthusiastically welcomed were the 122,093 Vietnamese fleeing the war between 1975 and 1989 (Gayral-Taminh 2010), Chileans after the 1973 military coup, persecuted Tamils in Sri Lanka and "Christians" in the Middle East. Between 2011 and 2015, France received a mere 10,000 Syrian refugees, while Germany hosted a million in 2015 alone.

Nationality/citizenship policy

The equal rights of all French nationals has been a major political issue since the adoption of the Civil Code in 1803: women, slaves (Larcher 2014), *indigènes* (Saada 2003) and naturalised people were the subject of legal discrimination that built the contours of a national citizenship based on racist and sexist criteria (Weil 2008). While categorised as 'nationals,' that is to say a legal relationship between them and the state existed, they were not however 'full citizens' enjoying legal equality in terms of political (right to vote and participate in elections) and social rights (including employment). The nationality/citizenship policy here has been the result of the struggle to define external and internal boundaries of the nation, which had evolved considerably in French history.

Since the late nineteenth century, there have been three modes of securing French nationality: by *ius sanguinis*, by 'declaration' (*ius soli* and marriage) and by naturalisation (Weil 2008). The acquisition of nationality has been a right of the children of French fathers since 1803, and children of French mothers married to foreigners since the Act of 1927. This right of blood has never been called into question because it constitutes the legal basis of the French nation. The great law of 1889 on nationality established *ius soli* – a child born in France of foreign parents automatically becomes French at adulthood – for political and demographic reasons (Noiriel 2007). Indeed, the majority of foreign children enjoyed the status of '*admis à domicile*,' intermediary between the French national and the foreigner, which enabled them to benefit from certain civil rights reserved for French citizens, while escaping French military service. Their legal situation gave them a more favourable position in the labour market, especially in border departments where the proportion of foreigners was significant. After the 'Universal' Male Suffrage was voted in 1848, border departments' *députés* were very anxious to win over a new electorate and chose to address the issue. Moreover, there were violent clashes between French and foreign workers (Dornel 2004), especially in the South, which were interpreted by demographic experts as the result of a 'race struggle' which was supposed to arise when the proportion of foreigners reached a certain threshold. The 'solution' advocated by demographers was the 'peaceful annexation' of foreign children through *ius soli*, which forced them to do military service and to turn them into 'good' French. The principle of *ius soli* remained unchallenged at the time, despite opposition from both the right and the far right. However, politicians' suspicions of children of North African descent led to questions about the automaticity of citizenship: from 1993 to 1998, the law changed and young people with foreign parents had to make register their interest between their 16th and 18th birthdays to become French, rather than it being automatically granted.

If *ius soli* is a right, this is not the case of naturalisation, which is considered as a 'favour' of the state. Since the nineteenth century, the requirements for securing citizenship have become increasingly complex, providing a broad range of discretionary powers to the administration in charge of naturalisations, which has always been suspicious of adult foreigners socialised abroad. Broadly, the foreigner seeking naturalisation should not be a minor, poor, illiterate, unmarried, condemned by justice, in poor health or 'un-assimilable' (Sayad 2004; Hajjat 2012). The first two requirements for naturalisation were the period of residence prior to application, and 'dignity' (no criminal record). The law of 1889 allowed a ten-year residence period, which was very high, and explains that, during the 1890s, the naturalisation average rose to only 2,000 a year. But the carnage of the First World War (1.3 million deaths) justified a massive naturalisation policy: the law of 1927 reduced to three years the residence period required to apply. The effect was immediate, with the average between 1928 and 1929 increasing to 22,500. However, the law of 1927 and its implementation demanded new requirements such as proof of income (contract from an employer), reproductive capacity ('familialism' that discriminated against unmarried and single women), health (the naturalised mustn't burden the nation) and assimilation (linguistic and 'cultural' differences). All these criteria, still present today in the nationality law, are combined according to historical periods and economic needs.

After the financial crisis of 1929, the Republican administration closed the doors to naturalisation and, after the 1940 defeat of France, the Vichy regime implemented a racial politics of citizenship under the law of 1927 resulting in the number of naturalisations decreasing from 47,000 in 1939 to 980 in 1942. The law of 22 July 1940 withdrew citizenship to the first *résistants* (including Charles de Gaulle, René Cassin, Pierre Mendes-France), 'un-assimilated' Jews, and 110,000 Jews of Algeria were deprived of their citizenship. In order to 'purify the French race,' the Naturalisation Review Commission reassessed 660,000 naturalisation files leading to 15,000 'denaturalisations.' This racist policy produced thousands of stateless persons, facilitating their expulsion and deportation to Nazi extermination camps.

If anti-Semitic legal texts were removed following the Liberation, the Ordinance of 19 October 1945 (the new nationality code) did not lead to a return to the highly liberal law of 1927. Indeed, the required period of residence was five years in 1945, instead of three, and most legal discriminations were maintained against the natives of the colonies (lack of political rights, special criminal regime) and the naturalised. Those naturalised had suffered discrimination since the nineteenth century: the law of 1849 barred them from the National Assembly for ten years after naturalisation, from the Senate entirely after the law of 1889, and the law of 1927 extended this discrimination to all elective offices (chambers of commerce for instance). The 'Daladier decree' of 12 November 1938 extended political exclusion to the right to vote for a period of five years. Naturalised people were also legally discriminated in the labour market: the law of 19 July 1934 denied them access for ten years to public service, state ministerial offices and bars; the laws of 21 April 1933 and of 26 July 1935 prohibited access to medical professions for five years. Thus, the 1945 law renewed the ten years' restriction period for elective positions or mandates, while decreasing restrictions on the right to vote and access to public service from ten to five years. This renewal demonstrates the absence of a complete break with discriminatory logic against the naturalised, and it was not until 1983 that parliament voted to repeal most of the legal discriminations targeting them.

This removal of restrictions is still not complete because the principle of deprivation of nationality, affecting only those within ten years of their naturalisation, has never been abolished. The laws of 7 April 1915 and 18 June 1917 introduced the power to remove French nationality from naturalised people coming from enemy countries (including Germany and Italy), reinforced by subsequent laws. It targets those naturalised considered as threats to the state's interest: 'spies,' 'deserters' and 'disloyal' people. It has not only been used by the authoritarian Vichy regime (446 removals of nationality for such reasons between 1940 and 1944) but also by Republican regimes (16 such actions between 1927 and 1940, 696 removals between 1945 and 1956, several dozen since 1956). The scarcity of removal of nationality shows that it is an exceptional procedure, strictly controlled by the judiciary, but public debate has emerged following the terrorist attacks of 13 November 2015 in Paris and Saint-Denis. Indeed, president François Hollande suggested a constitutional amendment introducing the extension of removal powers to dual nationals who have acquired citizenship by descent or *ius soli*. This initiative introduces a new discrimination within the national community by implying that the attackers are not really French and their actions are explained by their Muslimness. After a heated public controversy, the project was finally abandoned because the government failed to meet a sufficient majority in parliament to amend the constitution.

Migrants' political mobilisations and 'integration' policy

The final dimension of the migration issue is the interaction between migrants' mobilisations and integration policy. After the independence of the former colonies in the 1960s, many anti-colonial activists returned to their countries, but a new wave of migration came from the Maghreb and Africa, and the political opponents of the postcolonial regimes, swelled the ranks of unskilled workers in the automobile plants, steel, coal mining and the building sectors. Thus, immigrant workers were to play an important role in the largest social movement in the history of France after 1945, in May and June 1968 (Damamme et al. 2008; Artières and Zancarini-Fournel 2008; Gobille 2009; Jackson et al. 2011). Indeed, immigrant workers were involved in strikes and factory and university occupations, and bore the brunt of police repression as hundreds of them were deported (Vigna 2008; Gordon 2003). Demands related primarily to working conditions in general, workplace democracy, but also on specific aspects of their social conditions: lack of trade union rights, wage inequality, housing and the like. The 'breath of May 68' was extended to the subsequent years through an unlikely alliance of immigrant workers – such as the Arab Workers' Movement (Hajjat 2011) – and far left activists and leftist intellectuals like Jean-Paul Sartre and Michel Foucault (Gordon 2012). This alliance resulted primarily in the mobilisations against both racism – which prompted the passing of the law of 1972 that criminalised racist speech and acts – and the tightening of migration policy (movement of undocumented migrants).

In the early 1980s, the overriding image of immigration, that of the low-skilled worker, was replaced by a new one, that of immigrants' children. This corresponded to a profound transformation of the immigrant composition: since the 1970s, family reunification became common and a new generation reached adulthood in the early 1980s. A few years after the war in Algeria, this generation experienced an extremely virulent anti-Arab racism – 150 deaths in 1970s, 200 deaths in the 1980s – mass unemployment and a territorial stigma. They were invisible until they appeared in the public space during the 1983 March for Equality and against Racism and the famous 100,000-people demonstration in the streets of Paris (Hajjat 2013). The March was organised in the wake of urban rebellions in the Lyon region (Minguettes district in Venissieux) in 1981 and 1983, challenging the police and judicial brutality, social and racial discrimination in the labour and housing market, and the impunity of perpetrators of racist crimes. Thus, the immigrant issue is increasingly conflated with the racial issue as well as the issue of public policies for real equality.

Nonetheless, the state response to the claims of immigrants' children was very ambivalent. Indeed, the political anti-racism of immigrant organisations, such as the Movement of Immigration and Suburbs, has been short-circuited by the moral racism of SOS Racisme. For the former, there is a structural racism to be challenged by proactive public action. For the latter, racism is above all about individual attitudes to be fought over through communication campaigns. Thus, a clear division appeared within the space of anti-racist movements in the early 1980s and continues to this day. However, urban rebellions of 1990 in Vaulx-en-Velin (near Lyon), following the death of a working-class youngster, resulted in the creation of the Ministry of Cities (Tissot 2007). The issue of social and racial inequality has been filtered through urban policy, which was essentially geared to demolishing unsafe buildings and moving people in urban space. The question of integration was central to the result of the first affair of the Islamic headscarf in 1989, which inspired the creation of the High Council for Integration (HCI). Initially, responsibility for integration issues was returned to the state, which was judged accountable for not creating the conditions conducive to integration. But from the 2000s, the HCI reversed the burden of responsibility: it was ultimately immigrants and their children who were now responsible for their problems because their 'integration efforts' were unsatisfactory. This reversal reflects the impact of the events of 9/11 upon the intellectual sphere, the coming to power of the French right in 2002, the impact of the 2005 urban rebellions, the 2015 terrorist attacks, the rise of Islamophobia. It has entirely transformed the thinking on integration, which has become an injunction to conform to majority norms, a way to produce racial difference against Muslims and to question their fundamental human rights as the right to education and the right to work (Hajjat and Mohammed 2013).

References

About, I. and V. Denis. 2010. *Histoire de l'identification des personnes*. Paris: La Découverte.

Artières, P. and M. Zancarini-Fournel. (Eds.). 2008. *68, une histoire collective (1962–1981)*. Paris: La Découverte.

Damamme, D., B. Gobille, F. Matonti and B. Pudal. (Eds.). 2008. *Mai-Juin 68*. Ivry: Éditions de l'Atelier.

Dornel, L. 2004. *La France hostile, sociohistoire de la xénophobie 1870–1914*. Paris: Hachette Littératures.

Gayral-Taminh, M. 2010. Voyage au bout de la mer: les boat people en France. In *Hommes and Migrations*, 1285, 163–171.

Gobille, B. 2009. *Mai 68*. Paris: La Découverte.

Gordon, D. 2003. 'Il est recommandé aux étrangers de ne pas participer': les étrangers expulsés en mai–juin 1968. In *Migrations Société*, 15:87–88, 45–65.

Gordon, D. 2012. *Immigrants and Intellectuals: May '68 and the Rise of Anti-Racism in France*. London: Merlin Press.

Hajjat, A. 2011. The Arab workers' movement (1970–1976): sociology of a new political generation. In J. Jackson, A-L. Milne and J. Williams (Eds.), *May '68: Rethinking France's Last Revolution*. Basingstoke: Palgrave Macmillan.

Hajjat, A. 2012. *Les frontières de l' "identité nationale."* Paris: La Découverte.

Hajjat, A. and M. Mohammed. 2013. *Islamophobie*. Paris: La Découverte.

Jackson, J., A-L. Milne and J. Williams. (Eds.). 2011. *May '68: Rethinking France's Last Revolution*. Basingstoke: Palgrave Macmillan.

Larbiou, B. 2003. *Connaître et traiter l'étranger. Les constructions sociales d'un savoir politique sur l'immigration*. Thèse de science politique, université Montpellier I.

Larcher, S. 2014. *L'autre citoyen. L'idéal républicain et les Antilles après l'esclavage*. Paris: Armand Colin.

Laurens, S. 2009. *Une politisation feutrée*. Paris: Belin.

Lochak, D. 1985. *Étrangers, de quel droit?* Paris: PUF.

Noiriel, G. 1999. *Les Origines républicaines de Vichy*. Paris: Hachette.

Noiriel, G. 2007. *Immigration, racisme et antisémitisme (XIXe-XXe siècle)*. Paris: Fayard.

Paxton, R. O. 2001 [1972]. *Vichy France: Old Guard and New Order, 1940–1944*. New York: Columbia University Press.

Saada, E. 2003. Citoyens et sujets de l'Empire français. Les usages du droit en situation coloniale. In *Genèses*, 4:53, 4–24.

Sayad, A. 2004. *The Suffering of the Immigrant*. Cambridge, UK: Polity Press.

Siméant, J. 1998. *La cause des sans-papiers*. Paris: Presses de Sciences Po.

Spire, A. 2005. *Étrangers à la carte*. Paris: Grasset.

Tissot, S. 2007. *L'État et les quartiers*. Paris: Seuil.

Torpey, J. 2000. *The Invention of the Passport: Surveillance, Citizenship, and the State*. Cambridge: Cambridge University Press.

Valluy, J. 2009. *Rejet des exilés. Le grand retournement du droit de l'asile*. Broissieux: Editions du Croquant.

Vigna, X. 2008. Une émancipation des invisibles? Les ouvriers immigrés dans les grèves de mai–juin 68. In A. Boubeker and A. Hajjat (Eds.), *Histoire politique des immigrations (post)coloniales, France, 1920–2008*. Amsterdam: Editions Amsterdam, 85–94.

Weil, P. 2005. *La France et ses étrangers*. Paris: Gallimard.

Weil, P. 2008. *How to Be French? Nationality in the Making since 1789*. Durham, NC: Duke University Press.

7

THE POLITICAL TRANSVERSALITY OF ISLAMOPHOBIA

An analysis of historical and ideological foundations

Marwan Mohammed

Islamophobia is a complex process of 'othering' based on the indication of actual or perceived affiliation with Islam. The term 'othering,' or racialisation, refers to the act of seeing the intentions, social conduct and perceptions of those who are (or are assumed to be) Muslim as essentialised religious behaviour. This process overlooks the plurality, divisions and complexities of this group (or at least limits them to a binary contrast between 'good' and 'bad' Muslims) on, for example, a social, economic, theological, ideological and identity-related level.[1] Islamophobic 'othering' results in a representation, which – by amalgamation – groups together individuals, communities and populations that have little in common, linking them to various acts of violence carried out by individuals and groups who claim to be acting in the name of Islam. Islamophobia is therefore a sociopolitical phenomenon which has little to do with the balanced analysis of religions and religious dogmas and institutions – a wholly legitimate process.[2] Nor is the phenomenon of Islamophobia limited solely to actions (such as discrimination and physical or verbal attacks, which, according to many sources, are becoming increasingly frequent) whose legitimisation must also be explored. In France, Islamophobia is one of the consequences springing from the construction of a 'Muslim problem' by a significant number of elites.

It is possible to object that Islamophobia is a product of the rising number of violent acts shrouded by Muslim religious discourse (for example the attacks in Paris in 1995–1996, New York and Washington in 2001, Madrid in 2004, London in 2005, Paris in 2015) or of certain changes in the status and forms of Islam in France (more places of worship, the emergence and development of discourse and lines of thought that recommend breaking away from society, etc.). These tangible realities should be considered alongside the different forms of political violence around the world and alongside the changes in Muslim religious practice in Europe. It is also true that for prejudice to work it must first be endorsed by the members of the group that is being targeted. Even if their power is limited, these 'endorsers' are essential when it comes to delegitimising their own group – a role carried out by a certain number of 'representatives' chosen and championed by the same elites that promote the 'Muslim problem.' Furthermore, there are numerous examples of violent behaviour or of non-Muslim religious practices that are, in fact, not deemed to be a public issue (or at least not to the same extent), such as the spread of

Catholic traditionalist demonstrations, the rise in power of the African Pentecost movement in working class areas, the over-representation of 'separatist' movements in comparison with other 'terrorist' acts reported by Europol, even though they cause fewer deaths. The Utøya massacre carried out by Anders Breivik, classed as the deadliest in Europe in recent decades, was not made out to be a 'white' or a 'Christian' problem.

There is nothing organic about the 'Muslim problem' and it has not simply appeared out of the blue. We must remember that social phenomena are not, by default, a public issue, and that for the general public to believe there is a problem three conditions must first be met (Gusfield 2009): the condition of awareness, starting with categorising and interpreting social phenomena; an effort to mobilise different types of actors and supporters, who, without working together but by influencing one another, will come to agree that Islam poses a problem; lastly, a condition concerning norms or, in other words, the series of rules and values that serve to define the problem. That which is presented to us as being a 'problem' hides the unknown, thereby meaning that its scope and its social or health-related impact may be far greater.

Yet, in contemporary France, Islam 'poses a problem.' Today, this idea has become widespread if we are to go by the prolific spread of negative images and discourses regarding the presence of Muslims in France and more widely in Europe. It is even an example of social 'evidence,' in line with the philosopher Fernando Gil's (1993) definition of the word: not an irrefutable argument, but rather a belief that is so deeply engrained that it does not require verification and, as a result, foregoes reason. In fact, in the French context, it is striking to note that the regular and voluntary reinforcement of this 'Muslim problem' is rarely the result of rational exchanges, robust arguments or well-supported explanations. This atmosphere of 'paranoia,' as described by Raphaël Liogier (2012), spans from the far right of the political spectrum to the far left, and across all European countries. The fact that this kind of transversality is possible indicates that modern Islamophobia is based on different foundations. Indeed, how can a social group stir so many negative and transpartisan opinions within French society when rejection of the Other is generally seen as a dividing factor in politics?[3] Here, this chapter is not claiming that 'everyone is Islamophobic' and that Islamophobia shares the same foundations for left- and right-wing sympathisers, both of which would be false and lazy assertions. On the contrary, its aim is to explore the different mechanisms that facilitate the politically transversal nature of hostility towards Islam and Muslims. In this instance, the term 'mechanism' refers to the main ideological and symbolic frameworks around adhesion to Islamophobia.

The main historical foundations of contemporary Islamophobia

Several historical movements – which date back to different points in history and which have evolved over time – have facilitated the expression, dissemination and spread of Islamophobia today. This anti-Muslim archive, at times referred to, must not force us to adopt an outdated stance based on an unhistorical view of spoken, written or visual Islamophobia. It would be wrong to think that there is a sort of general Islamophobia that has been around forever and is intrinsic to European identity; one that has supposedly been expressed throughout history with unconscious and recurring hostility that has remained unchanged since the Middle Ages (Dakhlia and Vincent 2011). The long history behind the Muslim problem in Europe is anything but linear, yet in many ways, it remains a contentious topic.

Indeed, France's first encounter with Islam came not with the emergence of the colonial empire or the arrival in the last century of indigenous migrants who had come for military or economic reasons. The long history between the two has created a unique archive of material, portraying Islam and Muslims as a dangerous and/or inferior 'other' in Western theological and political thought. This anti-Muslim archive was made up of the ideological or iconographical works of a wide variety of actors (theologians, philosophers, erudites, diplomats, in addition to politicians, scientists, journalists, and the like) working in particular social and historical fields (the reaction to the Muslim conquests, the Crusades, the decline of the Ottoman Empire, European and American imperialism, immigration from Muslim countries to Europe, geopolitical and conflict-related reshuffling after the Cold War, etc.).

Since the Middle Ages, religious and political conflicts have given rise to different types of European discourses that have aimed to counter and delegitimise a new opposing and heretical religion, to justify social segregation and to legitimise military conquests. This discourse regarding Islam and Muslims has generated a pool of ideas, representations and images, which has been used by different generations of public actors according to their social standing, their interests and their historical and political contexts.

Shortly after the emergence of Islam in the seventh century, political and religious authorities in Christian Europe drew up various strategies to fight the spread of Islam around the world, including the theological denial of the Crusades, the sending of missionaries, etc. The earliest representations of Islam and Muslims in Europe are to be found in the works of Christian writers (seventh to twelfth centuries) living in Christian and Muslim Europe (Spain, the Balkans) or in territories of the Islamic Orient. The main aim of these works was to fight against a rival Muslim dogma and to avoid conversions in conquered territories, to justify military conquests that made it possible to face a political enemy whose power was growing, and finally, to legitimise the different forms of segregation (legal, spatial) of Muslim subjects under Christian princes. This Muslim enemy has been assigned several names over time and depending on geographical area, including Arabs, Saracens, Moors, Ishmaelites, Agareniens and Turks.

Thus, for Norman Daniel, these writers built up a 'set of beliefs,' an 'arsenal of polemical images' and, according to John Tolan, 'intellectual weapons,' which revealed a feeling of superiority in the West over Muslims and Arabs (see Daniel 1993; Tolan 2003). At the time, this superiority was mainly defined in religious terms, and the arguments lodged against Islam and Muslims were largely theological. Across the board, Christian discourse formed opposing patterns of thought, which became central to popular perception of Islam and Muslims. On the one hand, Islam was dismissed as being tantamount to irrationality, passion, emotion and barbarism, whilst on the other, Christianity was said to represent reason, civilisation and spiritual truth. Some of these patterns were in line with the discourse on the Saracen people, considered to be a 'perfidious race' by one Riccold de Monte Croce (1243–1320). According to the historian John Tolan, the negative representations and beliefs that were deeply rooted in people's minds up until the eighteenth century only underwent 'minor changes' up until the Enlightenment, and even as late as the twentieth century: 'Little truly new was written about Islam between 1300 and the Enlightenment' (1993: 364). Nevertheless, the period between the Reformation and the Enlightenment was marked by a greater diversity in European discourse concerning Islam and Muslims. Traditional prejudices were still rife, but the unanimity of European discourse was interrupted by conflict within Europe itself (protestants and philosophers against the Catholic Church), a shift in relations between international forces with the rise and fall of the Ottoman Empire, and, lastly, an increasing drive for knowledge that characterised, for example, Orientalism.

Thereafter, negative representations of Islam and Muslims tended to stay separate from religious or spiritual influences and started to become more diverse. The 'anti-Mohammed' phenomenon gave way to the construction of a negative Muslim 'otherness' originating from the arts, literature and, increasingly, science. The role of orientalist writers would prove to be crucial;

they saw the East as an area shaped by different communities that were to be explored and colonised for economic (raw materials, workforce and other resources) and political reasons (power struggles between Western states). These colonial discoveries brought about a global tripartition: civilised Western Europe, the history- and culture-deprived world of the 'uncivilised' and, between the two, the East, made up of great civilisations in decline. While allowing for a whole host of discoveries relating to Eastern communities, Orientalism led to the scientific legitimisation of colonial conquests and also took an active role in them. The desires for knowledge and for power are often linked.

In particular, orientalists helped to establish the idea that religion had to feature in all analyses of the history of oriental societies. They played down political, technological, economic and social factors because they felt that spirituality and religion took precedence in oriental cultures, in contrast to the West, which was going through a process of secularisation (Said 1980). Even today, this view helps to legitimise the idea that the individual and collective behaviours of Muslims are determined primarily by their religious affiliation, and not by political, economic or social determining factors. This unhistorical perspective on the history of the Muslim world leads on to a second assumption: that of the existence of different races within the human race, each one with inherent biological and psychological characteristics. By picking up on the 'War of the Races' theory and the pseudo-scientific works of racial anthropology, orientalists see the historical trends of the Muslim world as a struggle between religious movements, which is also a race struggle (see Reynaud-Paligot 2006). By connecting religion and race, they thereby help to racialise religious affiliation, which has become an intrinsic characteristic of Muslim populations. From this perspective, colonial domination is based on a racial definition of nationality and citizenship. For example, in 1830, indigenous Muslim populations that were overpowered following the conquest of Algeria were, from a legal point of view, both nationals (subjects of the empire) and non-citizens (without the right to vote or to be elected) who were subject to a unique penal code (the *code de l'indigénat* or Indigenous Statute). This legal discrimination can be explained by the colonists' desire to maintain their grip on political power, but also by the belief in the civilisational and racial inferiority of Algerian Muslims.

From xenophobia to anti-clericalism: main contemporary foundations

Of course, the small number of historical points highlighted here do not give a comprehensive account of the link between the past and present of Islamophobia; they simply allow us to perceive the periods in which more material was added to the anti-Muslim archive. We are reminded to what extent the status of Islam in France can be partly described in view of this past by the hostility towards Islam in certain traditionalist Christian communities; the recurrence of prejudices and the faults attributed to the Muslim "other"; the hegemony in the French media of neo-orientalist interpretations promoted by various experts and public speaking professionals; or the perpetuation – more than half a century after the Évian Accords – of a specific legal and political way of dealing with Islam used by successive governments.

Since the beginning of the 1980s, this belief in the existence of a 'Muslim problem' has brought about numerous public issues and controversies: an 'integration' problem concerning the inter-generational reproduction of a certain form of religiosity judged to be incompatible with overarching concepts of citizenship, assimilation and national identity; a problem of modernity based on Muslims' supposed rejection of democracy, secularism and gender equality; a fear of over-population and even population transfer; a security problem centred around the threat of Islamic terrorism (Bigo et al. 2008). Discourse and imaging has aided the construction of an 'imaginary Islam,' which was opposed to the French 'Republic,' the 'state,' 'secularism' and the 'nation' (Deltombe 2005). 'Muslims' themselves, although not against the 'French people,' are frequently divided into two broad categories: 'extremists' ('Islamists' or 'fundamentalists') on the one hand and 'moderates' on the other. This logic is binary and essentialist, and it completely overlooks the nuances and complexities uncovered by an increasing number of social science studies on the Muslim phenomenon (Göle 2015). In reality, there are several forms of Islamophobia, which are driven by different forces, and which highlight the transpartisan reach of this phenomenon. Here, we will discuss some of these forms.

Above all, Islamophobia subscribes to nationalist, racist and xenophobic traditions. It forms part of the extension of racism, covering other minorities that are judged to be undesirable on national territory. Here, Islam is seen as the extension of the other's religion. We will only briefly discuss this form of Islamophobia (or rather Islamo-xenophobia), which sits at the right end of the political spectrum. The confusion caused by the appropriation of secular and feminist struggles by the far right and the hard right must not obscure these racist foundations. Numerous observers have highlighted the importance of anti-Arab racism – or even the targeted rejection of Algerians following decolonisation – as a way of understanding contemporary Islamophobia. To be convinced of this truth, it is enough to note the overlap in the family histories and political engagements of current Islamophobic figures, such as Eric Zemmour or Robert Ménard. However, this is only part of the picture.

Islamophobia is also boosted by societal dynamics, allowing it to make a wide-reaching impact. In fact, for several centuries, at least since the Revolution, French society has been shaped by a deep secularisation movement, characterised in particular by the loss of influence of religious norms in daily life, the political decline of church authorities, in addition to the decline in religious practice and the vocational crisis. While the nineteenth century was marked by important battles between the different factions of the secularisation movement and the supporters of a return to the *Ancien Régime*, the subsequent century seemed to be one of institutionalisation with the establishment of a peaceful compromise written into the law of 9 December 1905 (Baubérot 2011). This law failed to put a definitive end to the conflict between the 'two faces of France' – anti-clerical and Catholic – but it did establish a definite balance between the factions and, at the time, the French Republic. Even though several events meant that the stability of 1905 was called into question, it was never a matter of restricting the religious freedoms guaranteed by the founding texts of modern secularism, which was vigorously defended by Aristide Briand before the Chamber of Deputies. Up until the Second World War, it was essentially the survival of a Christian form of anti-Judaism that led the theme of religion to be seen as a marker of racism (although this dimension was present in Nazi anti-Semitism). The relevance of this theme was subsequently questioned with the preparation of the law against racism of 1 July 1972 (Calvès 2011). Speaking on this matter, Jean-Pierre Delannoy said that legislators 'feared discrediting the plan by focusing on such a dated hypothesis' (Delannoy 2005). The religious theme was eventually taken into account in 1972, but its 'dated' nature would reveal the general acceptance of reduced religious visibility in public (places of worship and religious institutions, clothing and even special public demonstrations like processions, festivals, etc.). Yet, at the end of the 1980s, the emergence of a new type of religious visibility – regarding clothing in particular – and the widespread, negative media coverage it received, once again brought this topic to the attention of the French people. This turning point – marked by the first 'veil controversy' in Creil in 1989, the year of the fall of the Berlin wall and the bicentenary of the Revolution – was to destabilise those who maintained that the secularisation of the twentieth century and the shift in cultural attitudes (in particular with regard to women) had already been achieved in the 1960s. Several individuals, who had based their political careers on opposing the tradition and norms of the Church, looked very unfavourably upon the public emergence of new forms of religiosity among younger generations.

These dynamics of secularisation and secularism, at the heart of the universalist myths of the Jacobin Republic, can also be linked to virulent anti-clericalism, which draws inspiration from a highly anti-religious interpretation of historical materialism (Tévanian 2013). Certain theoretical approaches that are inspired by this concept often see religiosity as an obstacle to openness, and to being aware of 'true' social relationships and the forms of domination that are fostered between them. Moreover, assuming the importance of class relations and the social question, these heterogeneous approaches are sometimes used to downgrade, rather than analyse, what is revealed by the dynamics of race and religion compared with what is revealed by socio-economic standing. As a result, theoretical, political and moral considerations are blurred, making it difficult to carry out a balanced analysis of Islam's place in society. On the far left, Islam is often accused of impeding the course of social and revolutionary emancipation, and of stopping the unification of the working class. It is therefore hard to see this 'suspect Islam' as a source of victimisation, in contrast to other markers of rejection, such as background or skin colour.

The attitude that should be adopted with regard to Islam and Muslims has significantly divided feminist, anti-racist and anti-clerical groups – considered to be progressive – in light of the numerous controversies that have plagued the public sphere for 30 years. Similarly, aside from openly racist and xenophobic movements, political organisations and trends from the far left through to the centre right have all had to endure debates, deep-rooted disagreements, reconfigurations and even outright division, which have given rise to forms of Islamophobia that cannot solely be described as xenophobia. Recognising religion to be a marker of the rejection of others, much like race, gender or social class, is the cause of similar debate. Religious affiliation is considered to be an acquired marker, which is the result of a personal choice deemed to be reversible. It does not have the same status as ascriptive markers, like gender, disability or skin colour, because these are considered to be hereditary and exterior to the individuals in question. Yet, in France, Muslim visibility was constructed as if it had emerged from bottom-up *islamisation*, that is to say, as the symbolic marker of politico-religious movements. Generally speaking, it is also seen as a movement that goes against women's rights. As a result, the various spiritual and moral aims of Muslims – which often correspond to the characteristics outlined in empirical research on Islam and which are accepted by Muslims themselves – stand in stark contrast to the view held by the dominant and hegemonic community, which equates Islam with a questioning of the historical movement of secularisation, with 'failed integration' and with the rising power of Islamism, which is seen as a threat to individual liberty.

Conclusions

In contrast to what might be implied by the change in status of Muslims in Europe as a result of a chain of violent military events here and particularly in those countries of the Middle East and Africa with substantial Muslim populations, the ideological foundations of Islamophobia have been set for a very long time and have been discussed differently since the beginning of the 1980s. Without doubt, the numerous sources of contemporary political and geopolitical upheaval have added to our concerns and our fears, which are manipulated by a number of political and media personalities in hopes of increasing their own popularity and the levels of hostility towards Muslims. However, let us not forget that the first modern version of the 'Muslim problem' was used in the factories of the automotive industry, just as the left-wing government shifted towards ultra-liberal rigour. Faced with North African skilled workers and the General Workers' Confederation (CGT), the Mauroy government decided to move away from a traditional trade union movement centred around protecting jobs, in particular those of North African workers, by putting a religious slant on strike action. They became 'holy strikes,' 'Shiite strikes,' which resonated with the international press, even though the North African workers were Sunnis. In this regard, this period in social history represents a sort of contrast that simultaneously reveals the issues of legitimacy that link the presence of migrant workers to their economic purpose, demonstrating the effectiveness of using identity as leverage in dividing the working classes, and unveils the impact of exclusion based on Islam. The role of employers, the government and a part of the press in the stigmatisation of strikers and the trade unions that supported them invites us to think about the overlaps between economic and social agendas, and the emergence of public scandals. Yet, in more general terms, what is most striking is this refusal, this incapacity to envisage a shared future and a common imagination that includes the Muslim population of France. This is because, fundamentally, the solutions to the 'Muslim problem' are mainly centred around control (of the cult, the mosques, the training of Imams, etc.) or prohibition (through legal discrimination); they are based on disciplining the minds and bodies of those men and women who are believed to be Muslims. Nevertheless, they imply that these supposed Muslims are not here to stay and can be deported. This is what an increasing number of disinhibited Islamophobic individuals are openly hoping for and what an increasing number of French people defining themselves (or perceived) as being Muslims are fearing.

Translated by Steven Wonnacott

Notes

1 This chapter picks up on the analyses presented in «*Islamophobie*». *Comment les élites françaises fabriquent le 'problème musulman'* (Hajjat and Mohammed 2013) and on my introduction to the sociology of Islamophobia (Mohammed 2014). The reader can refer to these in order to further explore the analyses outlined in this chapter and to access a more complete bibliography. For the purposes of readability, we have kept bibliographical annotations to a minimum.
2 This is the case even if the content of these analyses is sometimes a way of disguising hate speech.
3 The reader might want to refer to the opinion polls carried out by the *Commission nationale consultative des droits de l'homme* (CNCDH), the French Advisory Commission on Human Rights.

References

Baubérot, J. 2011. *La Laïcité falsifiée*. Paris: La Découverte.
Bigo, D., T. Deltombe and L. Bonelli. 2008. *Au nom du 11 septembre. . . . Les démocraties à l'épreuve de l'antiterrorisme*. Paris: La Découverte.
Calvès, G. 2011. Les discriminations fondées sur la religion: quelques remarques sceptiques. In E. Lambert Abdelgawad and T. Rambaud (Eds.), *Analyse comparée des discriminations religieuses en Europe*. Paris: Société de législation comparée, 9–23.
Dakhlia, J. and B. Vincent. (Eds.). 2011. *Les Musulmans dans l'histoire de l'Europe*. Paris: Albin Michel.
Daniel, N. 1993. *L'Islam et l'Occident*. Paris: Éditions du Cerf.
Delannoy, J-P. 2005. *Les religions au Parlement français. Du général de Gaulle (1958) à Valéry Giscard d'Estaing (1975)*. Paris: Éditions du Cerf.
Deltombe, T. 2005. *L'islam imaginaire. La construction médiatique de l'islamophobie en France 1975–2005*. Paris: La Découverte.
Gil, F. 1993. *Traité de l'évidence*. Grenoble: J. Millon, Coll. "Krisis."
Göle, N. 2015. *Musulmans au quotidien. Une enquête européenne sur les controverses autour de l'islam*. Paris: La Découverte.
Gusfield, J. 2009 [1984]. *La Culture des problèmes publics. L'alcool au volant: la production d'un ordre symbolique*. Paris: Economica.
Hajjat, A. and M. Mohammed. 2013. *Islamophobie*. Paris: La Découverte.
Liogier, R. 2012. *Le mythe de l'islamisation: essai sur une obsession collective*. Paris: Seuil.

Mohammed, M. 2014. Un nouveau champ de recherche. In *Sociologie*, 1:5.

Reynaud-Paligot, C. 2006. *La République raciale. Paradigme racial et idéologie républicaine (1860–1930)*. Paris: Presses universitaires de France.

Said, E. W. 1980. *L'Orientalisme. L'Orient créé par l'Occident*. Paris: Seuil.

Tévanian, P. 2013. *La haine de la religion*. Paris: La Découverte.

Tolan, J. 2003. *Les Sarrasins*. Paris: Flammarion.

8

THE NEW POLITICS OF RACIALISATION IN FRANCE

The Roma, territorialisation and mobility

Marion Demossier

Over the last three decades, notions of both belonging and identity have attracted a great deal of interest and generated intense public and academic debate. Recent political events, such as the Brexit vote in the UK or the election of president Donald J. Trump in the US, have been accompanied by a rise in new forms of identity claims from neo-nationalism and expression of sovereignty to the anti-globalisation movement. Individuals and groups increasingly take for granted public claims and expressions of national belonging, even to the extent of committing appalling acts in their name, while social media have facilitated hate speech, sometimes disguised as the exercise of free speech. Such actions have taken place against the background of the pro-liferation of new forms of media, which have permitted the banalisation of violence, be it verbal or physical, that is now visible from the comfort of our living rooms. France has not escaped this phenomenon and it could be argued that here, with the renegotiation of the Republican model and the threat of terrorism, a new form of racism has accompanied the development of targeted attacks against specific ethnic groups. Both Europeanisation and globalisation accompanied by neo-liberal policies have been the backbone of these movements.

Mobility, residency, citizenship, social rights and territory have become central to these debates and a means of defining who does, or does not, belong, and place has become one of the salient features of arguments about belonging. Akhil Gupta (1997) has, for example, criticised anthropologists for considering place as a given factor without bothering to understand how it is perceived, constructed and experienced. The idea of culture was traditionally understood in national terms with an expectation of historical roots and a stable territorialised existence (Clifford 1988: 338), while globalisation was often described in terms of a clash of cultures or as the result of the external forces created by sovereign rule, market rationality and regimes of citizenship. These external pressures have had a profound impact on communities, nation states and social life. Most of the sociological literature refers to the intensification of global interconnectedness, suggesting 'a world full of movement and mixture, contacts and linkages, and persistent cultural interaction and exchange' (Inda and Rosaldo 2002: 2). It is against this background that new forms of radicalised identities have emerged, ever more aggressive, visible and vociferously articulated.

In France, these striking new features of contemporary Western society have provoked intense existential debates. For the French, concepts of territory, soil and terroir have a particular resonance and are closely linked to the French national state-building project (Bérard 2016:

72–92). Since the nineteenth century, France has been shuttling back and forth between the general and the particular, and preoccupation with locality persisted throughout the twentieth century against the background of a country with a long history of centralisation. This obsession with place and locality has, for example, been associated with regionalism and the Vichy regime when glorifying the agrarian past, folklore and traditionalism. This close relationship to a physical territory could also be read, for example, through the politics of *terroir* and its more contemporary global deployment illustrating a renewed interest in local and sustainable forms of production and consumption. The local has become extremely popular and fashionable, especially as a response to globalisation. As Paola Filippucci (2004: 72) has argued, this is also part of cultural heritage, broadly defined as a complex set of objects and practices that embody the unique characteristics and enduring presence of a collective, typically a nation or an ethnic group, at once founding and displaying its 'identity.' It is often presented as harmonious, coherent, respectful, original, natural, a setting in which people, space and time are organically connected (Filippucci 2004: 79).

Yet this renewed interest in locality is also becoming more visibly articulated through a politics of exclusion directed towards specific groups. France has witnessed a rise in assertions of belonging through the specific lens of societal ethnic divisions and their visible growing articulation in the public sphere. As illustrated by the tragic attack on the French satirical magazine *Charlie Hebdo* on 7 January 2015, or more recently the terrorist massacre in Paris of 13 November 2015, claims of belonging and not belonging, inclusion and exclusion have assumed a new transnational dimension. In France itself, these terrorist attacks have obscured broader issues of inequality, power and rights in the context of a country where seemingly perennial ideas of *liberté, égalité, fraternité* are both deeply entrenched and divisive, but have never been fully translated into the social and political spheres (Hannoum 2015). Moreover the global nature of the *mise en scène* of these extreme forms of belonging has heightened our sense that ever more violent and disturbing crises are constantly flickering across our screens. To understand this current situation, the anthropologist, Thomas Eriksen, uses the term schimogenesis developed by Gregory Bateson and defined as the destructive spirals of distrust. Today's intercultural encounters, he writes, are 'self-reinforcing, spiralling conflicts' (Eriksen 2016). Yet in the case of the Roma, cultural contacts take another form as it is mainly about a violent process of othering through a scapegoating and alienating process.

This chapter seeks to engage with this shift in the politics of racialisation which has developed in France over the last ten years by focusing more specifically on the Roma,[1] which have been the subject of debate since the enlargement of the European Union in 2007. They can be analysed as an ethnographic window into how the state deploys new social categories which racialise public discourse and policies. As a result of this state obsession, the debate on the Roma has focused on the legitimisation and institutionalisation of a new set of territorial policies. The ethnography of the Roma in France thus offers an opportunity to examine the debate on the complex and changing nature of the nation state against the background of French Republican ideology. The chapter argues that a complex and multilevel process of re-nationalisation and securitisation has taken place, which has led to a rise in racial discourse and hate crimes against groups which are defined as non-territorial and are easy to target because of the deep prejudices circulating around them and their lack of political representation and power.

Territorialisation, nation state and the trope of mobility

On 31 December 2014, the mayor of Champlan in Essonne refused to bury a baby named Maria Francesca, born on 14 October to a Roma family, who had tragically died from cot death, on the grounds that priority had to be given to local taxpayers. The family had lived for the past eight years in a shanty town at the edge of the commune located 16 kilometres to the south-west of Paris, in the Essonne department of the Île-de-France.[2] The event mobilised NGOs and local associations as well as some liberal newspapers, but it remained largely marginalised in the French political sphere. Yet in this case, notions of death, citizenship and belonging called into question the much-vaunted human rights tradition of the French Republic and the essence of *liberté, égalité, fraternité*. This episode is revealing of the entrenched perceptions attached to the Roma in the French collective psyche, which was clearly articulated by a policymaker during a workshop organised in Paris in 2015 by *Counterpoint*[3] '*Les maires, ils ne font rien, ils ont peur*' (the mayors they do nothing, they are frightened).

In French law, the authorisation to be buried has to be submitted to the mayor of the commune of the chosen cemetery, usually that linked to individual residency. The deceased may be buried in the commune where he/she lived, or died, but also where the family vault is located, enabling the anchorage of the family genealogy into a specific site of remembrance. The burial is also possible in another commune, but the mayor may refuse. If the deceased is resident abroad, he/she can be buried in the cemetery of the town in which he/she is registered on the electoral list, even though he/she has no family grave. Often it is the case that the deceased will go back to the family vault or will be buried where most of the deceased lineage members are. Traditionally, cemeteries were a point of physical and symbolic significance for the understanding and binding together of family identity. Today they are still an important point of national anchorage.

However, an IFOP survey[4] published in 2010 on the 'French and Death' underlines how the views of the French on the issue have changed. When the French think of their own funeral, it is first and foremost in terms of ceremony (75%), to determine whether it will be religious or civil, as well as in terms of organ donation (more than half of the French have already thought about it (57%)). Concerns about the place of burial or destination of ashes are now far behind in terms of priorities (IFOP 2010: 9). At a time of intense debate over the place and nature of religion, the French demonstrate an unusual spirit of tolerance by estimating (for 62% of them) that the confessional squares, specific space reserved for the members of a same religion in a cemetery (IFOP 2010: 11), are generally a good thing. Despite these shifts in attitudes towards death and bereavement, the Roma seem to be completely excluded from this new liberal mood. So the question remains: why are they the object of a different societal treatment?

The French media construction of Roma has produced its own economic, cultural and political imaginary landscape through specific relational practices embedded in institutional arrangements that construct essentialised subjects – Roma, securitisation and the French nation – in reference to each other (Demossier 2014). Here Roma are constructed as 'aliens,' a cause of economic and social instability, displaced bodies without territorial roots who are denied their national, European and even human rights. McGarry and Drake described them as trapped in a cycle of exclusion:

> A marginalised group with policymakers and activists ontologising them as a 'problem' community, elaborating policy interventions and articulating interests, respectively, which reinforces the status-quo.
>
> *(2014: 78)*

Moreover, the debate over the Roma crisis has been constructed around a confused amalgam of populations – Gypsies, *gens du voyage, gitans, Manouches* and migrants who, in reality, have little in common. The newspaper *Le Monde* has even devoted several articles to the terminology around these populations. According to Paloma Gay y Blasco:

> The resilience and dominance of the image of the wandering Gypsy needs to be investigated and its effects closely examined, if only because today the majority of European Roma are not nomadic and because the Roma populations of many European countries have been sedentary for several centuries.
>
> *(2008: 299)*

This kind of confusion is also found in the discourse on securitisation, and this presents the opportunity to direct policies against different categories. The EU played a major role in constructing the Roma 'question' and defining Roma rights in a post-national context. Approximately ten to twelve million Roma[5] reside in Europe, mostly in EU Member States and comprise up to 10% of the total populations in historical settlement societies such as Bulgaria, Slovakia, Romania and Hungary; in Western European countries such as Spain, Roma comprise approximately 2% of the total population (these figures do not include Kosovo Roma categorised as asylum seekers). As Guglielmo and Waters (2005), argue, many Roma communities reject the notion that they share a single identity. Wagner (2011: 16) notes that most of his interviewees primarily identify themselves as members of their national communities and only then as Roma. According to the Organisation for Security and Co-operation in Europe (OSCE), the Roma diaspora comprises an extremely heterogeneous set of communities speaking 50 to 100 dialects as well as their national language (Kovats 2002). *Gens du voyage*, on the other hand, refers to an ill-defined administrative category of people under French law who are itinerant within France. They are not fully fledged citizens as their lack of a permanent residence curtails the right to vote, for example. *Gens du voyage* is often taken to also denote *Manouches*, a term for Sinti and Cinti, partly nomadic people who are also referred to under the broad and controversial label 'Gypsies.'

By coupling Roma with *gens du voyage*, they both become part of a wider threat to the fragile nation and its evanescent nature. As Gupta and Ferguson (1997: 4) argue, the Hobbesian idea of culture as orderly and set against the ever-present threat of chaos and anomie is a powerful and prevailing idea in Western thought and politics. Yet here it takes a new form: Roma are presented as being without a national territory like the *gens du voyage*, in constant transit and escaping any national order or categorisation; their social construction is constantly on the move, which resonates with the main features of economic globalisation and grates against French national ideology (Demossier 2014).

If we push the analysis further, it could be argued that they form a new category of representation which is founded on a more archaic, dehumanised and historicised construction of otherness that relies on national psyche. Leonardo Piasere (2013) argues that the rise of *antitsiganisme* is one of the many spectres that haunts collective European minds. The paradox lies with their perceived invisibility and the difficulties in defining the community despite it being the object of intense policing. Leonardo Piasere described them as:

> Sometimes they succumb, sometimes they flee. Now and then they adapt and sometimes they become stronger than ever. The earthly existence of many Rom, Sinti, etc. depends on self-defence and every day they are obliged to use their intelligence to contain the anti-gypsyism that pursues them.
>
> *(2013: 7)*

They are therefore constructed as escaping the rational order of the nation state and the easy to categorise labels used for traditional statistical registers of nationals and foreigners.

The tropes of mobility, nomadism and deterritorialisation all contribute to their lack of analytical and ontological essentialism prescribed by the state, and the Roma defy the traditional canons of the nation state. As a result, they have become an easy target of public discourse, particularly as they are not politically represented at national or transnational levels. Interestingly enough and despite the heterogeneity of the Roma as a cultural group, a degree of confusion has permitted the French state to treat them on equal footing with the *gens du voyage*. This confusion is part of the new French policy landscape. While the Roma of Eastern European origin or from Kosovo have been portrayed as living in camps, the *gens du voyage*, Gypsies and *gitans* who are French citizens, have been the object of local policymaking in relation to access to traveller sites. For the *gens du voyage*, the *Besson* Law[6] obliges towns of more than 5,000 inhabitants to provide a site. However, only a small proportion of towns have implemented this law and as a result, the *gens du voyage* in France have had a complicated relationship to the state in relation to residency and rights. The state has also kept their presence quasi-invisible for decades.[7] Interestingly, both *gens du voyage* and Roma are presented as problems in terms of the management of urban space while their living conditions differ radically (Commission Nationale Consultative des Droits de l'Homme 2008).

Locality, fictions and territorial frictions

As Gullestad argues:

> Cultural fundamentalism and the essentialism which goes hand in hand with it does reify culture, but it is, in reality, about relationships between cultures understood as bounded, internally homogenous, integrated and exclusive entities. As a result, forms of behaviour and meaning attached to the definition of the nation are thought to be inevitably threatened by foreigners who by definition have a different culture.
>
> *(2002: 176)*

The term 'Roma' used in the context of the recent French crisis of securitisation is characterised by great heterogeneity and cultural diversity. Most commentators surprisingly have accepted the state recognition that Roma and *gens du voyage* are synonymous, while their socio-historical trajectory and self-definition differ radically. *Gens du voyage* refers to both a self-identification process of labelling the group against the others the *gadjé* (the French), but also to an ill-defined administrative category under French law that includes those who are itinerant within France. The *loi de circulation* (Law of Circulation) was defined in 1969 to replace that of 1912 on 'nomads.' Both laws focused on how the state should manage the *gens du voyage* as 'others,' especially their itinerant way of life. They are not fully fledged citizens, as their lack of a permanent residence curtails the right to vote. Until comparatively recently, they had to possess a *carnet de circulation* (circulation permit) when they moved from one site to another, and it needed to be signed by the prefecture on arrival at a new site. The carnet was repealed by the French government in June 2015 following the pressure of the NGOs.[8] *Gens du voyage* defines, however, a heterogeneous cultural and social group which historically had a long presence on the French territory: some of them having integrated French society by owning a house and living in communities, while others have opted for an itinerant lifestyle in the proximity of towns and urban centres. *Gens du voyage* is also often taken to denote *Manouches*, a term for Sinti and Cinti, partly nomadic people who are also referred to under the broad and controversial label 'Gypsies.' Moreover, Gypsies or *Manouches* are often referred to as Roma today, though they tend to refute this categorisation.

Throughout the crisis, a great deal of confusion in the French terminology around *gens du voyage, Roms* and *Manouches* has been displayed by the political class, and especially by former president Nicolas Sarkozy and his ministers (Marthaler 2008), something which was also witnessed amongst academics and policymakers. I have discussed the construction of the crisis elsewhere (Demossier 2014). The confusion has contributed to the social construction of Roma as a security and economic threat in territorial, social and national terms that is regularly repeated (Mayer et al. 2014). A report drafted by the *Commission Nationale Consultative des Droits de l'Homme, Etudes et propositions sur la situation des Roms et des gens du voyage en France*, the text of which was adopted by the National Assembly on 7 February 2008, argues that in order to characterise Roma identity the metaphor of a mosaic is a useful one: 'Each piece has its own profile which makes sense only as a whole' (*Commission Nationale Consultative des Droits de l'Homme* 2008). Yet in policy terms, questions could be raised about the impact of a measure aiming at 'a one size fits all' and about the wider treatment of these European citizens in France (McGarry and Drake 2014; Demossier 2014; Nacu 2011; Carrera and Atger 2010).

What is central, however, to the treatment of the Roma by the French state is related to the issue of the lack of a home address as well as a taxable citizenry. Territorial belonging and residence are central to processes of French naturalisation. The politicisation of the Roma and *gens du voyage* focuses mainly on the issue of residency and its impact on the locality (Legros 2011). Most French commentators describe it as an urban problem which needs to be addressed for broader political reasons, such as social order, private law and the management of urban wasteland. A report produced by the *Commission Nationale Consultative des Droits de l'Homme* underlines the growing complexity of the law applicable to both *gens du voyage* and Roma. There is a new legal emphasis on their lack of housing rights and their mobility – both of which are exacerbated by the constant waves of expulsions. In terms of human rights, the laws have to conform to the *champ d'application* of EU citizenship and free movement by prohibiting discrimination on grounds of race, ethnic social origin or membership of a national minority (Article 21 of the EU Charter). Yet the economic and social situation many Roma face is well below the minimum provisions for human rights as illustrated by recent ONF reports. Their treatment under both Nicolas Sarkozy and François Hollande's governments has been consistent, and reinforced the growing marginalisation of the Roma. Parallels could be established with the treatment of migrants in Calais.

In a recent article, Olivier Legros and Martin Olivera (2014), who both have a long experience of examining urban public policies and the situation of the Roma in the Paris suburbs, have argued that they are actually facing, like other migrants and *banlieusards*, the struggle of residential choices in order to establish, improve or develop their socio-economic positions. Yet they have also been the subject of continuous waves of expulsions and their situation is still characterised by fear, danger and intolerance. In their study of a group of Roma from Romania over a period of several years, Legros and Olivera (2014) demonstrate how these family groups have been skilful in managing local resources and using their connections to survive in a rather hostile context. Scott talks of veritable strategies of subsistence (2013: 28). They have learned to know 'how to find, open and maintain a squat' in the context of local power which oscillates between acceptance and expulsions. While some cities and towns, often in the proximity of the major French cities, do not tolerate their presence at all, others agreed to collect their waste and have helped them find accommodation and send their children to school (Lille or the Seine-Saint-Denis, for example).

A variety of situations characterises their treatment from expulsions to integration (Legros and Olivera 2014). Tensions between different local approaches towards the Roma can be detected through an examination of access to housing which is crucial for the acquisition of social rights based on residence. When the Roma are expelled from urban space or wasteland, pushed from one place to the next, they are unable to acquire the fixed residential status required by the French authorities and are rendered 'nomads' *malgré eux*. The list of legal texts around the Roma deals mainly with issues such as residency, education and use of travellers' sites (Legros 2011). The lack of a coherent framework and a clear and organised political mobilisation coming from the Roma themselves illustrates the state of confusion and fear which has spread in France and serves as a background to the intensification of racism against them. Like the *gens du voyage*, they face administrative and institutional obstacles constitutive of the process of othering and alienating. They are thus defined as *hors d'ici* (not belonging here) and their status is reduced to nothing. Roma are constructed as 'aliens,' a cause of economic and social instability, displaced bodies without territorial roots who are denied their national, European and even human rights. At the same time, they are presented as a threat to both French cultural essentialism and republicanism with their territorial forms of belonging and citizenship (*jus solis*). As a result, Roma incarnate non-territorial belonging. They appear to have all the characteristics of nations but lack geographical integrity, as illustrated through the refusal to bury the deceased child mentioned previously.

Cultural racism: acts and representations

Behind the wide range of local situations facing them, the Roma have not only suffered racism but also experienced growing support for their cause. Since their emergence in public discourse following the policies implemented under Sarkozy (Demossier 2014), they have found themselves represented in the public sphere by an extreme polarisation, stretching from targeted explicit racism to exhibitions intended to educate the wider public. This polarisation is documented through the examples which include videos on Youtube such as *Ras -le-bol* Marseille[9] introducing Geoffrey de la Gasnerie's website which documents how the local population has reacted to the presence of the Roma. Against the background of this difficult cultural encounter, several major exhibitions have also been organised throughout France by agencies and European stakeholders telling the story of a cultural tale.[10] Another powerful example of this process is provided by the video *Pas de roms dans le pastis*, recounting a catalogue of banal racism witnessed in the suburbs of Marseille.[11] This dualism characterising the visual construction of the Roma as both a threat but also as human cultural beings, contributes to the perpetuation of enduring clichés attached to their essentialisation. Their mediatisation has also been largely the work by others.

In French public discourse, popular attitudes equate the group of Roma with Gypsies and, thus, refer back to a past they do not wish to relive in the context of the Holocaust, which is still kept hidden in the collective European memory. Because public memory is an important symbol of belonging in European societies, the lack of endorsement of Roma Holocaust commemoration at the national level constitutes a refusal of national belonging (Gay y Blasco 2008: 300). Both the European Union and its institutions have simultaneously approached the Roma in terms of European political and cultural integration (van Baar 2011: 3) through, for example, Holocaust remembrance and minority/majority cultural dialogue, but this is still limited to the Europe Union rather than being debated at the national level. This reflects their position in the heritage landscape as a diaspora. Yet there is a disjuncture between the collective mobilisation at the European level around their historical treatment, especially during the Second World War, and their elusive status at national and local levels. The place they occupy in the French political imagination is therefore characterised by contradictions and paradoxes feeding into a space full of ambiguities, fears and invisibility.

This construction of the Roma in the national imagination relies on a deep historical collective process of societal exclusion and the alienation of the group presented as being incapable of integrating any nation on the grounds of cultural and social difference. According to Valeriu Nicolae (2006), dehumanisation through animalisation is the central pivot of *antitsiganisme*. Some arguments used to illustrate this dehumanisation refer to their alleged lack of hygiene, the illnesses they bring with them, the state of their children, the erratic sexual behaviour of women who are often described as prostitutes, the fact that the men steal and lie, as well as a quasi-animality attached for example to the ways in which they treat their children, which supposedly characterises them. A woman recently interviewed commented: 'they do not bother anybody but the problem is everything that gravitates around them: prostitution, begging and all the children. Look at all the children who run and they have tuberculosis.'[12] Didier Bigo (2014: 184) has argued that the role played by specific experts in criminology has undeniably contributed to the construction and dissemination of a discourse of justification concerning the criminalisation of the Roma, presenting them as a transnational group of criminals stealing, occupying urban fringes, a no man's land. The anthropologist, Jean-Pierre Liégeois (2009), speaks of 'the gypsy as not defined in its real and concrete being, but as how they need to be defined for sociopolitical reasons' (my own translation).

Conclusions

The Roma crisis was embedded in a wide constellation of meanings, representations and discourses carefully orchestrated by the French government to facilitate its construction as a zero-sum game in which the Roma were constructed as a nomadic yet invisible group within the French nation (Demossier 2014). Since the election of president François Hollande in 2012, the daily news media have been more generous towards the Roma following increasing denunciation of their ill-treatment, but in practice this has not led to any substantial signs of improvement. Since the 2017 elections, the Macron government has continued to close down the camps. The role of the media and the local work of associations and NGOs has certainly helped to transform the landscape that the Roma have to confront on a daily basis. Yet, if recent surveys are encouraging it is nevertheless the case that the political context in which these performative crises of the state are played out and performed are indicative of a broader and more global polarisation of identity claims which, in return, have an impact on national politics.

The work of political scientists Nonna Mayer, Guy Michelat, Vincent Tiberj and Tommaso Vitale on the Roma in France (2016) recently argued for the emergence of more nuanced feelings. If they were seen by 77% of those interviewed as not able to integrate French society in 2014, that figure fell to only 57.4% in 2016. According to the authors, what has changed is the decline in the offensive stereotypes attached to the Roma, especially in relation to delinquency and other social problems. The idea that the Roma are relying essentially on stealing and trafficking is shared by 57% compared to 78% in 2013 (Mayer et al. 2016: 339). The authors of the report attributed this change in French public opinion to the reaction following the death of Maria Francesca, as well as a strong local associative mobilisation defending Roma rights, which has become even more active since. Similarly the Roma have started to organise and mobilise public opinion more effectively at a local level in order to be more actively represented and heard.[13] Yet there is still a long way to go before the Roma are treated as European citizens on equal footing with other EU nationals. Surveys are also no more than snapshots and are limited in their ways of understanding the nature of the new fears emerging at global level.

As Legros (2011) pointed out, the Roma illustrate the problems attached to urban space and its management, as well as the migratory flux and the question of French hospitality. In this context, the discussion could be opened to the broader changes affecting France, that is to say its inability to integrate citizens of North African descent, migration policies and the treatment of foreigners. Camps like Calais offer another example of how the French state struggles to manage migration and to think about these crises as performative politics rather than key areas of political and ideological positioning. Only time will tell if the Roma will be offered a genuine French hospitality enjoying the same rights as others.

Notes

1 For a discussion on these categories, see the work of Gay y Blasco. Academics and others face difficulties in their choice of terminology and intersect with issues of representation, authorship and effect (Gay y Blasco 2008: 298). Herein, I refer to the terminology used by the various actors because it is an intrinsic part of my analysis. However, terms such as 'Roma' or 'Gypsies' remain the subject of much debate.
2 'Le maire de Champlan refuse d'enterrer un bébé rom dans sa commune,' in *Le Monde*, 3 January 2015. www.lemonde.fr/societe/article/2015/02/18/enterrement-d-un-bebe-rom-l-enquete-preliminaire-classee-sans-suite_4578989_3224.html [Accessed: 10.11.2016]. For further information around the controversy, see http://rue89.nouvelobs.com/2015/01/05/refus-dinhumer-bebe-rom-trois-versions-forcement-deux-mensonges-256909#! [Accessed: 10.11.2016].
3 See workshop organised in Paris by Counterpoint. Building Bridges. http://counterpoint.uk.com/ [Accessed: 11.11.2016].
4 www.ifop.fr/media/poll/1283-1-study_file.pdf [Accessed: 11.11.2016].
5 See ec.europa.eu/justice/policies/discrimination/docs/com_2011_173_en.pdf [Accessed: 11.11.2016].
6 For more details, see www.legifrance.gouv.fr/affichTexte.do?cidTexte=JORFTEXT000000583573 and www.senat.fr/lc/lc145/lc1450.html [Accessed: 11.11.2016].
7 I lived between 1981 and 1990 with a group of *gens du voyage* who were semi-sedentarised and travelled during the summer for their professional activities. Often we went with other members of the extended family and stayed in local campsites in caravans. As a *gadjé* living with a gypsy, I experienced racism, but also how invisible the group was at an institutional level.
8 www.lemonde.fr/societe/article/2015/06/10/l-assemblee-vote-la-suppression-du-livret-de-circulation-pour-les-gens-du-voyage_4650732_3224.html [Accessed: 18.01.2017].
9 www.bing.com/videos/search?q=ras+le+bol+Marseille+Roms&view=detail&mid=87923D0E0A44 AA2B968387923D0E0A44AA2B9683&FORM=VIRE [Accessed: 18.01.2017].
10 See for example in Lyon in 2010. www.citizenside.com/fr/photos/culture/2010-11-22/31619/ exposition-sur-les-roms-au-centre-d-histoire-de.html#f=0/198406 [Accessed: 18.01.2017].
11 www.youtube.com/watch?v=fmf3RK_MR6M [Accessed: 18.01.2017].
12 www.bing.com/videos/search?q=ras+le+bol+Marseille+Roms&view=detail&mid=87923D0E0A44 AA2B968387923D0E0A44AA2B9683&FORM=VIRE [Accessed: 18.01.2017].
13 See for example https://romsaction.org/ [Accessed: 18.01.2017].

References

Bérard, L. 2016. Terroir and the sense of Place. In D. Gangjee (Ed.), *Research Handbook on Intellectual Property and Geographical Indications*. London: Edward Elgar, 72–92.
Bigo, D. 2014. Security, IR and anthropology: encounters, misunderstanding and possible collaborations. In C. Frois, M. Maguire and N. Zurawski (Eds.), *The Anthropology of Security: Perspectives from the Frontline of Policing Counter-Terrorism and Border Control*. London: Pluto Press.
Carrera, S. and A. Faure Atger. 2010. *L'Affaire des Roms*: a challenge to the EU's area of freedom, security and justice. Available at: www.ceps.be/ceps/download/3746 [Accessed: 29.06.2012].
Clifford, J. 1988. *The Predicament of Culture. Twentieth-Century Ethnography, Literature, and Art*. Harvard: Harvard University Press.

Commission Nationale Consultative des Droits de l'Homme. 2008. *Études et proposition sur la situation des Roms et des gens du voyage en France.* Texte adopté en séance plénière, 7 February. Available at: www. cncdh.fr/sites/default/files/08.02.07_etude_sur_la_situation_des_roms_et_des_gens_du_voyage_en_france.pdf [Accessed: 2.02.2014].

Demossier, M. 2014. Sarkozy and Roma: performing securitization. In C. Frois, M. Maguire and N. Zurawski (Eds.), *The Anthropology of Security: Perspectives from the Frontline of Policing Counter-Terrorism and Border Control.* London: Pluto Press.

Eriksen, T. 2016. Globalisation. *Eriksen's* blog. Available at: https://thomashyllanderiksen.net/tag/globalisation-2/ [Accessed: 01.02.2017].

Fillipucci, P. 2004. A French place without a cheese: problems with heritage and identity in northeastern France. In *Focaal,* 2004:44, Winter, 72–86.

Gay y Blasco, P. 2008. Picturing 'Gypsies.' In *Third Text,* 22:3, 297–303.

Guglielmo, R. and T-W. Waters. 2005. Migrating towards minority status: shifting European policy towards Roma. In *Journal of Common Market Studies,* 43:4, 763–786.

Gullestad, M. 2002. Invisible fences: egalitarianism, nationalism, and racism. In *Journal of the Royal Anthropological Institute,* 8:1, 45–63.

Gupta, A. and J. Ferguson. 1997. Culture, power, and place: ethnography at the end of an era. In A. Gupta and J. Ferguson (Eds.), *Culture, Power, Place: Explorations in Critical Anthropology.* Durham, NC: Duke University Press, 1–29.

Hannoum, A. 2015. Cartoons, secularism, and inequality. In *Anthropology Today,* 31, 21–24.

IFOP. 2010. Sondage 26 Avril. Intentions de vote à l'élection présidentielle. Available at: https://www.ifop.com/publication/intentions-de-vote-a-lelection-presidentielle/ [Accessed 20.10.2017].

Inda, J-X. and R. Rosaldo. (Eds.). 2002. *The Anthropology of Globalization,* 1st edition. Malden, MA: Blackwell Publishing.

Kovats, M. 2002. The European Roma question. Working Paper, No. 31. London: Royal Institute of International Affairs.

Legros, D. 2011. Roma villages or the reinvention of *cités de transit.* Available at: www.l.metropolitiques.eu/Roma-Villages-or-the-Reinvention.html [Accessed: 19.11.2011].

Legros, O. and M. Olivera. 2014. La gouvernance métropolitaine à l'épreuve de la mobilité contrainte des Roms migrants. In *EspacesTemps.net,* rubrique "Travaux." Available at: www.espacestemps.net/articles/lmobilite-contrainte-des-roms-migrants-en-region-parisienne/ [Accessed: 15.01.2015].

Liégeois, J-P. 2009. *Roms et Tsiganes.* Paris: La Découverte, Coll. "Repères Sociologie."

Marthaler, S. 2008. Nicolas Sarkozy and the politics of French immigration policy. In *Journal of European Public Policy,* 15:3, 382–397.

Mayer, N., G. Michelat, V. Tiberj and T. Vitale. 2014. Un refus croissant de 'l'autre.' In *La lutte contre le racisme, l'antisémitisme et la xénophobie.* Année 2013. Commission nationale consultative des droits de l'homme. Paris: La Documentation française, 157–208.

Mayer, N., G. Michelat and T. Vitale. 2016. Des sentiments plus nuancés envers les Roms. In *La lutte contre le racisme, l'antisémitisme et la xénophobie.* Année 2015. Paris: La Documentation française, 335–339.

Mc Garry, A. and H. Drake. 2014. The politicisation of Roma as an ethnic 'other': security discourse in France and the politics of belonging. In U. Korkut, G. Bucken-Knapp, A. Mc Garry, J. Hinnfors and H. Drake (Eds.), *The Discourses and Politics of Migration in Europe.* New York: Palgrave Macmillan, 73–91.

Nacu, A. 2011. The politics of Roma migration: framing identity struggles among Romanian and Bulgarian Roma in the Paris region. In *Journal of Ethnic and Migration Studies,* 37:1, 135–150.

Nacu, A. 2012. From silent marginality to spotlight scapegoating? A brief case study of French policy towards the Roma. In *Journal of Ethnic and Migration Studies,* 38:8, 1323–1328.

Nicolae, V. 2006. Towards a definition of anti-gypsyism. Available at: www.ergonetwork.org/media/userfiles/media/egro/Towards%20a%20Definition%20of%20Anti-Gypsyism.pdf [Accessed: 15.01.2017].

Piasere, L. 2013. Un racisme méconnu: l'antitsiganisme. In *Regions: Tests of Constrict, Conflict and Contact Theory, Social Science Research,* 40, 1091–1107.

Scott, J. C. 2013. Zomia ou l'art de ne pas être gouverné. Traduit par Nicolas Guilhot, Frédéric Joly et Olivier Ruchet. Paris: Seuil.

Van Baar, H. 2011. Cultural policy and the governmentalization of Holocaust remembrance in Europe: Romani memory between denial and recognition. In *International Journal of Cultural Policy,* 17:1, 1–17.

Wagner, F-P. 2011. Citizenship as Europeanization, Europeanization as citizenship: challenges, opportunities and realities of a European post-national political space and the question of the integration of European Roma, Sinti and Traveller communities. Paper presented at UAECS the Academic Association for Contemporary European Studies Conference, 5–8 September, Cambridge.

9

YOUTH AND POLITICS IN FRANCE

Democratic deficit or new model of citizenship?

Anne Muxel

Transformations in the relationships between young people and politics are obvious in all European democracies. Engagement in traditional political institutions has declined. Partisan and social allegiances have become looser. Our democracies have become more reflective and the links that ordinary citizens establish with the political system have become more individualised. In terms of social politicisation, experimentation has won out over identification and affiliation among the younger generations. Increasingly, political involvement takes place by means of many different types of expression and action. Abstention continues to grow, acquiring an increasing level of democratic legitimacy. It is clear that the endemic economic crisis that many European countries are currently facing has had an impact on political attitudes and behaviour.

This new political context has led to what some have seen as a crisis in citizenship. However, these transformations can be interpreted differently and instead be seen more as a sign of the emergence of a new model of citizenship than as a democratic deficit. This chapter will focus on these political transformations. It will present the empirical results from quantitative and electoral surveys conducted in France at the CEVIPOF to explore what is so special about young people's electoral behaviour in the French context; how we can explain that the most attractive political party in France today among the young is the Front National (the now Rassemblement National); and what the chances of so-called political resilience among the younger generations are despite their deep mistrust of politicians and representative democracy.

Towards a new model of citizenship

Transformations in political attitudes and behavior are not limited to young people and can be observed among the entire population. However, young people function as a kind of magnifying glass reflecting change in the relationships between ordinary citizens and politicians, but also change in the practice of politics and political policy. The transformations observed today will have an impact on the way politics is practiced and the expression of political choices, but also, more broadly, on the future of democracy. The three most relevant characteristics that reveal what could be seen as a new citizenship model in our advanced European democracies are political mistrust, intermittent voting, and the increased legitimacy of protest. While I will essentially focus on France, most of the traits I will discuss can also be observed in other European countries (Norris 1999, 2011).

Political mistrust

There is a distance, even a lack of understanding towards the political sphere shared by many French citizens today. Rarely has politics been associated with such a negative image of both its actors and its program objectives. This widespread credibility gap, which has taken a rather firm foothold, is often cloaked in a discourse of disenchantment. Dissatisfaction with political representatives can be detected in citizens of all ages. In France today, almost two-thirds of the population (65%) does not trust either the left or the right to govern (CEVIPOF 2015). More than eight out of ten respondents think that politicians do not deal with their problems and their difficulties (CEVIPOF 2015). There is a very wide gap between the elites and ordinary people: two-thirds of the population believe that politicians are corrupt and do not do their jobs with integrity and honesty. Young people share the same attitudes and begin their lives as citizens with this very negative perception of the political sphere.

This new framework clearly reveals the difficulties and dangers at hand. In order to function, democracy needs mutual trust between citizens and their representatives. Setting aside the negative consequences of generalised political distrust for the moment (populism, political crises, civic defection), it could also be argued that such distrust provides an opportunity for the political system to be more demanding of its institutions and the people who govern. Keeping this optimistic view of the future of democracy in mind, this generalisation of mistrust in the socialisation process could clearly lead to more critical citizens, who both support democratic ideals and are critical of the political system.

Intermittent voting

Abstention has constantly increased in most European countries over the last 30 years, and particularly in France (Cautrés and Muxel 2011). In the recent period, voter turnout levels have been at their lowest, whatever the type of election, particularly among young voters. The 2015 mid-term regional French elections witnessed record levels of non-voting. More than six out of ten young voters aged 18–24 years, did not cast a ballot. Sociological reasons for abstention do still exist. They include lower levels of social integration (among young people, women, the less well-educated, the unemployed and so forth) and social divides which cut across age categories. During the 2012 presidential election, 62% of students said that they voted in all elections, while only 49% of young people in employment said the same, and 42% of the unemployed; 26% of students recognised they were hesitant about who to vote for right up until election day, making their final choice at the last minute, 27% of young people in employment said the same, as did 34% of the unemployed; 75% of voters born before 1945 said their choice was made a long time prior to the election compared to only 45% of voters born after 1980 (–30 points) (CEVIPOF 2012).[1] Nevertheless, social factors are not sufficient to explain why citizens abstain more, despite the fact that levels of education continue to improve, with 35% of students abstaining in the first round of the 2012 presidential elections in France. In the first round of the last presidential elections in 2017, which is usually an election that mobilises more than any other, one-third of young people abstained (32%), ten points more than the entire electorate (22%), and much more than older people (17% of people aged 65 and over) (IFOP 2017).

Abstention from political life is prominent in all segments of society. Voting patterns across all forms of election have become intermittent at best, and abstention is increasingly an expression of discontent and political protest. The average voter has become more unpredictable, and potentially more volatile in his or her choices. This has led to a profound change in how the act of voting is interpreted. The idea of voting as a civic norm encompassing the notion of duty is disappearing. The political socialisation of younger generations has given rise to a new framework. Although voting is still considered as the most effective democratic tool, it is no longer considered only as a moral duty citizens must carry out in democracy, but increasingly as a right, suggesting a more expressive and individualised bond with politics. Half of French teenagers (14–17 years old) see voting primordially as a right (50%) and only half as above all a duty (49%) (CEVIPOF/Ministère de la Défense 2015). Nevertheless, young people still consider voting to be important. The young may not always exercise their right to vote, but that does not mean that they do not regard voting as being useful: more than three-quarters (77%) considers it to be very or extremely important for democracy.

If voting is increasingly seen as a right, so is abstention, considered as the right not to vote. Abstention can be used to express political dissatisfaction and protest about the candidates and parties on offer in an election. The growth of this political use of abstention suggests that it is a behaviour used and legitimised increasingly often and above all by young people. Stepping into this new model of electoral behaviour, young people will adopt the habit of voting or not voting depending on the importance they attach to the result of the election. They tend not to consider mid-term elections such as European elections as crucial. In France, only presidential elections are perceived as being more decisive. Therefore, intermittent voting has become the normal way to practice one's civic duty. This toing and froing between voting and non-voting constitutes real political change and redefines the democratic tools citizens use to express their opinions. Obviously, the consequences of an early socialisation towards abstention among younger generations, and above all its legitimisation, will change the rules of the democratic game and will have an impact on the electoral system and competition. If systematic abstention constitutes a real danger for democracy, in that it threatens the legitimacy of democracy itself, one could also strongly suggest that the growth of the political and intermittent expression of abstention could on the contrary be a sign of political vitality.

Legitimacy of protest

The development of participatory protest

Voting, although still regarded as useful and effective by the young, is no longer considered to be the sole means of civic involvement. Young people have a set of proprietary characteristics that translate into non-institutional forms of political participation, rather than institutional and electoral participation. According to Eurostat, less than 4% of young Europeans declared that they took part in the activities of political parties or trade unions (Eurostat 2011). Expression of political awareness is emerging and protest is increasingly seen as legitimate. Non-conventional participation is on the increase in all European countries. This is predominantly a generational phenomenon: members of the older generations are unlikely to be involved in protests, baby boomers more likely and young people today more likely still: increasing involvement in protest is a continuing trend.

In France, half of young people have taken part in a street demonstration. Even very young teenagers have engaged in this type of protest: 20% of 14–17-year-olds, of which 44% declare themselves to lean to the left, and 28% to the right. Protest is becoming a very familiar form of political expression, and fully part of the ordinary process of political socialisation among younger generations (CEVIPOF/Ministère de la Défense 2015). Their familiarity with protest attitudes and behavior is also strengthened by the specific political climate which has characterised the relationship between French citizens and politics for decades. Today, half of French people (51%) declare themselves to be ready to demonstrate to defend their ideas. Even if it is strongest among the young, this prevalent feeling is shared by all age groups (CEVIPOF 2017).

Conventional participation (voting) and non-conventional participation (demonstrating) are not rival options; they are closely linked and often complement each other. Protest movements cannot be seen as an alternative to electoral turnout: the more citizens value conventional participation, the more they also regard participating in protests as important.

This protest-style politicisation can also be found at the ballot box. Many European countries have seen extremist parties or parties outside the system achieve electoral success. In the same way that abstention has become frequently used as an instrument to express political protest, the vote has become a means of protest that expresses a rejection of government parties and the conventional political system. During the 2012 presidential elections, many young people voted for far right or far left candidates. More than a third of them (35%) used the election to express their discontent and vent their concerns, in the process disregarding the '*vote utile*' (tactical vote), which in the past has been taken for granted by the two main parties. In 2007, only 20% of young people ventured from the mainstream parties. In 2017, more than half of young voters (51%) voted for Jean-Luc Mélenchon or for Marine Le Pen (respectively 30% and 21%) in the first round.

Through these means, protest can be a conventional means of participation. Within this new model of citizenship, conventional and non-conventional types of involvement are not mutually exclusive but rather have become more and more intertwined. The range of tools used in democratic expression has diversified hugely.

Vanishing of ideology and weakening of the left-right cleavage

Great political narratives have faded and no longer provide a readable map of systems of belonging to which individuals can attach themselves and become involved. Members of most adult age groups, particularly those which include the parents of today's youth, began formulating their views in a world where ideological labels, the division between the left and the right, and the definition of competing international power blocs were all well established. But this is no longer the case for younger generations.

Young people in Europe today have been socialised in a period when the ideologies which structured political debate and the face-off between capitalism and socialism during the twentieth century have waned. They have assimilated a certain amount of disenchantment with politics. This does not mean a lack of beliefs and values but rather a rejection of all the crimes engendered by totalitarianism. Although they are deeply attached to democracy, they also tend to develop a more critical vision of what political power is and what it can ultimately achieve. In a sense, they are both idealistic and realistic. As 'critical citizens' they are more lucid and less credulous about the political discourses and electoral promises they hear.

Today's young people live in a very different world: political experimentation is the order of the day. Although older generations are also becoming involved in more autonomous and spontaneous initiatives, they still recollect traditional forms of political activism and allegiance, whereas today's young form their political views without the aid of clearly established reference points. Their political socialisation is more experimental and less structured by party or trade union politics, and tends to focus on mobilisation around quite specific issues and debates. Moreover, it is increasingly difficult to differentiate between left- and right-wing political values. In present-day France, Republican values are drawn on by both the left and right. And the Front National shows great expertise in drawing on them. Human rights, solidarity, democracy, secularity, the market economy, tackling unemployment, rising insecurity are now all recurrent mobilising themes in the discourses of most French political parties.

As a result of the blurring of ideological boundaries and the growing tendency of voters not to situate themselves on the traditional right–left axis, there is an increasing difference in how generations identify themselves on the political spectrum. In 1978, a comparison of the positioning of young French people vis-à-vis their elders revealed that fewer young people positioned themselves as neither on the left nor on the right than their older cohorts. This would suggest that they were more politicised than their elders. Now, in the space of 40 years, the refusal to position oneself on the left–right axis is more pronounced among young people when compared to the entirety of the population, and especially among the youngest: 42% of 16- to 21.5-year-olds position themselves as neither left nor right and 35% of 21.5-year-olds do so. Compared to older citizens (65 and over), only 27% of whom do so, there is a clear vanishing of ideological identifications and a weakening of the left–right cleavage (CEVIPOF 2016). This change concerns the entire population, but is more pronounced among the youngest generations.

As an example of this, the weakening of support for the left among young French people is part of a long-term generational shift which points to the transformation of political identification. Clearly, the relative shrinkage of support among young French people for the left reveals an ideological generational realignment. Even if the contexts are different, their electoral choices in the last two presidential elections reveal this growing distance from the left and also from institutional parties. Let's begin with 2012. One of the paradoxes of the 2012 French presidential elections is that young people, despite their traditional orientation to the left, and the fact that they are bearing the brunt of the fall-out from the economic crisis, contributed less to the victory of François Hollande than their elders. However, this occurred in a context where François Hollande placed a new generational pact at the heart of his election campaign.

In the first round of the presidential election, of all age groups, it was the youngest voters who voted the least for Hollande: 22% of 18- to 24-year-olds compared to 27% of 25- to 34-year-olds, 29% of 35- to 49-year-olds, 29% of 50- to 64-year-olds and 31% of those over 65 (Figure 9.1). Throughout the campaign, while the Front de Gauche candidate Jean-Luc Mélenchon attracted a non-negligible share of the left-leaning youth in his first-round total of 11% (16% of the 18- to 24-year-olds vote, +5 points compared to 2007), François Hollande's appeal

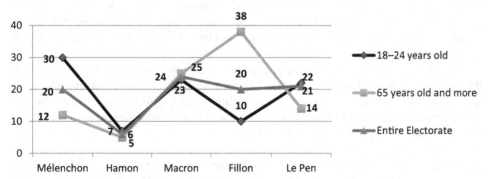

Figure 9.1 Electoral choices at the presidential elections of 2017.

(Electoral Survey ENEF/CEVIPOF 2017 Wave 14)

to young people was relatively unsuccessful. Young people expressed radical choices during the first round, also choosing the far right. As many as 17% voted for Marine Le Pen (+11 points compared to 2007). During the second round, among 18- to 24-year-olds, François Hollande practically tied with Nicolas Sarkozy (51% compared to 49%). With the exception of the oldest group of voters (65+), who voted clearly in support of Sarkozy (56.6% vs. 43.3%), all other age groups opted for the Socialist leader (59% of 25- to 34-year-olds, 54.4% of 35- to 49-year-olds and 53.6% of 50- to 64-year-olds). To put this in perspective, in the second round of the 2007 presidential election, Ségolène Royal, the Socialist candidate, garnered 63% of the young people's vote (as against only 37% for Nicolas Sarkozy).

At the last presidential elections, the left performed a little better than in 2012 among the young. Jean-Luc Mélenchon, the radical candidate of la France Insoumise, did particularly well (30% of the 18- to 24-year-olds who voted and 20% of the entire electorate). On the other hand, the candidate of the Parti Socialiste, Benoît Hamon, obtained only 7% of their vote (5% of the whole electorate). Young people also expressed radical choices, voting for Marine Le Pen as much as the electorate as a whole (respectively 22% and 21%). François Fillon, the candidate of Les Républicains, did only half as well amongst young people as compared with the whole electorate (10% compared to 20% of the entire electorate). The most interesting result is the relatively poor support for Emmanuel Macron amongst young people. Given the image of renewal that he wanted to engender, and also because he was the youngest candidate, one could have expected a stronger echo from the youth. In the first round, the 18–24 vote was on par with the overall electorate (respectively 23% and 24%). There was therefore no specific youth effect. Even if the radical left seems to have increased its attractiveness among the youngest generations in France, these latest results confirm that they seem to be more or less following the electoral trends of the electorate as a whole. These trends are also more protest oriented than ever.

An increase in political radicalism? The seductive power of the *Front National* in France

In today's time of economic and cultural crisis, young people seem to be more motivated by their individual circumstances. This in turn will stimulate extremism and populism as the overall political context of Europe has been radically modified. Today in France, a quarter of young people (25%) have to deal with unemployment. Young people are faced with the malfunctioning of political systems in which affiliations and identifications are more random and less clearly stated. When making political choices, especially at election time, a growing number of individuals use criteria which have less to do with commitment to or support for a particular political stance. Electoral voting behaviour, in particular, is greatly influenced by this kind of 'negative politicisation,' though the consequences and impact of this phenomenon on different generations vary greatly.

The growing lack of confidence in politicians and governments progressively undermines the legitimacy of political institutions themselves, particularly in the eyes of young people. When questioned, only 44% of the youngest voters declare themselves to be satisfied with the way democracy functions today in France. And only a third (33%) say they are satisfied with Emmanuel Macron as president (CEVIPOF 2017).

The general mistrust of politics and politicians in France, as well the lack of support for political institutions and for representative democracy, has generated more populist attitudes and more radical behaviours. The widespread echo of the Front National, and its normalisation, indicates that a large part of the French population expresses dissatisfaction and anger. The appeal of political radicalism, populism, and the far right among the young is not new. The

Vote for the Front National at the first round of the presidential elections (1988–2017) (%)

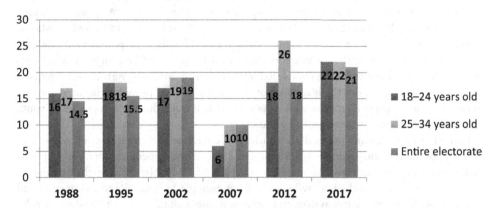

Figure 9.2 Evolution of the vote for the Front National by age groups as percentage of the vote at presidential elections since its inception.

(CEVIPOF Electoral Surveys : Sofres (1988, 1995, 2002), IFOP (2007), Opinion Way (2012), IPSOS (2017))

Front National has played a determining role in the French political and electoral landscape for almost 30 years. In the first round of the 1988 presidential election, 16% of 18- to 24-year-olds voted for Jean-Marie Le Pen, 18% in 1995, 17% in 2002, 18% in 2012, and 22% in 2017. 2007 is an exception (only 6%) due to Nicolas Sarkozy's personal ability to capture this section of the electorate (Figure 9.2).

The Front National (and now the Rassemblement National) is better able than its competitors to maintain the ambient disillusion with the left–right cleavage and more generally with the political system, and to take advantage of it. The Front National has taken advantage of social disaffiliation, the fear of losing social status and the feelings of vulnerability that the economic and social crisis has given rise to, but it has also positioned itself very well as a refuge for those who have become alienated from politics. Throughout Europe, the rise of populisms and far right parties can be witnessed, and France is no exception. However, this is part of a long-term process. The electoral success of the Front National has been built over a period of 30 years. It has a well-consolidated electoral base and can count on strong support within the French youth.

Social and political cleavages at work

Young people do not form a homogenous group when it comes to politics. The social divides that cut across the young reflect real political divides. Level of education is an important determinant of voting behaviours and attitudes. Employment status, which is tightly correlated to level of education at this age, reveals deep divisions in partisan identification as well as other characteristics of politicisation. As shown previously, the Front National is more attractive to less-well-educated young people, even if the party is also gathering strength among the student population. Level of education consistently leads to a wide gap in the way young people consider politics: young people with lower levels of education, whether they work or are unemployed, are less interested in politics, tend to abstain more often at elections, and are more likely to refuse to position themselves on a left/right scale. They are also less likely to demonstrate than students. Their relationship with the political system is weaker and more distant. When they do participate, a significant number of them choose to cast a protest vote rather than to demonstrate. But using voting to protest and choosing mainly populist leaders expresses a lack of trust in democratic regimes. Radicalisation has also become prevalent among the younger population working in the least advantageous jobs or experiencing unemployment. A quarter of young workers without education (23%) and half of young unemployed voters (51%) voted for Marine Le Pen in the first round of the last presidential election. This far right populist radicalisation is not so significant among the student population who are protected by a higher level of education. Only 16% made the same choice (CEVIPOF/ENEF 2017). Nevertheless the renewal of the Front National under the leadership of Marine Le Pen has proved to be attractive to a number of young people disappointed with government. It can seduce new segments of youth with its anti-system rhetoric and protest attitude.

Beyond this electoral and political division, level of education and employment status engender a number of relevant cleavages within the value system young people adopt. Younger generations are always less authoritarian than their elders (Figure 9.3). Nevertheless, the demand for authority is higher among the less-well educated. For example, both employed and unemployed young people are more numerous than students in agreeing with the idea that 'the death penalty should be reinstated' (respectively +18 points and +24 points), that 'nowadays parents no longer have any authority' (respectively +14 points and +18 points), that 'France should have a strong leader who doesn't need to concern him/herself with parliament and elections' (respectively +20 points and +8 points). It should be noted that this inclination towards more authority within political leadership is felt by half of the French population as a whole (52%). This result confirms the profound crisis of political representation in France today and the overall disappointment of the electorate with the socialist government and the executive power. The same trends can be observed concerning attitudes to immigration (Figure 9.4). Rejection of immigration is always more pronounced among less-well-educated young people, whether they are employed or unemployed, than among students: respectively +10 points and +18 points agree

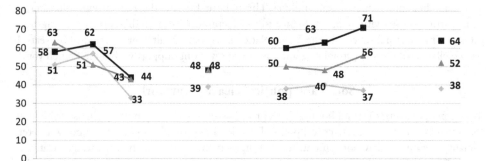

According to employment status

Figure 9.3 Attitudes towards questions around authority in France expressed as percentage.

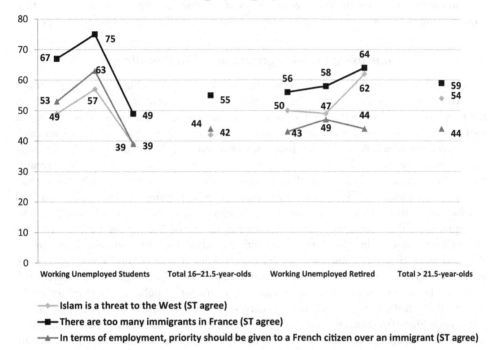

According to employment status

Legend:
- Islam is a threat to the West (ST agree)
- There are too many immigrants in France (ST agree)
- In terms of employment, priority should be given to a French citizen over an immigrant (ST agree)

Figure 9.4 Attitudes towards immigration and Islam according to employment status, expressed as percentage.

that 'Islam is a threat to the West,' respectively +18 points and +26 points consider that 'there are too many immigrants in France.'

As a result, a wide gap can be observed in the conception of democracy itself. The most highly educated members of the younger generations, though highly critical of politics, are deeply attached to representative democracy. Their internalisation of universalist values, through which they interpret political issues, compensates for their scepticism of politics, and underpins their unwavering attachment to the current system of representation. As for less-well-educated young people, although they more readily embrace universalist values than older people with the same level of education, these values are not sufficiently strong to compensate for their relative rejection of politics. Their trust in representative democracy has been more seriously undermined, and their estrangement from politics extends to a weakening of their belief in democracy itself. When compared to their highly educated contemporaries, they are less likely to be involved in any kind of civic participation, such as voting and political protest, and are more likely to view the kind of authoritarian regimes which rely on charismatic and populist personal leadership and are based on limiting the power of democratically elected bodies such as parliament in a favourable light. The danger of an increasing deficit is greatest among this category of the young. Whereas only 43% of the most highly qualified young people do agree with this kind of authoritarian regime (a significant figure in itself), the percentage increases to 63% (+20 pts) among those with little education who are already at work. Two co-existing trends which create tension, and risk widening intra-generational divisions, can therefore be observed:

on the one hand, among the most highly educated young people, an increasingly strong identification with democracy, underpinned by values of tolerance and openness and, on the other, a questioning of the principles of representative democracy by their less-well-educated peers.

Conclusions: disengagement or political resilience?

This general overview of the transformations at work in the relationships young people entertain with politics provides a number of clues to defining what kind of citizens they will be in the future of our old democracies. The politicisation of young people today is less normative, more expressive and freer from institutional and organisational norms. Such a climate conditions an engagement which is on the one hand individualised, and on the other hand collectively more reactionary, more critical and more protest oriented. The triptych − mistrust, intermittent voting, protest − is common to all categories of present-day young people. It characterises their politicisation, even if it is more or less pronounced depending on social status and level of education. This explains why the triptych constitutes a new framework for citizenship. The widespread idea that young people are no longer political is false. Young people are indeed critical and distrustful of politicians, parties and politics, but they also want something from politics. Pragmatism, efficiency and autonomy are key concepts in a type of political action that is more experimental than it was in the past, since it continually needs to be renegotiated and readjusted. Socialised in an atmosphere of disenchantment and mistrust of politics, and characterised by high levels of disillusionment and social anxiety, young people have built a new approach to politics combining intransigence on matters of principle and a desire for pragmatism, demands for values to be upheld and for real effectiveness. The young are indeed marked by a certain withdrawal from involvement in elections and by a civic moratorium. However, on the other hand they are very present on the collective scene and have proved themselves to be extremely reactive politically. Clearly, the protest culture deeply internalised by younger generations has created a critical political spirit which can, in turn, strengthen a democratic spirit as well. Such a protest culture allows citizens to become ever more vigilant about what democracy can accomplish and guarantee. In that sense, mistrust, intermittent voting, and protest, can be considered as tools of political and civic resilience for the future of democracy. However, we should not minimise the fact that this protest culture also reflects a democratic malaise and a crisis within political representation − an inherent part of democracy. The rise of populist parties all over Europe, and the rebirth of extremist behaviors and ideas, poses a threat to the future of democracy. Young people must take up the challenge of defining a new citizen's pact laying down the building blocks for the future of our European democracies. Such a pact must bring together citizens who are more critical and demanding, and who will remain so. But it must also be able to rely on citizens building a constructive (and not only a reactive) dialogue with those who govern them, and who have confidence in the ability of politics and public policy to improve the societies we live in. In a period during which two-thirds of the entire French population, including the young, believe that young people today have less chance of succeeding in life than their parents did at the same age, finding an answer to this challenge is more crucial than ever.

Extremisms of both left and right continue to attract young people in France who are not yet convinced by the reforms and pragmatism embodied by the new president. Emmanuel Macron's political challenge during his mandate will be to rally them. Young people demand that politics is both effective and meaningful. While it is possible to bring them back into the fold, Macron must not underestimate their performance requirement or the strength of their discontent. Protest as a means of democratic expression and a tool for political action remains their first political response, and young people will continue to act and vote as 'critical citizens' in the France of tomorrow.

Note

1 Post-electoral Survey 2012, CEVIPOF. The '−30 points' indicates the difference between the 75% of voters born before 1945 who said their choice was made a long time prior to the election and the 45% of younger voters born after 1980 who said the same (−30 points).

References

Cautrés, B. and A. Muxel. (Eds.). 2011. *The New Voter. France and Beyond.* New York: Palgrave Macmillan.

CEVIPOF. 2012. Political Trust Barometer, Wave 4. December. Paris: CEVIPOF.

CEVIPOF. 2015. Baromètre de la Confiance Politique. December.

CEVIPOF. 2016. Electoral Panel, Wave 2. January.

CEVIPOF. 2017. Political Trust Barometer, Wave 9. December.

CEVIPOF/ENEF. 2017. Survey of public opinion.

CEVIPOF/Ministère de la Défense. 2015. Baromètre de la jeunesse, Wave 2. December.

Eurostat. 2011. Report on public opinion.

IFOP. 2012. Post-electoral survey. April.

IFOP. 2017. 'Le profil des électeurs et les clefs du premier tour de l'élection présidentielle'. April.

Norris, P. (Ed.). 1999. *Critical Citizens: Global Support for Democratic Government.* Oxford: Oxford University Press.

Norris, P. (Ed.). 2011. *Democratic Deficit: Critical Citizens Revisited.* Cambridge: Cambridge University Press.

10

ANTI-RACISM, RACE AND THE REPUBLIC IN CONTEMPORARY FRANCE

Tom Martin

Few would disagree that political debate in contemporary France is subject to a so-called Republican consensus. That is to say that a prerequisite for mainstream credibility is the acceptance of a set of principles seen as resulting from the Enlightenment and the Revolution of 1789: *liberté, égalité* and *fraternité*, as promised by the Republican slogan; to which has increasingly been added *laïcité*, a strict form of state secularism. Particularly salient to the discussion in this chapter is the conception of citizenship which results from these principles: the Republican citizen is individual, abstract and universal, with no affiliation to organised 'communities' based, for example, on religion or ethnic origin. France's national specificities have a significant impact on anti-racist discourse and strategy, and this chapter aims to examine the complex and contradictory relationship between the anti-racist movement and Republican ideology in contemporary France, focusing particularly on the effect that differing organisations' relationships with the concept have on their utilisation of the idea of 'race' itself. As we will see, the central paradox behind the discussion in the chapter is this: on the one hand, mainstream anti-racist groups have had a tendency to conceive of France's Republican political culture as inherently compatible with their aims, thus seeing themselves not as challenging the political system and its ideological basis, but as part of the same system and the same traditions. On the other hand however, coexistence of a consensus on the language of republicanism and a lack of consensus on its underlying meaning leads to a situation in which this language – with its basis in Enlightenment, the universalism and rejection of 'difference' and particularist identities – can be used as rhetorical cover for almost any political position, including ones which serve to stigmatise and exclude minority populations.

This chapter is made up of two sections. The first section focuses on defining and analysing the central concepts of anti-racism and republicanism, and the way in which these ideas are tightly interlinked in the French context. This section will go into further detail on the paradox introduced previously. Having discussed the theoretical issues, the second section considers how they play out in practice, via a case study of two French anti-racist organisations with highly contrasting views on republicanism: the mainstream, consensus-seeking SOS Racisme (SOS), founded in 1984, and the radically postcolonial Mouvement des Indigènes de la République (MIR), founded in 2005. This section will consider these organisations' positions on the issue of 'race,' the effect it has on society, and whether the acknowledgement of ethnic difference has any part to play in the anti-racist movement. Let us begin, then, with the relationship between anti-racist activism and France's Republican political culture.

Anti-racism and republicanism

Anti-racism can be a surprisingly difficult concept to pin down. Certainly, it is possible to establish a minimal definition, and certain points of convergence amongst the majority of anti-racist organisations. Alastair Bonnett, for example, defines the fundamental meaning of anti-racism as 'those forms of thought and/or practice that seek to confront, eradicate and/or ameliorate racism' (2000: 4), and argues that nearly all forms of anti-racism agree that 'racism is an intellectual error'; that 'racism distorts and erases people's identities' and that 'racism is anti-egalitarian and socially unjust' (2000: 6). Even within this minimal definition of anti-racist beliefs, however, it is possible to find contradictions, particularly relating to the status of 'race': as Bonnett notes, 'If we accept that the notion of race is an intellectual error and a cause of both inequality and the destruction of identity, then it follows that enabling people to express their own racial identity and to be accorded equality, and rights, *as races* is problematic' (2000: 7). The question of how French anti-racism deals with 'race' is a key issue in this chapter so will not be developed further at this point. It should however be noted in passing that the mainstream political cultures in different national contexts lead to widely varying responses on anti-racist strategy and the place of race and ethnicity – a point which complicates further any attempt to define the essence of anti-racism. Anglophones may well take it as read that the fight against racism and discrimination involves the recognition of ethnic or religious 'communities' and the keeping of ethnic statistics in order to target action taken and judge its effectiveness, but in the French context such practices are seen by most Republican analysts as highly dangerous to national cohesion and the ideal of a purely equal and neutral form of citizenship (see Favell (1998) for a nuanced comparative analysis of French republicanism and British multiculturalism). Having said this, the form taken by anti-racist discourse and action in a given society is not entirely determined by national political culture: while mainstream social movements may work within the political system and accept its consensual terms of reference, more radical anti-system movements may reject such 'common sense' entirely, and argue that discrimination and inequality are embedded within the supposedly liberal and egalitarian structures of society. As Alana Lentin puts it:

> Just as racism could be differentially conceived as either fundamentally opposed to the ideologies of the state or undeniably grounded within them, so too anti-racism could be interpreted as either upholding the values of the West incorporated in the state or as a challenge to their usage in practice. These values – democracy, freedom, fraternity, human rights, equality – could at once be seen as the very principles upon which the modern state is built and, therefore, the ideals that an anti-racism that seeks widespread public support should uphold, or alternatively, as the hypocritical anchorings of the state in principles of equality and rights that belie the selective nature of their application.
>
> *(2004: 310)*

In the French case, republicanism has historically been seen as inherently compatible with anti-racism. Mainstream anti-racist organisations such as LDH, MRAP, LICRA[1] and SOS Racisme have – broadly speaking, and allowing for certain differences in orientation beyond the scope of this chapter – presented racism as contrary to Republican values, and argued that it should be fought through a reassertion of such values, seen as naturally egalitarian. Contemporary republicanism is thus placed in a historical lineage which presents 'Frenchness' as progressive and emancipatory, drawing on touchstones such as the Enlightenment, the 'universal' Declaration of the Rights of Man of 1789, the defence of Dreyfus[2] and the resistance to Nazi occupation during World War II. To quote Lentin again:

> French conceptualisations of anti-racism are to a great extent tied to the republican ideologies that are central to the public political culture of that country. [. . .] The importance periodically placed on anti-racism in French post-war politics reflects the extent to which, rather than being the preserve of groups of the racially marginalised, it has been constructed as inherently French, and therefore hegemonic. The ideals of anti-racism have been construed as universally applicable though their connection with the republican principle of liberty, equality and fraternity.
>
> *(2004: 115)*

A further impact of Republican ideology on the form taken by anti-racism in France relates to the conception of citizenship noted in the introduction: because the French citizen is purely individual, with no legally recognised community attachments, action taken by Republican movements against racism and discrimination is strictly colour-blind, in accordance with article 1 of the French constitution. The use of positive discrimination, quota systems or ethnic monitoring designed to gauge the effectiveness of anti-discrimination policies is therefore seen as inherently dangerous and anti-Republican, as we will see in the case study of SOS Racisme later in the chapter. In an essay arguing against any use of ethnic statistics in the fight against discrimination, for example, the public intellectual and Republican fundamentalist Elisabeth Badinter argues that this practice 'facilitates the formation of ethnic, cultural, racial and religious communities,' which leads to 'the division of France' (2009: 25); the 'institutionalisation' of difference – that is to say, a situation in which France's 'ethnic minority' inhabitants cease to be seen as individuals, and as either current or potential citizens benefiting from equal rights, and begin to be seen solely as faceless representatives of their allotted 'communities' (2009: 11) – and the promotion of *communautarisme*.[3]

A French Republican form of anti-racism, then, has historically been one which takes the Republic's proclaimed values – freedom, equality, secularism and so on – at face value, thus seeing racism as a contradiction to or perversion of such values. Furthermore, it draws on the Republic's traditions of individual, 'universal' citizenship, being strongly 'colour-blind' and hostile to multiculturalism, in contrast to the US and UK where movements are frequently organised on an ethnic or religious basis. A worldview in which individuals are seen as equal, undifferentiated citizens rather than being judged by race or religion may, in theory, sound appealing. There are several major contradictions, however, between theory and practice. Firstly, the historical mythology used to support the idea of the Republic as progressive and emancipatory is decidedly rose tinted. Certainly, it is true that the Republic's high-minded ideals of freedom, equality and universal human rights have provided inspiration for combats against oppression and injustice, during the Dreyfus Affair or the Occupation, for example. At the same time, however, Republican regimes were also responsible for the forced 'civilisation' of supposedly 'inferior races' – i.e. non-white ones – during the colonial period,[4] a point forcefully made in the rhetoric of MIR, as we will see in the case studies shortly (it can also be noted in passing that the Republic has historically been far from progressive in its treatment of women, but that is another question).[5] Secondly, the 'Republican consensus' in contemporary French politics has substantial implications for movements attempting to use the language of republicanism for progressive ends. Almost every political party and social movement aiming to participate in the mainstream attempts to lay claim to Republican values, a state of affairs made possible by the inherent flexibility of the concept: does equality, for example, just imply theoretical equality of opportunity and equality before the law, or does it imply active efforts to fight inequality and social injustice? Is secularism simply neutrality towards religion, or should the secular state forcibly emancipate its citizens from the supposed backwardness and ignorance of religion and deliver them into the light of progress and reason?[26] It is this combination of consensus and flexibility which leads to a situation in which different political groupings use the language of republicanism for seemingly irreconcilable purposes: as Sarah Waters argues, at the same time as the left's debates around republicanism 'often involve a re-examination of political traditions, the legacy of the Revolution and the significance of republican values in order to devise responses to today's social problems' (2012: 43), the right is able to use the Republic 'to justify the most hardline and discriminatory laws against immigrants, implemented in the name of strictly defined republican ideals and in particular the principle of secularism' (2012: 42). This can be seen, for example, in the discourse of Nicolas Sarkozy, France's president from 2007 to 2012, who argued in a 2007 campaign speech in Caen that the opposite of the Republic is represented by:

> Someone who does not respect our values of liberty, who rejects humanism and universalism, who rejects reason, who wants to abolish the heritage of the Enlightenment and the Revolution, who does not want to recognise that women are equal to men, who wants to shut his wife away indoors, and make his daughter wear the veil, or submit to female circumcision or forced marriage.
>
> *(in Noiriel 2007: 95)*

In this kind of discourse then, the definition of the Republic is clear: it is the opposite of Islam, evoked as something medieval and barbaric through a mixture of exaggerations, stereotypes and innuendo. This of course poses substantial problems for the anti-racist movement: how is it possible to use the language of republicanism to fight racism when it is so frequently used, in mainstream political debate, to stigmatise minority populations?

Finally for this section, the tenability of Republican 'colour-blindness' as a basis for anti-racist action can perhaps be questioned. The official invisibility of 'ethnic universalist republican ideology' theoretically leads to them being treated as equals. Some analysts, however, argue that it may actually serve to harm these populations, by 'disarming them when faced with the effects of an ethnic and racial hierarchisation hidden behind formal equality' (Simon 2006: 162). According to this viewpoint, those who argue for a 'colour-blind' Republican response to racial discrimination are to some extent in denial of reality: just because ethnic categorisation and hierarchies *should* not exist, this does not mean they *do* not exist. As Koopmans et al. point out:

> [T]he French approach has difficulty in dealing with the fact that cultural group differences, which are denied as legitimate policy categories, do form the basis of discrimination and racism from the side of the majority population. [...] Insisting on the equal treatment of all and loathing group-specific approaches, France to some extent ties its own hands when it comes to combating forms of social exclusion that are rooted in ethnic and cultural differences.
>
> *(2006: 14)*

How, then, is it possible to fight discrimination based on race and ethnicity, using the tools provided by a political ideology which refuses to take race and ethnicity into account? This is a key question for SOS, as we will see in the following case study.

Case studies: SOS Racisme and the Mouvement des Indigènes de la République

Let us now move on, then, to the case studies, which consider how the issues of race and republicanism, and their place in anti-racism, play out in the discourse of two contrasting anti-racist movements in contemporary France: SOS Racisme (SOS) and the Mouvement des Indigènes de la République (MIR). I will begin by considering SOS, still perhaps France's best-known anti-racist association.

SOS Racisme was founded in 1984. Closely linked with François Mitterrand's Socialist Party in a political climate marked by the increasing influence of the far right Front National (FN), it quickly became associated in the public mind with its telegenic founding president Harlem Désir; its massive, highly mediatised public events (a free music festival at the Place de la Concorde in 1985 attracted 300,000 people); and the promotion of a form of liberal multiculturalism known as 'the right to difference' (*le droit à la différence*). This discourse on the 'right to difference' did not, however, last long. By the early 1990s, the window on any putative rethinking of republicanism and its universalist conception of citizenship seemed to be firmly shut, the political class collectively deciding, over the course of several high-profile commissions on nationality, citizenship and the place of religion, that it was necessary to reinforce the 'Republican consensus' – and, thus, the official hostility to manifestations of 'difference' – in the face of the FN threat (Favell 1998). For its part, SOS – as a mainstream movement with links to one of France's major parties – went along with this consensus,[7] thereafter articulating a discourse stressing equality of opportunity, *laïcité*, and 'colour-blindness' in relation to race (SOS Racisme 2006).

In its twenty-first-century incarnation, then, SOS is representative of the kind of mainstream, Republican anti-racist movement whose strengths and weaknesses were considered in the first section. As such, it takes at face value the idea that Republican values are naturally progressive, seeing its role as promoting and protecting such values, and ensuring they are properly applied throughout society by the political authorities. As the association's 2007 'mission statement' puts it, 'To defend the Republic is to make it be seen as a source of emancipation; it is to make it credible by ensuring that its values are lived by everyone, everywhere in day-to-day life.' And one of the values it sees itself defending is the egalitarian colour-blindness proclaimed by the constitution. As the same document states: 'Anti-racism, for us, has always been the desire to see everybody live with equal dignity in society, whatever their origin, their religion or their cultural practices' (SOS Racisme 2007).

This positioning on the part of SOS can be illustrated by examining the association's reaction to the possibility of using ethnic classifications and statistics in the fight against racial discrimination, and the measures it proposes to take against such discrimination itself. For SOS, the idea of distinguishing between France's inhabitants on the basis of ethnicity is seen as inherently incompatible with Republican ideals; and as France does not officially recognise or monitor ethnic groups, neither should the anti-racist movement. Indeed, SOS presents such classifications as contrary to French identity. As the current SOS president Dominique Sopo argues, France is a 'terre de métissage'[8] (SOS Racisme 2006: 96). And if this is the case, then taking into account ethnic difference is automatically contrary to the underlying ideological essence of French society. As Sopo's argument continues, classifying populations in this way 'would push populations into referring to particularist categories, and no longer to the category of citizenship. But one of the great strengths of France [. . .] resides precisely in the fact that, in our country, ethnic, cultural and religious barriers are highly porous' (SOS Racisme 2006). For SOS, therefore, there must be no deviation from what could be called the 'universal citizen' proclaimed theoretically by the French constitution. That is to say, race, ethnicity and religion should all be subordinate to the greater ideal of French citizenship, and no forms of community organisation based on these categories should intervene between the citizen and the 'universalist' state. As Sopo argues elsewhere:

> To invite people to live as if they belonged to this or that 'ethnic category' or 'community' (which would be defined over the heads of those involved) is of course to take the risk of creating barriers and therefore, under the cover of fighting against discrimination, to fall into a 'communitarianised'[9] society which in no way corresponds to our ideals.
>
> *(Manifeste pour l'égalité 2007: 43)*

It is the view of the movement, then, that ethnic classification – even if brought in with the aim of fighting discrimination – is highly dangerous, as it leads to 'visible minorities' being seen not as true citizens but as undifferentiated members of 'communities.' It is seen as leading to a situation in which the identities of minority populations become racialised, which leads in turn to such populations racialising their *own* identities, making them inflexible and unchangeable.

This being the case, much of the action proposed by SOS against discrimination focuses on anonymisation: that is, making ethnic origin invisible to gatekeepers of social opportunity. A recurrent demand of SOS, for example, is for anonymous CVs: the logic being that because CVs under this proposal would contain no name, address or photograph, potential candidates could not be stereotyped by employers and thus rejected without an interview.[10] Similarly, the organisation has argued (for example in its 'Manifesto for equality' published ahead of the 2007 presidential election) for the anonymisation of applications for social housing, in the hope of promoting 'social mixing' and fighting the 'ghettoisation' of poor minority populations (2007: 140). The movement's strategy can therefore perhaps be seen as a literal enforcement of the Republic's proclaimed 'colour-blindness,' leading it to conceive of the fight against discrimination in territorial and socio-economic, rather than ethnic, terms.

So far in this chapter we have mainly been considering the Republican, colour-blind form of French anti-racism, as represented by a movement like SOS. As noted in the first section however, social movements can of course choose to act outside the system and challenge the mainstream political culture of the country in which they operate. This is the position taken by the Mouvement des Indigènes de la République (MIR).

MIR was founded in 2005 by a group of anti-racist, anti-colonial and radical left activists, many of North African origin, who published an appeal which denounced the widespread racism and discrimination faced by postcolonial immigrant-origin populations. This discrimination, it was argued, was the result of logics, processes and stereotypes which had their origins in the colonial era, hence the use of the term *indigène* in the name of the movement: the term can be taken to refer to a non-white inhabitant of the French colonies who is denied full citizen status, denied equality in a supposed hierarchy of civilisations, and denied equality before the law through subjection to the *code de l'indigénat*.[11] As Sadri Khiari, one of the founders of the movement, puts it:

> 'We are the Natives of the Republic' signifies this: the Republic claims to be universal and egalitarian; and the *indigène* no longer exists as a juridical status. However, in renewed and often unprecedented ways, the regime of the *indigénat* continues to haunt institutions, practices and ideologies.
>
> *(2006: 17)*

As we have seen, the assumption underlying mainstream political discourse in France is that republicanism is, by definition, universal: there should be no differentiation between France's inhabitants based on ethnicity or origin. MIR, however, reverses this assumption by referring to 'white universalism' and the 'white Republic.' As the movement's leader Houria Bouteldja puts it:

> In France, the *Indigènes* have taken up the weapon of race in order to fight the stubborn rhetoric of universalism: a white universalism which masks and denies the structural hierarchies which constitute the French Republic.
>
> *(indigenes-republique.fr 2011)*

In other words, for MIR the 'universalist' principles inherited from the Enlightenment, which went on to form the basis of Republican ideology, were only ever truly applicable to white populations of European origin, as shown by the Republic's history of colonial racism and exploitation, dressed up in the paternalistic language of a 'civilising mission.' What is more, Bouteldja argues, the widespread belief in the universalist nature of Republican values has served to cover up the systemic nature of race and discrimination in French society.

The movement's view, then, is that the Republic is not a safeguard against racial inequalities; it is fundamentally based on racial inequalities – as is the modern nation state in a wider sense. As Florence Bernault writes of the movement:

> For the Indigènes, race is not prior to, or distinct from, the project of modern nation-building, but has historically emerged as a state-sponsored tool of distancing and othering, while the French republican order, under the pretence of imposing universal civil rights over cultural and racial loyalties, has essentialised racial and cultural differences.
>
> *(in Tshimanga, Gondola and Bloom 2009: 129)*

And this situation has led to the existence of ingrained racial hierarchies, which the movement has frequently proclaimed the need to end. This is perhaps easier said than done, as such hierarchies are rarely, if ever, explicitly stated: rather, they are made up of generations of stereotypes embedded in the subconscious mind of the population, and/or disguised as something else, such as a discussion of the incompatibility of various 'immigrant' cultures with that of France. Nevertheless, it is clear that the *Indigènes* see movements like SOS, which refuse – on the grounds of fidelity to Republican values and fear of endorsing *communautarisme* – to differentiate between races as fundamentally in denial of social reality.

As such, the focus of MIR is not specifically on the 'social question' – that is, fighting inequality on socio-economic grounds, with racial issues addressed only as a by-product. Rather, for MIR the 'racial question' is paramount, with class, wealth and social opportunity seen as subsets of this central issue. As Bouteldja states in a 2011 interview with the author:

> It is necessary to understand systems of domination and the divides in society. For us the central divides are racial, and colonial. That is to say, class divides – left/right, rich/poor – are not sufficiently pertinent to understand the situation of *indigènes* in France. [...] And we say that, if you want to fight against discrimination, and for more justice between whites and non-whites, you must the racial divide; the racial fracture. That race, as a socio-historical phenomenon, exists.
>
> *(Interview August 2011a)*

A major difference between the positions of MIR and SOS can be summed up by the reference here to 'systems of domination.' Broadly speaking, for SOS, racism is something that takes place between an individual and an individual, or an individual and an institution (employers, housing associations, schools, etc.), and can be fought against via legal action, and state action in favour of equality. For MIR on the other hand, racism is systemic, or even intrinsic to the formation of the modern nation state. It is the movement's argument consequently that 'universalist' or 'consensual' conceptions of anti-racism are by definition inadequate: this form of anti-racism is seen as choosing deliberately to decontextualise the acts of discrimination it targets, by focusing on the acts themselves rather than the racial power relations which underpin them. A colour-blind form of anti-racism, therefore, is clearly insufficient when society is not 'colour-blind' in reality.

Linked to MIR's analysis of racial power relations in French society, and to their connected analysis of the dominant/dominated relationship within racism – according to which white people are 'dominant' and hold the vast majority of power in every field; while non-whites, particularly 'postcolonised' blacks and Arabs, are 'dominated,' holding very little power – is the idea that all white people, regardless of social class, benefit from social privileges due to their race. As Khiari puts it, 'Certainly, not all white French people are racist. At the same time, though, they all benefit indirectly and involuntarily from the postcolonial regime' (2006: 90). Similarly, the MIR-affiliated sociologist Pierre Tévanian (2008: 74) argues that like 'black' or 'Arab,' 'white is not a racial category, but a social category' – but unlike the privileges that arise from being part of the visible majority, non-white populations suffer from disadvantages in society based on their skin colour. In this type of argument, MIR shifts the argument about racism away from individual agency, and posits it instead as something entirely systemic: white populations benefit from the postcolonial, whether they like it or not, and conversely, non-white populations suffer from it. If MIR's argument is correct therefore, movements like SOS are missing the point by seeing racism as something that can be isolated and legislated against: rather, mainstream politics must admit the continuing influence of race on society, in order to begin 'deracialising' and 'decolonising.' Hidebound by Republican ideology, however, it is collectively unwilling or unable to do so.

Conclusions

These case studies illustrate the complex and contradictory relationship that French anti-racism has with republicanism, and consequently with the idea of race itself. Certainly, Republican values – *liberté, égalité, fraternité*, secularism, 'colour-blind' universalism and so on – may seem in theory to be favourable to anti-racism. In practice, however, they have frequently proved to be anything but favourable, being used historically as an alibi for the forced 'civilisation' of 'inferior races,' and still being used in contemporary France as a means of stigmatising immigration and Islam, presented as an inherent threat to Republican identity. As Max Silverman notes, the French state has for much of its history 'preached inclusion according to universalist criteria,' while simultaneously 'practising exclusion through racialising the French community and its other' (1992: 9). What, then, should be the goal of French anti-racism? Should it redouble its efforts to make the self-proclaimed principles of the Republic a genuine reality? Or should it question these principles, the uses they have been put to, and the social and racial power relations which lie behind them? In a political context where the 'Republican consensus' appears to be becoming stronger and stronger, and less and less tolerant of any manifestation of 'difference,' it perhaps seems unlikely that any group taking the second of these options will have much impact in public debate – and indeed, MIR has always been very much a minority voice. This does not mean, however, that these are not important questions to ask.

Notes

1 Respectively: Ligue des Droits de l'Homme (Human Rights League), founded in 1898; Mouvement contre le Racisme et pour l'Amitié entre les Peuples (Movement against Racism and for Friendship between Peoples), founded in 1949; and Ligue Internationale Contre le Racisme et l'Antisémitisme (International League against Racism and Anti-Semitism), founded in 1927.
2 Alfred Dreyfus (1859–1935) was a Jewish officer in the French Army who was falsely accused of treason in a highly anti-Semitic political climate. His cause was taken up by a number of prominent republicans, most notably Émile Zola. The LDH, touched upon earlier, was founded as a result of this case.
3 There is no single term in English which captures all the connotations of *communautarisme*: it refers to populations seeing their primary loyalty as being towards an ethnic or religious 'community' rather than to the Republic, and is frequently used as a polemic term to attack the supposed 'refusal to integrate' of France's Muslim population.
4 This is not an attitude which was euphemised by republicans of the late nineteenth and early twentieth centuries. For example, one of the most celebrated figures in the history of French republicanism, Jules Ferry (1832–1893), was at the same time a fervent secularist, the father of the modern French education system and a promoter of colonial expansion who argued that 'superior races [. . .] have the duty to civilise inferior races.'
5 See for example Gill Allwood's chapter in the present volume (Chapter 5).
6 This is a caricature of Republican attitudes towards religion, but only slightly: it was this kind of logic which underlay the anti-clericalism of the revolutionary period (post-1789) and the Third Republic (1870–1940), and which still frequently serves as a justification for Republican hostility towards Islam.
7 A decision also influenced by the fact that it had found itself on the wrong side of prevailing opinion in relation to the Gulf War – SOS had opposed it, while the majority had supported it – and perhaps most importantly, in relation to the first 'headscarf affair' in 1989: SOS had supported the right of three Muslim schoolgirls to wear the veil in class, while many prominent republicans, such as Alain Finkielkraut, opposed it with almost astonishing vehemence. By 2004, when the affair cropped up again, SOS was in line with the Republican logic that the veil should be outlawed in schools in order to defend secularism and equality.
8 Literally 'land of mixing.' What is meant here is that France is – or should be – a country where citizens of different ethnicities and religions freely mix, because they are unencumbered by particularist identities which confine them to fixed 'communities.'
9 The original French word used is 'communautarisée.' As noted earlier, *communautarisme* is not a term which translates smoothly into English, as the danger it is seen as representing, and the intensity of the debate it provokes, are so specific to the French context.
10 See for example *Le Nouvel Observateur*, 10 July 2014. http://tempsreel.nouvelobs.com/societe/social/20140710.OBS3414/cv-anonyme-ce-n-est-pas-la-solution-magique-mais.html [Accessed: 20.10.2015].
11 This was a code of law used in the French colonies, which was notable for creating offences that could only be committed by 'natives,' and for the fact that colonial administrators could apply disciplinary sanctions without judicial procedure. Equality before the law, it should be noted, was proclaimed as a 'universal' human right by what is arguably the foundational text of modern France, the Declaration of the Rights of Man of 1789.

References

Badinter, E. et al. 2009. *Le retour de la race: contre les 'statistiques ethniques.'* Paris: Éditions de l'Aube.
Bernault, F. 2009. Colonial syndrome: French modern and the deceptions of history. In C. Tshimanga, D. Gondola and P. J. Bloom (Eds.), *Frenchness and the African Diaspora: Identity and Uprising in Contemporary France*. Bloomington: Indiana University Press.
Bonnett, A. 2009. *Anti-Racism*. London: Routledge.
Bouteldja, H. 2011a. Interview with Houria Bouteldja (Parti des Indigènes de la République, spokesperson), conducted by author 9 August.

Bouteldja, H. 2011b. Le 'racisme anti-blanc' des Indigènes de la République. Available at: www.indigenes-republique.fr/article.php3?id_article=1345 [Accessed: 20.01.2015].

Favell, A. 1998. *Philosophies of Integration: Immigration and the Idea of Citizenship in France and Britain*. Basingstoke: Palgrave Macmillan.

Khiari, S. 2006. *Pour une politique de la racaille*. Paris: Textuel.

Koopmans, R. et al. 2005. *Contested Citizenship: Immigration and Cultural Diversity in Europe*. Minneapolis: University of Minnesota Press.

Lentin, A. 2004. *Racism & Anti-racism in Europe*. London: Pluto Press.

Morice, L. 2014. CV anonyme: 'Ce n'est pas la solution magique mais. . . .' In *Le Nouvel Observateur* 10 July. Available at: http://tempsreel.nouvelobs.com/societe/social/20140710.OBS3414/cv-anonyme-ce-n-est-pas-la-solution-magique-mais.html [Accessed: 20.01.2015].

Noiriel, G. 2007. *À quoi sert 'l'identité nationale.'* Paris: Agone.

Silverman, M. 1992. *Deconstructing the Nation: Immigration, Racism and Citizenship in Modern France*. London: Routledge.

Simon, P. 2006. L'arbre du racisme et la forêt des discriminations. In N. Guénif-Souilamas (Ed.), *La République mise à nu par son immigration*. Paris: La Fabrique.

Sopo, D. 2007. *Manifeste pour l'égalité: 60 propositions pour que ça change*. Paris: Éditions First.

SOS Racisme. 2006. *Qu'est-ce que SOS Racisme*. Paris: l'Archipel.

SOS Racisme. 2007. *Nos Missions*. Available at: www.sos-racisme.org/Nouvel-article,30.html [Accessed: 20.01.2015].

Tévanian, P. 2008. *La mécanique raciste*. Paris: Éditions Dilecta.

Waters, S. 2012. *Between Republic and Market: Globalization and Identity in Contemporary France*. London: Continuum.

PART III

Spaces of political and cultural contestation

11

LA FRANCE DANS LA RUE

Chris Reynolds

The weekend of 10–11 January 2015 saw reportedly up to four million people take to the streets of France in 'Republican marches' as a response to the horrific terrorist attacks of the previous three days. On 7 January, two gunmen made their way into the offices of French satirical magazine *Charlie Hebdo* where they slayed the core of the editorial team. After having taken 12 lives in this attack, the Kouachi brothers then fled Paris, and during an interminable two days on the run, were finally tracked down and killed by the police following a shoot-out at a print works in Seine-et-Marne. During this hunt, an accomplice of the brothers shot and killed a police officer on the morning of 8 January before attacking a kosher supermarket the next day. He took several hostages and killed four people before finally, around the same time as the demise of the Kouachi brothers, meeting his own violent end in a police raid. In total, 17 people lost their lives in what was a terrifying and shocking three days for France.[1] During this period, France was shaken to the core as these horrific events were played out on mainstream media with the terrorists even at one point taking to the airwaves. As information leaked out, it became clear that France was under attack by home-grown jihadists and it was immediately obvious that, on top of the human cost and the horrific violence, this incident was going to spark much debate and soul-searching in a country already, for many, considered to be in an era of decline (Ly 2015).[2]

Once this incident had been brought to a conclusion, a sense of 'what next' filled the void. The reaction came the following day (Saturday 10 January) when, across the country, from Nantes to Toulouse, from Paris to Lille, reportedly 700,000 people took to the streets. On Sunday 11 January, an even greater outpouring was in evidence with a reported four million people across France hitting the street in what has been described as the biggest ever demonstration in French history.[3] There has been much debate related to the so-called *esprit du 11 janvier*.[4] In particular, much discussion has centred on how inclusive these marches were, how much of it was exploited by politicians and how one should understand/interpret such a reaction. Such debates are hardly surprising given the uncertain times France has been experiencing and in particular in relation to themes of national identity, secularism, freedom of expression, not to mention the malaise created by the financial crisis and its fallout. Whilst such uncertainties are undeniably important to understanding the significance of these events, one enduring French characteristic was consolidated – the power of the street. That the spontaneous reaction of so many people, all over the country, was to take to the street should not really be that surprising. It was the latest – albeit spectacular and exceptional in its own right – example of how 'la rue' is a central part of life in France and French politics. It is a critically important arena for the people of France to express their frustrations, concerns and desires.

This chapter will explain how and why the street has become – and remains – such an important element in France. It will begin with an examination of the extent to which this prevalence for protest can and should be considered as a specifically French phenomenon, before offering structural reasons to explain it. However, the central argument will be that such structural conditions do not tell the whole story and instead (or in addition), one must consider the weight of history. Via a tour of seminal moments that have embedded the propensity to hit the street as part of French national identity, combined with an obsession with the past, it will be argued that the street is and will continue to be a central factor in how France functions.

The prevalence of protest

At the forefront of those characteristics that help define our understanding of France is the idea that it is a nation with a strong propensity for protest. Statistically, there is some debate. For example, in his 1994 article, Frank L. Wilson argued that the French were 'no more contentious than other Europeans' (Wilson 1994: 24). To back such an assessment, he drew on a particular dataset that argued that both in terms of types and frequency of protest, France was no more than average, if not in the lower echelons, when compared to its European counterparts. On the other hand, it is possible to look elsewhere for evidence that reveals an alternative perspective. The annual data from the European Social Survey (ESS), which since 2002 has been asking populations about their participation in 'lawful public demonstrations,' enables a comparison across European nations. As Table 11.1 demonstrates, in the period between 2002 and 2014, France figures amongst the top countries in terms of protest participation. In fact, if we remove Spain, where the economic crisis has led to a huge and exceptional surge in protest, France is consistently the country where protest is most prevalent.

These two examples demonstrate the difficulties of only relying on a statistical approach to make sense of the French specificity relating to protest. The explanation lies well beyond statistics. One only has to consider a number of recent examples to take stock of how the idea that the French are always protesting is more than a simple impression.

On Sunday 15 March 2015, after a long period of fragmented discussion and growing tension over the *loi santé* (adopted by parliament on 8 April[5]), the streets of France rang out to the sound of doctors, nurses, surgeons, students and dentists in protest. Between 20,000 and 50,000 people, following a call from all the major trade unions, were reportedly on the streets of Paris.[6] Such

Table 11.1 Taken part in lawful public demonstration last 12 months (as percentage of people surveyed).

	2002	*2004*	*2006*	*2008*	*2010*	*2012*	*2014*
France	17.9	12.8	16.5	15.3	17.7	11.7	13.5
Germany	10.6	8.5	7	8.1	8.4	9.1	9.6
Greece	4.5	5		6.1	10		
Ireland	7.1	5.9	5.2	9.8	7	11.5	13.1
Portugal	1.3	3.5	3.1	3.7	2.4	6.9	7.1
Spain	17.5	24	17.8	15.9	18.3	25.9	23.2
Sweden	6.4	7.5	4.8	6.4	4.9	7.9	11
UK	4.4	3.7	4.4	3.8	2.4	3.1	5.7

Source: European Social Survey (www.europeansocialsurvey.org/ [Accessed: 01/06/2016]).

demonstrations did little to prevent the law being adopted by parliament but inevitably led to the continuation of street protests such as those in the provinces in October 2015 following the Senate's decision to adopt the law. In the summer of 2015, France was gripped by an outbreak of protest within the taxi industry. Fearing being outpriced and marginalised by the UBER model, the reaction of the taxi drivers was inevitably to take to the streets. Throughout the summer, in all major French cities, *les chauffeurs de taxis* brought the country to a standstill with a whole raft of protests – often quite violent. At its height, the upheaval saw a reported 3,000 taxi drivers demonstrating in France using tactics such as go-slows, blocking airports and even attacks on the competition.[7] On 17 September 2015, the movement against Najat Vallaud-Belkacem's *collège* (school) reform[8] began with a day of protest across the country. Depending on reports, there was somewhere between 15% and 30% of teachers on strike, and demonstrations were held in cities such as Paris, Bordeaux, Rennes and Marseilles. This day of action, called for by all major trade unions, was the latest opportunity for teachers to set out their arguments against the reform.[9] The familiar sight of French teachers protesting was replayed on Saturday 8 October when between 8,000 and 15,000 protestors hit the streets of Paris as the protest rumbled on.[10] On 5 October 2015, after a period of building tension with rumours of massive job losses, a group of *Air France* employees decided to take a very direct form of action. During a meeting of the company's senior management team brought together to put the finishing touches to a package of changes, worried workers intervened and physically attacked their bosses. Protesting against the restructuring plan that threatened a two-year period of redundancies across the company from pilots to ground staff, the band of a 100 or so protestors stormed the meeting and (symbolically) ripped the shirts from the directors' backs.[11] For foreign commentators, the images of the shirtless executives fleeing the protestors by desperately climbing fences were lapped up and circulated widely.[12] October 2015 was a decidedly busy month for protest in France. It began with a four-day strike by Parisian refuse collectors. Refusing to collect rubbish in the capital, the strong percentage of those on strike were protesting for improved salaries and career prospects.[13] On 12 October, 300 striking employees from the company *Française des Roues* took to the streets of Chateauroux in the latest episode of a long struggle over the future of their jobs. Highly critical of the unjust pressures faced by their company, employees were particularly critical of the actions of companies like Renault and PSA in forcing down profits in the interests of their own bottom line.[14] On Wednesday 14 October, a reported 7,500 members of the police force assembled at the Place Vendôme in Paris whilst similar protests took place around the country.[15] Monday 19 October saw the announcement of a general strike by *les avocats de Paris* (Paris Lawyers) in protest to a change in how the justice system would be financed, with justice minister Christine Taubira the focus of protestors' ire.[16]

As the preceding demonstrates, one only has to present a relatively short snapshot to understand just how prevalent protest is in contemporary France. What is more, beyond the stereotypical image of the striking worker protesting about the imminent closure of their factory, very noteworthy is the sheer breadth of those protesting. From refuse collectors to lawyers, from teachers to police officers, or taxi drivers to airline employees, the inclination to protest transcends sectors and social class. It is very difficult to identify another country where the prevalence of protest is so obvious and widespread. Also interesting is the diversity in terms of forms of action across the different movements mentioned. Go-slows, occupations, strikes and blockages; the repertoire of collective action is broad and is clearly something that has evolved significantly over the years (Mathieu 2011). However, if it is possible to discern one common denominator in the gamut of action forms, it is clear that the street remains a very potent and well-trodden arena for protest, regardless of who is involved or what is at stake. It would appear, given the reflex to organise demonstrations, that despite the passage of time and the evolving repetoires of action, the street remains a constant for all French people in their desires to make their voices heard. The remainder of this chapter will make sense of just why the street has acquired such a role and managed to remain the home of France's undeniable prevalence for protest. Before outlining how much of this can be explained via a look back at history, there are a number of structural considerations that require attention.

Structural conditions

This section, through an examination of the make-up of the French state and the role played by trade unions, will argue that there are perfectly logical, structural reasons for the Gallic tendency to protest. Firstly, let us consider another important and related factor – the idea of '*la grève*' (the strike). If France is so often held up as a nation of protests, an accompanying element is that such protests are linked to the prevalence of industrial action and in particular the propensity to go on strike. One only has to consider the comparative data to confirm that this is more than a hunch.[17] Stéphane Sirot's research on '*la grève*' in France, which neatly divides the history of strikes into three eras dominated by the themes of '*exclusion*' (exclusion), '*permissivité*' (permissiveness) and '*institutionnalisation*' (institutionalisation), sheds some light on this French specificity (2011).

The age of *exclusion* runs between the French Revolution of 1789 and 1864, during which time strike action was perceived as running contrary to the principles of the Revolution and the Republic, unconstitutional and subject to prosecution. This did not prevent strikes continuing and eventually forced the 1864 law that, whilst stopping short of legalising strike action, de-penalised it and therefore helped open the era of *permissivité* that would stitch strike action into the social and industrial fabric of France. Its growth was only halted by the exceptional circumstances of Occupied and Vichy France. The *institutionnalisation* process started in the postwar era when the act of striking was held up as a fundamental right requiring protection. This explains how France started to set itself apart, in particular by writing the (conflictual) right to strike into the constitutions of the Fourth and Fifth Republics. Strike action became the norm during the period of unprecedented growth that was *les trente glorieuses*. However, once the crisis of the 1970s took hold and the neo-liberal model started to dominate, attitudes towards collective action unsurprisingly changed. Sirot argues that such developments explain current-day difficulties and growing opposition towards strike action. The 2007 law on minimum service is described as an *encadrement renforcé* (strengthened containment) seeking to exploit changing attitudes and something that ultimately strips strike action of its very *raison d'être* (Sirot 2011: 110). Nevertheless, despite such changes, the intensity of the debate surrounding *le service minimum* (minimum service) and the ongoing prevalence of strike action today, it is hard to disagree with the assessment that it remains a core feature of how France functions. The right to strike and how this has become embedded cannot be understood without a consideration of the role of trade unions. Their historical trajectory very much mirrors that of strike action and this is of course not a coincidence. However, there are some interesting divergences that help us further understand the characteristics of collective action in France today.

The period following the Revolution, characterised by negative perceptions of collective action, meant that the emergent working class, wishing to come together, was forced to exist on the margins, engaged in clandestine activity with a profound lack of trust in the state and politicians. When strike action was de-penalised in 1864, the period leading up to the relatively belated legalisation of French trade unions in 1884 was inevitably one that saw those wishing to act revert to the only option available – thus (further) explaining how striking became the default form of action in working class militancy. The period between 1884 and the end of the

Second World War saw further anchoring of the key characteristics of the French trade union movement. The fact that French union activity had been legalised later than their European counterparts helps explain why, by the time they did, the trade union/state relationship was one that was much more conflictual than elsewhere. The early twentieth century saw some attempts at unifying the various strands of the movement but, overall, fragmentation soon developed as the norm and was undoubtedly a contributing factor behind the decline in membership in the aftermath of the First World War (Sowerine 2009: 117–132). High points such as the 1936 Popular Front movement and important advances in labour relations in the interwar period helped consolidate the place of trade unions before the onset of the Second World War and the halt it brought to any such progress.

The post-war period, and in particular *les trente glorieuses*, appears on the surface to have been somewhat of a golden era with high points including the 1968 legalisation of union activity (Séguy 2008: 148–169). However, other interpretations posit this period as one that institutionalised trade unions and goes a long way towards explaining how and why the current day movement is so often described as being in a state of crisis (Baumgartner 1994: 90). The widespread prosperity is said to have disguised the erosion of unions' conflictual edge, something that only became evident once the economic crisis of the 1970s stripped away the veil of stability. The period since is commonly described as one of crisis in France in general; the plight of trade unions is just one part of this. With the onset of economic problems, and in particular the question of unemployment, one would have thought that there was perhaps more than ever a need for trade unions. Instead, the already relatively low membership has continued to suffer (Lindvall 2011: 297). This of course has happened across Europe but France seems to have been hit hardest. How can this be explained?

The easy answer is to point to how the demographic make-up of society has stripped away the traditional bedrock of membership. Furthermore, the neo-liberal, capitalist monolith has encouraged increasing atomisation and individualism, reducing the collectivist tendencies that underpin the essence of union activity and draining away the attractiveness and perceived utility. In the French case, as well as the enduring characteristics of low numbers and fragmentation, the inability of the unions to break out of their institutionalisation, achieved during *les trente glorieuses*, has rendered them weak, ineffective and less of a counterbalance to the state. This explains how in recent times the government has been willing to allow movements to burn themselves out. They are no longer effective as they are increasingly presented and perceived as sectorial and far from representing the majority of workers' interests. Sirot argues that in order to overcome this situation, trade unions have had to change their message and approach, moving away from their conflictual essence and instead become more reformist. Depoliticised, their mission has changed. Today they work within the system and not against it (Sirot 2011: 344). One would be forgiven for suggesting that continued protest in an age of declining trade union membership and significance is somewhat of a paradox. However, and as cogently argued by Lindvall, such developments have only served to further marginalise the people, leading to a set of circumstances whereby 'such organisational weakness is a part of the explanation for the high level of protest activity' (Lindvall 2011: 297).

This overview of the development of French trade unionism certainly helps us understand how and why a certain propensity to contest has characterised the world of labour over the years and, together with the reasons behind the prevalence of strike action, provides part of the answer as to why the street is so important in France. However, the current crisis situation of trade unions and the blunting of strike action has not eroded any of the importance of the street. Furthermore, as outlined earlier, not all street protests are the result of – or accompany – industrial action. A further consideration is that which relates to the make-up of the French state.

Given the characteristics just outlined in terms of the embedded conflictual relationship, it becomes easier to make sense of the prevalence of protest in France. In fact, as argued elsewhere, it is reasonable to assume that such protest has almost become part and parcel of the reform process (Tilly 1986; Fillieule 1997). The reasons for this are numerous but also include some reference to the make-up of the French state and in particular its very highly centralised nature. It is widely recognised and accepted that France is a profoundly centralised country (Ancelovici 2008: 74; Knapp and Wright 2006: 22). The reasons for this go back, as ever, to the Revolution, and it is a characteristic deeply embedded in the Republican psyche. Such a particularity certainly must be borne in mind when trying to make sense of the evidently specific relationship France has with protest (Baumgartner 1994: 93). This centralisation of powers in the capital has meant that it is equally possible to concentrate the effectiveness of protest. Paralysing Paris paralyses France. One must not forget also the ease with which media coverage of such protest is facilitated by this centralised nature (Baumgartner 1994: 85; Wilson 1994: 24).

Furthermore, the overly centralised make-up of the French state contributes to the idea of it being closed to society (Ancelovici 2008: 79–80; Wilson 1994: 32–33). As argued by Ancelovici, France is the poster child of such an approach, minimalising what is known as institutional access where 'closed, exclusive states foster disruption' with the inevitable consequence of an increased propensity to protest (Ancelovici 2015: 197). Indeed, 'the closed manner in which the state manages the country leaves little space for civil society actors to access the policymaking process, thereby fostering the use of extra-institutional, contentious modes of collective action' (Ancelovici 2011: 127). A factor further compounding this closed nature of the French state is, as Lindvall argues, the majoritarian electoral system and weak parliament that create the grounds for opposition from trade unions and pressure groups (Lindvall 2011: 298).

Despite the long, rich and ongoing debate around Political Process Theory (PPT) that has dominated discussions on social movement mobilisation, there remains a certain degree of value in citing the work of McAdam et al. (2001) in helping us make sense of the unquestionable French exceptionalism under scrutiny here. In an ever-evolving debate that has seen many developments over the years, a constant theme relates to the notion of 'political opportunity.' The basic idea is that one (of several) important elements that must be taken into consideration is how the actual context creates the grounds for protest to exist. One significant feature is the extent of the openness or closure of the institutionalised political system. As outlined previously, the heavily centralised nature of the French state is such that it has created a firmly closed system, restricting institutional access and therefore heightening the propensity to protest. Lindvall's assessment of French protest culture being best understood as resulting from issues over trust and distrust nevertheless accepts that the absence of political opportunities created by the inherently closed-off nature of the French state, arguing that 'there would be fewer protests if the social groups that trade unions and other interest organisations represent had more effective representation within political institutions (Lindvall 2011: 299).

The combination of the preceding factors certainly goes a long way towards helping us argue that certain structural characteristics lie behind the French propensity to protest and the significance of the street. Despite today lacking the relative weight in terms of numbers, French trade unions have a very important role to play. This role and their relationship are defined by notions of contest where the historical importance of strike action is firmly stitched into their *modus operandi* (Tartakowsky 2006: 23–27). However, this only tells part of the story. Not all protests are the result of industrial action and the frequency of strikes is on the wane, and yet, the importance of the street persists (Ancelovici 2011: 127). To make sense of this, one is obliged to take stock of the heavily centralised nature of the French state that excludes society from the decision-making process. This is an enduring characteristic of the French Republican system but also one that continues to define French society today. Having taken such considerations on board, one is closer to understanding how and why the street is so prominent. However, there is one final element requiring our attention, without which the explanation would be incomplete – the weight of history.

The weight of history

A number of significant, foundational moments in the history of the French Republic highlight just how the street has been a key arena and demonstrates why it has become progressively stitched into the very fabric of French society. The inevitable starting point is of course the French Revolution (Evans and Godin 2014: 1–18).

The storming of the Bastille on 14 July 1789, however mythical, has come to represent the will of the people to physically seize power. Such direct action set an example taken up across the country and helped ensure that the French Revolution would bring an end to the monarchy and ultimately lead to the creation of the Republic. It is therefore unsurprising that it has left such an important legacy (Tartakowsky 2006). Furthermore, it set a precedent whereby the will of the people expressed via direct action, and in particular by taking to the street, would become an important, recurring feature (Tilly 1978). The year 1848 witnessed the spread of revolution throughout Europe and in France was the culmination of a period of instability and mounting tension started in 1814 when the Restoration brought about the creation of a constitutional monarchy led by Louis XIII (Gildea 2003: 83–104). Following a co-ordinated programme of protests that were progressively outlawed, the people took to the streets. Building barricades and clashing with forces of order, they drew a violent and fatal reaction from the authorities with over 50 people killed. This heightened the resolve of the people, who redoubled their ownership of the streets, eventually forcing Louis Philippe to abdicate and creating the grounds for the birth of the Second Republic. Twice the Republic had been born and twice it was ultimately the will of the people and the power of the street that had tipped the balance. It is no surprise then that the next moment in the evolution of the Republic was also played out on the street.

The Franco-Prussian War was declared on 18 July 1870. After an embarrassing and chaotic effort, the French were defeated by September 1870, leading to the end of the Empire and the creation of the Third Republic (Sowerine 2009: 11). Following the signing of the armistice, the working-class people of Paris, frustrated with the defeat, took control of the capital in what would become known as the Paris Commune (Ross 2015). The Commune left a durable and important legacy in France and beyond for many reasons, and in particular, through how the Communards physically made Paris, its quarters, and its streets their own. When repression came, the Communards attempted to defend their space, most symbolically from behind barricades. The Commune may well have been defeated and short-lived but it left an indelible mark that lives on today.

Coming between the two world wars and triggered by the Third Republic's distinct inability to deal with the fallout of the global financial crisis and subsequent rise of fascism, the ephemeral hiatus of 1936, known as the Popular Front, is unquestionably one of the foundational moments of contemporary France (Jackson 1990). It very much continued the Republican tradition – so embedded by this stage – of the ability of the people to rise up and take control. The street was once again pivotal, as it was the arena for a protest by far right-wing groups known as *ligues* on 6 February 1934 that set in motion the process that would culminate with the emergence of a Popular Front government. Throughout this period, the emphasis on people taking ownership was symbolically represented through strikes, occupations and the continued significance of the street (Tartakowsky 1998: 85–118). The next cornerstone moment for the Republic saw strong overlap and connections to this momentous interwar period.

The seminal events of 1968 further consolidated the centrality of the street (Mathieu 2008: 195–206). Taking their suburban revolt from Nanterre to the Sorbonne in early May, the initial student protestors sought to render their revolt more visible via action in important sites in the heart of the capital. As the events quickly escalated, hardly a day would pass without a demonstration. May and June 1968 provided the latest in a long line of examples of how the French, feeling ignored, powerless and marginalised from state levers of power, resorted to the one source that has consistently proved effective in making sure their voices and desires were heard. De Gaulle's eventual success in turning the situation on its head (ironically confirmed initially by the silent majority hitting the street) did not prevent May '68 becoming a watershed moment right across French society (Artières and Fournel 2008). By 1968 street protest had become tightly woven into the fabric of how France operated and *mai–juin 68* only served to help further confirm this status.

Over 50 years on from the tumultuous events of 1968, France has not experienced anything on the same scale. That is not to say that protest has stopped since then, on the contrary. May '68 confirmed the potency of protest and the power of the street. When the Devaquet protests of 1986, the anti-pension rebellion of 1995 or the anti-Le Pen mobilisation of 2002 occurred, there was evidence that the memory of the '68 events still weighed heavily (Duclaud-Williams 1989: 43–61; Cohen 2008: 19–28). This was true in the nature of the protest but also in the evident fear of the political elite for any repeat of *mai 68*. However, what happened in 1968 must not be considered in isolation (Baumgartner 1994: 94; Wilson 1994: 30). As argued previously, it was just the latest in a long line of foundational moments where protest and the street took centre stage and became part of the way France operates and functions. References to 1968 in '86, '95 or '02 were not simply nods to this specific period, they were nods to the long-established and ongoing tradition that dictates how and why the street matters in France. Wilson argues that, so embedded has protest become in the French psyche, it has in many ways become a means for 'contemporaries to relive and participate in these grand events' (Wilson 1994: 35).

As time has passed, the reasons that have brought about collective action have obviously changed and evolved. It is of no surprise that such developments have fed into the way in which protest has been conducted in France (Hayat 2006: 31–44). As Tilly has argued, the repertoires of collective action have and will continue to change and develop (1986). However, certain forms of action have become embedded and the durable common denominator from the Revolution until today is unquestionably the street. The central argument here is that, as well as the structural reasons discussed earlier, one cannot truly understand the importance of the street without considering the weight of history. Wilson argued that it is the significance of history that really sets France apart: 'It is, perhaps, the importance of this ritual of protest that makes protest in France, where the incidence and success rates of protest are little different from other western democracies, so prominent a feature of French politics' (Wilson 1994: 36). However, France is not the only nation with a history of protest and yet it is claimed and largely perceived as a case apart. In order to make sense of this conundrum one must take into consideration the fact that France, arguably more so than any other nation, places a heavy emphasis on the significance of its past (Howarth and Varouxakis 2003: 2–4). One only has to consider just how present the past is in France – a fact exemplified by almost every presidential address emphasising the need to linger on, and remind citizens of, the importance of French history. In order to understand why this is the case, one must consider the importance of the notion of the French collective memory in shaping how France sees itself on the global stage today.

It is difficult to disagree that since the onset of the First World War, France has been experiencing a decline in its position as a global power. When the period of conflict was finally brought to a close in 1945, France was no longer able to use its standing to argue for the continuation of its prominent place amongst the world's leading nations. As France and Europe climbed up from their knees in the post-war period, any hope of future *grandeur* lay not in its current predicament but in its prestigious place in history. Since then, the actual place of France, whilst undoubtedly making dramatic progress under de Gaulle during *les trente glorieuses*, has not come too far. In fact, the onset of economic crisis in the 1970s only served to further accentuate the decline of France. And yet France has somehow managed to hold on to its place as a world leader. It has done so by relying on past glories and its undisputedly central role played in defining and determining the contemporary global order. This explains why French leaders have been and continue to be so keen to remind everyone of France's golden history. The jewel in the historical crown is undoubtedly the French Revolution of 1789. How many times are we reminded of how this event established France's role as the beacon of democracy and human rights?[18] The Republic, as consequence of the Revolution, has become a byword for all that is good in terms of France, thus explaining why the term is no longer a divisive one but something that is arguably the focus of everyone's desire (Chabal 2015). This desire to emphasise the glorious past in order to ensure continued prominence in the present and the future is also an important consideration for understanding the enduring centrality of the street. By consistently emphasising the importance of the Revolution, there is an indirect legitimisation of the street. The Revolution as *the* foundational moment of the French Republic places a revolt by and of the people, where the street was so important, in a position of irrefutable credence (Hayat 2006). By emphasising the importance of the Revolution, there is an implicit acceptance that the street had and continues to have an important role to play.

Conclusions

The nature of the 2016 *Nuit Debout* movement and the accompanying references to France's long history of protest served as a reminder of the ongoing tradition as highlighted in this chapter (Reynolds 2018). Furthermore, despite the initial positivity surrounding Emmanuel Macron's election as president, and as so effectively demonstrated by the 2018–2019 *gilets jaunes* movement, the street nevertheless continues to be an important arena for the French to express their frustrations, discontent and desires.[19] Whilst some studies may suggest that France is no real exception when it comes to protest, one cannot help but feel that such a tradition is quintessentially French. The fact that the statistics are unhelpful in capturing this exception lends weight to the argument that something more fundamental is at play. The importance of structural concerns around French specificities created by the place and role of trade unions, the history of strike action and the heavily centralised nature of the state have been highlighted as going some way towards helping us make sense of the centrality of the street. However, it has been argued that such considerations do not tell the full story.

Instead, one is obliged to look to history for two particular reasons. Firstly, ever since the foundational moment that was the French Revolution, France has arguably only ever progressed thorough periodic moments of protest (Cole 2005: 45–48). Whilst forms of action have evolved across periods such as 1848, the Commune, the Popular Front and May '68, the enduring common denominator has been the street. As such, it has secured its place as an indisputable venue with credible legitimacy in ensuring the advancement of France. Secondly, as France has sought to keep hold of its place as a nation with a key role to play despite its unquestionable decline, the past has been used to justify the maintenance of France's prominent position. The cornerstone of this narrative is the French Revolution that gave birth to the Republic and placed France at the heart of modern democratic values. The glorious past versus the declinist present explains why the former is significant for France, as exemplified by the consistent emphasis placed on it by France's political elite. In so doing, a certain legitimacy is indirectly afforded to the means of the Revolution's success: the people and the street. To understand the power of the street in the present one must look to the past. It is difficult to see how this will change in the future.

Notes

1 There exists a vast amount of material on this horrific day. Particularly noteworthy is the documentary *Du coté des vivants*, 2016. www.youtube.com/watch?v=TiqI_BJD7bA [Accessed: 01.07.2016].

2 C.f. for example Zagato, A. (Ed.). 2015. *The Event of Charlie Hebdo*. New York: Berghahn; Wieviorka, M. 2015. *Retour au sens pour en finir avec le déclinisme*. Paris: Robert Laffont.

3 'Marche républicaine à Paris: une ampleur "sans précédent,"' in *Libération*, 11 January 2015. www.liberation.fr/societe/2015/01/11/en-direct-la-place-de-la-republique-noire-de-monde_1178277 [Accessed: 05.07.2016]; 'Contre le terrorisme, la plus grande manifestation jamais recensée en France,' in *Le Monde*, 11 January 2015. www.lemonde.fr/societe/article/2015/01/11/la-france-dans-la-rue-pour-defendre-la-liberte_4553845_3224.html [Accessed: 05.07.2016].

4 C.f. for example Todd, E. 2015. Qui est Charlie? Sociologie d'une crise religieuse. Paris: Seuil.

5 'Les principales mesures du projet de loi santé,' in *Libération*, 14 April 2015. www.liberation.fr/france/2015/04/14/projet-de-loi-sante-l-heure-du-vote-a-l-assemblee_1240694 [Accessed: 24.06.2016]; 'Ce que la loi santé va changer pour les Français,' in *Le Figaro*, 14 April 2015. www.lefigaro.fr/conjoncture/2015/04/14/20002-20150414ARTFIG00049-ce-que-la-loi-sante-va-changer-pour-les-francais.php [Accessed: 24.06.2016]; 'Ce que le projet de loi santé va changer au quotidien,' in *Le Monde*, 14 April 2015. www.lemonde.fr/sante/article/2015/04/11/ce-que-le-projet-de-loi-sante-va-changer-au-quotidien_4614241_1651302.html [Accessed: 25.06.2016].

6 'Forte mobilisation contre le projet de loi santé,' in *Le Monde,* 14 March 2015. www.lemonde.fr/sciences/article/2015/03/14/forte-mobilisation-contre-le-projet-de-loi-sante_4593562_1650684.html [Accessed: 25.06.2016].

7 'Les taxis contre Uber,' in *Le Monde*, 8 June 2015. www.lemonde.fr/les-taxis-contre-uber/ [Accessed: 21.06.2016]; 'Taxis contre Uber: «Ne cédez rien, c'est votre dernière chance!»,' in *Libération*, 26 June 2015. www.liberation.fr/futurs/2015/06/26/taxis-contre-uber-ne-cedez-rien-c-est-votre-derniere-chance_1337819 [Accessed: 26.06.2016]; 'Offensive d'Uber en france@ taxis et VTC en colère contre le gouvernement,' in *Le Figaro*, 8 June 2015. www.lefigaro.fr/secteur/high-tech/2015/06/08/32001-20150608ARTFIG00339-offensive-d-uber-en-france-taxis-et-vtc-en-colere-contre-le-gouvernement.php [Accessed: 26.06.2016].

8 See www.education.gouv.fr/cid86831/college-mieux-apprendre-pour-mieux-reussir.html [Accessed: 28.06.2016].

9 'Réforme des collèges: les raisons de la nouvelle grève des enseignants,' in *Le Monde*, 17 September 2015. www.lemonde.fr/education/article/2015/09/16/nouvelle-journee-de-greve-des-enseignants-contre-la-reforme-des-colleges_4759927_1473685.html [Accessed: 28.06.2016].

10 'Cette réforme du collège qui ne passe toujours pas,' in *Le Figaro*, 10 October 2015. www.lefigaro.fr/actualite-france/2015/10/09/01016-20151009ARTFIG00337-cette-reforme-du-college-qui-ne-passe-toujours-pas.php [Accessed: 28.06.2016].

11 'VIDEO. Le jour où des salariés d'Air France ont arraché la chemise du DRH,' in *Le Nouvel Observateur*, 5 October 2015. http://tempsreel.nouvelobs.com/societe/20151005.OBS7068/video-air-france-le-drh-se-fait-arracher-la-chemise-par-des-salaries-et-s-enfuit.html [Accessed: 29.06.2016].

12 'Air France protests – in pictures,' in *The Guardian*, 5 October 2015. www.theguardian.com/world/gallery/2015/oct/05/air-france-protests-job-losses-charles-de-gaulle-airport-paris [Accessed: 30.06.2016]; 'Angry Workers Storm Air France Meeting on Job Cuts,' in *New York Times*, 5 October 2015. www.nytimes.com/2015/10/06/business/international/angry-workers-storm-air-france-meeting-on-job-cuts.html [Accessed: 30.06.2016].

13 'A Paris, les éboueurs mettent fin à leur grève,' in *Le Monde*, 8 October 2015. www.lemonde.fr/societe/article/2015/10/08/a-paris-les-eboueurs-mettent-fin-a-leur-greve_4785856_3224.html [Accessed: 29.06.2016].

14 'Thierry Morin reprend Française des Roues,' in *Le Figaro*, 16 October 2015. www.lefigaro.fr/flash-eco/2015/10/16/97002-20151016FILWWW00382-thierry-morin-reprend-francaise-des-roues.php [Accessed: 29.06.2016].

15 'Le gouvernement sommé de soigner ses «bleus»,' in *Libération*, 14 October 2015. www.liberation.fr/france/2015/10/14/le-gouvernement-somme-de-soigner-ses-bleus_1404099 [Accessed: 29.06.2016].

16 'La grève des avocats prend de l'ampleur,' in *Le Nouvel Observateur*, 20 October 2015. http://tempsreel.nouvelobs.com/topnews/20151020.REU8623/la-greve-des-avocats-s-etend-a-la-province.html [Accessed: 29.06.2016].

17 Strikes in Europe (Version 2.1, January 2015). www.etui.org/Topics/Trade-union-renewal-and-mobilisation/Strikes-in-Europe-version-2.1-January-2015#use [Accessed: 30.06.2016].

18 For example 'Discours du président de la République devant le Parlement réuni en Congrès,' in *Versailles*, 16 November 2015. www.elysee.fr/declarations/article/discours-du-president-de-la-republique-devant-le-parlement-reuni-en-congres-3/ [Accessed: 20.06.2016].

19 'Yellow vest protests': it goes far beyond the fuel tax,' in *France 24*, 8 December 2018. www.france24.com/en/video/20181208-yellow-vest-protests-it-goes-far-beyond-fuel-tax [Accessed: 09.01.2019].

References

Ancelovici, M. 2008. Social movements and protest politics. In A. Cole et al. (Eds.), *Developments in French Politics*. Basingstoke: Palgrave Macmillan, 74–91.

Ancelovici, M. 2011. In search of lost radicalism: the hot autumn of 2010 and the transformation of labor contention in France. In *French Politics, Culture and Society*, 29:3, 121–139.

Ancelovici, M. 2015. Crisis and contention in Europe: a political process account of anti-austerity protests. In V. Guiraudon, C. Ruzza and H-J. Trenz (Eds.), *Europe's Prolonged Crisis: The Making or the Unmaking of a Political Union*. Basingstoke: Palgrave Macmillan, 189–209.

Artières, P. and M. Zancarini-Fournel. 2008. *68. Une Histoire Collective [1962–1981]*. Paris: La Découverte.

Baumgartner, F. R. 1994. The politics of protest and mass mobilization in France. In *French Politics and Society*, 12:2/3, 84–96.

Chabal, E. 2015. *A Divided Republic: Nations, State and Citizenship in Contemporary France*. Cambridge: Cambridge University Press.

Cohen, E. 2008. L'ombre portée de Mai 68 en politique. Démocratie et participation. In Vingtième Siècle. Revue d'histoire, 98:2, 19–28.

Cole, A. 2005. *French Politics and Society*. Harlow: Pearson Longman.

Duclaud-Williams, R. 1989. Student protest: 1968 and 1986 compared. In D. L. Hanley and A. P. Kerr (Eds.), *May '68: Coming of Age*. London: Macmillan, 43–61.

Evans, M. and E. Godin. 2014. *France since 1815*. London: Routledge.

Fillieule, O. 1997. *Stratégies de la rue. Les manifestations en France*. Paris: Presses de Sciences Po.

Gildea, R. 2003. *Barricades and Borders: Europe 1800–1914*. Oxford: Oxford University Press.

Hayat, S. 2006. La république, la rue et l'urne. In *Pouvoirs*, 116:1, 31–44.

Howarth, D. and G. Varouxakis. 2003. *Contemporary France: An Introduction to French Politics and Society*. London: Arnold.

Jackson, J. 1990. *The Popular Front in France: Defending Democracy, 1934–38*. Cambridge: Cambridge University Press.

Knapp, A. and V. Wright. 2006. *The Government and Politics of France*. London: Routledge.

Lindvall, J. 2011. The political foundations of trust and distrust: reforms and protests in France. In *West European Politics*, 34:2, 296–316.

Ly, M. 2015. Attaque meurtrière contre *Charlie Hebdo*: La France face au défi du vivre ensemble. In *Médiapart*, 9 January.

Mathieu, L. 2008. Les manifestations en mai-juin 68. In D. Damamme et al. (Eds.), *Mai Juin 68*. Paris: Atelier, 195–206.

Mathieu, L. 2011. *La démocratie protestataire*. Paris: Presses de Sciences Po.

McAdam, D., S. Tarrow and C. Tilly. 2001. *Dynamics of Contention*. Cambridge: Cambridge University Press.

Reynolds, C. 2018. From mai-juin '68 to Nuit Debout: shifting perspectives on France's anti-police. In *Modern and Contemporary France*, 26:2, 145–163.

Ross, K. 2015. *Communal Luxury: The Political Imaginary of the Paris Commune*. London: Verso.

Séguy, G. 2008. *Résister: De Mauthausen à Mai 68*. Paris: l'Archipel.

Sirot, S. 2011. *Le syndicalisme, la politique et la grève. France et Europe: XIXe-XXIe siècles*. Nancy: Arbre bleu.

Sowerine, C. 2009. *France since 1870*. Basingstoke: Palgrave Macmillan.

Tartakowsky, D. 1998. *Le pouvoir est dans la rue. Crises politiques et manifestations en France*. Paris: Aubier.

Tartakowsky, D. 2006. Quand la rue fait l'histoire. In *Pouvoirs*, 116:1, 19–29.

Tilly, C. 1978. The routinization of protest in nineteenth-century France. CRSO Working Paper, No. 181, October.

Tilly, C. 1986. *The Contentious French: Four Centuries of Popular Struggle*. London: Harvard University Press.

Todd, E. 2015. *Qui est Charlie? Sociologie d'une crise religieuse*. Paris: Seuil.

Wieviorka, M. 2015. *Retour au sens pour en finir avec le déclinisme*. Paris: Robert Laffont.

Wilson, F. L. 1994. Political demonstrations in France: protest politics or politics of ritual. In *French Politics and Society*, 12:2/3, 23–40.

Zagato, A. (Ed.). 2015. *The Event of Charlie Hebdo*. New York: Berghahn.

12

THE FRENCH 'BANLIEUES'

Realities, myths, representations

Christina Horvath

In January 2015, just a few days after the attacks on the offices of *Charlie Hebdo* and the kosher supermarket, Hyper Cacher, French prime minister Manuel Valls used the word 'apartheid' to describe the deep-seated territorial, social and ethnic divides that separate the disadvantaged urban fringes called 'banlieues' from the rest of the country. The polemical term was deliberately chosen to shock French audiences grown accustomed to the word 'ghetto.' Since the 1980s (Vieillard-Baron 2011; Robine 2004), French politicians have increasingly resorted to derogatory terms with regard to working-class suburbs, the most memorable example being the word *racaille* ('scum') used by Nicolas Sarkozy to qualify the authors of the 2005 banlieue uprisings. This deprecating rhetoric has indisputably contributed to stigmatising the predominantly high-rise social housing estates and turning the originally neutral term 'banlieue' into a byword for ethnic and territorial segregation, in which 'ban' no longer stands for the perimeter around a town falling under the jurisprudence of the local authority, but for banishment (Belhaj Kacem 2006).

This chapter aims to evaluate how official representations of the banlieues and counternarratives relate to myths and reality. It will show how, since the 1980s, banlieues have been turned into France's major social problem by biased political and media representations and urban policies promoting a territorial approach to ethnic and socio-economic inequalities. The first section will focus on the rise of the banlieue myth and examine the suburbs' progressive decline in public imagery. The second will look at major public debates which have been shaping the banlieues' image in recent years. Finally, the last section will explore how a range of counter-narratives have been developed by residents and artists in response to the myth of the ghetto.

The planning of a social problem

The construction of French banlieues arose from centralised urban planning, guided by political and economic influences emanating from the centre (Angélil and Siress 2012). The relegation of poor communities to the urban margins began with the major modernisation of Paris between 1852 and 1870. The works undertaken by Baron Haussmann resulted in a lasting divide between the city core and the margins, replacing previous forms of vertical segregation with a horizontal one (Merlin 2012: 9). Geographer David Harvey sees this division as an organised spatial hierarchy in which the 'dangerous classes,' insalubrious housing and polluting industries were evicted from the city core while power was asserted through the polarisation of centre and periphery (Harvey 2003).

France responded to the post-war housing shortage by constructing government-subsidised housing on a large scale. Between 1945 and 1975, thousands of housing units were constructed in the periphery of most French cities, taking Le Corbusier's *Radiant City* (1935) as a blueprint for social change. The Swiss architect recommended free circulation, abundant green spaces and separate function-based zones for dwelling, work, recreation and transport. However, in order to quickly resorb the population of substandard housing and slums, quantity was prioritised over quality.

Whether banlieues were originally constructed to become ghettos is a much debated question. According to Merlin, the initial population of the 'grands ensembles' were predominantly middle-class families with young children (2012: 54) who moved out when this form of sub-urban living had become unpopular. Tissot (2007) claims that there was a fair degree of social diversity among the initial banlieue residents and it was not before the sanitisation of the slums in the mid-1970s that immigrants, especially those from North Africa, were let into the public housing estates. However, Angélil and Siress argue that many 'cités' were originally intended to keep workers from the former colonies at a safe distance from the city centre (Angélil and Siress 2012: 59–60). Annie Fourcaut proposes a more nuanced vision by revealing that working-class housing estates on the so-called red belt[1] around Paris were not just places of territorial exclusion but also privileged sites for the integration of successive waves of migrants from France and elsewhere. They facilitated the emergence of working-class elites and the formation of political opinions (Fourcaut 2004: 196). This view is also supported by Dikeç, who sees banlieues not only 'as "badlands" but also as sites of political mobilisations with democratic ideals' (Dikeç 2007: 22).

The first critiques of large-scale banlieue construction emerged in the 1960s. They pointed to the monotonous architecture as well as the absence of some essential facilities including businesses, public services and initially even schools. The decline of banlieue architecture, however, was due to economic factors rather than to the residents' discomfort. In the early 1970s, the oil crisis marked the end of 30 years of economic prosperity in France. A major shift in the government's approach to housing made low-interest loans available to many middle-class families, enabling them to buy their own homes (Merlin 2012: 71–80). Then, the first wave of urban violence in the 1970s inspired state responses in the form of urban policies, initially conceived for the 'social development of the neighbourhoods' and later aiming to reconquer no-go areas (Dikeç 2007: 15).

Urban policies

Desponds (2015) distinguishes three main phases of the policies conceived to tackle urban segregation in banlieues after the 1979 urban unrests in the Lyon suburb of Vaulx-en-Velin. The first phase started in 1973 with the Guichard report announcing the fight against segregation. During the following decade, the construction of new housing estates was abandoned and significant inter-ministerial funding was allocated to improve the infrastructure and to combat urban decay, discomfort, sociocultural exclusion and poverty in 39 selected areas.

The second phase, concerned with urban renewal, lasted from the Vénissieux riots in 1981 until the creation of the ANRU (Agence Nationale pour la Rénovation Urbaine; National Agency for Urban Renovation) in 2003. In his 1983 report commissioned by the socialist government entitled 'Ensemble refaire la ville' ('Let's remake the city, together'), Dubedout, the mayor of Grenoble, advocated social development and recommended proactive urban policies to extend the 'right to the city' to all. However, the new focus on at-risk neighbourhoods (called *quartiers sensibles*, or 'sensitive neighbourhoods') implied centring state action on specific urban spaces rather than the entire national territory. As a consequence, social disadvantage became increasingly territorialised. In Tissot's words, 'poverty, inequality or unemployment are no longer discussed, or rather, they are discussed only through territorial categories' (Tissot 2007: 2). During this period, the number of neighbourhoods supported by urban regeneration programmes rose from 148 in 1984 to 751 in 1996 when these areas of intervention were named *Zones Urbaines Sensibles* ('Sensitive Urban Areas') or ZUS. In 1991, the Ministry of Urban Affairs was created, acknowledging that the 'banlieue question' had become one of France's most burning social problems. A new vocabulary was adopted, in which some banlieues were labelled 'difficult' or 'disadvantaged.' This change of terminology was indicative of the increasing ethnicisation of the debates on poverty and the emergence of a state discourse linking the question of 'quartiers sensibles' to immigration rather than economic hardship (Tissot 2007: 19–49).

Finally, the current phase started in 2003 with the adoption of a National Programme of Urban Renovation (PNRU), whose objective was to 'break up the ghettos' through physical renovation, economic development and restructuring. To achieve the ideal of 'social mixity' (Avenel 2005: 65), the 2003 Borloo Law introduced large-scale demolition and redevelopment projects. The so-called GPUs (Great Urban Projects) linked to city contracts on 50 designated sites expected to produce 200,000 demolitions, 200,000 rehabilitations and 200,000 new social housing units between 2004 and 2008. The CUSCs (Urban Contracts of Social Cohesion) were introduced in 2006, and then abolished in 2014 along with the ZUS, supplanted by the new *Quartiers Prioritaires* (QPs), reducing the number of targeted neighbourhoods from 2,492 to 1,300 (Desponds and Bergel 2015). Today the geography of urban interventions relies on one single criterion, low income, and targets areas where the residents' revenue does not reach 60% of the national average.

The French state's approach to urban inequalities has been heavily criticised by a number of commentators. Tissot's analysis reveals how, between the mid-1980s and the mid-1990s, the welfare state and its redistributive policies based on urban planning were abandoned in favour of urban policies relying on the ethnic stigmatisation of social problems. Dikeç associates the shift with the adoption of neo-liberal strategies driven by the logic of competition and effectiveness instead of caring. Urban neo-liberalism manifests itself through the institutionalisation of urban policies based on the market, sharpening socio-economic inequalities and new, aggressive strategies of policing and surveillance aimed at particular groups (Dikeç 2007: 25–26), as well as the criminalisation of poverty and the increased use of the penal system. These analyses concur in their denunciation of hardening public policy discourses that stigmatise banlieue residents while occulting the challenges they face, such as domination, poverty and unemployment. Most commentators agree on the systemic disadvantage and ethnic discrimination resulting from place-based rather than people-based social policies and condemn the abandonment of the welfare state in favour of increasingly repressive policies.

Media representations and the myth of the ghetto

Audio-visual media are believed to have also significantly contributed to the current predominantly negative perception of the banlieues in the public imagination. The shift, which occurred around 1980 in journalistic practices, can be held responsible for the prevailing biased treatment of the suburbs. According to Champagne (1991, 2011), events are produced by journalists collectively. Local and national newspapers, news magazines, public and private radio stations and television channels participate in the selection, classification and ranking of news items that will be turned into events, while they themselves are subjected to pressure from advertisers, pollsters, politicians and audiences. Synchronisation and focalisation are two journalistic processes that have resulted in the relative uniformity of themes and interpretative frameworks used across the French journalistic field.

Until the 1980s, 'serious' news media with high symbolic capital were able to impose a predominantly political vision on events. However, the privatisation of TF1 and the rise of private channels increased the influence of economic priorities on the production of information. This new economic logic prompted journalists to dramatise events to provoke collective emotions while the pressure to cover events rapidly before other media captured them significantly reduced investigative journalism and in-depth analysis. In addition, initial representations often persist, even after they were proven inaccurate and revoked, since the prejudices on which they were based are constantly reactivated.

Sedel (2014) analyses how media treatment of the banlieues has evolved since the 1970s. Journalists' initial interest in deficient public transport links, poverty, delinquency and immigration was supplanted in the 1980s by the emerging new theme of 'banlieue youth.' In the 1990s, when anti-racist movements lost their impetus, urban violence and delinquency became the dominant themes (Sedel 2014: 52), followed by insecurity; a topic introduced during the 2002 electoral campaigns. Mutations in the framing prompted a shift in the ways in which information was collected and processed. Treatment of the banlieue became less political while empathic approaches gave way to a new ethos that Sedel describes as 'fact fetishism' (Sedel 2014: 53). Since then, banlieue-themed articles have been increasingly delegated to less prestigious services and less specialised and experienced journalists, whose main informants are no longer community leaders, teachers or social activists but police officers and law courts. Editors in chief encourage exclusive focus on extraordinary events such as riots or cases of delinquency while more ordinary events are no longer worth of coverage. Nevertheless, as Garcin-Marrou (in Carpenter and Horvath 2015) and Turpin (2012) show, differences in the framing do persist. They depend on the type of the media (written/audio-visual) as well as their political orientations (left wing/right wing).

According to Champagne (1991), marginalised populations have very little influence over their own media image. They do not have sufficient command of the forms of expression specific to the media and even tend to borrow from dominant discourses to speak about themselves. For example, by adopting the self-definition 'banlieue youth,' the journalists of the Bondy blog, an alternative media created by the Swiss news magazine *Hebdo*, have subscribed to a designation that was imposed upon them (Sedel 2011). As a result, the bloggers' identity remains vague and subject to tensions between their personal experience and professional journalism, popular slang and legitimate language, and working-class roots and middle-class aspirations. Consequently, the public representations of working-class banlieues remain largely dominated by binaries (Vieillard-Baron 2011: 28) and the myth of the banlieues, inscribed in a specific ideological context and fostered by a range of stereotypical images and cultural references 'tends to elude the complexity of urban dynamics, the rich input of immigration and segregating processes emanating from the centre' (Vieillard-Baron 2012: 39).

Banlieues at the heart of contemporary debates

Since the 1980s, banlieues have been at the heart of many public debates. This section attempts to sum up some of the current polemics that continue to shape the perception of the suburbs, incessantly adding new features to the myth of the ghetto. First we will consider whether banlieues are actually the lawless ghettos or no-go zones depicted in some media-political discourses. Then we will focus on what sets apart the repeated waves of urban violence occurring in banlieues from other forms of violence generally recognised as political protest movements. Finally we will examine whether working-class suburbs present a higher concentration of gender discrimination than other areas in France before scrutinising recent stereotypical representations of banlieues as fertile places for radical Islam and breeding grounds for terrorism.

Since the 1980s, banlieues have been increasingly compared to ghettos by politicians, journalists and researchers. The 2002 election campaign, in which most parties denounced ghettoisation, was a turning point in the vulgarisation of this metaphor. The word was first used by SOS Racisme in 1987 (Robine 2004) to justify their transformation into a permanent organisation. The leaders of the association argued that most inequalities in France originate from unequal access to urban space. They denounced racist practices in social housing allocation and warned against school segregation as well as the rise of ethnic communities which challenge Republican unity. According to Robine, this discourse was deliberately vague to allow SOS Racisme to discredit other political forces, raise funding and shape the representations of the periphery to conform to their needs (Robine 2004: 146).

Many researchers reject the word 'ghetto' as illegitimate in the French context. They point to the banlieues' great ethnic and social diversity, arguing that the integration and dispersion of immigrants are still ongoing processes. Vieillard-Baron (2011) shows that neither economic disadvantage nor foreign nationals were sufficiently concentrated to justify the use of this term while other criteria – geographic segregation, stigmatisation and belonging to the same ethnic and religious community – were simply not met. Wacquant (1992) also contests the analogy between France and the United States, not only because of the two countries' different levels of poverty, exclusion, dereliction and marginalisation but also because banlieues, unlike the African-American ghettos, concentrate populations of different ethnicities who belong to similar social classes. Racial polarisation is deeply rooted in North American history and is inscribed in institutions as well as in mindsets, far more than in France. Importing such foreign concepts without regard for their original use and context is perilous, not only because it blurs the understanding of territorial segregation in France but also because it aggravates the banlieues' symbolic stigmatisation.

In the 2000s and 2010s, however, the rising violence, segregation and radicalisation in French banlieues were interpreted by some as the signs of a process of ghettoisation. Kokoreff and Lapeyronnie (2013) distinguish three phases of this process: the age of '*galère*' (slang word for 'difficulty') in the 1970s and 1980s, the age of 'violence' in the 1990s and, finally, the age of the 'ghetto' from the 2000s. According to sociologists, the violent riots, deepening gender divides, radical forms of religiosity, and hostility towards the state and its institution indicate the banlieues' increasing isolation from the rest of French society. Far from being unanimously adopted, the idea of ghettoisation has been frequently used in dominant discourses to obscure the banlieues' great diversity and to justify the state's top-down, territorial approaches to social inequalities despite evidence of their inefficiency.

Are riots political protests or acts of aimless violence?

Another much debated question is whether riots should be interpreted as political protests. Rioting in banlieues started in the late 1970s and it has continued ever since, reaching an unprecedented peak in November 2005 with three weeks of uninterrupted unrest spreading across France and provoking a state of emergency. Since the 1981 unrests in the Lyon suburb of Minguettes, riots have essentially followed the same pattern: they occur in former working-class neighbourhoods hit hard by unemployment. They involve young men, mostly of immigrant origin who are often subjected to humiliating stop and search practices performed by the police. According to Mucchielli (2012), most unrest is triggered by the accidental killing of youths by the police. The 2005 riots started after the teenagers Bouna Traoré and Zyed Benna were electrocuted in an electric sub-station in Clichy-sous-Bois, chased by the police. Riots generally have no leaders nor political claims and consist mostly of torching vehicles and throwing projectiles at the police, although they may occasionally also include vandalising buildings or ransacking businesses.

While Nicolas Sarkozy and other political leaders viewed the 2005 events as the work of experienced delinquents and mafia-like organisations, some social scientists propose different interpretations. Murphy (2011) shows that the French model of public contestation requires announced intentions, established spokespersons, well-disciplined membership with relatively high social standing, clear management and supervision of the protest, as well as claims about the general interest. Since the events of November 2005 did not follow this model, they were almost unanimously condemned as acts of aimless violence, revealing an important divide between marginalised postcolonial populations designated as the 'internal enemy,' and the police violating banlieue residents' rights instead of protecting them.

Mucchielli (2006, 2012) suggests that banlieue upheavals express the despair of marginalised youths who suffer from long-term unemployment as a result of failing at school and suffering from racial and social discrimination. Other commentators (in Waddington et al. 2009: 107–123) argue that the 2005 riots were a reaction to urban renovation operations which, after the adoption of the Borloo Law in 2003, endeavoured to solve social problems by demolishing and reconstructing high-rise social housing estates, thereby increasing the vulnerability of the most insecure groups threatened by expulsion. Moran (2011) emphasises the media's responsibility in the upheaval by demonstrating how the foregrounding of sensationalist material by journalists encouraged large-scale destruction as a way of gaining public visibility, venting anger and articulating concerns about salient social issues in the banlieues. Kokoreff, Mouhanna, Rigouste, and Mohammed (in Waddington et al. 2009) conclude that the primary motivation for rioting was a deep-seated feeling of rejection and injustice, which constitutes a common experience among the children of postcolonial immigrants involved in strained relations with everyday institutions.

Many commentators highlight that, rather than being part of the solution, the police have worsened the problem. Mouhanna (2009) demonstrates that the maintenance of public order and the tight control of protesters through space saturation techniques and intimidation are major priorities for the French police while mediation, negotiation and prevention are neglected. Often fearful of the residents, police officers regard themselves as outsiders and show contempt for ethnic minority youths who, in their view, do not qualify for full citizenship rights (Waddington et al. 2009: 179). As a result, police conduct is undoubtedly an important catalyst for the unrest.

Is gender segregation specific to banlieues?

In December 2016, a report broadcast on France 2 revealed that female clients were not welcome in a Muslim-owned café in Sevran, Seine Saint-Denis. By suggesting that women in French banlieues were intimidated by mostly Muslim men of North African origin, the programme reactivated earlier polemics about gender segregation specific to postcolonial populations in France, including debates about headscarves at schools and burkinis on French beaches. While some reactions relied on the interpretative framework of the Islamic threat, others interpreted this event through the prism of the 'virtuous mask of Republican racism,' elaborated by Nacira Guénif-Soulaimas (2006b) after the publication of the manifesto 'Ni Putes Ni Soumises' in 2003. This highly visible protest movement, which called for a demonstration 'against the ghettos and for equality' and denounced the recrudescence of violence against women in ban-lieues (Amara and Zappi 2003), caused a profound divide among social scientists and intellectu-als. Some warned against the 'Orientalist notion of a "victimised Muslim woman," who must be rescued by Westerners' (Selby 2011: 446) and cautioned against viewing certain forms of gender violence as specific to banlieue populations while obscuring others. They also highlighted the symbolic and political advantages some assimilated minority ethnic women gain in France from displaying their eroticised bodies as a sign of Republican loyalty (Guénif-Souilamas 2006a).

Other commentators, like Alidières (2010), however, caution against underplaying female suffering in the banlieues. They insist on including an ethno-cultural or ethno-religious dimen-sion to the study of gender violence in banlieues (Alidières 2010: 71), even if this involves the risk of ethnicising gender violence and stigmatising postcolonial males. The discriminatory nature of this suggestion is highlighted by Delphy (2006) and Fernando (2014, 2016), who criti-cise the majority ethnic French feminists for discriminating against veiled Muslim women by excluding them from the fight against sexism.[2] Fernando in particular demonstrates that gender discrimination is always linked to other forms of discrimination 'as long as racism exists, the critique of indigene patriarchy is a luxury' (Fernando 2016: 42).

Are banlieues breeding grounds for terrorism?

Finally, the latest debates are concerned with home-grown terrorism. In a speech following the terrorist attacks in November 2015, Emmanuel Macron alluded to the responsibility of French society for letting a breeding ground ('terreau') develop on which Islamic radicalisation could prosper. Although Macron did not mention whether this breeding ground had a connection to the banlieues (the word itself does not even feature in the speech in which only the word 'faubourg' is mentioned on one occasion), he alluded to France's increasingly endogamous elites enjoying the 'luxury of [. . .] living further away from the locations where the Republic had sur-rendered' and social mobility had faded away (Macron 2015). This statement established a causal link between the failed social mobility of banlieue youths and their radicalisation. Is there, how-ever, any evidence supporting that working-class banlieues with high concentrations of Muslim populations are turning into breeding grounds for terrorism?

Muslim religiosity has been widely associated with segregated lifestyles, susceptibility to vio-lent terrorism, and the rejection of European values and identity (Koopmans 2013). For many commentators who have analysed terrorist profiles in the aftermath of the 2015 and 2016 ter-rorist attacks, there is undoubtedly a link between radicalisation and growing up in poor and dysfunctional immigrant families in working-class banlieues. Identifying similarities in the ter-rorists' background and trajectories, Mouterde and Baruch (2015) reveal that those who expe-rienced learning difficulties at school and spent some time in penitentiaries are more likely to become radicalised. This is also confirmed by Khosrokavar (2013), whose research shows how the overcrowding and understaffing of French prisons, along with the high staff and inmate turnover, the rigid application of secular principles and the lack of acceptable means for many inmates to practise their religion facilitate conversion to radical Islam. Seen by some as the 'religion of the oppressed' (Khosrokavar 2013: 288), Islam channels the deep frustrations among inmates. Khosrokavar notes a shift in recruitment strategies in that recruiters tend to form duos or trios rather than larger groups and are more discreet about their radical views. He reveals that, paradoxically, a radical form of Islam, Salafism, 'is the most potent obstacle towards radicalization in the sense that it absorbs many young people's need for a new identity in rupture with society and transforms it into a non-violent sectarian attitude' (Khosrokavar 2013: 305).

Other researchers have challenged the widespread belief that in France, a country where traditions of secularism conflict with some Muslims' desires to make claims about the social or political value of their religious practices, Muslims are alienated from mainstream society due to their religiosity. On the contrary, as Maxwell and Bleich (2014) show, many Muslims are strongly attached to their Frenchness and factors associated with immigrant integration are more relevant for their self-identification as French than religiosity (Maxwell and Bleich 2014: 156).

Counter-narratives in rap and popular culture

While the aforementioned debates have influenced how banlieues are perceived in the public space, they have also triggered responses from suburban populations who are more often objects than subjects of discourses formulated about them. Some of these representations produced by residents and artists do little more than reproduce widespread clichés. Other discourses produced by rap musicians, film-makers and writers, however, reflect an internal vision of the banlieues and function as counter-narratives that challenge official narratives and stereotypical images.

In her recent book, Bettina Ghio (2016) sheds light on rhetoric strategies used by rap artists to depict the suburbs. She dispels the myth that rap always has a testimonial value and provides an authentic insight into banlieue life. She shows that rappers frequently resort to commonplace metonymies and metaphors by equating banlieues with concrete and prisons. The fact that these images have hardly changed over the last three decades demonstrates their symbolic rather than realist nature. Ghio also reveals that lyrics by La Cliqua, NTM, IAM, Sinik, La Rumeur or Casey have not been produced in isolation. These artists have established multiple links with French literature, which has been an important source of inspiration for them.

Another genre turned towards banlieue life is ethnic stand-up comedy. Laurent Béru's 2011 study highlights how the North American genre has been appropriated by a new generation of minority ethnic comedians from the banlieues. Béru focuses on the French television show Jamel Comedy Club (2006–2008), which was successful in launching a new generation of young comedians, such as Thomas Ngijol, Wahid Bouzidi, Fabrice Éboué, Paul Séré, Sébastien Dedominicis, Blanche Deconnick, Nouhoum Diawara, Amelle Chabi, Frédéric Chau, Patrice Kouassi and Youssoupha Diaby. These artists share similar demographics and have a strong interest in ethnically connoted musical genres like rap, zouk or dombolo. Ethnic stand-up comedies often use slang and neologisms and imitate oral speech. They speak about banlieues and denounce racial discrimination, colonial history and racial segregation by playfully overstating clichés and parodying mainstream discourses about immigrants, banlieue youths and Islamic radicalisation in peripheral neighbourhoods. Both popular genres use the word 'ghetto' as a form of self-identification. They draw inspiration from hip-hop culture and North American contra-hegemonic movements to promote the use of culture as a tool to enact social change in marginalised communities.

Banlieue cinema

French films also engage with the banlieue both as a theme and a setting. Higbee (2007: 38) finds this engagement 'problematic, in the sense that these representations risk falling into the same over-determined clichés of the rundown *cité* as the emblematic site of exclusion, criminality and "otherness."' While suburban housing estates have been present in the French *cinéma d'auteur* (Godard, Carné, Brissau, Le Péron) since the 1960s, it is only in 1995, after the simultaneous release of Dridi's *Bye-Bye*, Chibane's *Douce France*, Bouchaala's *Krim*, Gilou's *Raï* and, most importantly, Kassovitz' *La Haine*, that the term banlieue cinema was coined. Tarr

(2005) note the importance of the intersecting categories of banlieue and French-Maghrebi film-making, even though this production only represented about 5% of the national cinematographic production until 2000. Reeck (2018: 78) explains this low percentage with French society's resistance to the sociopolitical themes (economic integration, social mobility, cultural differences) these films tend to focus on.

More recently, banlieue film-making has taken two opposite directions: some directors have allied themselves with mainstream comedy while others have turned to drama and guerrilla film-making. Ferenczi (2015) notes that since the 2010s the suburbs have established themselves as popular settings for TV series and box office successes like *Intouchables* (2011) or *De l'autre côté du périph* (2012), where the daily life of those living in banlieues is no longer shown. Guerrilla films, such as Djaïdani's *Rengaine* (2012) or Tessaud's *Brooklyn* (2014), provide a correction to this by renewing 'with the type of social and committed cinema that shows its times' (Reeck 2018: 78) whereas a second shift is concerned with the emergence of female directors who disrupt the banlieue film's traditionally male-centred aesthetics. Tarr (2005) notes that female characters first appear in 'white male-authored films' (Tarr 2005: 111) such as *Samia* (Faucon 2001) and *La Squale* (Génestal 2000), however the recent success of *Bande de filles* (Sciamma 2014) and *Divines* (Banyamina 2016) points to a rise of a more inclusive visual culture in which there is more room for minority ethnic female protagonists and for engaging with the challenges of female coming of age in the urban periphery.

Banlieue narratives in literature

Banlieue literature started around the new millennium, a few years after the emergence of the banlieue film. Its development was triggered by a new territorially rather than ethnically defined identity and interethnic camaraderie, which was first depicted in Charef's *Thé au Harem d'Archimed* (1984) and Kassovitz' *La Haine* (1995). Since their beginning, banlieue narratives have developed strong links with rap, ethnic stand-up and banlieue film. Ironically, their focus on a generation of young people brought together by shared space and class belonging rather than ethnicity has mirrored the French state's territorial approach to socio-ethnic inequalities. In a context of rising inequalities, banlieue literature has attempted to voice new, hybrid, postcolonial identities and denounced socio-ethnic discrimination and French colonial nostalgia.

This new literary production has gained greater visibility with the manifesto *Qui fait la France?*[3] published in 2007 by Karim Amellal, Jean Eric Boulin, Khalid El Bahji, Faïza Guène, Dembo Goumane, Habiba Mahany, Samir Ouazène, Mabrouck Rachedi, Mohamed Razane and Thomte Ryam in a book of short stories entitled *Chroniques d'une société annoncée*. The manifesto states the signatories' ambition to reintroduce social criticism into the contemporary literary agenda. They accuse mainstream literary productions of obstinately turning toward middle-class individualism and identified nineteenth-century realist novelists engaging with major social issues as their literary models. The manifesto constitutes a brief moment of solidarity and alliance between writers pursuing similar objectives and aesthetic principles.

Banlieue narratives written from an internal viewpoint can be divided into various categories, including fiction and testimonies, single-author texts and collective publications, life writing (biography, autobiography, Bildungsroman) and other literary subgenres (crime fiction, anticipation novel, science fiction). Although banlieue fiction draws on the traditions of the 'beur generation,' around the new millennium, it freed itself from the models established in the 1980s and 1990s. Rachid Djaïdani's first novel *Boumkœur* (1999), prefaced by the rap group Suprême NTM, marked the beginning of a new literary production which aims to express the thoughts, cultural references and everyday experiences of youths living in the French urban periphery. This marketplace success, selling more than 100,000 copies, was followed by a series of narratives by Djaïdani (2004, 2007) as well as by Mouss Bénia (2003, 2006), Thomté Ryam (2006), Mabrouck Rachedi (2006, 2008), Skander Kali (2008), Insa Sané (2006, 2008, 2009, 2010, 2012), Mohamed Razane (2006), Karim Amellal (2006), Ahmed Djouder (2006) and others, focusing not only on young male characters living in France's underprivileged housing estates and voicing their concerns about institutional racism, discrimination and police violence targeting banlieue youths but also on their affective attachment to their neighbourhoods, solidarity with their group of peers and even love for French culture, language and literature. Soon after their emergence, banlieue narratives began to diversify. Female authors such as Faïza Guène (2004, 2006), Houda Rouane (2006), Habiba Mahany (2008, 2010) and Isabelle Pandazopoulos (2009) produced first-person narratives focusing on female coming of age in the banlieues and reflecting on particular challenges facing young Muslim women seeking love, independence and integration in a society that tends to stigmatise them.

From the late 2000s onwards, both male and female novelists started experimenting with new genres and aesthetics. Kaoutar Harchi's *Zone cinglée* (2009) is a dystopian novel reminiscent of Classical myths that depicts a war-ridden banlieue in which young men are attracted to and consumed by the hostile city centre while mothers seek to set up an army of children to protect the living from the dead. Cloé Korman's *Les Saisons de Louveplaine* (2013) is a gothic novel that explores the mysteries of an ordinary banlieue where illegal dogfights and drug trafficking coexist with neighbourhood conviviality and academic excellence. Rachid Santaki's crime novels (2011, 2012, 2013, 2014) explore crime, boxing and police corruption in the city of Saint-Denis. Sylvain Pattieu's *Des Impatientes* (2012) shows how two teenage girls excluded from their suburban high school for misconduct become strike leaders in a central Paris furniture store where they find employment. In the 2010s there emerges a stream of witness narratives including *Les Gars de Villiers* (2011) and *Nous ... la cité* (2012) in which groups of banlieue youths explore their everyday experience in writing, supported by journalists, educators and writers.

Most of these narratives share a plethora of writing strategies, including the use of slang and neologisms to imitate oral speech, humour to parody clichés and verbal violence to denounce mainstream discourses about the periphery, an emphasis on young characters' lives to show the challenges banlieue youths face, the representation of everyday life to contest the medias' exclusive focus on spectacular events and the representation of dramatic events which appeals to the reader's sympathy and identification with the suburban protagonists' struggle for recognition and respect.

Conclusions: diversifying representations of the French urban periphery

As we have seen previously, official representations of the working-class suburbs in media-political discourses and neo-liberal urban planning agendas concur to depict banlieues as homogeneous no-go zones where France's main economic and social problems are concentrated. The myth of suburban ghettos, where delinquency, crime, and Muslim fundamentalism prosper, are deeply rooted in a long genealogy of discourses established since the nineteenth century about the 'dangerous classes' living in the periphery. These discourses encourage top-down approaches focusing on security and control instead of integration, social mobility and bottom-up community initiatives.

Current debates about the banlieues are characterised by a tension between validating the myth of the ghetto and resisting it. While discourses about ghettoisation and aimless violence, de-politicisation and religious practices defying Republican principles tend to homogenise the urban periphery, resistance to this bias seeks to demonstrate the diversity that characterises the peripheral space and its inhabitants and show the great variety of practices and identities that develop in France's working-class suburbs.

Residents whose ordinary lives are rarely depicted in the media, have attempted to express their own vision of the banlieues. They have developed new forms of journalism using blogs, social media, YouTube channels and other online platforms. Artists emerging from banlieues have also engaged in various art forms, ranging from music and stand-up comedy to film and literature to reach out to wider audiences and subvert some of the dominant discourses. The residents' discontent has also recently been expressed in organised forms of political action, such as militancy and social activism. An example of this is ACLEFEU (Association Collectif, Liberté Égalité Fraternité Ensemble et Unis, pronounced '*assez le feu*' or 'no more burning'), a movement promoting voter registration in banlieues, as well as collecting citizen grievances across France and organising neighbourhood debates to give voice to marginalised working-class populations. Although these reactions have difficulty matching the broad reach of dominant narratives, they have contributed to diversifying the ways in which the urban periphery is represented.

Notes

1 Working-class suburbs around Paris where the Communist Party was deeply rooted and wielded municipal power since the 1920s and 30s.
2 See Gill Allwood's chapter in the present volume (Chapter 5) for a further overview of the ways in which gender parity in French politics has largely favoured women from superior socio-economic groups rather than women from more diverse backgrounds.
3 A play on the words '*qui fait*' and '*kiffer*,' which can be translated as 'Who makes/loves France?'

References

Alidières, B. 2010. Face à l'insécurité et aux violences faites aux personnes de sexe féminin en banlieue: éléments pour une approche géopolitique des représentations. In *Hérodote*, 136:1, 56–75.

Amara, F. and S. Zappi. 2003. *Ni Putes Ni Soumises*. Paris: La Découverte.

Angélil, M. and C. Siress. 2012. The Paris banlieue: peripheries of inequity. In *Journal of International Affairs*, 65:2, 57–67.

Belhaj Kacem, M. 2006. *La psychose française. Les banlieues: le ban de la République*. Paris: Gallimard.

Carpenter, J. and C. Horvath. 2015. *Regards croisés sur la banlieue*. Bern: Peter Lang.

Champagne, P. 1991. La construction médiatique des 'malaises sociaux.' In *Actes de la recherche en sciences sociales*, 90, 64–76.

Champagne, P. 2011. Le coup médiatique. Les journalistes font-ils l'événement? In *Sociétés et Représentation*, 2:52, 25–43.

Delphy, C. 2006. Antisexisme ou antiracisme? Un faux dilemma. In N. Guénif-Souilamas (Ed.), *La République mise à nue par son immigration*. Paris: La Fabrique, 81–108.

Desponds, D. and P. Bergel. 2015. 'La banlieue': des dynamiques complexes derrière un mot trop ordinaire. In J. Carpenter and C. Horvath (Eds.), *Regards sur la banlieue*. Brussels: Peter Lang, 23–38.

Dikeç, M. 2007. *Badlands of the Republic*. Oxford: Blackwell.

Ferenczi, A. 2015. Vingt ans après 'La Haine,' les cités, toujours grandes absentes des écrans.' In *Télérama.fr*, 1 June.

Fernando, M. L. 2014. *The Republic Unsettled: Muslim French and the Contradictions of Secularism*. Durham, NC: Duke University Press.

Fernando, M. L. 2016. Liberté, égalité, féminisme? In *Dissent*, 63:4, 38–46.

Fourcaut, A. 2004. Les premiers grands ensembles en région parisienne: ne pas refaire la banlieue? *French Historical Studies*, 27:1, 195–218.

Ghio, B. 2016. *Sans Fautes de frappe: rap et literature*. Marseille: Le mot et le reste.

Guénif-Souilamas, N. 2006a. La Française voilée, la beurette, le garçon arabe et le musulman laïc. Les figures assignées du nouveau racisme vertueux. In N. Guénif-Souilamas (Ed.), *La République mise à nue par son immigration*. Paris: La Fabrique, 109–130.

Guénif-Soulaimas, N. 2006b. The other French exception: Virtuous racism and the war of sexes in postcolonial France. In *French Politics Culture and Society*, 24:3, 23–41.

Hargreaves, A. G. 2014. De la littérature de 'beur' à la littérature de 'banlieue': des écrivains en quête de reconnaissance. In *La Marche en héritage*, *Africultures*, 97, 144–149.

Harvey, D. 2003. *Paris, Capital of Modernity*. New York: Routledge.

Higbee, W. 2007. Re-presenting the urban periphery: Maghreb-French filmmaking and the *banlieue* film. In *Cinéaste*, Winter, 38–43.

Horvath, C. 2015. L'authenticité des 'voix de la banlieue' entre témoignage et fiction. In J. Carpenter and C. Horvath (Eds.), *Regards sur la banlieue*. Brussels: Peter Lang, 183–198.

Horvath, C. 2016. Écrire la banlieue dans les années 2000–2015. In B. Wallon (Ed.), *Banlieues vues d'ailleurs. Les Essentiels d'Hermès*. Paris: CNRS Editions, 47–68.

Horvath, C. 2017. Droit de cité au féminin: femmes, espace et violence dans les récits de banlieue contemporains. In E. Faure et al. (Eds.), *La ville: quel genre?* Paris: Le Temps des Cerises, 69–97.

Khosrokhavar, F. 2013. Radicalisation in prison: The French case. In *Politics, Religion and Ideology*, 14:2, 284–306.

Kokoreff, M. and D. Lapeyronnie. 2013. *Refaire la cite*. Paris: Seuil.

Koopmans, R. 2013. Fundamentalismus und Fremden-feindlichkeit: Muslime und Christen im europäischen Vergleich. In *WZB Mitteilungen*, 142, 21–25.

Macron, E. 2015. Speech at the University of Gracques on 21 November 2015. Available at: https://en-marche.fr/articles/discours/discours-a-luniversite-des-gracques [Accessed: 31.01.2018].

Marlière, É. 2005. *Jeunes en cité: diversité des trajectoires ou destin commun?* Paris: l'Harmattan.

Maxwell, R. and E. Bleich. 2014. *What makes Muslims feel French?* In Social Forces, 93:1, 155–179.

Merlin, P. 2012. *Des Grands ensembles aux cités: L'avenir d'une utopie*. Paris: Ellipses.

Moran, M. 2011. Opposing exclusion: The political significance of the riots in French suburbs (2005–2007). In *Modern and Contemporary France*, 19:3, 297–312.

Mouhanna, C. 2009. French police and urban riots: Is the National Police Force part of the solution or part of the problem? In D. Waddington, F. Jobard and M. King (Eds.), *Rioting in the UK and France: A Comparative Analysis*. Portland, OR: Willan Publishing.

Mouterde, P. and J. Baruch. 2015. Y at-il un profil type des djihadistes français? In *Le Monde*.

Mucchielli, L. 2006. *Quelques reflexions critiques sur la 'psychopathologie des banlieues'*. Paris: J.-M. Tremblay.

Mucchielli, L. 2012. *Le scandale des 'tournantes': Dérives médiatiques, contre-enquête sociologique*. Paris: La Découverte.

Murphy, J. P. 2011. Protest or riot?: Interpreting collective action in contemporary France. In *Anthropological Quarterly*, 84:4, 977–1009.

Reeck, L. 2011. *Writerly Identities in Beur Fiction and Beyond*. Plymouth: Lexington Books.

Reeck, L. 2018. Gender and genre in banlieue film, and the guerrilla film Brooklyn. In *Journal of Romance Studies*, 36:1–2, 76–90.

Robine, J. 2004. SOS Racisme et les 'ghettos des banlieues': construction et utilisations d'une representation. In *Hérodote*, 2, 134–151.

Sedel, J. 2011. *Bondy Blog*. Le travail de représentation des «habitants de la banlieue» par un média d'information participative. In *Réseaux*, 170:6, 103–133.

Sedel, J. 2014. Les ressorts sociaux de la médiatisation des banlieues. In *Savoir/Agir.*, 28:2, 51–56.

Selby, J. A. 2011. French secularism as a 'guarantor' of women's rights? Muslim women and gender politics in a Parisian *banlieue*. In *Culture and Religion*, 12:4, 441–462.

Tarr, C. 2005. *Reframing Difference: Beur and Banlieue Filmmaking in France*. Manchester: Manchester University Press.

Tissot, S. 2007. *L'État et les quartiers. Genèse d'une catégorie de l'action publique*. Paris: Seuil.

Turpin, B. 2012. *Discours et sémiotisation de l'espace: Les représentations de la banlieue et de sa jeunesse*. Paris: L'Harmattan.

Vieillard-Baron, H. 2011. *Banlieues et périphéries*. Paris: Hachette.

Wacquant, L. 1992. Banlieues françaises et ghetto noir américain: de l'amalgame à la comparaison. In *French Politics and Society*, 10:4, 81–103.

Wacquant, L. 2016. Revisiting territories of relegation: class, ethnicity and state in the making of advanced marginality. In *Urban Studies*, 53:6, 1077–1088.

Waddington, D., F. Jobard and M. King. (Eds.). 2009. *Rioting in the UK and France: A Comparative Analysis*. Cullompton: Willan.

13

THE GOOD, THE BAD AND THE UGLY

'Banlieue youth' as a figure of speech and as speaking figures

Fabien Truong

Today, in France, the stereotype of 'banlieue youth' structures the media agenda and national imagination. From the 2005 protests to the wave of assaults starting in January and November 2015, it has increasingly important effects in the social world. In ten years, from 'the rioter' to the 'Islamist terrorist,' the figure of the *'banlieusard-de classe populaire-d'origine-immigrée-musulman'* (a person from the suburbs with working-class Muslim migrant background) has been established as the face of imminent danger. It penetrates prevailing discourse and shapes ways of seeing, thinking and believing.

The spread of neighbourhood identity police checks represents the archetype of this shaping influence. They are recurrent humiliations at an age when young people are trying to find their feet to shape their personality, particularly through opposition towards adults. This presumption of guilt is one of the reasons why some young people run away – including when they have not done anything wrong – like Zyed Benna and Bouna Traoré, who were electrocuted by an electricity transformer at the ages of 15 and 17 when they were looking for somewhere to hide to avoid a police inspection in Montfermeil on 27 October 2005. These two deaths triggered a wave of urban violence throughout France.

This stereotype is never so keenly perceived as when it stands against a positive corollary: Zinédine Zidane, Jamel Debbouze, Omar Sy, anonymous Sciences Po students who got there because of priority education conventions. Without diminishing the exemplary value of these *made-in-France success stories*, the subtext shall also be acknowledged. The 'jeunes de banlieue' can achieve excellence by exploiting their specific qualities – playing sports, cracking jokes, acting funny – recognised by positive discrimination at school. The blueprint, despite having laudable intentions, remains largely the same: 'us' and 'them.'

Deconstructing this blueprint necessitates questioning the symbolic borders on which a certain ordering of French society rests. It is also a gesture that refers to a collection of debates, in social sciences, on ways of envisaging the true–false contradictions between individual and society, practice and representation, free will and determination, the empirical and theoretical. The stances taken on the subject result in ways of observing, thinking and writing that are never neutral and often irreconcilable. It is important to recall that the tensions that play out here go far beyond the 'jeune de banlieue,' as we have got so used to making this figure of otherness bear all the evils of the nation, justifying an exceptionality that especially denotes an ordinary underlying miserabilism or populism (Grignon and Passeron 1989).

The good, the bad and the ugly

To the left of the political spectrum, the pessimists see in the 'jeune de banlieue,' an adolescent without means, more lacking in capital than young people from privileged areas. Their criminal activity and behaviours could be both a cause and a consequence of this initial deficit. Such an interpretation posits that these young people are, through no fault of their own, socially condemned to be 'the bad' or 'the ugly.' And if there are good ones, it would obviously be because sociological rules do not exist without exceptions. Optimistic populism is the romantic-revolutionary face of the same essentialist, leftist coin: 'good' may come out from the transgressive, rebellious figure of 'the bad' – or even 'the ugly.' They therefore embody rupture with an unjust social order which must, eventually, disappear. This last point assumes that a transgression of the law is a transgression of the social order, which is more of a syllogism than a balanced argument. For 15 years, this argumentative register has been progressively dismantled, appearing electorally ineffective for the Parti Socialiste in front of the fear incited by the 'scum' and 'the sociological excuse' that could be given to them (Wacquant 1999).[1]

On the right, a symmetric line of essentialism opposes vandalism and legitimism. From the point of view of the law and of morality, it is imperative to monitor and punish the bad and ugly, a mob of vandals who steal, pillage and make too much noise in public, in the name of the very protection of the good who form a silent and legitimist majority, those who work and perform – or try to – in respectful silence (*la majorité silencieuse*). On the left, defending equality: on the right, defending liberty. A question of political sides, historical traditions and prerogatives whose borders are largely porous nowadays, as sanctioned, in a certain way, by the victory of Emmanuel Macron against Marine Le Pen in the second round of the 2017 presidential elections.

The essentialist assumption asserts that young individuals always operate between the good, the bad and the ugly, without any possibility of peaceful coexistence. Indeed, there is not a good, bad or even less an ugly one *in itself* and *once and for all*. That is precisely what is forgotten by this caricatural vision of juvenile delinquency, which has become short-sighted on its left and long-sighted on its right. In only seeing all-powerful society or the king-individual as an explanatory premise there where there are actually only adolescents, these young people are no longer envisaged as *men and women of the future*. Not observed enough from the angle of their individual and social trajectories, they are observed through the prism of an instantaneous cliché, devoid of all ethnographical context.

What would have happened if Zyed Benna and Bouna Traoré had not jumped across an electricity transformer? At the time of writing, they would have been 27 and 29 years old. Where would they have lived? Would they have passed the baccalaureate exams like they too had hoped? Who would they be working for? Would they be young dads? These questions torment their loved ones. They are the simplest and most important questions that the surging discourses on banlieues practically never ask. What becomes of young people from working-class neighbourhoods?

From figures of speech to speaking figures . . .

To try to respond to these questions, I take the approach of patient observation through ethnographic investigation. I am a sociologist who has been going into working-class neighbourhoods of the Parisian banlieues for more than ten years. In brief, I observe and I participate in the social life of people who inhabit the world differently to me. Everything started in 2005 in Seine-Saint-Denis, in the north banlieue of Paris, where I was posted as a teacher in several *lycées* located in neighbourhoods where the statistical indicators fooled no one: a large majority of immigrant families, parents who were in poorly paid jobs when they were not unemployed, lower academic success rates than the national average and inversely proportional to the surrounding economic poverty. After having left my last post in *lycée* for a university post in 2010, I continued to follow the lives of around 40 of my former pupils. I learned to move with them, in time and in space. The confidence that they willingly gave me was constructed by the chance of an imposed situation: the classroom. It became stronger over time, as the stages and masks changed, the former teacher became an investigator, a confidant, an advisor, then 'someone who writes books.' At the same time, I regularly stayed in several neighbourhoods. Time there was therefore punctuated by chance encounters. My repeated stays had produced its lot of habits and customs. The 'newcomer,' through his blunders and his curiosity, had progressively made a place for himself and some allies. It is like this, in the field, that I endeavoured to question boys' transition to delinquency (Truong 2013), participation in urban protests (Truong 2017), academic trajectories (Truong 2015), growing desires for Islam or processes currently labelled as 'radicalisation' (Truong 2018).[2]

Expanding spaces, or the plurality of stages

A first key element involves *expanding the observation focus as much as possible in space,* in order to provide the means to understand the multiplicity of stages in which young people talk to each other and 'show off.' In the words of Erving Goffman (1991), the 'fields of experience' are plural. Within the same neighbourhood, several social stages exist, never occupied by each person in the same way. In that, the lexicon of 'la' cité/ 'la' banlieue (the estate/ the outskirts) is rather misleading as it consists of multiple stages which determine and predefine divided behaviours: stages concerning parents, siblings, public space, same-gender peer groups, mixed-gender peer groups, the community network, and sports clubs, relationships with young people, with old people, romantic stages, religious stages and 'business' relationships for those concerned. In Durkheimian terms, it is 'abnormal' for a young person to be able to adopt the same behaviours and the same language within different stages. What is normal is negotiating the change from one register to another and managing loyalty conflicts, that which, contrary to the image of young people as prisoners of their 'culture de banlieue,' requires fluid interactional and dispositional abilities.

It is then imperative to go beyond the topographical limits of the immediate universe of the estate. Firstly, because other stages, just as central, exist beyond its walls, primarily school. It is striking to observe that even when a school institution is physically located amid the rows of high-rise buildings, it never seems to form an integral part of 'la' cité. It always appears as an enclave, a place which drives hope as much as resentment. What occurs there marks young people in the long term, particularly because unfortunate experiences are numerous and recurrent. The experience of failure – all so relative and variable over time – is a primary biographical marker (Amrani and Beaud 2005; Le Goaziou and Mucchielli 2007), which effectively demonstrates the extent to which this situation matters. The blueprint of antagonism ('the street' against 'the school') provides narrative structure but nevertheless has its limits. Without denying the intensity of these confrontations, they end up being thought of in terms of *durable and meaningful relationships,* particularly in acknowledging the pivotal role of school (and, more generally, of public services) in young people's lives. The principle of such an opposition even acts as a departure point in my book, *Des capuches et des hommes,* contrary to common sense – starting with mine. While Radouane, Tarik and Eliott are three boys who, in the academic stages, appear to me to be rather 'good' ('deserving,' 'serious' and 'invested'), the investigation led me to understand these three pupils in a new light. I discovered that while they played the game of school in my lessons, they were also engaged at various stages in petty crime. This dichotomy of façade between the 'good' and the 'ugly' could be observed in other social stages, for example, romantic, volunteer or even sporting. Not directly opposing 'the street' with 'school' and observing, conversely, their dialectical relationships therefore makes it possible to identify better the processes of entering/ 'withdrawing' (Mohammed 2012) delinquency and assessing the stakes of schoolwork.

Finally, young people living in Parisian banlieues are not just assigned to their neighbourhood. They move about the capital, which is thus divided into a collection of subspaces that authorise each different type of practice, investment and projection (the 'Blanc Paris' [White Paris], the 'Paris Poubelle' [Garbage Paris] and the 'Paris quotidien' [Everyday Paris]; Truong 2012). They move about even more in the metropolitan area, particularly in other *banlieues* or in suburban areas further away. There are also logics of diaspora, chronic returns to the family country of origin and, for a non-negligible proportion of those pursuing their studies, journeys abroad (out of the 20 young people monitored in *Jeunesses françaises*, 11 'travelled' during the investigation). Understanding these movements makes it possible to understand why the presentation and definition of self is *malleable* and has to be *contextualised* for these young people. In *Jeunesses françaises*, Youssef presents himself differently depending on the various social stages on which he is playing. When I talked with him about schoolwork, the baccalaureate or the capital's museums, he defined himself as a 'banlieusard' and told me that he could never say that he was a 'Parisian.' When we talked football, he defined himself as a *marseillais* (a supporter of Olympique de Marseille) in opposition to his banlieusard friends who become in turn 'Parisians,' because they supported Paris Saint Germain. When we brought up his family in Tunisia and his links to their village, he defined himself by contrast as 'Parisian' because living near touristic monuments makes it possible to portray a certain image of social success and makes the objective distance from the village family acceptable. The same applied to his links to the feeling of national belonging. For example, Youssef was one of the young people who booed the national anthem at the Stade de France during the France-Tunisia football match in 2008. Analyses that only focus on the stadium tend to describe a feeling of direct opposition to France, whereas a wider observation in space (for example, Youssef wears a French football shirt printed with his name at the *lycée*) makes it possible to understand that something else other than 'identity' is occurring when he booed, in particular subjective self-evaluation of his social position in a country that he never rejects, doubled with a temporary correction/inversion of stigma.

Drawing out time, or the plurality of trajectories

Advocating the observation of the plurality of social stages, an interpersonal and process-led approach is favoured over a culturalist and fixed one. It also calls for *drawing out time*. Carrying out a study over time and on time seems to me to be the only possible strategy to re-establish 'youth' as a moment – of which the social meaning and connotation translate into a certain state of power ratios in the social world and not into a single state (Bourdieu 1984). Re-establishing the pathways of young banlieusards over time is all the more important as they are never linear, including for those who 'succeed.' The quest for qualifications and for a 'position' in the working world is carried out through a series of trials of adjustments and turnarounds. It simply *takes time*, the reason why one-off observations or observations of too short a duration run the risk of reifying that which is the order of passage and of categorising that which is only a stage, in a more comprehensive process.

Therefore, it is around the organisation of time, represented by higher education, that the subject matter of *Jeunesses françaises* is organised. In following the succession of the same collective chronological sequences (*lycée* [secondary education for children between the ages of 15 and 18] and the baccalaureate, the bac+3 path [3 years at university following the baccalaureate], the bac+5 path [5 years at university following the baccalaureate]; entry into working life), it is possible to see how these temporal markers structure the same generation of pupils. In addition, it can be understood why, between these different boundaries, that time never passes as 'quickly' and as 'positively' for each and every person. The question of reconfigurations between expectations and aspirations does not nevertheless change in the case of pursuing studies. In order to learn to study, it is necessary to come to rationalise studying in an effort of reframing which happens both on the content and the container of the lessons given. This aims to comprehend why expectations – that correspond to the desire to finish or to the need to continue – will never be completely satisfied. It explains, in large part, the many dropouts, breaks and other retakes, that the frequent recourse to paid employment emphasises, the back-and-forths between student status and employee status contributing to a smokescreen effect. We are far from the official temporal blueprint that governs the underlying rationale of higher education: straightforward journeys where knowledge is accumulated in order to maximise young people's future.

These discontinuities help to underline the micro-differences between banlieusards. It can be observed that, at comparable lower social conditions and positions, the gradients of individual trajectories operate fully. Small initial advantages end up making significant differences (association of trailblazers, thwarted academic pathways among parents projected onto their offspring, professions with small advantages in kind, family diaspora, comparative advantages of certain types of 'casual work,' ability to travel, upkeep of 'erotic capital,'[3] religious or voluntary engagement). But they only become active if other processes are set in motion in parallel. It is not possible to observe what the effects of these micro-differences are in the short term, precisely because, unlike 'major capitals' whose profitability is sufficiently substantial to appear relatively quickly to the external observer, small resources generate small profits and are never *immediately* profitable. They differentiate little when compared between those (and at the beginning of their journey) which are further from criteria of social and academic legitimacy. And yet, they matter, producing their effect and making consequential differences in the medium term.

An observation over a period of seven years after the bac also facilitates the conclusion that the 'lower qualifications,' despite deceptions and disillusions, always pay off a little. In *Jeunesses françaises*, those surveyed who stopped before the bac+3 nearly all managed to convert the general baccalaureate and the fact that they had studied for a few years afterwards into objective professional resources: Kader (dropped out during L2, the second year of university) passed a competitive exam for the Civil Service; Hakan (dropped out during the second year of STS [*sections de techniciens supérieurs* – a type of vocational course]) landed a permanent contract in sales; Hacene (did not drop out but did not make any progress in L2) won the confidence of an events organisation who sponsored his training in logistics; Fanta (failed to reach L3, the third year of university, after the BTS [*brevet technicien supérieur* – a qualification like the Higher National Diploma]) lined up temporary contracts without ever experiencing a period of prolonged unemployment. The question of course remains of knowing whether what has been gained is as much as what had been hoped for. But observing what these young people became over a prolonged period helped to put the 'difficult' initial years back into perspective. The discourse on the 'failure of integration' therefore becomes more nuanced and the frustrations and the feeling of 'duty done' appear for what they are: social constructions and symbolic rationalisations. 'Integration' is only mysterious if one tries to envisage it as an objectifiable state – that is, as a collection of de-contextualised or quantified data to be evaluated.

The plurality of trajectories makes it possible to understand why the ways in which each social situation is invested are never fixed over time. If we take for example the mental map of Paris, it can be observed that as time passes, '*le Blanc Paris*,' '*le Paris poubelle*' and '*le Paris quotidien*' change in meaning, grow larger or contract, and that the amplitude of these changes is strongly linked to academic trajectories. With regard to turning to Islam – a subject on which the most fixed and caricatural remarks are made (Hajjat and Mohammed 2013) – the variety of do-it-yourself practices, the relative intensity of ostentatious practices, the more or less significant importance of religious belief and the ability or inability to delimit a certain number of practices through time encourage reconsideration of social practices which are mobilised above all as resources in changing situations. In *Radicalized Loyaties*, we also clearly see the extent of the difference between decided and faltering entries into religion – very often experienced by boys as an about-turn or a show of rebellion – and the routinisation of religious practice which subsequently begins. Once the excitement of conversion ends, a more ambivalent moment of 'reconversion' through Islam follows. It is precisely during this lengthy period of reconversion that the transition from an exclusive and excluding religion to a more tolerant religion takes place. It is also during this lengthy period that it can be understood how 'the same causes' do not always have the 'same effects' – like in the case of Adama, a close friend of Amédy Coulibaly, who, although he experienced the same 'difficulties,' did not take the same deadly path. Finally, these processes always gain from being re-situated in the drawn-out time of history and in the memory of the observed communities and neighbourhoods, the family dynasties, the history of colonisation and 'long-term crisis' (Beaud and Pialoux 2013).

Surveying individuals, or the plurality of cases

Having 'expanded space' and 'drawn out time,' ethnography proves to be particularly invaluable when it 'thinks by case,' to adopt Jean-Claude Passeron and Jacques Revel's phrase (Passeron and Revel 2005). Studying cases *comparatively* transforms the density of observations into effective resources for considering the consistency and the disparities with the norm and for comprehending the dialectics between categories and their 'loop effects.' At this point, comparison is essential: it is the way in which a case is made a case, in other words an element that only exists in relation to another and makes it possible to grasp that uniqueness is constructed around a collection of generic attributes and statistical regularities.

'Thinking by case' also makes it possible to have an approach that is less overarching and more detailed with regard to mechanisms of domination, particularly when there are so many of them. The 'jeunes de banlieues' must construct themselves in relation to racism, territorial stigma, class contempt, cultural illegitimacy and phobias related to immigration or to the practice of Islam – forms of subordination which also take different forms depending on gender relations. These cases help to guard against poor uses of intersectionality which view plurality of levels of legitimacy either as an accumulation of 'handicaps' or as an opposition of contradictory principles ('class' against 'race,' 'gender' against 'race,' etc.). Indeed, detailed observation shows that in terms of stigma, reversals and fluctuations are never synchronous. Trajectories, just like configurations, perceptibly alter the respective power of stigma and the room available for manoeuvre. Using cases also makes it possible to see how young banlieusards learn to *progressively* 'rock' between the different borders which make up the social world and to see how certain dispositions are accrued, mobilised in certain situations and left on standby at other times. It is the 'rocking horse' mechanism described in *Jeunesses françaises*. Looking at cases makes it possible to report sociologically on statistically unlikely pathways (for example, it is possible to consider the case of Irfan who became a schoolteacher after failing the bac three times). Uniqueness is not constructed against but on social determinations. Finally, it is what the cases explain when they illustrate the fact that young people in banlieues do not only characterise themselves by what differentiates them from other young people in France: the lack of symbolic and political perspectives, the fear of 'corporate life' and of the precariat, disenchantment with regard to the meritocracy that I was able to observe absolutely not being *banlieue specific*.

Conclusions

It is stupefying to see to what extent the passionate bursts about the disappearance of national identity are the discourses taking place from 'up high' in the name of 'France below.' What is said by the sycophants of roots identity does not refer to working class banlieues. They produce images from other images which say more about their own social and individual attributes and about their deep concerns. The pertinent question is not that of belonging and roots, but of the way in which adolescents from working-class neighbourhoods find their place despite everything. A place which moves over time, depending on different stages and interlocuters. In the facts, the bodies and time, it is never a question of 'integration' (present or absent), but of relationships, learnings and attitudes. It is here that isolation and impossibility can be understood. Delinquency, physical or verbal violence and academic failure are anchored in the landscape of working-class neighbourhoods. But instead of attacking or defending, taking distance makes it possible to situate. For example, while the fear of Islam has become widespread, we must return to the facts and the practices. What can be observed? That for juvenile delinquents, escaping delinquency often occurs through involvement with religion, all the more effectively when it is combined with professional integration and a lasting love story. For banlieusard students, religious practice helps them to confront difficulties. Religion offers, under certain conditions, favourable contexts for starting work and for academic cultural integration. It presides there where, in other configurations, different social practices cause the emergence of similar levers: self-confidence, certainty of having made the 'right choices,' organising work, behavioural routines. Establishing candidate profiles for Jihadist terrorism does not suggest anything else. Religious practices depend on context, on encounters, on the slope of trajectories and on the emptiness that they replace. So many nuances that are erased by debates about 'radicalisation' when this term becomes a new black box for commentators in a rush. Navigating in between 'the good,' 'the bad' and 'the ugly' may demonstrate our capacity to change collective representations and to not fear nuance and ambivalence. It is a great challenge, commensurate with the simplicity of the high priests of identity politics.

Translated by Georgia Corp

Notes

1 The speech of socialist prime minister Valls on 25 November 2015 which strongly criticised the 'social, sociological and cultural excuses' appears from this point of view as a grand finale for the Parti Socialiste. On the progressive imposition of the international rhetoric of the 'criminalisation of misery' in public debate and on how it shows a widespread reconfiguration of the penal state in contemporary neo-liberal capitalism, see Wacquant, L. 1999. *Les prisons de la misère*. Paris: Raisons d'agir.

2 Truong, F. 2018. *Radicalized Loyalties: Becoming Muslim in the West*. Cambridge: Polity Press. A section of this book is dedicated to carrying out a post-mortem ethnography of Amédy Coulibaly, one of the three perpetrators of the January 2015 terrorist attacks, through interviewing his close relations and through trying to respond to the reverse question: 'What happened to the boy "of before"?'

3 On the controversial question of 'erotic capital' and on the idea that it is utilised more by men than women, see Hakim, C. 2011. *Erotic Capital: The Power of Attraction in the Boardroom and the Bedroom*. New York: Basic Books.

References

Amrani, Y. and S. Beaud. 2005. *Pays de malheur! Un jeune de cité écrit à un sociologue.* Paris: La Découverte.

Beaud, S. and M. Pialoux. 2013. *Violences urbaines, violence sociale: genèse des nouvelles classes dangereuses.* Paris: Hachette.

Bourdieu, P. 1984. *Questions de sociologie.* Paris: Minuit.

Goffman, E. 1991. *Les cadres de l'expérience.* Paris: Minuit.

Grignon, C. and J-C. Passeron. 1989. *Le savant et le populaire: misérabilisme et populisme en sociologie et en littérature.* Paris: Gallimard.

Hajjat, A. and M. Mohammed. 2013. *Islamophobie: comment les élites françaises fabriquent le "problème musulman."* Paris: La Découverte.

Hakim, C. 2011. *Erotic Capital: The Power of Attraction in the Boardroom and the Bedroom.* New York: Basic Books.

Mucchielli, L. and V. Le Gouziou. 2007. *Quand les banlieues brûlent. . . Retour sur les émeutes de novembre 2005.* Paris: La Découverte.

Mohammed, M. (Ed.). 2012. *Les sorties de délinquance: théories, méthodes, enquêtes.* Paris: La Découverte.

Ott, L. 2007. Pourquoi ont-ils brûlé les écoles? In V. Le Goaziou and L. Mucchielli (Eds.), *Quand les banlieues brûlent . . . Retour sur les émeutes de 2005.* Paris: La Découverte, 126–144.

Passeron, J-C. and J. Revel. (Eds.). 2005. *Penser par cas.* Paris: Éditions de l'EHESS.

Truong, F. 2012. Au-delà et en deçà du Périphérique. Circulations et représentations territoriales de jeunes habitants de Seine-Saint-Denis dans la métropole parisienne. In *Métropoles*, 11 [Online].

Truong, F. 2013. *Des capuches et des hommes: Trajectoires de 'jeunes de banlieues.'* Paris: Buchet-Chastel.

Truong, F. 2015. *Jeunesses françaises: Bac+ 5 made in banlieue.* Paris: La Découverte.

Truong, F. 2017. Total rioting: from metaphysics to politics. In *The Sociological Review*, 65:4, 563–577.

Truong, F. 2018. *Radicalized Loyalties: Becoming Muslim in the West.* Cambridge: Polity Press.

Wacquant, L. 1999. *Les prisons de la misère.* Paris: Raisons d'agir.

14
NIGHTCLUBS AND NATIONAL BELONGING

Malek Boutih's solutions for personal and national insecurity

Mehammed Mack

I'm not a theorist, but I think it's paradoxically easier to talk about discrimination at work, in terms of housing, and other things, than to speak about . . . nightclubs. Why? Because it goes back to the sexual question. And it's obvious that within the question of racism, at its heart, there is a fear, a fear of the male person of color who comes to fuck (*baiser*) the white woman, and vice versa. [. . .] And in the nightclubs if there is so much tension, such a racism problem, it's because it's linked to that.[1]

Zinédine Zidane, a French football star of Algerian background who may retain the greatest name recognition among Frenchmen outside France, has long been considered a symbol of the beauty of French diversity, if not an outright sex symbol. He has several times been voted France's most handsome athlete (Editors sport.fr 2002), was deemed the sixth most handsome man in the world in a 2005 TF1 poll, and second most handsome Frenchman (behind only Patrick Bruel, also of Algerian descent) among French voters (Editors comlive.net 2002). He has appeared in 'Sexiest Man Alive' lists almost every year thereafter, and not just in France. There was a time in the not so distant past, however, when it was rare to find men of Arab or North African descent at the top of any such French lists, a time when Arab physiques, features, or clothing styles were aesthetically denigrated in popular culture and common parlance, as attested to in the body of memoirs and childhood narratives often referred to as *beur* literature.[2] The topics of self-perception and body image among Arabs in France have often been vexed since immigrants as well as French Algerians arrived in great numbers from North Africa in the 1960s. They have been especially vexed for the descendants who followed in their footsteps, left to compare themselves with unspoken but ever-present standards of beauty in fashion and advertising that remain principally tall, white and thin, this despite French demographic studies suggesting the unacknowledged centrality of *métissage* (that is to say racial and cultural mixing), foreign origins (concerning one out of three French nationals according to Gérard Noiriel 2006) and mixed marriages in the national make-up, not just during the postcolonial period but also over the course of the *longue durée* (Noiriel 2006).

A central focus of this chapter is a dramatic exchange from the year 2000 on evolving notions of Franco-Arab body image that speaks volumes about the aesthetic depreciation and sudden revalorisation of Arabs and banlieusards[3] as possible sources of beauty. The printed exchange, now out of print and unavailable online, took place between two prominent French anti-discrimination activists early on in their careers: Malek Boutih, then president of SOS Racisme and a fixture of the centre left Parti Socialiste (PS), and Fouad Zeraoui, a nightlife entrepreneur behind a popular and long-lived gay club night called 'Black Blanc Beur' in Paris. Zeraoui is also the founder of an expansive online social network for French men of colour and their admirers, called *Kelma*, or 'word' in Arabic. The premise and also title of their exchange was 'Homophobia in the banlieues,' the banlieues being working-class suburbs and housing projects with high concentrations of residents of North African and sub-Saharan African descent. Zeraoui and Boutih discuss how minority self-perception can be reflected in clothing choices and behaviour in nightclubs, a terrain common to both Boutih and Zeraoui.[4] Their exchange is notable for its intimate frankness in addressing painful notions of body shame, internalised self-hatred and racism. The interview took place in 2000, originally published within the pages of Zeraoui's now defunct publication *Baby Boy* (once available in Paris gay nightclubs and gay-interest stores), at a time when SOS Racisme, an anti-discrimination group connected to the state, seemed to be making overtures to its LGBT activist peers. The interview had been posted to the Kelma.org website, and has appeared in several other academic bibliographies, but it has since mysteriously been removed, while articles from the same *Kelma* media archive it originally appeared in have remained.

In this chapter, I argue that activists of a certain stripe, whose mission it is to advocate for sexual and ethnic minorities in France's multi-ethnic suburbs, tend to stigmatise locals' efforts to conceive of their own beauty and self-worth, because it would too proudly resemble communitarian pride, the enemy of Republican unity. I use a discourse analysis and cultural studies approach to examine seemingly innocuous rhetoric about fashion and beauty to extract far from harmless conclusions about the futility and morbidity of banlieue and Arab life trajectories. This is also a story that relates how an insider political operative who symbolically represents France's diversity (selected due to his spotless, secular, anti-communitarian credentials) has no choice but to adopt rhetoric that denigrates non-white forms of beauty because of these credentials. While recognising the need to restore the self-esteem of constantly scrutinised banlieue populations, Boutih's ideological commitments to anti-communitarianism[5] inhibit his efforts and produce not only cognitive dissonance but the opposite of his aims: a population made to feel that it has no intrinsic worth. At the point of his utmost prominence in 2015, when he was commissioned by former prime minister Manuel Valls to produce a report on the radicalisation of French youth (*Génération Radicale*; Boutih 2015), Boutih found himself making connections between societal rejection at both the professional and romantic levels. More profoundly, I argue, he warned of this 'sacrificed' generation's pathways towards self-destruction, pathways whose logical outcomes tend toward nihilistic urban riots and, finally, (suicide) terrorism.

Boutih inadvertently produces a stigmatisation of the communities he tries to defend through his anti-discrimination campaign, a stigmatisation that especially targets the way young Arab and black French youth 'style' themselves. He details how sartorial expression and body language can be indicative of a larger social isolation: for Boutih, banlieue youth's physical envelope becomes a transmitter of social messages conveying hostility not only toward greater France but also to oneself. Clothing style is one of Boutih and Zeraoui's concerns primarily due to their familiarity with nightclub spaces, which have been an important site for Boutih's anti-discrimination campaigns. Nightclubs also constitute an exhibition space for the banlieusard street style that Zeraoui observes weekly, a style faulted by many outside observers as 'aggressive' but which has nevertheless inspired many an haute-couture designer and film-maker. My intervention examines more broadly a pattern according to which anti-discrimination activists aiming to combat

social alienation and segregation in the *banlieue* actually reify them through Othering vocabular-
ies of gender that pathologise Arab-authored dress, self-styling, customs of salutation and body
language. The exchange that occurred in 2000 ('*l'homophobie en banlieue*') illuminates the seeds
of the model-minority-tough-on-his-peers-persona that the then activist Boutih would later
incarnate as a seasoned politician in 2015, tasked with crafting the nation's response to Islamic
terrorism in the wake of the *Charlie Hebdo* attacks.

Boutih and Zeraoui's respective backgrounds help put into context this exchange, especially
because their itineraries exemplify the various cross-pollinations that can occur between anti-
racist and anti-sexist groups. Boutih held political office as a congressional deputy representing the 10th conscription of the Essonne department, from 2012 to 2017. He was the party's
national secretary in charge of social issues from 2003 to 2008, and also served on the Commission for the Armed Forces and National Defence at the National Assembly. Boutih has in
recent history developed professional links with high-profile anti-sexism activists working in
the banlieues, the most well-known being former government minister Fadela Amara, founder
of the banlieue women's rights group *Ni Putes Ni Soumises*, who declared him one of her first
major supporters (Amara and Zappi 2004: 89). After Amara and Rachida Dati (who were ushered into the Sarkozy administration in a then unprecedented push for diversity), he is one of
the most visible Franco-Arab politicians, but also one of those most criticised by Franco-Arab
commentators and other scholars of immigration, mainly due to his assimilationist politics, and
his willingness to say out loud what other politicians might only think or whisper, especially
when making generalisations about banlieue residents, Islam or the politics of security.[6] Like
Amara, Boutih came into politics from activist roots in the banlieues, but later in his career opted
for a stridently critical turn in regards to banlieue 'delinquents' as he approached the political
centre. This 'tough' approach, which banked on community self-criticism, afforded him the
appearance of greater integrity and granted him greater visibility and responsibility in the Parti
Socialiste, especially when he was tasked with commenting on issues related to diversity and
immigration. However, Boutih's arguably assimilationist path through the fair-weather friend-
ships of French party politics was not without setbacks and rejections from both the banlieue
base and the political elite. His attempts to appeal to greater France did not always achieve
their desired objective, as controversial remarks from Gérard Longuet made clear in a speech in
March 2010, when Longuet was lead senator of the right-wing UMP (Union pour un mouvement popuaire) party. At the time, Boutih was running for a spot on the HALDE,[7] an administrative body responsible for monitoring discrimination: 'It would be better for someone from
the traditional French social body (*du corps français traditionnel*) to be responsible for welcoming
all our compatriots. [. . .] If you put someone symbolic and exterior there, you risk failing the
operation' (Editors saphirnews.com 2010). Boutih's sometimes bumpy political itinerary makes
his interview remarks on how Arab youth do not 'fit in' all the more notable. In his exchange
with Zeraoui, who advocates for gay banlieue youth of colour, Boutih first articulates in striking fashion the same essentialist critiques of immigrant 'sexism' that were later reproduced by
feminist and LGBT activists like Fadela Amara and Franck Chaumont. Some have suggested that
their highly critical and inflexible approaches to their target populations helped them eventually
get recruited for important positions in government (Marteau 2006).

Boutih's interviewer, Fouad Zeraoui, has been an unmistakable face in Paris gay nightlife
circles, ever since his famed Black Blanc Beur dance party launched in the mid-1990s. The club
night opened its doors to a mix of 'out' as well as discreet patrons who flocked to its doors for
various reasons: they did not want to run the risk of being discovered in areas publicly known
as gay, they found the 'gay ghetto' of the Marais to be a discriminatory environment, they liked
the 'tea dance' hours (7 pm to midnight originally) that allowed patrons to catch the last train

from Paris back to the banlieues (Garcia 2002). In newspapers and several gay-interest films where it appeared, Black Blanc Beur was heralded as a place of joyful inclusivity and diversity in a mostly white nightlife scene, a refuge for those rejected, exotified, or taken for sex workers in the Marais. While Zeraoui launched his club to offer patrons a sanctuary from sometimes hostile families and neighbourhoods, more recently Zeraoui has tried to offer French gay men of colour sanctuary from discrimination and also criticism emanating from the homonormative mainstream, in which 'outness' is required and where Islamic cultures often face condemnation. Zeraoui has always paid keen attention to incidents of homophobia in the banlieues, but more recently (2009) he has become sensitive to the instrumentalisation of homophobia toward xeno- phobic and anti-immigration ends: gays and lesbians from the banlieues have been shamed for the supposed anti-modernity of their attachments to community, religion and discretion, as seen in the exposé about gay life in the banlieues *Homo-Ghetto*, which still serves as the main refer- ence on the topic (Chaumont 2009). In a 2010 interview in *Têtu* magazine, Zeraoui contested the ideas that the banlieues were completely inhospitable for homosexuals, and that children of North and West African immigrants were the most homophobic: he even went so far as to say that the banlieue's gay and lesbian population were able to 'make it' (out of the banlieues, or in terms of professional and social success) in ways that their heterosexual counterparts could not (Chaumont and Zeraoui 2009).

The seeds of Zeraoui's eventual change of heart are apparent, ten years earlier, in this exchange with Boutih. The exchange importantly gives insight into how those activists who have got their start advocating against sexual intolerance in communities of colour can, through repeated exposure and disillusionment with the campaign against the very wrong one is try- ing to combat, make a 180-degree turn. In so doing, they can break partnerships with previous allies, allies whose criticism of a given community is not always motivated by reasons of personal concern for that community. Zeraoui seemed to have realised a decade into his activism that former allies against banlieue sexism did not seek to bring sociocultural reform and education initiatives to banlieues so as to make them more hospitable for women and homosexuals, but rather to recommend ways 'out.' This opposition between goals is a reiteration of the escape nar- rative or '*Faut-il en sortir pour s'en sortir?*' question: does one have to leave it in order to make it?

Boutih's commentary, both in the 2000 exchange and his later rhetoric, is especially remark- able for how exhaustively it fleshes out the sexual demonisation of immigrant and banlieusard communities that had been building up since the 1960s. Sexual violence, harassment, machismo, gang rapes, together become representative behaviours of a 'sick' rapport to gender and sexual- ity that has crossed the Mediterranean and infected Europe (Daoud 2016). Contributing to the negative portrait of banlieue youth is a pattern of representation collectively understood as *misérabilisme* (a loose equivalent to the 'culture of poverty' in the US), defined by its insist- ence on cyclical failure, suffering, impossibility of resilience, bleak professional and roman- tic horizons, all of which are to blame on the population in question. Sexual demonisation and *misérabilisme* are an aggressive/passive couplet that would together result in the social and romantic rejection that befall banlieue youth in nightclubs, as discussed in Boutih and Zeraoui's exchange. However, one might be justified in hoping that their encounter could be generative of something more productive: the anti-discrimination group SOS Racisme is dealing here with a sister organisation of sorts (*Kelma* working to stop a different but no less insidious type of discrimination: homophobia), and this permits some important conceptual breakthroughs, some 'aha' moments that illuminate the commonalities between discriminations based on race, class and sexuality, in other words, their intersectionality. Through speaking with the founder of *Kelma*, the SOS Racisme activist comes to realise the centrality of sexuality to the social issues under his purview: especially as regards nightlife discrimination, their common terrain. In this sense, talking about homosexuality (the premise of their interview) allows them to broach the sexual undercurrents of issues like nightlife discrimination. This breakthrough constitutes a type of 'interpenetration' – or productive encounter of active minorities in public space, as described by Nilüfer Göle (2005).

With such familiarity and solidarity between groups also come several asides that seem perhaps too raw, too expository: secrets uttered in the company of friends that depart from the politically cautious tones usually adopted by SOS Racisme. That organisation has long been considered by more radical members of the anti-racist community in France to be a co-optation of the ethnic solidarity marches and movements of the 1980s, such as the *marches pour l'égalité et contre le racisme* of 1982 and 1983. It is an organisation that aims for a race-blind universalist society and discourages ethnic and community pride as a form of political mobilisation. The accusatory and harsh tones taken by Boutih when it comes to the topic of Franco-Arab groups and gangs follow from the nature of SOS Racisme's strong anti-communitarianism agenda. This tone is surprisingly discriminatory for an anti-discrimination activist, as I intend to show, because it zeroes in on Arab and banlieusards' stylistic choices as particularly representative of a pathological groupthink in which the group always eclipses the individual, a groupthink that reflects a toxic communitarianism.

Nightclubs, beauty and selectivity

One of the high points of Boutih's career at SOS Racisme was the implementation of a discrimination-monitoring mechanism called 'testing.' Testing was a method by which anti-discrimination groups would send out identically dressed parties of patrons to nightclubs, at a time interval, with the sole difference between the two groups being their racial composition, all this in order to monitor discrimination. Other such 'testing' experiments targeted job and housing discrimination: identical applications were sent to the offices in question with the only difference being the ethnic or religious origins suggested by the applicants' names.[8] Boutih's activism also secured the judicial recognition of the testing technique as admissible evidence in court. Testing is all the more of an accomplishment as it allowed for the measurement of discrimination without soliciting anyone for their racial or religious affiliations, a practice forbidden under French law (a considerable limitation when it comes to measuring discrimination overall). In the *Baby Boy* exchange, Zeraoui emphasises 'testing,' one of Boutih's most creative and successful campaigns, in order to highlight the intersection of the spaces (nightclubs) that he and Boutih inhabit, and to raise more importantly the issue of Franco-Arab image and its sometimes vexed correlation with access to nightlife. This allows the conversation to turn to self-presentation and self-image: unavoidable concerns when one is grooming oneself in preparation for a night on the town. Zeraoui uses the feel-good example of Zidane as his entry point:

ZERAOUI: There is something which has fascinated me, what some have called the World Cup effect of 1999. We place much emphasis on the impact of the 'Black Blanc Beur' team that notched the victory, but one effect less noticed is the Zidane effect, but for other reasons. Zidane was the great goal-scorer of France's team, but Zidane is also a beautiful guy. He made the covers of magazines, he did publicity campaigns for Dior, and I don't think this has made an impact yet in French minds, that a *beur* could be handsome, 'beautiful' (*in English*). And that [...] don't you think these are things which can help the thingamajig progress (*faire avancer le schmilblick*)? We don't say it enough. It's almost a taboo. A desirable *beur*.

BOUTIH: And why is it a taboo? That's also one of my analyses, one of my observations. I believe that within the crisis that exists in the banlieue, what I call the identity crisis, it's not a crisis simply in social, and intellectual terms etc. It's true that people rarely say it, but I don't have any shame in telling you: the people are closing in on themselves (*se referment sur eux-mêmes*). These youth have a physical complex. They have ended up internalising the bad image they have of themselves.

Boutih attributes banlieusards' inability to recognise their own beauty to a 'physical complex' which causes a self-isolation that is both geographic (the banlieues are cut-off from the city) and personal (banlieusards have turned inward and become hermits out of supposed shame). Notably, Boutih rewords Zeraoui's phrase about a 'desirable beur' being 'almost taboo' such that it is no longer society that is at fault for its failure to recognise Arab beauty but rather the fault of French Arabs themselves. This rephrasing permits the introduction of 'blameworthiness': are French-Arabs blameworthy for the way they approach nightclubs and, more importantly, themselves?

Zinédine Zidane's beauty – a topic that seems random at first but then begins to make sense once the question of discriminating door policies at clubs comes up – provides an interesting response to (and rebuttal of the terms of) this last question. In Zeraoui's mind, the Zidane era of multicultural celebration and the rallying slogan 'Black Blanc Beur' (Tiloune 2006) is one in which a France newly energised by the salutary promise of multi-ethnicity would cease to discriminate at its elite establishments and would instead embrace Arab beauty as something to prize and feature in selective spaces like nightclubs – keep in mind this interview took place less than two years after France's victory in the World Cup. This slogan was popularised during the celebratory atmosphere following the French national football team's 1998 victory, but Zeraoui predated this usage, employing it as a moniker for his club night as early as 1996. Nightclubs, not only in France but around the Western world, will often proclaim unashamedly, 'we maintain the right to be selective,' thus enveloping in the private sphere the right to discriminate based on external factors like dress code, which can very often cloak discriminations based on class, gender and race, all used to streamline a certain clientele. These factors intermingle in one of the most recognisable bogeymen of sexual stigmatisation, the Arab sexual menace, a stereotype informed by an enduring legacy of emphasising Muslim/Arab sexual aggressivity (Shepard 2017). Recognising Arab beauty at the nightclub door, however, might possibly work to reduce nightlife discrimination. With his universal(ist) desirability, Zidane undoes the damage of an ego-puncturing amalgamation Zeraoui and Boutih often worry about: the connection of nightclub rejection to feelings of ugliness and lack of social worth.

The costly consequences of nightclub rejection have recently become a focus of social science. The French sociologist Eric Marlière (2011) authored a book-length study on 'youth and the discotheque,' which looks at two nightlife spaces within the Paris agglomeration (Paris' Bastille neighbourhood and the north banlieue of Cergy), and focuses on the incidence of violence, competition, aggressive flirting, as well as on the security arrangements and relations among peer groups that structure and divide these spaces. As seen in Marlière's book, the judgments (resulting in rejection) made at nightclub entrances are often shrouded in the management's right to maintain a selective dress code. These rejections can produce resentments that reinforce other rejections, creating a snowball effect whose gravity quickly escalates: rejected club patrons 'loiter' around the areas in question and loudly ruminate in their frustration, disturbing the peace. The Bastille neighbourhood, located within a hip and very policed part of Paris, is an area where these youth run the risk of attracting negative attention, possibly risking arrest. The doorpersons' decisions are not without consequences for the neighbourhoods in question and can foster ethnic enmity between the nightclub clientele and local residents. The rejected patrons go, in the space of a night, from an attitude of aspirational assimilation into the beautiful crowd, hoping to join the nation at the level of the dance floor, to reinforcing society's stigma of banlieusard populations by incarnating a stereotype of rage (*la haine, avoir la rage*), precisely out of frustration with that very stereotype (which had been a basis for rejecting them from the club in the first place). In his 2015 'Génération Radicale' report, Boutih labelled the snowball-ing movement from rejection to rejection and failure to failure *l'effet cicatrice* (the scar effect), for the way it mines the confidence of youth and creates permanent social damage (Boutih 2015: 13). In this way, the rejected illustrate the tragic phenomenon of the *absence de souci de soi*, as articulated by Nacira Guénif-Souilamas (2004), a process by which those stigmatised by society respond by adopting risky behaviours that are bound to provoke serious social opprobrium and legal consequences for themselves, in a way that eventually exacerbates the first stigmatisation, the first rejection. Boutih himself echoed this in his 2015 report, underlining one diagnostic that found French youth to be 'careless (*insouciant(e)*), so much do certain of their behaviours betray a manifest denial of danger, but also an increasing lack of well-being' (Boutih 2015: 15). Alarm-ingly, the values that animate 'dangerous' behaviour (especially at the sexual level) in nightclubs are exactly those ordinarily commissioned to reinforce the self-esteem of French youth, as Boutih concludes in his report:

> The thirst for peer recognition and the valorisation of one's image – which boils down to mastering one's reputation, to be high-performing – stems from a logic of domina-tion: the imperative to affirm virility for boys and only radical choices (all or nothing) in terms of sexuality for the girls.
>
> *(Boutih 2015: 21)*

These imperatives feed into the pressure cooker that is the modern nightclub, a place where competitive tensions can boil over into violence. Boutih emphasises both in the 2000 exchange with Zeraoui and in his 2015 report the idea that the best way to alleviate the 'sexual misery' afflicting French youth from underprivileged backgrounds (males in particular) is sexual educa-tion. He proposes a radical solution to the problem of young men being 'deprived of encounters with women of their generation,' one that calls for increased *mixité* (or co-ed mingling) in all manner of social and cultural activities:

> We must favour *mixité* in sports, at school, and especially at the level of leisure activities. Why not experiment with, on this topic, opening 'nightclubs' managed by associations and publicly financed. The hatred that erupts in 'rejects' from nightclubs carries enor-mous frustration and hatred (his repetition). The more you meet young people your age, the more one flirts, the more exchanges one has, the more you take an intimate distance from the logic of radicalisation.
>
> *(Boutih 2015: 54)*

The state can seduce youth away from the lure of radicalisation by seducing them at a more physical level. Fifteen years after his first interview with Zeraoui, the primacy of nightclubs as a social barometer that takes the temperature of race relations has not lessened; on the contrary, the stakes are mortally higher, at the level of national security and terrorism prevention. While recognising beauty and aesthetic merit at the nightclub door might otherwise seem a trivial issue, nightclubs, as Boutih and Zeraoui show, are often the site of a first rejection on a tragic trajectory that later leads to violence and possibly mass killing (Richet 1997).

Zeraoui's surprise at the notion that a beur could be beautiful might itself seem surprising to outside observers of France not already exposed to a certain tradition of insults in argotic

French lore (Elbadawi 2014). Various pejoratives for the epithet 'Arab' have often been synonymous not only with racial disparagement but also ugliness, otherness, dirtiness, and animalisation ('*bougnoule*,' '*raton*,' '*bicot*,' '*métèque*' and '*sale arabe*'). Sensitivities today have mercifully done away with the acceptability of such terms in articulating racial difference as aesthetically and hygienically compromised, at least out loud. Generations of Franco-Arab writers and filmmakers, however, remember so viscerally being at the receiving end of such epithets that these memories show up recurrently in cultural production as traumatic episodes in playground, classroom, and public transport scenes.[9] Such self-consciousness about the aesthetic 'devaluation' of ethnic difference is evident, for example, in the elaborate manoeuvres by which literary and film protagonists of North African background conceal their ethnicities in order to appear more attractive. In the cinema of Malik Chibane, for example, they pose as Italians, usually to avoid anticipated rejection by women:[10] this ethnic drag technique was taken to comical extremes in the film *L'Italien*,[11] in which actor Kad Merad must come out of the closet as an Arab after using an Italian cloak to meet his career and relationship goals. Doubly ironic is the fact that Kad Merad, who is of Algerian descent, has been a symbol of success among Franco-Arab actors, due to being cast in mostly non-Arab roles, thus escaping the sentence of 'ethnic' type-casting which severely limits one's options for roles.

As if to rectify years of aesthetic depreciation, it is pertinent that Zeraoui chose as a motto for the promotion of his Black Blanc Beur club night the slogan 'beur is beautiful,' a message that borrows from the 1960s and 1970s US ethnic pride movements that valorised African-American beauty and afrocentrism in the US ('black is beautiful'). This constitutes yet another instance of cultural importation among banlieusard subjects of American self-valorisation and self-actualisation techniques. Generally speaking, mainstream French and American mentalities differ radically when it comes to the concept of 'pride,' at the heart of expressions like 'beur is beautiful.' It is here where Boutih (a strident Republicanist) and Zeraoui (sympathetic to banlieusard claims of ethnic affirmation) begin to diverge. Boutih's conclusion about 'a community closing in on itself' reinforces a point that he develops over the course of the interview: the danger of communitarianism. As the corollary of the supposedly 'excessive' pride evidenced by Franco-Arabs, communitarianism would really just constitute a compensation technique masking an essential shame, a 'physical complex' that would seem to explain other, more first-degree frustrations like social and professional immobility. This dismissal of the desirability of beurs and pride in Arab beauty is inseparable from Boutih's campaign against the ethnic communitarianism in the banlieues that might encourage that sort of pride.[12] In what seems at first like a misstatement, Boutih explains that Arab beauty is 'surprising' because banlieue youth have internalised 'the bad image they have of themselves' rather than the 'bad image' of banlieue youth society has produced: this choice of terminology underlies his belief that dismissal is produced from within ethnic enclaves and not exclusively from the 'outside,' thus becoming blameworthy. In this way, a strong sense of ethnic community would not make the recognition of that ethnicity's beauty potential more likely, rather, the congregation of people belonging to the same ethnicity would render the recognition of their beauty less likely because that beauty, seen everywhere in the community, would be more mundane. This line of thinking echoes that found in novels touting social realism like Chimo's *Lila dit ça*, in which 'brown' is the most common of colours in the banlieues and 'white' is in danger of extinction, more rare and thus more beautiful.

Style, body image and acceptance

Just as Boutih notices the harmful effects of the aesthetic devaluation of Arab beauty in comparison with white standards, he underlines that Arabs cannot be deemed beautiful without first passing through whiteness. Boutih fleshes out this idea when asked to dig deeper into the extent of internalised 'ugliness':

BOUTIH: Yes. There is a complex. I myself am not willing to believe that all the phenomena linked to shaved heads, to making hair disappear, to dressing a certain way, etc., don't stem from a certain shame in regard to the body, to its visibility, to its colour etc. And it's true that one of the ways of resolving this problem, is to find a certain beauty in these physical criteria. And it's true that Zidane is a part of that. And it's true that somewhere, for those who are attentive observers of French society, little by little, Arab beauty is starting to emerge within French beauty. In the same way that, undeniably, it has happened with the black population at a certain moment in the eighties and nineties, through what Jean-Paul Gaultier did with a certain number of models, and others too. The motto 'black is beautiful' played a part. Obviously, because it allows for *métissage*.

We have to tell people, you are beautiful. If we don't tell them they are beautiful, we have said nothing. The start of the beginning (of change) is the fact of feeling free to own up to one's physical difference. If we don't start by saying that, we are closing people in, we are leading them to believe that somewhere, the only beauty that exists is white. It's not true.

ZERAOUI: It's what the media, the ads, and the television would have us believe . . .

Here, Boutih entertains larger notions about what the self-stylings of Franco-Arab youth socially represent. His remarks suggest that shame regarding the visible markers of 'Arab' ethnicity (curly hair, dark beards, brown skin) cause subjects to seek their erasure through excessive self-tailoring and shaving ('making hair disappear'). One can read his commentary differently, however: the focus on purely physical development would provide a means to excel at a universalist endeavour, that is, we can all sculpt our bodies regardless of ethnicity. In this scenario, body sculpting would serve to make ethnic markers irrelevant when compared with the accomplishment of a self-styled body or face. Such self-tailoring would draw attention away from ethnic particularity, and would even serve to conceal or distract from ethnicity. Such shame might paradoxically be reflected in the prideful and 'combative' social stance evident in the banlieusard street fashion Boutih elliptically mentions ('all the phenomena. . .'), which changes over the years but can be variously composed of buzz cuts, mohawks and faux hawks, sculpted facial hair, eyebrows shaved through the middle to resemble a battle scar, all of which involve the removal of hair.[13] These stylings complement the form-fitting leather jackets, upturned collars, and the athletic-wear panoply of sneakers, sweatpants, hoodies, white athletic socks pulled up high, and baseball caps that round off the list (far from exhaustive) of banlieue street style's most common elements (Mack 2017). The effort and aesthetic maintenance involved in sustaining this 'aggressive' social posture would make these subjects' inferiority complex all the more apparent in Boutih's view, for the overcompensation it would involve.

Quite recently, banlieusard street style came under similar attack from an author with decidedly different political leanings, in Laurent Obertone's *La France Orange Mécanique* (2013), a fear-inducing tally of the alleged rise of serious crime among populations of 'immigrant origin.' In a passage justifying ethnic profiling by the French police, Obertone, who writes under a pen-name, states that banlieue youth are drawing attention to themselves, and their tendency toward criminality, via their clothes:

Most of the individuals (more than half) stopped by the police are stopped because of their 'hip-hop' clothing style (backwards cap, socks pulled up over fluorescent sweats, chains of jewels, etc.). A CNRS[14] study, published in 2009 by the Open Society

Institute, found that in Paris near Les Halles, 'blacks' were stopped six times more frequently than 'whites,' and 'Arabs' eight times more. However, those individuals who 'dress young' (10% of the population) represent half of the police stops. 'The clothing style of the youth in question is just as predictive of a stop as racial appearance is.' Two thirds of individuals who 'dress young' belong to racial minorities. Can one forbid the police from stopping individuals who 'dress young?' Obviously, these youth expect to be stopped, just like a kid picking his nose in front of his teacher expects to get slapped.

(Obertone 2013: 286)

Rather than conclude that clothing styles have been racialised, Obertone uses these ambiguous statistics to state instead that race does not quantitatively matter in police stops. He thus defends the police against accusations of racism, burying specific findings about race within the much larger category of 'youth.' It should be noted, however, that in many media and political contexts, '*les jeunes*' acts as code for youth of colour or banlieusards. The epithet 'young' is not devoid of ethnic profiling, as it goes part and parcel with characterisations of banlieusards (who in the popular imagination are mostly made up of people of colour) as forever juvenile no matter their age, locked in a state of dependency. Obertone's image of a social aggressivity mirrored in clothes is one that Boutih fleshed out a decade earlier; it so happens that in *La France orange mécanique*, Boutih is the Franco-Arab politician Obertone cites the most, recycling his most self-critical comments (self-critical in the sense of Boutih commenting on a community he also belongs to), always making sure to underline Boutih's ethnic origins to defend against the idea that only white commentators would draw analogies between ethnicity and crime (while Obertone does so explicitly, Boutih does so indirectly, and is careful to avoid mentioning race and ethnicity too much). Boutih has often played this role, used as a vessel for right-wing politicians to anchor their critiques of banlieue youth in an irreproachable shroud of ethnic 'authenticity.'

Another reading of the social significance of clothes is possible, however; one that does not psychologise clothing choices as perpetuating stigmas that reinforce failure and rejection. The very clothing choices that Boutih has called symptomatic of internalised Arab 'ugliness' have had their connotations flipped through a reinterpretation of self-tailoring not as erasure of ethnicity but as its opposite. This reinterpretation transforms the self-tailoring that supposedly came in reaction to shame (and aimed to erase Arabness) into a sign that signifies 'Franco-Arabness' and banlieusard belonging in a novel and decisive way, one that is more emic than etic. In other words, an action that comes in reaction to the supposedly unbearable visibility of Arabness – like shaving off one's curls – can come to signify Arabness. This is evident, for example, in the fact that fashion observers have come to recognise the 'Arab' or 'black' stamp on this hair styling, such that shaved heads or close-cropped cuts then come to signify a multi-ethnic banlieue look. The same could be said of any other of the aforementioned components of the athletic banlieusard look. These stylings would not stand in relation with white French standards of beauty, but would rather stand in cross-pollination and conversation with the aesthetics favoured by Europeans of colour as well as transatlantic hip-hop cultures, without being simply derivative of American styles (as many street fashions that exist in Europe, but not the United States, make clear). By the measure of tastemakers and fashion monitors, these multi-ethnic youth have produced an asceticism and discipline of the body which is now considered beautiful and sought after as something emanating from ethnic enclaves that are seen as creative rather than limited spaces of expression, and thus commodifiable.[15] The pursuit of body and face sculpting, previously connoted in Boutih as the pursuit of the non-ethnic universal, has here attained a degree of ethnic particularity. In 2004, *Vogues Hommes* picked up on this 'ethnic' character of face, hair, and body hyper-styling, famously dedicating an entire issue to celebrating the beauty of the Arab male, but more particularly the French Arab banlieusard male. The issue featured the Olympic gold medallist boxer Brahim Asloum on the cover with a grill and a buzzed blond hairdo, under the caption, 'Ch'Adore!,' a play on words combining the Tchador and the French for 'I love it!' (Editors Vogue Hommes 2003–2004). Other photospreads show Arab and black men with eyebrows split down the middle, designs stencilled into their scalps (hairstyles known as 'tribales'), wearing form-fitting sportswear or baggy hip-hop gear, arms locked in brotherly gestures that are at once reflective of North African homo-social customs as well as gang handshakes (clearly exploited for their homo-eroticism by the photographers): all in all the images derive from an urban Atlantic that borrows equally from Casablanca and the Bronx (Mack 2017). In each photo, hair is either bleached blond, removed, or hyper-tailored: the removal of hair as an ethnic marker, however, only underscores ethnic and banlieue belonging by drawing attention to other physical and sartorial features through its absence.

While Boutih struggles to articulate an Arabness that might be beautiful in and of itself, this has definitely not been the case for many gay-identified directors, artists and authors who have, for quite some time already, saluted the embattled beauty of the banlieusard social posture described by Boutih.[16] Admirers of successful performances, these directors appreciate the 'work' involved in banlieusard self-styling, seeing in it something accomplished rather than a false screen compensating for an internal vacuum. Boutih himself refers to gay tastemakers and cultural actors like Jean-Paul Gaultier, as we have seen, in explaining just how the advent (rather than recognition) of 'ethnic beauty' can be engineered by those in the fashion avant-garde. Often lifting cues from the stylings of immigrants, minorities, and banlieusards, fashion designers around the world bank on the creativity of populations that Boutih finds sartorially homogenous, more 'uniform' in all senses of the word.

Conclusions

Unlike *Vogue* magazine, Boutih believes Arab beauty has yet to fully come into being: in nascent formation, he uses the present participle ('is starting to emerge') to describe it. And if it is beautiful at all, Arabness is beautiful for its contribution to *métissage*, or the production of a third hybrid body that attenuates the particularity of the first two bodies. Beauty is located in the non-particularity of the *métis* or mixed-race subject as a universal figure. Even though it is borrowed from the Americans, for Boutih 'black is beautiful' is a worthwhile slogan because it allows for *métissage*, as he explains: the purpose of recognising black beauty is not empowerment of that 'beautiful' racial group so much as empowering the black populations' ability to attract other groups. In the analogy, Arab beauty emerges solely as a subcomponent of 'French beauty,' part of a melting pot whose components cannot be isolated after mixing, with the threat of that beauty's particularity neutralised. In contemporary France, '*métissage*' has become a buzzword for the French centre and left – Boutih even underlines it as a societal goal on his government profile: 'In his battle against racism and its roots, [Boutih] counts on the mixing of populations and the struggle against violence.'[17] However, a critique can be made of the otherwise laudable encouragement of '*métissage*' here: *métissage* is only laudable when it passes through the national centre, and thus, whiteness; other forms of *métissage* that occur between minorities in the banlieues, or between Muslims of different races, are not always graced with the term '*métissage*' even though they correspond with it factually, because they appear to be communitarian rather than universalist acts of *métissage*.

Pride in a community's internal beauty, in an ethnic beauty which is not part of a *métissage* equation, is precluded in Boutih's argument. All uniform ethnic pride is merely compensation, in the sense of the rationalisation of a disadvantaged situation. In such a view, Arab men could never find themselves beautiful, because appreciating the way they look could only stem from isolation and lack of exposure to other types of beauty, an isolation which results in their collapse upon themselves, which then results in communitarian pride, which results in more compensation, and the cycle goes on in this circular and highly alienating argument. Yet Boutih's recommendation – that they must find beauty in themselves – still stands. Hidden within this framework is the idea of 'neediness': needing others to validate one's beauty, through a kind of Republican marketplace where *métissage* finalises optimal transactions. Communitarianism leads to low self-esteem, in Boutih's argument, even though it is based on pride, because those that judge their own beauty without recourse to the (white) centre can only have an impoverished idea of beauty. However, in the logic of the argument at hand, an appreciation of beauty could only become manifest through *mixité*, through an outside assessment by the Other, never from within. This places the Franco-Arab subject in a conundrum also perilous for self-worth, that of having to resort to the Other for a valorisation of the self, prolonging a trend Boutih already recognises to be dangerous, that of Arabs internalising the image with which larger society frames this group.

Notes

1 Zeraoui, F. (interviewer). n.d. Malek Boutih, Président de sos racisme: L'homophobie en banlieue. www.kelma.org/PAGES/DOCUMENTS/malek_boutih.php [Accessed: 14.02.2012]. Note: All translations, unless otherwise stated, are my own.

2 For some of the most widely read examples: Begag, A. 2007. *The Shantytown Kid*. Translated by A. Hargreaves. Lincoln, NE: Bison Books; Guène, F. 2006. *Kiffe Kiffe Tomorrow*. Translated by S. Adams. Boston, MA: Mariner Books. French titles: Begag, A. 2005. *Le gone du Chaaba*. Paris: Editions du Seuil; Guène, F. 2006. *Kiffe Kiffe Demain*. Paris: Livre de Poche.

3 Residents of the French multi-ethnic and working class housing projects and suburbs.

4 Zeraoui, Malek Boutih, Président de sos racisme: L'homophobie en banlieue, op. cit.

5 Unlike in the US, the word 'community' has a mostly negative connotation (except when making reference to the national community) in France. '*Communautarisme*' refers to the tendency of minorities to associate only with members of the same minority, as well as ethnic separatism, and has often been associated with reluctance to assimilate, competing systems of law that are intolerable for the Republic, and Islamic fundamentalism. Communitarianism, however, can also result from government-engineered policy decisions to concentrate the urban poor and immigrants in certain areas.

6 Collectif Les mots sont importants. Malek Boutih et ses amis: présentation de la rubrique. 8 July 2003. http://lmsi.net/Presentation-de-la-rubrique [Accessed: 14.12.2017].

7 High Authority for the Struggle Against Discrimination and for Equality (*Haute autorité de lutte contre les discriminations et pour l'égalité*).

8 See the deputy's government profile: www.boutih.fr/mon-parcours/.

9 Observable in the repeated flashbacks to playground and public transport scenes in 'beur' literature, wherein the authors recall how their physical appearance had been denigrated by white peers (Guène). This representational trend is especially observable in some controversial novels of unknown authorship but purporting to represent an Arab point-of-view (Chimo), or memoirs in which a white author posed as Arab (Smaïl), in which the Arab protagonists repeatedly associate their "Arab" features to ugliness or average looks, and venerate European whiteness as the reference for all standards of beauty, or establish blondness as being pure angelic, and virtuous, under threat of being desecrated by immigration. Chimo. 1997. *Lila dit ça*. Paris: Pocket; Guène, *Kiffe Kiffe Tomorrow*, op. cit.; Smaïl, P. 1997. *Vivre me tue*. Paris: Balland.

10 Chibane, M. (Dir.). 2007. *La Trilogie Urbaine (Hexagone, Douce France, Voisins Voisines)*. Bac Films.

11 Baroux, O. (Dir.). 2010. *L'Italien*. Eskwad.

12 Boutih takes a position against communitarianism and affirmative action: 'In France, minorities don't exist! We are not an endangered species. If we start speaking Arabic or Mandingo, Breton or Corsican, we'll shatter the national community,' 'Mon parcours,' op. cit.

13 For a visual and insistently homo-erotic illustration of the parallels between hair removal and combative social postures, see the film *Le Clan*, whose English title is *Three Dancing Slaves*: Morel, G. (Dir.). 2004. *Le Clan (Three Dancing Slaves)*. TLA Releasing.

14 Centre National de la Recherche Scientifique, a reputed government body that sponsors academic research.
15 Film director Sébastien Lifshitz documented just such a gay fascination with this look, through the character of Laurent in *Les Terres Froides*: LAURENT: 'You know what fascinates me with blacks and beurs? It's their way of always being strong even when nothing's going right. Even when they are in the worst shit they'll never let themselves sink . . . they are all super-physical, you see them at the gym, the way they walk. I want to be like that you see, hard as concrete . . . in any case it helps me. They are role models.' Lifshitz, S. 1999. *Les Terres froides*. Agat films et Cie.
16 See the chapter 'Le cinéaste gay et le garçon arabe,' in Cervulle, M. and N. Rees-Roberts. 2010. *Homo Exoticus: Race, classe et critique queer*. Paris: Armand Colin.
17 c.f., 'Mon parcours.'

References

Amara, F. and S. Zappi. 2004. *Ni Putes Ni Soumises*. Paris: Éditions la Découverte.
Baroux, O. (Dir.). 2010. *L'Italien*. Eskwad.
Begag, A. 2007. *The Shantytown Kid*. Translated by A. Hargreaves. Lincoln, NE: Bison Books.
Boutih, M. 2015. Génération Radicale. June. Available at: www.gouv.fr [Accessed: 01.12.2018].
Cervulle, M. and N. Rees-Roberts. 2010. *Homo Exoticus: Race, classe et critique queer*. Paris: Armand Colin.
Chaumont, F. 2009. *Homo-Ghetto: Gays et Lesbiennes Dans Les Cités: Les Clandestins de La République*. Paris: Le Cherche Midi.
Chaumont, F. and F. Zeraoui. 2009. Débat Têtu: Gays de Banlieue Faut-Il En Sortir Pour S'en Sortir? In *Kelma.org* online newspaper, November. Available at: http://blog-gay.kelma.org/gays-en-banlieue [Accessed: 01.12.2018].
Chibane, M. (Dir.). 2007. *La Trilogie Urbaine (Hexagone, Douce France, Voisins Voisines)*. Bac Films.
Chimo. 1997. *Lila dit ça*. Paris: Pocket.
Clair, I. 2008. *Les Jeunes et l'amour dans les cités*. Paris: Armand Colin.
Collectif les mots sont importants. 2003. Malek Boutih et ses potes. In *lmsi.net*, 7 March. Available at: http://lmsi.net/-Malek-Boutih-et-ses-potes- [Accessed: 14.12.2017].
Daoud, K. 2016. Opinion | La Misère Sexuelle Du Monde Arabe. In *The New York Times*, 12 February, sec. Opinion. Available at: www.nytimes.com/2016/02/14/opinion/sunday/la-misere-sexuelle-du-monde-arabe.html [Accessed: 01.12.2018].
Editors. 2002. Sondage: Zidane Le plus Sexy. In *www.sport.fr*, 7 June. Available at: www.sport.fr/football/Sondage-Zidane-le-plus-sexy-22399.shtm [Accessed: 01.12.2018].
Editors. 2003–04. Ch'adore. In *Vogues Hommes International*, Fall/Winter.
Editors. 2005. Le plus Bel Homme Du Monde (sur tf1). In *www.comlive.net*, 2 March. Available at: www.comlive.net/Le-plus-bel-homme-du-monde-sur-tf1,58116.htm [Accessed: 01.12.2018].
Editors. 2009. Hortefeux: 'Quand Il Y a Un Ça Va . . . C'est Quand Il Y En a Beaucoup Qu'il Y a Des Problèmes!' In *Archives-Lepost.huffingtonpost.fr*, 10–9. Available at: http://archives-lepost.huffingtonpost.fr/video/2009/09/10/1690452_hortefeux-derape-serieusement.html [Accessed: 01.12.2018].
Editors. 2010. Malek Boutih, Président de La HALDE? Il Ne Ferait Pas L'affaire, Selon Longuet. In *www.saphirnews.com*, 11 March.
Elbadawi, S. 2014. Beur is not beautiful? In *Africultures*, 97, 9 February, 118–125. doi: 10.3917/afcul.097.0118.
French Government. 2015. *www.boutih.fr*. Available at: www.boutih.fr/mon-parcours/ [Accessed: 20.06.2015].
Garcia, D. 2002. L'Avant-garde soluble dans le Marais? In *Le Nouvel Observateur*, 28 February–6 March.
Göle, N. 2005. *Interpénétrations. Islam et l'Europe*. Paris: Galaade Editions.
Guène, F. 2006. *Kiffe Kiffe Tomorrow*. Translated by S. Adams. Boston, MA: Mariner Books.
Guénif-Souilamas, N. 2004. *Les Féministes et Le Garçon Arabe*. La-Tour-d'Aigues: Editions de l'Aube.
Honoré, C. (Dir.). 2010. *L'homme au bain*. Les films du Bélier.
Jazdzewski, C. 2010. Carnets de Mode: Le Style Gaultier. In *Palace Costes Magazine*, December 2009–January 2010.
LeBon, G. 2010. *The Crowd: A Study of the Popular Mind*. CreateSpace (Latest Edition).
Lee, D. 2010. Don't ask, just tell: sexual racism is at the core of what many gay men believe to be 'preferences.' In *Metroweekly.com*, 23 September. Available at: http://metroweekly.com/news/opinion/?ak=5613 [Accessed: 01.12.2018].

Lestrade, D. 2010. La moustache et les gays. In *didierlestrade.fr*, 2 December. Available at: http://didierle strade.fr/porno/article/la-moustache-et-les-gays [Accessed: 13.02.2012].

Lifshitz, S. (Dir.). 1999. *Les Terres froides.* Agat films et Cie.

Mack, M. 2017. *Sexagon: Muslims, France, and the Sexualization of National Culture.* New York: Fordham University Press.

Marlière, E. 2011. *Les Jeunes et la discothèque: Entre fêtes urbaines et violences ritualisées.* Paris: Editions du Cygne.

Marteau, S. 2006. Ni Putes Ni Soumises: Un Appareil Idéologique d'Etat. In *www.Mouvements.Info.* Available at: www.mouvements.info/Ni-Putes-Ni-Soumises-un-appareil.html [Accessed: 01.12.2018].

Morel, G. (Dir.). 2004. *Le Clan (Three Dancing Slaves).* TLA Releasing.

Noiriel, G. 2006. *Le Creuset Français.* Paris: Editions du Seuil.

Obertone, L. 2013. *La France Orange Mécanique.* Paris: Ring.

Patai, R. 1973. *The Arab Mind.* New York: Scribner.

Richet, J-F. (Dir.). 1997. *Ma 6-T va crack-er.* Actes Proletariens.

Shepard, T. 2017. *Sex, France, and Arab Men, 1962–1979.* Chicago and London: University of Chicago Press.

Smaïl, P. 1997. *Vivre me tue.* Paris: Balland.

Tiloune, J. 2006. Soirées homosexuelles 'Black Blanc Beur' à Paris.' In *www.afrik.com*, 21 October. Available at: www.afrik.com/article10577.html [Accessed: 01.12.2018].

Zauberman, Y. (Dir.). 1996. *Clubbed to Death.* Arthaus.

Zeraoui, F. n.d. Malek Boutih, Président de sos racisme: L'homophobie en banlieue. Available at: www. kelma.org/PAGES/DOCUMENTS/malek_boutih.php [Accessed: 14.02.2012].

15

LOCAL AND SOCIAL BELONGING IN THE CONTEMPORARY FRENCH RURAL WORLD

Nicolas Renahy

In comparison to the majority of European nations, the industrialisation and urbanisation of French society arrived later, not gaining momentum until the end of the nineteenth century. Nearly half of the population still lived in the countryside in 1946. While 77% of the population currently lives in conurbations of more than 2,000 inhabitants and while farmers represent no more than 2% of the workforce, what is the interest in studying the political and cultural situation in French rural areas today? Does the rural minority present sociologically significant characteristics in terms of training, education and access to leisure activities and culture in particular, while largely being under the influence of towns?

By concentrating on the practices of rural populations, this chapter presents an overview of rural studies which have witnessed a renaissance in recent years. First, the state of contemporary social structures of the French countryside will be examined. Emphasising the 'rural' category – or, in other words, defining populations by their place of residence alone without taking their social characteristics into account – always incurs the risk of essentialising physical spaces and reducing their inhabitants to pre-constructed representations. These representations might sometimes be pitiful ('countrified' or 'rooted' country dwellers) and sometimes populist (rural inhabitants with a 'traditional identity' or a naturalised 'heritage': Laferté and Renahy 2003). Conversely, such a social group will not have exactly the same characteristics and will not necessarily have the same aspirations depending on whether the group is located in a town or in the countryside. This is even more the case in a global context of increasing geographic mobility where forms of investment in places are being revived (Sencébé 2004). Local and social belonging must therefore be analysed in tandem (Chamboredon 1985).

The statistically larger group of workers (the scale of early industrialisation followed by the long process of leaving agriculture boosted the workforce of the working-class world over more than a century) will then be examined, a group which, like in towns, is suffering the effects of deindustrialisation. The constantly diminishing agricultural world is experiencing an important diversification. More generally, the revival of rural populations and the introduction of intercommunal services change forms of mobilisation and involvement in local politics, just as much as they change forms of sociability and leisure activities. Finally, even if the rural exodus seems to have come to a halt for the time being, the rural population continues to grow older. For that reason, it is also important to look at how end-of-life care is handled. Through the analysis of demographic and socio-professional change, support of rural populations, leisure and social practices over recent decades, the motivations underpinning social, political and cultural conflict in contemporary rural areas can be understood.

A specific social structure?

Even today, the adjective 'rural' is often synonymous with 'agricultural' in the French public forum, and there are always traditionalist and discrediting representations of 'la' campagne. The reality is more complex. Neither a reservoir of 'traditions' nor archaising isolates, French rural and suburban areas are very integrated in the national territory, yet, socially, they are very differentiated. This is what is being shown in the social sciences that are once again taking an interest in the subject after a long hiatus beginning in the early 1980s (Rogers 1995).

The concentration of farming activity continues to cause the number of farmers to fall; farmers who, in 2009, barely represented 10% of the rural population furthest from towns and 5.5% of the resident workforce in all 'predominantly rural areas'[1] (4.8% in 2014) even though inequalities within the profession are on the rise again (we will return to this question later). The continuous rise in the number of professional and intermediate fields and professions since the 1960s has only affected the countryside far from large towns to a lesser extent (Table 15.1). Conversely, the categories of employees and workers add up to over 60% of the workforce in predominantly rural areas (53% nationally). Between 1999 and 2009, the employed workforce continued to grow there while it decreased in towns, whereas the fall in the number of workers in the countryside was much less considerable. Today, these two categories are usually identified as making up the main part of the working classes, insofar as they group together the professions of the youth workforce that have some autonomy at work and are characterised more broadly by a social, economic and political position that is overlooked but often still produces certain

Table 15.1 Socio-professional categories in places of residence in 1999 and 2009 (in percentages).

Years	Centre of Paris		Large centres outside of Paris		Suburbs of large centres		Rural centres		Other suburbs		Remote rural areas		France	
	1999	2009	1999	2009	1999	2009	1999	2009	1999	2009	1999	2009	1999	2009
Farmers	0.0	0.1	0.5	0.4	4.1	2.7	2.2	1.6	9.8	6.4	12.9	9.5	2.5	1.7
Artisans, shopkeepers, company directors	5.1	4.4	5.9	5.3	6.9	6.3	7.9	7.3	7.6	7.2	9.3	9.1	6.4	5.8
Professional fields and occupations	22.2	27.6	12.1	15.2	8.6	11.6	6.7	8.1	5.1	6.9	5.0	6.4	12.1	15.3
Intermediate professions	24.8	25.8	23.4	25.4	21.6	24.9	17.8	20.3	16.2	19.7	14.5	17.3	22.1	24.3
Employees	30.2	27.6	31.8	30.6	28.1	28.3	30.1	30.8	25.1	27.1	26.2	27.6	29.9	29.2
Workers	17.6	14.6	26.3	23.2	30.7	26.3	35.2	31.9	36.1	32.6	32.1	30.1	27.1	23.8
Total	100	100	100	100	100	100	100	100	100	100	100	100	100	100

Sources: Insee, RP 1999; CESEAR 2009. Taken from Détang-Dessendre and Piguet (2016).

forms of cultural autonomy (Siblot et al. 2015).[2] As the number of farmers was divided by more than ten in the post–Second World War period, the social structure of rural areas has therefore lost its farming specificity very substantially. However, it cannot be assimilated with urban social structures: the further away from towns, the lower the prevalence of populations that are educated and situated at the top of the professional hierarchy. Even if today the rural population has stabilised and the suburban population is growing, the continuous urbanisation of French society has otherwise brought about an intensified dependence on towns. In fact, with the constant concentration of economic and cultural assets in cities, the restructuring of public services and the closure of small businesses happening since the 1980s,[3] the countryside is increasingly dependent on towns from a functional perspective. This phenomenon does not affect all social categories in the same way. While 'multi-territoriality' (the concept of frequenting different areas, owing to either a second home or daily travel for work), previously an upper middle-class privilege, has spread to the lower middle classes (Chamboredon 1985), the lower classes remain hugely attached to a form of localism. This is particularly true for the working-class world, the category of the workforce that is still the most represented in rural areas despite the effects of deindustrialisation.

The effects of the industrial crisis on the rural working-class world

Contemporary rural areas still seem to be more dependent on large towns. For the populations that live there, the majority having little or no economic or cultural capital, this situation can manifest itself as increased isolation. Throughout the economic growth of the post-war period, such an absence of legitimate capital was often compensated for by other types of resources, key to local belonging. Autochthony capital (Retière 2003) – all localised, social (access to the labour market, property, marriage, etc.) and symbolic (reputation linked to a name or a recognised involvement in local networks) resources – made up a fundamental asset for many young people who had little to no qualifications and were not inclined to move to towns. The case of young, sedentary workers shows that such an asset has lost its virtue and that geographic isolation developed into social isolation during the economic crisis of the 1980s (Renahy 2005).

In the 1970s, the young people living in Foulange, an industrial village in Burgundy with 600 inhabitants, were the products of itinerary stabilisation of the previous generation. Their parents had entered working life early, with few qualifications, owing to the paternalistic factory that would often take them on when they left school with their primary school certificate. They were married and had their first children young, often around 18 to 22 years old. The 1970s were also found to correspond to a certain zenith of the Welfare State implemented in the post-war period. The working-class families of Foulange were particularly helped by the creation of a social centre in the administrative centre of the canton in 1971. Local employers, who had preceded the state in these practices of helping the working classes, extended this assistance even further during this period (the factory brought in a village doctor at the end of the 1960s, for example). The local council was not going to be outdone as, between the 1950s and 1970s, it asked the Regional Public Office for Social Housing to come to the municipality and provided it with land on which to construct detached rental housing or to prepare areas for individual home ownership. From all points of view (including in terms of politicisation and access to a class conscience), the 1970s marked a zenith for this 'small' working-class world. In such a context, skill sets specific to the working-class world, namely manual expertise, found a particular environment in rural areas conducive to the re-appropriation of this know-how beyond the factory, for themselves and for their families, in do-it-yourself, gardening, woodcutting, etc. This is what Florence Weber (1989) called 'next-door work' in her analysis of labour consumption practices in the 1980s. The author positions her observations at the height of working-class culture, just before the economic crisis destabilised this balance. For the young people of the following generation who, in Foulange like elsewhere, were faced with a strong crisis in working-class employment, what is striking was the huge difficulty, or impossibility, of reproducing the characteristics of the parental model of reaching a respectable position at a young age (employee, parent, home owner). It was not until the age of 30 to 35 that many ended up stabilising their married lives by settling down truly independently. In a context of social weakening and putting off reaching independence, one of the only stages that procured a form of social 're-assurance' in its specific skills was between an adolescent and a post-adolescent being. This is of course down to objective facts: the expansion of trial periods, short contracts and temporary work. But it is also down to a more subjective weakness, linked to a childhood marked by parents' unemployment (what remained of the paternalistic factory in Foulange closed in 1981 before two small SMEs opened a few years later) just as much as it is linked to the hopes of leaving the working-class world. In this sense, and even if they retain the marked forms of working-class neutrality, they are young people like any others, affected by the 'expansion of a student model of youth' (Chamboredon 2015: 194): they also wanted to enjoy their youth, benefiting from long spans of free time and having access to leisure activities.

Therefore, for the most fragile members of the working classes, being 'local' is no longer enough to integrate socially and professionally. In many areas where youth employment has become virtually non-existent in public or industrial sectors, the professional trajectory of sedentary young people is intrinsically dependent on individual reputation and the state of the local social network. A recent survey carried out in Haute-Marne – a department with a particularly low population density – shows a revived desire to construct an autochthony amongst young people based on 'clans' that are particularly detached from the cultural petty bourgeoisie, which no longer seems to support the working classes there. A tendency to transition from a rationale of local belonging on an institutional basis (in the broader sense: businesses, associations, etc.) to a rationale of elective belonging has reappeared, in addition to a rejection of left-wing political theses ('the social') and a relative permeability to far right discourse (Coquard 2018). Owing to deindustrialisation and de-territorialisation of working-class work, but also to the 'restructuring' of the Welfare State services and to the extinction of old forms of managing young people (Catholic or municipal patronage, MJCs (*maisons des jeunes et de la culture*) and *mille clubs*) that were highly developed in rural areas in the 1960s and 1970s, the logics of knowledge between territories has been profoundly modified. We will see later that establishing municipal communities, which then withdraw from the power of action of smaller municipalities, also has an indirect role in contemporary forms of political participation. But first, the agricultural world will be analysed.

An agricultural world diversifying in social and trade union terms

Such opposition between social recognition on a local basis, on the one hand, and academically attested ability and entering a qualified profession, on the other, also affects the agricultural world. In 2010, three-quarters of farmers below the age of 40 had at least a baccalaureate level of agricultural training while, in 1975, three-quarters of those below the age of 30 had a qualification that was lower or equal to the school certificate. School capital has become a precious resource for farmers for maintaining relationships with professionals from the many structures that support them (Bessière et al. 2014). School contributes to new ways of differentiating between farmers, including when it comes to choosing a spouse: the most qualified and the owners of the largest farms are those who increasingly marry partners who work away from the farm (Giraud and Rémy 2008). Subsequently, for several decades, between small-scale farm workers and the established farming upper class, we have seen the arrival of farmers in the process of gentrifying, with qualifications in agricultural higher education, whose spouses work away from the farm, who travel on holiday, manage their stocks on the computer in accordance with market prices and invest their capital in the urban property market (Laferté 2018). It is evidently in the more specialised sectors, principally in cereal cultivation, that this type of profile is found. At the other end of this hierarchy, there are the less qualified small-scale farmers who are not so specialised (crop-livestock or milk production with extensive minimum working hours) and more oriented through inheritance towards a local network of relationships. But the growing demands of work and upheavals in forms of local sociability often increase their isolation: the abnormally high suicide rate of French men, farmers having the highest rate of all professions, is a particular sign of farmers 'being reduced to a minority in the rural world' (Deffontaines 2014: 20).

Internal variations, including academic inequality, economic heterogeneity linked to production types, growth of heterogamy and differentiated introduction of new workforce practices (particularly in terms of how weekends, holiday days and vacations are spent), also show a very disparate agricultural world. It is also increasingly disparate in terms of politicisation, while until the 1980s the representation of the profession was the monopoly of the *Fédération nationale des syndicats d'exploitants agricoles* (FNSEA). Even if this trade union still enjoys a majority, it is now rivalled. The *Confédération paysanne*, launched in 1987 but whose origin dates to the post-1968 anti-establishment turmoil, was founded by farmers who often inherited stable farms but who subverted the family inheritance by becoming 'leftist,' either as a result of the continued company of older, student brothers and sisters or because they themselves went to university (Bruneau 2015). The *Coordination rurale*, created in 1994, is the other minority trade union. It revives certain forms of reactionary engagement that draw on agrarianism. The space for the trade union representation of the profession has therefore progressively opened, even if the FNSEA remains very influential. That is a consequence of the relative diversification of how the profession is regarded. In this way, the supporters of organic agriculture, marginal for a long time in their professional universe, have now started to benefit from the progressive institutionalisation of this type of production. The organic market gardeners have thus ended up acquiring local and professional respectability (Nicolas 2016), which creates 'new competition for obtaining funding and/or of a lobbying position with public authorities' (Samak 2013: 146).

Upheavals in the local public sphere and in political participation

However, the public image of the French rural world remains marked by farmers' violence that has blemished current affairs since the beginning of the Fifth Republic by reviving the inherited fantasy of peasant revolts. The significant milk strikes of 2009 and the movement known as *Des Bonnets rouges* (the red caps) of 2013 (which united factories, the FNSEA and certain abattoir workers' trade unions) were the most recent protests. In particular, the milk strikes culminated in the destruction of milk by spilling or spraying it at the authorities, and *Des Bonnets rouges* culminated in the blocking of road bridges and the destruction of eco-tax toll gates that are supposed to regulate the pollution of heavy loads. Resorting to physical violence has to be understood as a reaction to symbolic violence and a feeling of collective depreciation (Duclos 1998). For example, the 2009 milk strikes aimed to capture the attention of the media using farmers who were destroying their own products (while it was the products of non-strikers being destroyed in the previous protests of 1964 and 1972). Personal tragedy thus illustrated the danger of the profession disappearing (Lynch 2013). This type of violent action is found in other marginalised rural social groups in the public space. In a similar way, the hunters who set fire to an ornithological observatory or massacred protected birds during dramatic action against EU directives believed they were acting in legitimate defence of their territory (Mischi 2013).

In the political sphere, the relegation of the agricultural world to a minority has now led to the erosion of farmers' dominance over town councils. While in 1983 45% of mayors of 36,000 French municipalities were farmers, this proportion was no more than 25% in 2008 (a fall of −57.4%: Koebel 2014). Progressively since the end of the 1970s, the sociology of rural public space has evolved in opposition to the sociology of social structures. This phenomenon is particularly noticeable in suburban rural areas where the proportion of intermediate fields and professions is more or less identical to the national average (Table 15.1). In this way, in a market town near Niort, retired farmers have for a time been able to continue exercising their local power via the perpetuation of the village fête, after the municipality was taken over in 1995 by a socialist group essentially composed of insurance company employees who had a strong presence in Niort (Schnapper 2019). But even this way of staging an agricultural autochthony (farmers' market, folklore parade, selling milk and puddings, football matches between farmers and traders, etc.) is subject to conflict. Farmers were excluded from the fête committee in 2015 and, in this market town, like in many places, they could no longer claim the symbolic monopoly of local belonging for themselves.

The effects of this process were evidently not only symbolic. The transfer of functions in municipalities towards inter-municipalities in the 2000s led to local public action becoming more complicated, transforming it into a 'democracy of expertise' where managerial skills of elected representatives took precedence over dedication within a sphere of inter-knowledge (Vignon 2010). While the economic bourgeoisie (entrepreneurs, liberal professions, large-scale farmers) has progressively withdrawn from the local political scene since the end of the 1970s, such an upheaval favours a cultural (teachers, public sector workers, etc.) and a technical (computer scientists, technicians, engineers, etc.) petty bourgeoisie gaining responsibilities. These groups have a past experience of urban life and are highly educated in comparison with a rural population which has few qualifications on the whole. Moreover, the former gives more prominence to personal skills as a result of professional know-how rather than simple dedication (Bruneau and Renahy 2012). Such an increase in the range of skills necessary for involvement in local political life also helps to explain the eviction of the working classes. Depending on the context (the influence of the workforce, the self-employed, etc.), it has led to both a revived political engagement in trade unions and leftist parties (Mischi 2016) and a rise in abstention and the increasing success of the Front National (FN) vote. The change of rationale of achieving local worthiness via politics has in effect intensified the feeling of rejection that spreads beyond just the unemployed and temporary workers. Far from a supposed 'authoritarianism' of the rural working classes, and it is important to note that it is the self-employed who vote the most often for the FN, it is the destabilisation of previously stable forms of relationships between social groups that drive political abstention and votes for the far right. Such rationales are also being observed in the villages of suburban areas of large cities where working-class households, slowly ascending socially and seeking respectability, buy private property more easily than in towns (Lambert 2015). As a result of the individualisation of work relationships, the value of personal merit and of forms of economic stabilisation, an aspiration is developing in such households that reinforces 'the awareness of certain right-wing values surrounding entrepreneurship [rather than] the collective defence of social groups [. . .]. Among certain [voters], the preservation of the social grouping of respectable households goes hand in hand with the rejection of precarious and racialised groups' (Girard 2017: 311–312). It has led to a mainstreaming of far right statements, strongly divided between areas that are subjected to deindustrialisation, more often situated in the east and north of France, and areas in the west with a more diversified economy (e.g. Schnapper 2019).

'My cows ain't majorettes.' Social activities and cultural practices

Beyond the elected representatives alone, the arrival of more qualified populations and the transformation of village social activities call into question the social activities established within a working-class social grouping. The practice of music in harmony, mainly anchored in the rural world and within the established working classes, has therefore continued to decline since the 1970s. Far from a model of musical excellence (its public image is that of old-fashioned and poor-quality music), such an amateur practice has particularly suffered as a result of the rise of music schools and the extension of education which culturally and physically distances young people from their municipality of origin (Dubois et al. 2009). This last factor means that more generally, and in comparison with the post-war years, the leisure activities of the rural population are experiencing a form of generational rupture. Even if some young students continue to take part in a village leisure activity for which they return at the weekend, the majority of those from the middle classes and established working classes quickly give up on village social activities. This is evidenced by the increase in 'fusions' of rural sports clubs and the fact that the social base of sports such as football has become impoverished (Renahy 2001). At the same time, sports and cultural opportunities are diversifying but they are concentrated in market towns and are bringing about a form of dilettantism.[4] This revival of rural social activities, marked by an increasing confrontation between rationales of local belonging and rationales of elective belonging based on forms of distinction, contributes to the marginalisation of the working classes, despite being the majority in rural areas as previously discussed; for example, the conversion of urban middle-class individuals into rural artisans making it a more socially heterogeneous profession (Mazaud 2013), or the arrival of this social group in a given rural area redefining what is a 'local' food product through the creation of purchasing groups of organic products (Malié 2016).

This evolution is evidently even more striking in touristic areas where recreational use of nature, the coast or mountains has been developed extensively. First, a sustenance practice, collecting fish products on the Atlantic coast – known as 'shore fishing' – also became a pastime in the 1950s and then a product aimed at tourists in the 1990s (Papinot 2003). Staged as 'local heritage' for the tourists, it became folklore and a source of development capitalised on by some elected representatives, in the same way as pastureland in the mountains is nowadays. In this way, the 'transhumances en Couserans' (Couserans Transhumance), established in 2000 in the Pyrenees, initially saw small-scale farmers engaging unwillingly in an event that was imposed on them: 'my cows ain't majorettes,' said one (Chandivert 2010). It was only after several years that they took over the celebration for themselves, taking the opportunity to make it their own collective festive event whilst keeping their distance (for example, the organisers asking that they speak in dialect can become insults aimed at tourists). Moreover, the perpetuation of the spatial appropriation of territory by the aristocracy and the upper class through the practice of fox hunting is the sign of the revived involvement of certain working-class groups (who attend the hunting voluntarily) in relations of personalised domination (Fradkine 2015). These last examples show that the marginalisation of less economically and culturally endowed rural populations is not necessarily systematic or unequivocal: dominated, they are still likely to re-appropriate cultural practices of which they are not the originators and, therefore, to retain degrees of autonomy in that domination (Grignon and Passeron 1989). But the rural working classes are nevertheless regularly robbed of their leisure activity practices, rivalled 'on their own territories.'

Home and care: growing old in rural areas

If, by and large, the population of rural areas is no longer diminishing, that population is, however, continuing to age. Nearly one-third of inhabitants in 'remote rural areas' are over the age of 60, the slowing of the rural exodus being the result of a net migration that has become positive (including in remote rural areas) since the 1990s with natural population growth remaining negative (Détang-Dessendre and Piguet 2016). The development of domestic help and retirement homes bear witness to this demographic evolution. While aging necessitates a level of care, an important difference between the 'local elderly' (locals who have remained or returned to the village) and those who arrived later in the rural area can be observed. For the former, in the same way that grandparents are called upon to look after grandchildren when their children remain nearby, intergenerational solidarity can still sometimes work with elderly people staying at home. In a similar way, networks of friends can make it possible to prolong local social activity, particularly through clubs of rural elderly people or senior citizens' clubs. When the time for less independence comes, social activities and solidarity remain very similar in terms of making dinner, going to the doctor or collecting medication from the pharmacy, for example. On the other hand, for those who arrived later, the geographic distance from their children means that family solidarity is more dispersed over time and it is stronger when celebrating or during holidays. Children are looked after for several weeks of the summer as opposed to the daily childcare provided by locals. When it comes to being less independent, it necessitates a systematic recourse to domestic help, social activities being more elective (a few friends in the vicinity) than local (in the neighbourhood), and children only being able to act from time to time when there are 'setbacks' (Mallon 2013).

When the level of independence determines the need to enter into an institution, solidarity essentially rests with the children, irrespective of their previous living situation. Children become the 'inheritors without inheriting' who have to manage the family heritage in addition to monitoring the parents' health. The gendered division of children's roles is therefore emphasised: daughters or daughters-in-law deal with the daily expenses while the sons manage the important expenses. But the division is also social: the differentiated social destinies of siblings playing a role in forms of commitment and decision making (in terms of selling the now-vacant parental home, for example). As well as the eldest being in a position of strength in relation to the youngest, the children with careers in administration will more willingly take charge of the management tasks (Billaud 2012).

Conclusions

A number of developments discussed in this chapter support the idea of a confrontation between local belonging and legitimate culture, in other words, between the regenerating familiarity of the sedentary working classes' local space and a space for the more urbanised and cosmopolitan practices of the middle and upper classes. While the former aspires to prolong social activities on a local basis, the latter puts more elective belongings in place. It is therefore through analysing the expression of social and local belonging that the field of French rural studies is revived, making it possible to grasp the intricacies of the motivations behind social, political and cultural conflict. Such a revival has been possible due to the epistemological breaking down of rural sociology, which is no longer only interested in farmers and no longer postulates a ruralist position that isolates 'rurals' on principle. The documented developments have not affected only the countryside: the analysis of its transformations could clarify questions concerning French society in its entirety. In this way, the continued development of urban utilisation of rural space provides information on the practices of certain groups of city dwellers (Chamboredon 1980); the analysis of the localism of the working classes is useful for understanding the development of forms of political and trade union engagement of their established groups in towns (Retière 1994) and in the countryside (Mischi 2016).

In the same way, the *gilets jaunes* movement during the 2018–19 winter, both suddenly and unexpectedly, places rural and suburban populations at the very centre of the stage. But if it indicates rural inhabitants' dependence, which has become total, on cars and the limited standard of living of a majority of residents belonging to the working class, its motivations can also be found in growing social and spatial distances between populations, in the concentration of political power and in a deficit of citizen participation which affect rural areas (Bruneau et al. 2018) as well as urban areas (Desage and Guéranger 2011).

The fact remains that this revival of the area of rural studies is recent, inferring a still-fragmented knowledge of contemporary rural worlds. For example, French social sciences currently have little to say about the poorest farmers, the development of the management and support of rural populations by the public services (police force, social services), and even about the practices of French or foreign second home owners and the relationships that they have with these populations. These are all elements that contribute to the shaping of political and cultural practices.

Translated by Georgia Corp

Notes

1 These areas include the 'rural centres' (with less than 10,000 jobs) and their surrounding areas ('other suburbs' in Table 15.1), as well as the 'isolated municipalities, outside the influence of the centres' (or 'remote rural areas'). This categorisation, adopted in official statistics since 1999, complicates the common definition of the threshold of 2,000 hectares which separates town and countryside, making it possible to measure the effects of distance from urban economic centres. In effect, it is based on concentration of employment, the suburban characterising municipalities where the level of the resident workforce working in the centres is higher than 40%. Many villages belonging to the category 'suburbs of the large centres' are also therefore considered here as belonging to 'urban areas' and not to the 'predominantly rural area,' owing to their proximity to the labour market of the 'large centres.'

2 However, the most fragile groups of the self-employed, farmers, artisans and shopkeepers, can also be included, as will be done in subsequent paragraphs.

3 In this way, Barczak and Hilal (2017) show that the closure of small businesses because of large retailers especially affects rural areas. Also, in terms of public services, between 1980 and 2013, 'the decline affected primary and nursery schools, which are disappearing in one in four municipalities (–24%), post offices (–36% of municipalities), tax offices (–31 %), police forces (–13%), train stations (–28%), maternity wards (–48%) and hospitals (–4%). This decline in services especially affects small rural municipalities, market towns and small towns.'

4 A manager who organised the fusion of two football clubs said in an interview (November 2008): 'at the rural level, we are in a cycle where we have fewer and fewer kids, where there are more and more sports, even in rural areas, and more and more associations. So, the kids are hopping from one thing to another.'

References

Barczak, A. and M. Hilal. 2017. Quelle évolution de la présence des services publics en France? In T. Courcelle and Y. Filjakow (Eds.), *Services publics et territoires: adaptations, innovations et réactions.* Rennes: Presses Universitaires de Rennes, 31–65.

Bessière, C., I. Bruneau and G. Laferté. 2014. Les agriculteurs dans la France contemporaine. In *Sociétés Contemporaines*, 96, 5–25.

Billaud, S. 2012. Gérer le patrimoine 'en fratrie' à la suite de l'entrée en institution d'un parent âgé. In *Informations sociales*, 173, 120–126.

Bruneau, I. 2015. The Confédération Paysanne and the political field: a conflicted history. In D. Strijker, I. Terluin and G. Voerman (Eds.), *Rural Protest Groups and Populist Political Parties*. Wageningen: Wageningen Academic Publishers, 101–124.

Bruneau, I., G. Laferté, J. Mischi and N. Renahy. (Eds.). 2018. *Mondes ruraux et classes sociales*. Paris: EHESS, 'En temps & lieux.'

Bruneau, I. and N. Renahy. 2012. Une petite bourgeoisie au pouvoir. Sur le renouvellement des élus en milieu rural. In *Actes de la recherche en sciences sociales*, 191–192, 48–67.

Chamboredon, J. 1980. Les usages urbains de l'espace rural: du moyen de production au lieu de récréation. In *Revue française de sociologie*, 21:1, 97–119.

Chamboredon, J. 1985. Nouvelles formes de l'opposition ville-campagne. In M. Roncayolo (Ed.), *Histoire de la France urbaine*, tome 5. Paris: Seuil, 557–573.

Chamboredon, J. 2015. *Jeunesse et classes sociales*. Paris: Editions Rue d'Ulm/Presses de l'ENS.

Chandivert, A. 2010. *Promouvoir les singularités locales: politiques de l'authenticité et usages sociaux du patrimoine en Couserans*. Ariège, thèse d'ethnologie, université de Montpellier.

Coquard, B. 2018. Faire partie de la bande. Le groupe d'amis comme instance de légitimation d'une masculinité populaire et rurale. In *Genèses*, 111, 50–69.

Deffontaines, N. 2014. La souffrance sociale chez les agriculteurs. Quelques jalons pour une compréhension du suicide. In *Études Rurales*, 193, 13–24.

Desage, F. and D. Guéranger. 2011. *La politique confisquée. Sociologie des réformes et des institutions intercommunales*. Bellecombe-en-Bauges: Le Croquant.

Détang-Dessendre, C. and V. Piguet. 2016. La population des villes et des campagnes: des mobilités qui comblent les disparités historiques? In S. Blancard, C. Détang-Dessendre and N. Renahy (coord.), *Campagnes contemporaines. Enjeux économiques et sociaux des espaces ruraux français*. Versailles: Quae, 9–22.

Dubois, V., J. Méon and E. Pierru. 2009. *Les mondes de l'harmonie. Enquête sur une pratique musicale amateur*. Paris: La Dispute.

Duclos, N. 1998. *Les Violences paysannes sous la Ve République*. Paris: Économica.

Fradkine, H. 2015. Chasse à courre, relations interclasses et domination spatialisée. In *Genèses*, 99, 28–47.

Girard, V. 2017. *Le vote FN au village. Trajectoires de ménages populaires du périurbain*. Bellecombe-en-Bauges: Le Croquant.

Giraud, C. and J. Rémy. 2008. Les choix des conjoints en agriculture. In *Revue d'études en agriculture et environnement*, 88, 21–46.

Grignon, C. and J. Passeron. 1989. *Le Savant et le populaire, misérabilisme et populisme en sociologie et en littérature*. Paris: Seuil – Gallimard.

Koebel, M. 2014. Le profil social des maires de France. In *Pouvoirs*, 148, 123–138.

Laferté, G. 2018. *L'embourgeoisement. Une enquête chez les céréaliers*. Paris: Raisons d'Agir.

Laferté, G. and N. Renahy. 2003. 'Campagnes de tous nos désirs' . . . d'ethnologues. In *L'Homme*, 166, 225–234.

Lambert, A. 2015. *'Tous propriétaires!' L'envers du décor pavillonnaire*. Paris: Seuil/Liber.

Lynch, E. 2013. Détruire pour exister: les grèves du lait en France (1964, 1972 et 2009). In *Politix*, 103, 99–124.

Malié, A. 2016. 'C'est local, c'est ce qui nous intéresse.' Etude des constructions et usages du 'local' à travers les pratiques alimentaires. In E. Aunis, J. Benet, A. Mège and I. Prat (Eds.), *Les territoires de l'autochtonie*. Rennes: Presses Universitaires de Rennes, 97–110.

Mallon, I. 2013. Vieillir en milieu rural isolé: une analyse au prisme des sociabilités. In *Gérontologie et société*, 146, 73–88.

Mazaud, C. 2013. *L'artisanat français. Entre métier et entreprise*. Rennes: Presses universitaires de Rennes.

Mischi, J. 2013. Contested rural activities: class, politics and shooting in the French countryside. In *Ethnography*, 14:1, 64–84.

Mischi, J. 2016. *Le Bourg et l'atelier. Sociologie du combat syndical*. Marseille: Agone.

Nicolas, F. 2016. Capitaux d'autochtonie et professionnalisation agricole. Le cas de l'agriculture biologique. In E. Aunis, J. Benet, A. Mège and I. Prat (Eds.), *Les territoires de l'autochtonie*. Rennes: Presses Universitaires de Rennes, 51–67.

Papinot, C. 2003. Requalification du littoral et conflits d'usage. L'estran-environnement et l'estran-territoire. In *Sociétés contemporaines*, 52, 105–121.

Renahy, N. 2001. Football et représentation territoriale: un club amateur dans un village ouvrier. In *Ethnologie française*, 31:4, 707–715.

Renahy, N. 2005. *Les gars du coin. Enquête sur une jeunesse rurale*. Paris: La Découverte.

Retière, J-N. 1994. *Identités ouvrières: histoire sociale d'un fief ouvrier en Bretagne 1909–1990*. Paris: L'Harmattan.

Retière, J-N. 2003. Autour de l'autochtonie. Réflexions sur la notion de capital social populaire. In *Politix*, 63, 121–143.

Rogers, S. C. 1995. Natural histories: the rise and fall of French rural studies. In *French Historical Studies*, 19, 381–397.

Samak, M. 2013. Quand la 'bio' rebat les cartes de la représentation des agriculteurs. L'institutionnalisation de l'agriculture biologique dans les Alpes-Maritimes. In *Politix*, 125–148.

Schnapper, Q. 2019. 'Ils ont volé l'identité de la foire aux agriculteurs!' Fête, défaites et luttes de pouvoir dans un bourg périurbain de Vendée (1980–2016). In C. Granger and L. Le Gall (Eds.), *L'élection au village. Quand les campagnes s'emparent de la politique, XXe-XXIe siècles*. Paris: Publications de la Sorbonne.

Sencébé, Y. 2004. Être ici, être d'ici. Formes d'appartenance dans le Diois (Drôme). In *Ethnologie française*, 34:1, 23–29.

Siblot, Y., M. Cartier, I. Coutant, O. Masclet and N. Renahy. 2015. *Sociologie des classes populaires contemporaines*. Paris: Armand Colin.

Vignon, S. 2010. Les élus des petites communes face à la 'démocratie d'expertise' intercommunale. Les 'semi-professionnels' de la politique locale. In S. Barone and A. Troupel (Eds.), *Battre la campagne. Elections et pouvoir municipal en milieu rural*. Paris: L'Harmattan, 189–224.

Weber, F. 1989. Le travail à-côté. Etude d'ethnographie ouvrière. Paris: INRA/EHESS.

16

GENDER AND CRISIS

Women's writing in French at the start of the twenty-first century

Shirley Jordan

Taking as axiomatic Simone de Beauvoir's observation that '[r]ien n'est définitivement acquis' [nothing is definitively acquired], the news magazine *Marianne* marked the transition from 2016 to 2017 with a 100-page special feature entitled 'Place aux femmes.'[1] Readers are reminded of the issues and victories that have defined women's ongoing battle for rights in France since the late 1960s, yet the tone is cautionary rather than celebratory: if *Marianne* sees in the new year with a focus on women, this is because of a freshly emerging sense that 'leur liberté est en danger' [their freedom is in danger] and that '[l]a grande régression des droits de femmes est en marche' [the great regression of women's rights is underway] (Gozlan 2016: 38). The same note is struck by feminist historian Christine Bard, who defines third-wave feminism as a largely defensive movement that combats an anti-feminist counter-revolution bolstered on an international scale by leaders such as Vladimir Putin and Donald Trump (Bard 2017: 50).

This chapter approaches the question of gender through a focus on tensions between constraint and freedom as explored in women's experimental writing in French at the start of the twenty-first century. It shows how current aspects of social change and prevailing values and ideologies concerning women are finding their way into literature and related scholarship. Its central thread is the idea of crisis, broadly understood: this includes the real experiences of gender-specific crisis that so frequently characterise women's lives and the perceived crises that are too readily attributed by society at large to women's ongoing attempts to reject restrictive, naturalised ideas of their role and 'place.' The period which serves as context and backdrop to the writings discussed is fraught with anxieties around identity politics. If France's pre-millennium moment was marked by some up-beat developments in terms of gender equality, including *la parité* (equal representation of women and men in parliament) and PACS (the '*pacte civil de solidarité*' which gave rights to cohabiting couples of both mixed and same-sex),[2] the early years of the twenty-first century have seen visceral division on the issue of same-sex marriage and parenting, and – more alarmingly – on the validity of gender theory as an area of study.

'Non à la théorie du genre!' [No to gender theory!] might seem a surprising slogan with which to take to the streets, yet it formed part of the soundscape of the 2014 mass political demonstration dubbed 'la manif pour tous' [the demonstration for all].[3] The thousands of protesters who demonstrated on the streets of Paris brandishing banners to promote the traditional family were also keen to denounce the supposedly corrosive nature of a field of enquiry which has been common currency in Anglo-American academia and popular culture since the 1980s.

Conservative groups deeply troubled by the theory's downgrading of biological distinctions and foregrounding of discursive practices and social constructions as a way of accounting for differences between the sexes were particularly angered by proposals to introduce such ideas to children as part of the primary school curriculum.[4] Their outcry is one instance of the way in which gender identities become scapegoats for more generalised anxieties in a country whose national identity is profoundly enmeshed with traditional views of femininity, masculinity and family (Perreau 2016; Zaretsky 2014).

In a climate of rising conservatism, thinking spaces provided by women's writing become especially vital. Experimental female-authored literature in France and beyond has a long history of providing sharply observant critiques and powerful arguments for change via embodied, intimate and complex accounts of individual lives. It is through such writing that private experiences which have been constructed as unspeakable and therefore unalterably confining become subject to debate, deconstruction and reframing. Literature thus remains critical to women's battles for rights, and the texts discussed in the current chapter are no exception. All share a preoccupation with the female body, perhaps the most familiar terrain of feminist debate. Women's bodies and who decides what happens to them constitute perennial subjects in women's literary accounts of their lives and continue to make headlines in new, often disturbing ways. Here I outline four recurring areas of body politics explored in recent women's writing in French. Each is specifically contemporary in emphasis; each is informative in terms of its departure from earlier accounts of women's embodied experience; and each entails forms of crisis into which women's bodies are thrown by cultural and societal pressures. These areas – mothering, sexual violence, eating disorders, and ageing – demonstrate certain continuities with women's body writing since second-wave feminist writings of the 1970s, but also show marked shifts in emphasis. For example, the celebratory trope of the mothering body as elaborated in *écriture féminine* has given way to multiple realist accounts of maternal ambivalence, while the physically explicit, often emotionally voided writing of sex that characterised taboo-busting female-authored works of the 1990s (Best and Crowley 2007; Jordan 2006) has given way to two different emphases: on the one hand a new curiosity about romantic love and affect (Holmes 2006); on the other a stark confrontation with sexual violence. Literary expressions of eating disorders and first-hand experiences of ageing are by contrast relatively new motifs, both notably expressive of early twenty-first-century concerns.

The backdrop to the literature examined in this chapter is the rapidly shifting, often conflicted configuration of third-wave feminism. One might sum up the third wave as pragmatic rather than programmatic, a mosaic of movements in which political theory and action are repeatedly peeled apart and assembled afresh in response to local circumstance (Bantegni et al. 2007). Of particular interest in today's multicultural France is intersectional feminism involving groups who seek to express the specificity of women's experience in migrant – especially Muslim – communities. The endangered freedoms referred to in the special feature of *Marianne* are those of all women, yet neo-feminist groups such as *Ensemble* [Together] and *Osez le féminisme!* [Dare to be feminist!] remain silent about the oppression of women in Islam for fear of stoking racism, thus placing France's secular, universalist vision of feminism under threat and doing little to address the problems of women who experience 'le cocktail explosif de l'Islamisme et de la pauvreté' [the explosive cocktail of Islamism and poverty] (Gozlan 2016: 53). Meanwhile distinctive feminisms are emerging within the Muslim religious world. Zahira Ali, author of the first book on Islamic feminism (Ali 2012) protests vigorously that all feminists should heed women's voices as they speak to us from France, Iran, Morocco, Syria and Egypt in order to 'décoloniser le féminisme hégémonique' [decolonise hegemonic feminism] (Ali 2012: 41) and give the lie to the prejudice that sees Islam and feminist activism as incompatible. Certain of the works examined in this chapter and the scholarship that sets out their importance are particularly concerned with the lives of Muslim protagonists and invite readers to locate the expressions of crisis that they explore on a continuum spanning culturally specific experiences in different areas of the francophone world. They share with all of the writings explored herein a determination to defy shame and to express publicly private experiences judged to be excessively intimate.[5]

Rewriting mothering

Much is invested in ideas of mothers and mothering, by society at large and by women themselves. This is strongly the case in France, a country with a distinctly Catholic and pro-natalist history where perceived disruptions of traditional mothering roles have often been fiercely contested, from battles over reproductive rights (contraception, abortion, new reproductive technologies and surrogacy) to current anxieties about same-sex parenting which, as Gill Rye points out, sets in train 'an interrogation of conventional parenting roles and a fundamental questioning of even who or what a mother is' (Rye 2013: 7). Notwithstanding the current rise of conservatism and populism in Europe, which may well erode women's freedom to make choices about motherhood and mothering, France is seeing sustained efforts on the part of some women to re-invent social perceptions of mothers through powerful, sometimes disturbing literary accounts. Analysing mothers as narrative subjects in turn-of-the-millennium French literature, Rye notes that although mothers have long been present in literature, they seldom speak as such: instead they are habitually 'objects of the narratives and discourses and of the fears and fantasies of others – of sons, daughters, husbands, lovers, of omniscient narrators, and of religions, ideologies and politics' (Rye 2009: 15). One of the most remarkable developments ushered in over the last three decades is the introduction of mothers' voices and perspectives in women's writing in French, whether fictional, autobiographical or auto-fictional. What does the world as focalised by mother protagonists and mother narrators look like? How are maternal subjectivities expressed in the text and what do they reveal about the complex experiences that come with mothering?

One might single out Marie Darrieussecq's novel *Le Mal de mer* (1999) as a hinge text since it straddles different 'takes' on the mother. The novel combines perspectives of child on mother and mother on child, this dual focalisation heightening the emotional and ethical stakes of a story concerning a woman who is ambivalent about mothering and who first abducts her infant daughter then abandons her – it seems definitively – at the novel's end. The reader's own investment in mother figures is put to the test by the access we are given to the inner worlds and unspoken needs of both child and woman. Darrieussecq's book therefore combines the traditional focalisation on the mother from the daughter's perspective, the newer phenomenon of women writing as mothers, and the still more recent trend of women writing about how they are shaking off ideologies of the family and eschewing the role of mother altogether (Edwards 2016). Darrieussecq's powerfully punning title, which relies on the often connected homophones *mer* (sea) and *mère* (mother), recasts familiar tropes connecting women and water and harnesses ideas of being at sea and of sea-sickness to characterise the mother/daughter relationship as a destabilising malaise for both parties.[6]

What is daring about many new narratives of mothering is that they bring vividly to expression the darker, unavowed aspects of maternal experience at the expense of the socially acceptable ideal. Several major writers – Darrieussecq, Christine Angot, Véronique Olmi, Camille Laurens, Marie NDiaye and Geneviève Brisac among others – have created a space in literature for exploring maternal ambivalence, for seeking new ways to mother and to talk about mothering, for voicing unspoken experiences such as the trauma of birth (Rye 2009: 54–74) and for investigating issues such as abortion or infanticide (Morello 2011). Women writers are also turning to literature to explore same-sex parenting (Payne 2016). In short, the conflicts and crises of mothering are increasingly being foregrounded, with the result that astonishing gaps in the articulation of women's bodily and emotional experience are now being filled. This is one important field wherein the symbolic value of literature constitutes a breach in the wider discursive fabric, making it possible to think and speak more openly about troubling private experience. Given the pressure on mothers to conform to their biologically and socially prescribed role, there is something even more transgressive about these new stories of mothering than about the narratives of sexual pleasure and promiscuity that were flagged up in 1990's France as so radical. Certainly the risk of stigma is greater and the liberating possibility arguably more profound. Collectively these works fracture the naturalised image of the ideal mother, throwing into question the oversimplified 'good mother'/'bad mother' binary, and problematising the knee-jerk attribution – and assumption – of maternal guilt.

Meanwhile the growing phenomenon of voluntary childlessness has begun to receive expression in French life-writing. In the first study of this phenomenon, Nathalie Edwards asks why some women in twentieth- and twenty-first-century France are deciding not to have children; how their rejection of motherhood is accounted for and explored in literary narrative; and how their writings begin to set out pathways for understanding women in ways that are not linked to their reproductive role (Edwards 2016). Importantly, the authors analysed in Edwards' book 'reframe their choice not to mother, turning it from something that consigns them as deviant to something that has the potential to destabilize current understandings of female identity' (Edwards 2016: 192). Here traditionalist assumptions that are so naturalised it can seem almost sacrilegious to call them into question – the unshakeable inevitability of mother love; the idea of 'maternal fibre' – are thrown into crisis not by dark, ambivalent or alternative accounts of mothering but by cogent accounts of decisions to eschew the experience in favour of a different way of life.

The aforementioned experiments do not of course mean that expressions of the powerfulness of maternal love disappear. Indeed, one of the most impassioned literary spats to take place in France in recent years was sparked by tensions around the perceived authority of mother narrators and the authenticity of stories of maternal loss. When Camille Laurens detected 'borrowings' in Darrieussecq's fictional *Tom est mort* (2007) from her own autobiographical story of maternal bereavement, *Philippe* (1995) complex and bitter debates were launched, fuelled not just by concerns about plagiarism or the fragile borderlines that separate fiction, autobiography and auto-fiction, but by the full force of maternal instinct (Barnes 2015). Laurens protected the closed circle of grief created between herself, Philippe her dead child and *Philippe* the book dedicated to him. Her avowed equation of boy and book perhaps accounts for the ferocity that characterised her attack on Darrieussecq. That said, what has become clear in the numerous alternative stories about mothering that mark recent literary production is that the pressure to conform to a maternal 'ideal' is vigorously challenged, as indeed is the perception that women who choose not to have children at all are an aberration.

Writing sexual violence

Statistics concerning sexual violence in France are alarming.[7] It is estimated that one woman is raped every seven minutes and that one in ten will be raped or undergo attempted rape at some point in her life (Foïs 2011). Research concerning the materiality of rape as a 'corporeal expression of gender divisions' in twenty-first-century France (Fayard 2013: 36) offers a chilling account of the prevalence of sexual violence and the numerous obstacles – symbolic, affective, practical and legal – that result in so few cases being pursued in the courts and even fewer convictions. A number of authors, some of them drawing on personal experience, have recently begun to respond to the silencing of sexual violence against women and to the consequent scarcity of literary representations, especially representations of rape. Author and film-maker Virginie Despentes scrutinises rape and tackles the challenge to expression that it presents, first in her landmark novel and film *Baise-moi* (2000) (translated in English as *Rape Me*) and more recently in her punchy feminist manifesto-cum-memoir *King Kong théorie* (2006: 35–57) (see Edwards 2013). Despentes provides an angry but clear-sighted analysis of rape's deeply rooted foundational role in sexual politics, its centrality to feminine identity, the circularity of the conspiracy that militates against its articulation, and its function in women's sexual fantasies. She also takes a bold stance in staunchly rejecting victim status. Other feminist critics too have sought to examine the idea of woman as intrinsically violable (Robson 2015). At around the same time Algerian-born French feminist activist Samira Bellil likewise spoke out about the phenomenon of *tournantes* (gang rapes), a distinctive part of the sexual violence associated with the disadvantaged North African and African immigrant suburbs that lie on the periphery of French cities (Bellil 2003). Her testimony drew public attention to the contempt and disgust with which women, their bodies and their stories are frequently treated in these communities. Bellil's case is all the more disquieting since her violators were known to her and since it was she, not they, who was disowned by family and community. Published shortly after the release of the film *La Squale* (2000) whose opening gang-rape sequence so shocked France, Bellil's book consolidates the sense that such rapes are endemic and highlights the unwritten law of silence that weighs upon victims.

The forms of sexual violence that are currently finding expression in literature include, then, those which 'affect foreign and ethnic minority women in specific spaces and ways' (Fayard 2013: 36) and which have been campaigned against by feminist groups such as *Voix d'Elles Rebelles*, *Rajfire* and *Ni Putes Ni Soumises*, a group which Bellil helped to found. Indeed some of the most explicit female-authored accounts of extreme sexual violence – for instance, rape as a tool of war and the brutal treatment of prostitutes – are written by women whose culture militates most strongly against their speaking out. The escalation of Islamic fundamentalism during the 1990's civil war in Algeria and the widespread abuse, torture, rape and murder of women that took place during the period are largely occulted in journalistic and official historical accounts, but in their experimental writings authors such as Assia Djebar, Latifa Ben Mansour, Leïla Marouane and Malika Mokeddem produce stories, generated by real-life experiences, which constitute counter-histories designed to address the period's violent excesses and to write women's experience authoritatively into history. These narratives have been described as 'fictionalized testimonial' (El Nossery 2012), a specific subset of women's writing whose delicate slippage between fact and invention establishes truths about what is unspeakable. Marouane's is one of the most powerful voices in terms of writing rape. Through allegory, metaphor and the fantastic, and always from the point of view of the victim, her intensely violent writing forges memorable accounts of rape's trauma, and does so in defiance of a culture in which a writing woman, deemed ideologically aberrant, writes at the risk of her life.

Writing in risk sums up the position of Iranian author Chahdortt Djavann who lives in exile in France. Her novel *Les Putes voilées n'iront jamais au Paradis!* (2016) interweaves the story of Soudabeh and Zahra, two adolescent girls forced into prostitution, with posthumous testimonies from prostitutes who were murdered, hanged or stoned in Iran. Based on first-hand experience of misogyny and sexual violence in Islamic culture, the novel depicts the raw brutality of sex orchestrated by men who are taught to despise the object of their desire, and women who have no choice but to let them carry out their fantasies. Djavann's female protagonists are beaten, whipped, incarcerated, drugged and reduced to sexual slavery. Meanwhile the men who commit such crimes on 'expendable' women keep their own women as chattels and guarantors of their honour. Sharia law deems the prostitute valueless and legitimises her murder, recasting it as 'sanitisation' or 'purification.' Yet the upshot of Djavann's swingeing attack on the various forms of violence meted out to women in radical Islam is to endow women with a distinctly powerful voice which goes some way towards writing them out of victim status. The virtuosity, wry irony and clear-sightedness of the novel's various storytellers constitute a powerful appropriation of experiences of abuse.

While the debates about women and misogyny raised by Djavann's courageous book are generated by its Iranian context, they cannot be peeled away entirely from the scenario in contemporary France. In French culture too the prevalent symbolic construction of rape is such that the legal system 'enables rape to be accepted as an inevitable fact of [women's] (private) everyday lives' (Fayard 2013: 49) and implicitly invokes the victim's consent so that even at the start of the twenty-first century 'the political will fully to recognize the reality of rape is still lamentably weak' (51). Further, the misogyny of *Les Putes voilées* lurks in recent attempts on the part of conservative Muslims in the outer-city areas of Paris and Lyon to ban women from certain public spaces. And according to one's views on the veil, it might also be detected in the fashion ranges recently launched by major brands such as Dolce and Gabanna or Marks and Spencer which are referred to as 'pudique' [modest], which include hidjabs, headscarves, burkinis and abayas, and which are reportedly taking off in France. Certainly Djavann's omnipresent leitmotif of the chador, which she sees as reducing women symbolically to the status of sexual objects and which serves tellingly as a murder weapon in her novel (prostitutes are strangled with it and their corpses wrapped in it), evokes the unresolved, often hysterical responses to the veiling and unveiling of the female body that characterise France's ongoing postcolonial struggle with pluri-culturalism. In conclusion, if sexual violence as experienced by women remains under-articulated and under-theorised (Higgins and Silver 1991; Mardorossian 2004; Robson 2015) accounts such as those just outlined show an increasing resolve to address the gap.

Eating disorders and disorderly eating

Disorderly eating in its various forms is a complex set of phenomena that blight individual lives and represent a major challenge to public health systems in France as in other developed countries at the start of the twenty-first century. Pathologies such as anorexia nervosa, bulimia and binge eating disorder, which are strongly gendered and almost overwhelmingly experienced by young women, are key instances of the body in crisis yet in spite of a raft of factors – the alarming statistics; the undeniably powerful experience of these disorders; the fact that they are now widely reported in the public domain and the evidence they give of severe, widespread malaise in response to a range of social factors – they have been extremely slow to find voice in literature. This is now changing in France as an increasing number of writers, often also sufferers, are rising to the challenge of bringing the experience to articulation. At the same time scholarship on such writing is growing, in part thanks to the current interest in the medical humanities.

Unsurprisingly most of this literature is produced by younger women writers, although there are some exceptions: it is notable for example that veteran life-writer Annie Ernaux, now in her seventies, recently wrote for the very first time about a period of her late teens and early twenties that was marked by an eating disorder (Ernaux 2016). Best-selling mainstream authors such as Amélie Nothomb, Marie NDiaye and Marie Darrieussecq have each produced creative, metaphorical explorations of women whose responses to food become disorderly. Nothomb's female protagonists habitually evoke the contentiously skeletal images of women in the fashion world, clinging to their androgynous childhood physique and expressing revulsion at the onset of womanhood (Damlé 2013); NDiaye's protagonist Olga in the short story 'Le Jour du Président' (2006) self-starves while the housewife Antoinette in the author's curious fable 'La Gourmandise' (1996) organises her day around secret orgies of binge eating. Finally, the protagonist of Darrieussecq's novel *Truismes* (1996) whose metamorphosing body famously serves as a magnet for multiple interpretations and debates as it shifts to-and-fro between woman and pig, presents with aberrant attitudes, desires and practices with regard to food so that one possible analysis involves casting her as a symbolic sufferer of bulimia and anorexia.

There are writings too which are much more clinically precise about the mechanisms of self-harm through food deprivation and which straddle the diary and the survival guide: Geneviève Brisac's *Petite* (1994), Marta Aleksandra Balinska's *Retour à la vie: quinze ans d'anorexie* (2003), Camille de Peretti's *Thorynitorynx* (2006), Mélanie Courtelle's *Journal d'une faim de vivre: témoignage* (2011) and Nicole Desportes' *Voyage jusqu'au bout de la vie; comment j'ai vaincu l'anorexie* (2016) are instances of personal testimonies which offer detailed, embodied descriptions of disturbed interactions with food including binge eating and vomiting. Each seeks to account for the pathology, to overcome its unspeakable dimension and to conjure shame. Each expresses the sufferer's desire for transparency, her loss of a sense of self, her deteriorating body, her avoidance behaviour around food, and a catalogue of routines, rituals, phobias and control mechanisms. A skeletal form may be adopted, giving the text little in the way of 'padding.' Thus Janine Teisson's *L'enfant plume* (2012), the poetic testimony of a mother, struggles to find a form that will lend the experience its full impact and offers the reader spare fragments redolent with unspoken emotion. Meanwhile, Marie Le Bars' *Appelez-moi plume* (2014) brings together a chorus of voices around an anorexic girl. Designed for patients, therapists and families, the book takes the form of an *abécédaire* [ABC], running from 'Aménorrhée' [Amenorrhea] to 'Vie' [Life], and is compiled as a collaborative venture, in part because words are 'les premières victimes de cette maladie' [the first victims of this illness], and '[l]es patients ne savent plus parler' [patients no longer know how to speak] (49).

If the pressures that engender eating disorders are notoriously difficult to pinpoint, causality becomes still more clouded where issues of cultural integration and postcolonial stigmatisation are part of the picture. Recent literature by women of North African origin offers instances of self-starving heroines whose pathologies present the reader with particularly pronounced interpretative problems (Meuret 2009; Bordo 2009; Hron 2005). In a study of French-Maghrebi writer Fawzia Zouari's anorexic protagonist Amira in *Ce Pays dont je meurs* (2000), Anna Kemp reads her starved body against the grain, resisting theory which sees the individual's physical disorder as expressive of the collective malaise of cultural 'others' and which 'limits them to speaking from a place of suffering' (2016: 50). Kemp shows how Zouari invites us to unpick such deceptively smooth interpretations, and how she harnesses the causal indeterminacy of anorexia to raise debates about gender, integration and identity that are more searching and troubling than those inscribed in, for example, the now familiar coming-of-age stories found in Beur fiction of the 1980s and 1990s. Growing up in a working-class family of Algerian immigrants, and the only member of that family to be born in France, Amira struggles against the confining stereotypes of class, race and gender. Indeed her illness itself is caught up in this debilitating mass of pre-formed conceptions, for it is, according to her family, '[u]n mal français' [a French sickness] (Zouari 2000: 77). Amira's thwarted desire for the anonymity and invisibility that French Republican ideology in theory promises her, results in a will to progressive disappearance which places her 'beyond easy recuperation by the politics of voice and visibility' (Kemp 2016: 57). Critically, Amira's diminishing body and crisis of self-harm take the reader beyond the habitual terms of the politics of pain that we expect to find inscribed in narratives of cultural otherness written by cultural others. The easy – and politically ineffectual – appeal to the reader's empathy in such literary accounts is short-circuited in this case by Amira's 'accusatory withdrawal from the reader's gaze' (62) and therefore, as Kemp suggests, it is usefully called into question as a general proposition. For Kemp, Amira's pathology thus serves as a way of highlighting the habitual pathologisation of immigrant writing and disturbing the unproblematised pleasures that identification with its protagonists can provide for readers.

Writers in France have, then, begun to thread their way down the difficult path of drawing eating disorders into literature and scholars of French and comparative culture are increasingly following (e.g. Cairns 2007, 2015, 2017; Robson 2016; Bagley et al. 2017). Such writings propose in-depth relationships with fictional or real sufferers, offering detailed phenomenological and experiential accounts of their disorders and raising fascinating issues in terms of interpretation and reception. Collectively, they are set to provide the general reader, the sufferer and the medical establishment with opportunities to enhance their understanding of the grave and all too often unspoken psychiatric disorders which are tellingly dubbed by Émilie Durand a 'folie ordinaire' [ordinary madness] (Durand 2006).

Ageing

A crisis in social care looms in France as in many other developed countries with rapidly ageing populations. Average life expectancy for women born in 2016 is 85 and women will form the majority of the predicted 270,000 centenarians in 2070.[8] If older people in France are becoming, in cultural and economic terms, 'an increasingly powerful and vocal section of the population' (Demossier and Milner 2000: 75), it nonetheless remains the case that in several key respects society is (paradoxically) youth-oriented, and old age devalued. It is not only the problem of care that needs addressing: the long-standing 'invisibility' of the old needs to be overcome so that ageing is articulated in the mainstream and society's symbolic representation of itself accommodates to its demographic shift. Yet there have been few literary depictions seeking to counter what remain overwhelmingly negative perceptions of life's late phases and the ageing subject has received little attention outside the social sciences (Davis 2006). Further, it remains the case that women's ageing is especially stigmatised: woman is 'encore perdante parmi ces perdants qui sont les vieux' [once again a loser among those losers that are the old] (Détrez and Simon 2006: 124) and feminist trailblazers have struggled with the issue as much as other women (Holmes 2012).

Simone de Beauvoir's pioneering exposure of the systemic devaluing of and contempt for the elderly in her philosophical, autobiographical and literary writing still sets the terms of debate to a great extent. Beauvoir's politically driven essay *La Vieillesse* (1970) sheds light on the shaming and shameful construction of the elderly as pariah, while *Le deuxième sexe* (1949), *La Femme rompue* (1967) and *La Force des choses* (1963) give wrenching accounts of women's distressing entrapment in ageing, and of ageing as a crisis of selfhood and an existential scandal. Against this backdrop, recent writing by authors such as Hélène Cixous, Annie Ernaux, Nancy Huston, Régine Detambel, Noëlle Châtelet and Dominique Rolin has grappled afresh with experiences of ageing, not only in an attempt to expose society's symbolic and material framing of older women but also to challenge perspectives on ageing as produced by anthropologists, philosophers and gerontologists and to change the way in which ageing is viewed (Boyer-Weinmann 2013).

There remain of course literary explorations of ageing which are dominated by a Beauvoirean sense of crisis. Self-styled libertine Catherine Millet, whose *La Vie sexuelle de Catherine*

M (2002) rewrote the script of women's sexuality, grapples with ageing in *Jour de souffrance* (2009) which narrates the sexual jealousy of an older woman; Annie Ernaux, who offsets her fear of both ageing and cancer by asserting the predominance of her sexuality and desirability in *L'Usage de la photo* (2005), opens and closes her autobiographical *Les Années* (2008) with disjointed fragments which convey her terror of dementia (Jordan 2011); while the narrator of Camille Laurens' fictional *Celle que vous croyez* (2016) invents a more youthful online identity which she uses to seduce her former partner of 20 years her junior, thus performing a thorough critique of women's categorisation and valorisation according to youth.

Creative challenges to deleterious conceptions of older female bodies are also in evidence in Darrieussecq's *Truismes*. The novel focuses on the enduring production of women's bodies as battlegrounds for a struggle against ageing, parodies the slogans and beauty product brand names that promote ideologies of youth in the feminine press and thus returns some 30 years later to a phenomenon that exercised Beauvoir as well as feminist writers Benoîte and Flora Groult (Long 2013). The heroine's physical symptoms – body hair sprouting in the 'wrong' places; redistribution of fat; inability to stand straight; joint pains; a sense of isolation and worthlessness; and internalised self-disgust – are (stereo-)typically associated with women's ageing. Certain symptoms specifically recall those of the menopause, an experience little covered in literature. If *Truismes* seeks to bring us up close to women's distressing estrangement from their own bodies, it also seeks to parody the discourses around that estrangement, to diffuse their potency and to satirise the social opprobrium which contains and condemns un-beautiful bodies. A further fictional feminine body in crisis is offered by Marie NDiaye's metamorphosing heroine Nadia in the novel *Mon cœur à l'étroit* (2007). Like Darrieussecq, NDiaye brings us up close to the materiality of her protagonist's body, perpetuating the troublingly excessive intimacy which is familiar in women's writing in French in the period under study. It remains unclear whether Nadia's changes denote menopause or pregnancy, but in either case her entourage persistently draws attention to them and as a woman in her middle years her sense of her own body is overwhelmingly negative. Both protagonists experience themselves as physical aberrations; both might be read as parodying the 'not-to-be-seen-ness' of older women and the shame-inducing nature of feminine ageing.

Writers concerned to cast women's ageing in more positive light include Noëlle Châtelet. Châtelet approaches the subject from a range of perspectives: that of daughter, mother and – a subject position that is much more unusual in literature – of grandmother, most notably in *Au pays des vermeilles* (2009) where the narrator's relationship with her granddaughter ushers in a period of extraordinary expansion and discovery. As Siobhán MacIlvanney points out, Châtelet's writing creates important new spaces of identification, her focus challenging prevailing stereotypes of 'the passive, asexual, unfulfilled older female,' her overarching emphasis falling not on the decline of the body but instead on 'psychic regeneration' and 'the gift of insight' (McIlvanney 2016: 987). If Beauvoir contends in *La Force des choses* that her ageing offers no compensation, Châtelet's account of old age all but bypasses ideas of compensation, caught up as its narrator is in the intense pleasures of relationality with her granddaughter.[9]

The creative writing of Régine Detambel is especially remarkable for its determined focus on perceptions of the elderly and on the institutions that are set up to care for them (Gil 2014). In her essay *Le Syndrome de Diogène, éloge des vieillesses* (2008) and numerous fictional works Detambel explores the stigmatisation of the elderly as liminal, disgusting, even contagious ('tous des lépreux' [all lepers] (2008: 12)) and tackles questions such as agency, power and sexual desire from their point of view. Her stories, at once particular and universal, are to be the stories of all of us notwithstanding variables such as education and affluence, yet many remain reluctant to recognise themselves in the elderly: instead the 'monstrueuse inculture' [monstrous lack of knowledge] (Detambel 2010) and narrow-minded fear that typify responses to ageing are perpetuated. Thus, 'on étouffe en soi l'être-en-devenir-vieux que nous sommes tous' [we suffocate the being-in-ageing that we all are] (Detambel n.d.: 11). Detambel's 'l'être-en-devenir-vieux' evokes the existentialist ideal of the subject as self-determining project, reminding us of, yet overriding, Beauvoir's insistence on ageing as the loss of the authentic self and reading like an answer to the unresolved tension evident throughout *La Vieillesse* 'between assuming one's old age and being lost in otherness' (Martin 2011: 128).

Conclusions

This chapter has discussed some of the key aspects of women's experience, each connected in some way with crisis, that are currently finding expression in contemporary female-authored writing in French. It has noted a prevailing fear of regression in terms of women's rights and freedoms. It has also suggested the critical role played by creative writing, and by the scholarship to which it in turn gives rise, in bringing unspoken issues to prominence and opening them powerfully to debate and re-framing through detailed, embodied accounts. Landmark volumes emerging from research conducted under the aegis of the Centre for the Study of Contemporary Women's Writing (e.g. Damlé and Rye 2013; Damlé 2013)[10] indicate the broader range of motifs and issues that have been gaining prominence in women's writing in French at the start of the new millennium, confirming persuasively the power of literature to expose otherwise hidden facets of experience.

Let me conclude with a coda: while compiling this chapter I signed an online petition to protest against conservative-driven proposals to cease funding gender studies in the Île-de-France region. Since 2006 gender studies have enjoyed the status of DIM (Domaine d'intérêt majeur [Domain of Major Interest]) in the region, but this is to be rescinded. Indeed, the key words 'women' and 'rights' have also disappeared from the programme (Daumas 2016). This stifling of research which by its very nature disturbs naturalised categories, distinctions and hierarchies, is deeply worrying since our understanding of the forms of oppression that are based on gender difference is sharpened not only by the kind of creative writing discussed in this chapter but also by critical and theoretical studies on gender identities across the disciplines. As sociologist Laure Bereni notes, gender studies constitute 'à la fois une formidable aventure du champ des possibles, et une forme de désenchantement du monde tel qu'il est' [both a fantastic foray into the field of the possible, and a form of disenchantment with the world as it is] (Bereni 2016). It is this combination of protest and investigation that drives much of the most powerful women's writing in French at the start of the twenty-first century.

Notes

1 No. 1030–1031, 22 December 2016–5 January 2017, pp. 36–127. 'Place aux femmes' may be translated 'Make way for women,' but the idea of women's 'place' also lingers within it.
2 The PACS bill was passed in 1999. For key issues concerning sex and gender at this moment in French history, see Cairns (2000).
3 So called in reference to the 'mariage pour tous' [marriage for all] law passed by François Hollande's socialist government in May 2013.
4 Experiments with a programme called 'The ABC of equality' were launched in late 2013 in a handful of schools, but were rapidly terminated.
5 See my *Private Lives, Public Display: Intimacy and Excess in French Women's Self-Narrative Experiment*. Liverpool: Liverpool University Press, 2018.
6 The title of the English translation, *Breathing Underwater*, relies similarly on the trope of maternal fluidity but harnesses ideas of drowning, or of survival in a hostile element, rather than sickness.

7 See www.haut-conseil-egalite.gouv.fr/violences-de-genre/actualites-69/article/violences-faites-aux-femmes-le-hce [Accessed: 01.06.2017].

8 www.insee.fr/fr/statistiques/2496218 [Accessed: 01.06.2017].

9 Grandmother figures also appear in the work of Dominique Mainard (see Anderson 2013).

10 http://modernlanguages.sas.ac.uk/centre-study-contemporary-womens-writing [Accessed: 01.06.2017].

References

Ali, Z. 2012. *Féminismes islamiques*. Paris: La Fabrique Éditions.

Anderson, J. 2013. No second chances? Grandmothering and storytelling in the work of Dominique Mainard. In G. Rye and A. Damlé (Eds.), *Experiment and Experience: Women's Writing in France 2000–2010*. Oxford: Peter Lang, 95–108.

Bagley, P., F. Calamita and K. Robson. (Eds.). 2017. *Starvation, Obsession and Identity: Eating Disorders in Post-1968 Women's Writing*. Oxford: Peter Lang.

Balinska, M. A. 2003. *Retour à la vie: quinze ans d'anorexie*. Paris: Odile Jacob.

Bantegni, G., Y. Benahmed Daho, J. Sorman and S. Vincent. 2007. *14 femmes: Pour un féminisme pragmatique*. Paris: Gallimard.

Bard, C., in interview with C. Boinet. 2017. Le Féminisme de A à Z. In *Les Inrockuptibles*, 1107, 15 February, 47–50.

Barnes, L. 2015. Truth, trauma, treachery: Camille Laurens v. Marie Darrieussecq. In *MLN*, 130:4, 998–1012.

Bellil, S. 2003. *Dans l'enfer des tournantes*. Paris: Gallimard.

Bereni, L. 2016. *Libération*. Available at: www.liberation.fr/debats/2016/12/14/pourquoi-la-theorie-du-genre-fait-elle-peur_1535293 [Accessed: 20.12.2016].

Best, V. and M. Crowley. 2007. *The New Pornographies: Explicit Sex in Recent French Fiction and Film*. Manchester: Manchester University Press.

Bordo, S. 2009. 'Not just a white girl's thing': the changing face of food and body image problems. In H. Malson and M. Burns (Eds.), *Critical Feminist Approaches to Eating Dis/Orders*. London: Routledge, 46–59.

Boyer-Weinmann, M. 2013. *Vieillir, dit-elle. Une anthropologie littéraire de l'âge*. Normandie: Champ Vallon.

Brisac, G. 1994. *Petite*. Paris: Points.

Cairns, L. 2000. Sexual fault lines: sex and gender in the cultural context. In W. Kidd and S. Reynolds (Eds.), *Contemporary French Cultural Studies*. London: Arnold, 81–94.

Cairns, L. 2007. *Dissidences charnelles*: the female body in revolt. In J. Baldwin, J. Fowler and S. Weller (Eds.), *The Flesh in the Text*. Oxford: Peter Lang, 205–225.

Cairns, L. 2015. Bodily dis-ease in contemporary French women's writing: two case studies. In *French Studies*, 69:4, 494–508.

Cairns, L. 2017. *Eating Disorders in Contemporary French Women's Writing*. Liverpool: Liverpool University Press.

Châtelet, N. 2009. *Au pays des vermeilles*. Paris: Seuil.

Courtelle, M. 2011. *Journal d'une faim de vivre: témoignage*. Paris: Editions Beaurepaire.

Damlé, A. 2013. The Becoming of Anorexia and Text in Amélie Nothomb's *Robert des noms propres* and Delphine de Vigan's *Jours sans faim*. In A. Damlé and G. Rye (Eds.), *Women's Writing in Twenty-First Century France: Life as Literature*. Cardiff: University of Wales Press, 113–126.

Damlé, A. and G. Rye. (Eds.). 2013. *Women's Writing in Twenty-First Century France: Life as Literature*. Cardiff: University of Wales Press.

Darrieussecq, M. 1999. *Le Mal de mer*. Paris: P.O.L.

Darrieussecq, M. 2007. *Tom est mort*. Paris: P.O.L.

Daumas, C. 2016. Pourquoi la "théorie du genre" fait-elle peur? In *Libération*, 14 December. Available at: www.liberation.fr/debats/2016/12/14/pourquoi-la-theorie-du-genre-fait-elle-peur_1535293 [Accessed: 17.12.2016].

Davis, O. 2006. *Age Rage and Going Gently: Stories of the Senescent Subject in Twentieth-Century French Writing*. Amsterdam: Rodopi.

de Beauvoir, S. 1949. *Le deuxième sexe*. Paris: Gallimard.

de Beauvoir, S. 1963. *La Force des choses*. Paris: Gallimard.

de Beauvoir, S. 1967. *La Femme rompue*. Paris: Gallimard.

de Beauvoir, S. 1970. *La Vieillesse*. Paris: Gallimard.

Demossier, M. and S. Milner. 2000. Social difference: age and place. In W. Kidd and S. Reynolds (Eds.), *Contemporary French Cultural Studies*. London: Arnold, 69–80.

Despentes, V. 1996. *Baise-moi*. Paris: Florent Massot.

Despentes, V. 2000. *Baise-moi* [Filmed adaptation of novel with Coralie Trinh Thi].

Despentes, V. 2006. *King Kong théorie*.

Desportes, N. 2016. *Voyage jusqu'au bout de la vie; comment j'ai vaincu l'anorexie*. Paris: Odile Jacob.

Detambel, R. 2008. *Syndrome de Diogène, éloge des vieillesses*. Arles: Actes Sud.

Detambel, R. 2010. Vieillesses créatrices. Available at: www.detambel.com/f/index.php?sp=liv&livre_id=62 [Accessed: 20.01.2017].

Detambel, R. n.d. Pour une vieillesse perfectionniste. Available at: www.detambel.com/images/30/revue_30.pdf [Accessed: 20.01.2017].

Détrez, C. and A. Simon. 2006. *À leur corps défendant: Les femmes à l'épreuve du nouvel ordre moral*. Paris: Seuil.

Djavann, C. 2016. *Les Putes voilées n'iront pas au Paradis*. Paris: Grasset.

Durand, E. 2006. *Ma folie ordinaire. Allers et retours à l'hôpital Sainte-Anne*. Paris: Empêcheurs de Penser en Rond.

Edwards, N. 2013. Rape and repetition: Virginie Despentes and the rewriting of trauma. In N. El Nossery and A. L. Hubbell (Eds.), *The Unspeakable: Representations of Trauma in Francophone Literature and Art*. Newcastle Upon Tyne: Cambridge Scholars Publishing, 211–229.

Edwards, N. 2016. *Voicing Voluntary Childlessness: Narratives of Non-Mothering in French*. Oxford: Peter Lang, Coll. "Studies in Contemporary Women's Writing, Vol. 3."

El Nossery, N. 2012. *Témoignages fictionnels au feminin: Une réécriture des blancs de la guerre civile algérienne* (Chiasma, 30). Amsterdam: Rodopi.

Ernaux, A. 2005. *L'usage de la photo*. Paris: Gallimard.

Ernaux, A. 2008. *Les Années*. Paris: Gallimard.

Ernaux, A. 2016. *Mémoire de fille*. Paris: Gallimard.

Fayard, N. 2013. Bodies matter: the materiality of rape in twenty-first century France. In M. Allison and I. Long (Eds.), *Women Matter/Femmes Matière*. Oxford: Peter Lang, 35–51.

Foïs, G. 2011. Le Viol en France: enquête sur un silence assourdissant. In *Marianne*, No. 727, October. Available at: www.marianne.net/Le-viol-en-France-enquete-sur-un-silence-assourdissant_a204395.html [Accessed: 02.12.2016].

Gil, C. 2014. Ecrire la viei/llesse dans l'oeuvre de Régine Detambel. In A. Damlé and G. Rye (Eds.), *Aventures et experiences littéraires: Ecritures des femmes en france au début du vingt-et-unième siècle*. Amsterdam and New York: Rodopi, 295–311.

Gozlan, M. 2016. Nos combats pour la liberté. In *Marianne*, No. 1030–1031, 22 December 2016–5 January 2017, 38–41.

Higgins, L. and B. Silver. 1991. *Rape and Representation*. New York: Columbia University Press.

Holmes, D. 2006. *Romance and Readership in Twentieth-Century France: Love Stories*. Oxford: Oxford University Press.

Holmes, D. 2012. Dealing with what is dealt: feminists and ageing. In M. Atack et al. (Eds.), *Women, Genre and Circumstance: Essays in Memory of Elizabeth Fallaize*. London: Legenda, 123–135.

Hron, M. 2005. Pathological victims: the discourse of disease/dis-ease in Beur texts. In *French Literary Studies*, 16, 159–174.

Jordan, S. 2006. Close-up and impersonal: sexual/textual bodies in contemporary French women's writing. In *Nottingham French Studies*, 45:3, 8–23.

Jordan, S. 2011. Writing age: Annie Ernaux's *Les Années*. In *Forum for Modern Language Studies*, 47:2, 138–149.

Kemp, A. 2016. 'Le passeport de la douleur ou rien': Fawzia Zouari's *Ce pays dont je meurs* and the politics of pain. In *Contemporary French Civilization*, 41, 49–67.

Laurens, C. 1995. *Philippe*. Paris: P.O.L.

Laurens, C. 2016. *Celle que vous croyez*. Paris: Gallimard.

Le Bars, M. 2014. *Appelez-moi plume*. Paris: Editions Fabert.

Long, I. 2013. Writing the material world: *Le féminin pluriel* by Benoîte and Flora Groult. In M. Allison and I. Long (Eds.), *Women Matter/Femmes Matière*. Oxford: Peter Lang, 87–102.

Mardorossian, C. 2004. Towards a new feminist theory of rape. In *Gender Studies*, 1:3, 251–285.

Martin, A. 2011. Old age and the other-within: Beauvoir's representation of ageing in *La Vieillesse*. In *Forum for Modern Language Studies*, 47:2, 126–137.

McIlvanney, S. 2016. Grandmother through the looking-glass: perspectives on (anti-) ageing in Noëlle Châtelet's *Au pays des vermeilles*. In *The Modern Language Review*, 111:4, 975–987.

Meuret, I. 2009. L'anoréxie: entre aliénation 'mentale' et revendication d'altérité. Le cas des écrivaines algériennes. In *International Journal of Francophone Studies*, 12:1, 17–35.

Millet, C. 2002. *La Vie sexuelle de Catherine M.* Paris: Seuil.

Millet, C. 2009. *Jour de souffrance*. Paris: Points.

Morello, N. 2011. Écrire le néonaticide maternel dans *Le Cimetière des poupées* de Mazarine Pingeot. In *Modern and Contemporary France*, 19:1, 53–68.

NDiaye, M. 1996. La Gourmandise. In J-P. Géné and M. NDiaye (Eds.), *Les Péchés capitaux: La Gourmandise*. Paris: Centre national d'art et de culture Georges Pompidou, 46–63.

NDiaye, M. 2006. Le Jour du Président. In P. Modiano, M. NDiaye and A. Speiss (Eds.), *Trois nouvelles contemporaines*. Paris: Gallimard, 51–67.

NDiaye, M. 2007. *Mon cœur à l'étroit*. Paris: Gallimard.

Payne, R. 2016. Lesbianism and Maternal Ambivalence in Hélène de Monferrand's *Les amies d'Héloïse* (1990) and *Les enfants d'Héloïse* (1997). In *Revue critique de fixxion française contemporaine*, 12, 120–129.

Peretti, C. de. 2006. *Thorynitorynx*. Paris: Belfond.

Perreau, B. 2016. Who's afraid of gender theory? In B. Perreau (Ed.), *Queer Theory: The French Response*. Stanford, CA: Stanford University Press, 17–74.

Robson, K. 2015. The subject of rape: feminist discourses on rape and violability in contemporary France. In *French Cultural Studies*, 26:1, 45–55.

Robson, K. 2016. Voicing abjection: narratives of anorexia in contemporary French women's (life-)writing. In *L'Esprit Créateur*, 56:2, 108–112.

Rye, G. 2009. *Narratives of Mothering: Women's Writing in Contemporary France*. Newark: University of Delaware Press.

Rye, G. 2013. Introduction. In G. Rye and A. Damlé (Eds.), *Experiment and Experience: Women's Writing in France 2000–2010*. Bern: Peter Lang, 1–10.

Teisson, J. 2012. *L'enfant plume*. Paris: Chèvre-feuille étoilée.

Zaretsky, R. 2014. How do you upset the French? Gender theory. Available at: www.bostonglobe.com/ideas/2014/03/02/how-do-you-upset-the-french-gender-theory/1DzXUKcQxBO1H [Accessed: 02.12.2016].

Zouari, F. 2000. *Ce pays dont je meurs*. Paris: Ramsay.

PART IV

Mediating memories and cultures

17

REMEMBERING THE FIRST WORLD WAR IN FRANCE

The Historial de la Grande Guerre and Thiepval Museum[1]

Nina Parish and Eleanor Rowley

The centenary of the First World War constitutes a key point in the memory of the conflict, contributing to what historian Jay Winter (2011, 2015) has described as a 'commemorative avalanche.' Memory theorist, Aleida Assmann, calls it a 'temporal watershed' as biological links to the event disappear: 'thereafter it will be of interest only to historians, unless it is also actively reconstructed and supported as an individual and collective memory along new lines' (2014: 58). In 2014, the British Prime Minister David Cameron pledged £50 million of public funds to a wide range of commemoration initiatives across the UK (Assmann 2014). Similar amounts were promised by France; and the Mission Nationale du Centenaire was established to oversee the centenary commemorations in France with historian Antoine Prost at its helm (Hanna and Horne 2016). The present moment of centennial First World War commemoration therefore provides an opportunity to shine critical light on heritage practices, where popular and formal as well as national and transnational conceptions of the past encounter each other. In this chapter, the Historial de la Grande Guerre, opened in 1992, will be examined in order to understand what representations of the First World War within the museum space can tell us about how France remembers the First World War.[2] The recently opened Thiepval Museum will provide a coda exploring contemporary reactions to the First World War.

In a comprehensive article entitled 'France and the Great War on Its Centenary,' Hanna and Horne map the transformations that the historiography of the First World War has undergone over the past 100 years. Reflecting a broad cultural turn in history writing since the 1990s, the focus of recent First World War scholarship has shifted from an emphasis on military tactics and political interpretations to cultural representations of everyman and everywoman (see also Jones 2013). At the centenary, the themes of reconciliation, war dead (1.3 million military dead in France) and national unity are key to how the French remember the First World War with the French president François Hollande emphasising the 'unity of the nation' and the 'common destiny of the French' in his speech at the beginning of the centenary commemorations (Hanna and Horne 2016: 233). In France, the history of the First World War is settled in comparison to the experience of the Second World War. It is thus used 'to express the general tragedy of war more readily than World War II, because while victory was achieved in 1918, the war's political agenda now seems remote whereas the war dead remain omnipresent' (Hanna and Horne 2016: 234). This history and in particular the suffering of soldiers (*le poilu* being a key figure in French popular memory) and civilians can serve to transmit a cosmopolitan message of peace and reconciliation across all nations, in keeping with the founding mission of the European Union. There also remain strong family links to memories of these soldiers' lives which are particularly prevalent at a local level (Hanna and Horne 2016: 235).

But how can we talk about history and memory when the past is evoked? In what ways do the tensions between them inform heritage practices? History and memory represent two valid and necessary orientations towards the past that are constructed in different ways and for different purposes (Wertsch and Roediger 2008). In the domain of public history, however, boundaries between the two categories often become blurred. Public history has traditionally been a national enterprise, institutionalised during the nineteenth century in the form of history education, museums, monuments and commemorations. It is this 'canonised' version of history, privileging coherent narratives, symbols and myths, that forms a core strand of cultural memory (Assmann 2008: 101) and contributes to a shared sense of national identity, famously reframed by Anderson as an 'imagined community' (1983). Memory is understood not as a static feature of social relations but as a process or range of practices. Collective memory, as theorised by Maurice Halbwachs, is a body of knowledge about the past shared by a memory community, which is maintained through social activities such as storytelling and commemorative rituals. More recent scholarship prioritises collective remembering, or the processes animating collective memory. This orientation emphasises the dynamic, political and contested nature of memory in its recognition that representations of the past are collectively constructed and reconstructed through processes by which some events or perspectives are privileged and others repressed (Wertsch and Roediger 2008). With memory viewed as a process through which social relations and cultural understandings are constructed and negotiated, critical attention has turned to how memory is articulated and mediated in an effort to understand how people use the past in everyday life. On the centenary of the First World War, the ways in which this conflict is remembered and commemorated need to be critically assessed, highlighting in the process the importance of remembering or forgetting responsibly.

Indeed, one distinction between history and memory is foregrounded through a discussion of forgetting (Assmann 2008; Lee 2012). Memory is necessarily selective, being negatively defined as that which is not forgotten. History, on the other hand, although privileging some information over others as more relevant, regards forgetting as perilous. History is a cumulative effort with many stories overlaid, and efforts to revise history include restoring perspectives that have been neglected or forgotten. Lee (2012: xi) distinguishes history as a 'public form of knowledge' based on a disciplinary apparatus that ensures minimum standards of validity and 'relationships to evidence that anyone can work with.' In addition, historians aim in principle to establish an accurate account of past events regardless of its convenience or relevance to present circumstances. By contrast, collective remembering is 'tied interpretatively to the present' (Wertsch and Roediger 2008: 320) and involves reinventing and reconstructing representations of the past to serve contemporary discourse and identity projects. In the context of First World War commemoration, we have already seen how collective memory has been instrumentalised by the French government to articulate messages of peace and European reconciliation. Later in this chapter, we will see how Hollande continued to deliver this message on the centenary of the Battle of the Somme when days before the British had voted to leave the European Union.

The origins of the Historial de la Grande Guerre

Whilst some heritage programmes have struggled to transcend the nation as the 'natural container' for narratives about the past, transnational and multiperspectival approaches to history have been gaining ground in a number of history museums across Europe. Kaiser draws upon an analysis of 92 history museums across 20 European countries in his observation that 'national master narratives are in retreat,' with museums increasingly giving space to transnational perspectives (2012: 10). Den Boer argues that 'the future of Europe requires a new kind of *loci memoriæ* [. . .] to learn how to forgive and forget' (2008: 24). Arguably this challenge has been taken up by a number of war museums in Europe. One such museum, established in 1992 in Péronne, in the Somme, is the Historial de la Grande Guerre. Here German, French and British artefacts are exhibited with equal emphasis in a manner that promotes cultural comparisons. With a discourse developed by an international team of professional historians recruited from France, Britain and Germany, the museum seeks to puncture national narratives of exceptionalism by highlighting a shared 'trench culture.' It similarly challenges what has been described as the 'Myth of the War Experience' (Mosse 1990) by focusing on suffering and the brutalising effects of total war. The creation of the Historial can be linked to the broader 'museum boom,' which took place in France from the 1970s onwards, and with the decentralisation reforms undertaken in the 1980s during the presidency of François Mitterrand. The process of establishing this museum and its permanent exhibition will be examined in order to understand how the history of the First World War is represented and mediated in this space.

The earliest origins of this transnational project are deeply local and can be traced to 1985 when the president of the General Council of the Somme, Max Lejeune, saw an opportunity to establish an international cultural centre dedicated to the memory of the First World War. The occasion arose when councillors from the east of the area raised concerns about the paucity of cultural and touristic development in their cantons compared to those in the west of the area. In responding to the councillors' concerns, Lejeune saw an opportunity not only to redress the imbalance of financial investment across the department but to correct a perceived injustice faced by the area in terms of historical memory (Becker 2008: 30; interviews with Annette Becker and Jay Winter). Although prominent in British memory of the Great War, the Somme was somewhat marginalised in French historical consciousness, with Verdun the focus of French First World War memory, memorialisation and 'trench tourism' (Prost in Nora 2008: 1761). Prior to 1992, the Somme lacked an institution providing orientation or interpretation for the surrounding landscape of battlefields, cemeteries and memorials, and this omission has been attributed to the relatively minor status of the Battle of the Somme in French memory compared with Verdun where a memorial museum had been established in the 1960s. Historian Jean-Jacques Becker writes of the Somme: 'Paradoxically enough, in this area so deeply scarred by battle, where towns and villages had had to be almost totally rebuilt, where the land was littered with military cemeteries [. . .] few efforts had been made to mark the memory of the Great War' (2008: 31).

In January 1986, on behalf of the General Council of the Somme, Lejeune commissioned a preliminary study into the establishment of a new cultural development dedicated to the history of the Battle of the Somme. Delivered in May of the same year by independent consultant Elisabeth Ramus, this document is the earliest available written record of many of the core principles that still underpin the Historial. Ramus' report expands Lejeune's idea to create a centre dedicated to the Battle of the Somme, and instead proposes a historical and cultural centre telling the story of the First World War as it was experienced in the Somme and Northern France. The report asserts that the project should focus on the daily life of both civilians and soldiers, on the battlefront, the home front, and in the occupied territories. Moreover, the centre should affirm the international character of the conflict by representing the experience of all the belligerent nations. Above all, Ramus emphasises the importance of an orientation towards the human experience of war (Ramus 1986: 26). The use of work by writers and artists of all nations who fought on the western front is proposed as a means of communicating this experience. Crucially, Ramus highlights the necessity of academic expertise, asserting that the programme should be entrusted to historians to ensure its quality and credibility (Ramus 1986: 28). The report was well received and provided the basis for a second phase of concept development. With a budget of 23 million francs, the museum was expected to open two years later, in time for the 70th anniversary of armistice day in November 1988.

Whereas museums usually grow out of an existing collection, the Historial began as an abstract idea and a collection that would animate the concept had to be built from scratch (Prévost-Bault 2008: 11; Sallois 2008). In 1987, a curator working for the General Council of the Somme secured the significant Van Treeck collection of almost 20,000 'prints, postcards and other two-dimensional objects' illustrating both the military and civilian war effort (Lévy 1995: 13). The purchase of these objects was enough to establish the intention to develop an important and distinctive collection. In this way, the museum was registered as a *musée contrôle* in October 1987.[3] By obtaining the status of *musée contrôle*, and thereby the support of the national body Musées de France, a series of benefits could accrue to the development. With *musée contrôle* status, a state subsidy would become available, and this would trigger a regional subsidy, which in turn would allow the General Council of the Somme to apply for additional funds distributed by the European Community.

Péronne was selected over neighbouring Albert as the venue for the development on the basis of its accessibility. Served by the TGV from Paris, and by the autoroute A1, Péronne was considered convenient to tourists from all regions of France, British tourists crossing the channel and to motorists from the Benelux countries and Germany. In addition, a unique opportunity materialised when Péronne's municipal council promised to cede its medieval castle to the project. The Historial is now designated the first station in the 'Circuit de Souvenir,' the 92-kilometre battlefields remembrance trail which starts in Péronne and ends in Albert and receives an estimated 200,000 visitors annually.

With the location settled and 10 million francs of the budget allocated to construction (the larger sum of 13 million francs was assigned to museography), an architectural competition was launched in 1987. The initial broadcast of the architectural competition was not ambitious, and neither were the submissions it attracted. Lévy (1995: 23) recounts the intervention of the Direction des Musées de France at this stage. It was recommended that the invitation to tender be redrafted in order to raise the profile of the competition. Moreover, an initiative to nominate the venture a 'grand projet' (an ambitious presidential enterprise to invest in new cultural developments and promote cultural projects) elevated the prestige of the project. The second diffusion of the architectural competition was much wider and more successful, with the prize being awarded to the firm of the renowned architect Henri Ciriani in 1987. As for the design for the permanent exhibition, following a stormy relationship with the first appointment, Gérard Rougeron and his company STORIA, a new firm, Repérages, set up by early career architects Adeline Rispal, Jean-Jacques Raynaud and Louis Tournoux, was chosen.

The historians, initially considered necessary as a measure of quality control, became instrumental in shaping the content and discourse of the museum. In 1986, Jean-Jacques Becker (an established French historian with expertise on the First World War), Wolfgang Mommsen (a German historian working on French history of the period) and Jay Winter (an American historian working on the First World War in Britain) were asked to identify an agreed set of principles that would inform the themes of a permanent exhibition. Following the official launch of the project the historians were asked to refine these themes and to produce fact sheets on each topic. At this stage, the team expanded to include Stéphane Audoin-Rouzeau (a former student of Jean-Jacques Becker, invited by the latter to assist him), Gerd Krumeich (a former student of Wolfgang Mommsen, invited by the latter to replace him) and later Annette Becker (Jean-Jacques Becker's daughter, trained in art history, invited by Jay Winter on account of her work on war memorials in France). These generations of respected historians have shaped the way we think about the First World War in France, Germany and the UK through their research, publications and the creation of this museum.[4] In keeping with this spirit, the Historial also comprises an onsite Documentation Centre and an International Research Centre, which has been described as the 'driving force in French historiography' of the First World War (Purseigle 2008). Several hundred historians are by now associated with the International Research Centre, and according to their expertise they are called upon to contribute to the development of themes and content for temporary exhibitions which reflect current research in diverse aspects of First World War Studies. Stéphane Audoin-Rouzeau, Annette Becker, Gerd Krumeich, Jay Winter and a number of other historians associated with the International Research Centre are also influential in the centenary project, being members of the scientific council of the Mission Nationale du Centenaire (http://centenaire.org/fr/espace-scientifique/le-conseil-scientifique-de-la-mission-du-centenaire).

'Histoire Autrement': the Historial's permanent exhibition

What then was the result of this planning? What are the distinctive characteristics of the permanent exhibition at the Historial de la Grande Guerre? It comprises four chronological rooms arranged in a propeller formation surrounding a central room dedicated to the museum's prized collection of 50 etchings by Otto Dix. Three levels of text are provided to orient the visitor: a headline text introduces each room whilst sub-chapters divide the rooms into themes. Finally, each object is numbered and given a corresponding label. In the first two rooms, both renewed since 2014, these labels give a brief explanation linking the objects to their corresponding theme, whereas in the last two rooms the object labels consist of one or two words. The first-level texts are a new (post-2014) addition to each room and are provided consistently in four languages: German, French, English and Dutch. The second- and third-level texts are provided consistently in the three languages: German, French and English.[5]

Each of the chronological rooms is organised into two zones representing the two fronts of total war: the military front is displayed horizontally in the centre and the home front vertically around the edges. In the two rooms treating the war period the key feature of the combatants' zone, and the trademark of the museum, is the use of open horizontal dugouts, or *fosses*, in the museum floor to display the relics of trench warfare. In the room treating 1914–1916 a German, a French and a British uniform are each recumbent in their own *fosse* and accompanied by a collection of items typically carried by a soldier of the corresponding army. The uniforms are given volume and weight, taking on the contours of a male body, though without faces or hands. Just as the uniforms are intact, shrouding invisible figures, the items accompanying them are displayed in orderly, schematic arrangements, rather than strewn haphazardly. Museographer Adeline Rispal indicates in an interview that the aim was to create in each case an 'abstract individual' that could stand for an unknown soldier.[6] Although the three soldiers lie in separate *fosses* and carry distinctive objects typical of their own national war cultures, the similarities between the three soldiers' belongings are striking. The similarities between these material remains extend in the visitor's imagination to a shared experience of trench life and trench warfare.

The *fosses* are lined with white marble, a material that contributes to a semi-sacred aura surrounding the unknown soldiers. Recalling a grave or an archaeological dig, the open *fosses* draw the gaze of the visitor down in solemn contemplation. The museographer points out that by putting these objects below the level of the museum they are not really in the museum space, but between the museum and the territory where the conflict played out. This idea to place the uniforms below the level of the floor arose from a sense of responsibility to return the soldiers to the earth.[7] The horizontal axis of display serves a further purpose, described by Jay Winter as the museum's moral imperative to avoid glorifying the war (2017: 162).[8]

The mobilisation of civilian society is represented around the edge of the rooms in show-cases, or *vitrines*, organised by nation across three levels with German objects at the top, French in the middle and British at the lower level. As the visitor advances along the *vitrines* new thematic 'chapters' are introduced with corresponding objects from each nation in close proximity. This scheme was developed in order to facilitate comparison across the warring nations of the social and cultural impacts and dimensions of events. The labels accompanying these objects provide a shared narrative in the form of short texts that are common in three languages, but the objects themselves develop the themes in multiple directions, providing a mosaic or a kalei-doscopic effect.

The museographers deliberately avoid building an atmosphere through the manipulation of artificial light and sound. Similarly, the museum avoids recreating the past by providing a voyeuristic experience. Rispal recalls that on first viewing the collections in storage it looked like a flea market, and she feared this would create distance between the viewer and the object. She wanted to ensure that in the museum the collection would be displayed cleanly, to allow the objects to communicate directly with the visitor.[9] The historians assert that the objects, having survived the conflict, carry narratives and biographies of their own. The visitors are invited to interrogate, receive and interpret these potentially powerful messages in a quiet and contemplative mode. The environment is deliberately sober and yet flooded with light, which represents the intention to offer up the history of the First World War to a new wave of scrutiny.

Displaying German objects alongside their French and British equivalents in such a delib-erate and sustained way was strikingly original and signaled an unwavering commitment to a comparative transnational approach. Similarly novel was the degree of focus on the home front and the meticulous attention to the ephemeral, banal, artisanal, and forgotten everyday objects of both fronts. These objects, although immediately recognisable as kin to objects that we still use in our daily lives, bear the imprint of a war culture that is more total than we might have otherwise imagined. The discourse of the museum was also particularly original in its restora-tion of the significance of the Somme to French historical consciousness. The museum's focus on the international character of the Somme unsettles the narrative associated with the Franco-German battle of Verdun that the First World War was a just war of defense against a barbaric Teutonic invasion; the museum rather promotes a message more familiar to the British that the First World War was a senseless war without justification. In its representation of the suffering of civilian populations during the First World War in the occupied territories it also attempts to rehabilitate the image of the German military of the First World War by illustrating that the Kaiser's army was not as monstrous as its reputation, and not equivalent to Hitler's army. Fur-thermore, the originality of the museum's approach was communicated through its motto: 'his-toire autrement' or 'history (done) differently.' This slogan was attached to the Historial through press releases, brochures, leaflets and a booklet available for visitors in the museum shop. The museum thereby self-consciously generated the news of its own originality, emphasising in its promotional materials not only its status as the first museum in France to tell the First World War history of the Somme but also as a new and unique historical and museographic concept in a destination building.

The Historial at the centenary

A recent article in the local press raises an accusation of elitism at the Historial, accusing the museum of neglecting its local audience.[10] This article raises the problem of missed visitation targets in the centenary year 2016 and suggests that the museum is out of touch with a public that finds its discourse inaccessible. Since the beginning of the centenary celebrations, a programme of renewal has been in place at the Historial in part to address these concerns which are far from new. In May 2015, a new permanent exhibition space, 'the Guardrooms' was opened in the castle. The largest change has been the *retournement*, or reversal of direction, in the permanent exhibition, whereby visitors now enter from what used to be the exit and the order of rooms is reversed. Two rooms have been fully updated with the addition of some new objects and more detailed labels. Two further rooms are scheduled to be renewed by the end of 2018. Since 2014, multimedia stations have been added to each room, providing information about objects and audio clips of contemporary recordings. A short film was introduced in a small auditorium at the entrance of the museum in 2014 to better orient visitors prior to their visit. The new film and multimedia stations are intended to provide 'historical contextualisation' (Historial de la Grande Guerre 2016: 4) and to 'better explain the topics and collections displayed' (François in Historial de la Grande Guerre 2016: 2). This programme of renewal therefore suggests a departure from the museum's initial anti-didactic approach, which intended to provoke questions and offer multiple readings rather than present a single explanation. Recent attempts to provide additional interpretation at the object level may make the collection more accessible to the visitor but they risk fixing the meaning of the objects and narrowing the available readings of the museum as a whole.

This shift in museological practice is also in evidence at the Historial's sister site at the nearby Franco-British Thiepval Memorial to the Missing of the Somme. The Commonwealth War Graves Commission and the Imperial War Museum originally opened a visitor centre here in 2004 as an orientation and interpretation centre for the large number of visitors to the site. This was extended, renovated and reopened by the Historial as Thiepval Museum in June 2016, a month before the centenary of the Battle of the Somme. The new museum has a permanent exhibition space of 400 square metres and focuses on the Battle of the Somme and 'the multitude of the missing.' There is also an exhibition on heroic aviators which includes a reconstruction of an aeroplane, which is a considerable departure from the authentic objects displayed at the Historial in Péronne, and the historians,' museographers' and curators' confidence in their storytelling abilities. The Péronne museum is likely to benefit in terms of visitor numbers from this association with Thiepval. The Historial receives an average of 75,000 visitors per year, with a majority of 67% being French (mostly from Northern France) and the second significant group being British (19%).[11] Visitation to the Visitor Centre at Thiepval has averaged 150,000 a year since 2004, with 90% being British (visitors to the Thiepval memorial, maintained by the Commonwealth Graves Commission, are estimated at 300,000 per year). The new Thiepval Museum received around 25,000 visitors in its first six months.[12] A dual ticket granting access to both museums was introduced as a strategic move to attract more British visitors to Péronne from Thiepval, and more French visitors to Thiepval from Péronne.

The Historial takes its name from a neologism combining the words for history and memorial. Upon its opening, the Péronne museum embodied an original attempt to recognise the importance of both of these orientations towards the past. Memory is served by the site-specificity of the museum and its role in orienting visitors to the surrounding landscape. In the authentic artefacts populating the vitrines and fosses visitors may also recognise objects that chime with personal and familial associations. Simultaneously, however, the museum is rigorous in its coolly scientific, interrogative discourse and museography. Although Thiepval Museum pays homage to the Historial, its discourse departs from that of the parent museum in significant ways. By illustrating the first day of the Battle of the Somme, Thiepval Museum answers questions about the representation of war that the Péronne museum prefers to leave open. Moreover an emphasis on the British experience in the depiction of the Battle of the Somme at Thiepval disrupts the tripartite equilibrium that is so crucial to the Historial.

Conclusions

It is to be expected that a new museum will seek to distinguish itself in an already saturated landscape. Interestingly the website that serves as a homepage for both museums (www.historial.org) today introduces the Historial de la Grande Guerre with the label 'L'Histoire' and Thiepval Museum with the term 'La Mémoire.' This distinction is reflected in the use of portraits and narratives to represent missing soldiers at Thiepval Museum. These techniques provide warmer, more straightforward opportunities for visitors to engage with the dead than the faceless archetypes displayed at Péronne. Whilst this may signify a shift in direction towards a greater prioritisation of memory, it could also be read as a response to the site of the new museum (in a promotional poster observed in Péronne recently, the Historial is referred to as 'Musée de collection' and the Thiepval Museum as 'Musée de site'). Given the role of the neighbouring Thiepval memorial, which is inscribed with the names of more than 72,000 British and Commonwealth soldiers, this warmer, memory-oriented approach hardly seems inappropriate. The museum building in Thiepval also houses databases for locating names on the memorial, or for tracing the graves of fallen soldiers where they are known. It is conceivable, therefore, that visitors seeking out sites of familial significance in the landscape will find resonance in the images and stories available at Thiepval Museum.

When the Historial opened, the local, national and international press coverage was unanimous in its praise of its original approach (Albaret 1998: 50). Some later articles place it in the context of France's rediscovery of the First World War[13] and the museum and remembrance tourism boom.[14] Several articles covering the inauguration highlight the message of peace given by representatives of different nations at the ceremony, whilst others underline the presence of Ernst Jünger who had not returned to the Somme since being deployed there during the Battle of the Somme (Albaret 1998: 50). The museum was thus portrayed as a symbol of peace and reconciliation. The communication of this message continued at the centenary of the Battle of the Somme which took place a week after the British voted to leave the European Union. François Hollande, David Cameron, Prince Charles, Camilla Parker Bowles, Prince William, Kate Middleton and Prince Harry were all present at this ceremony, where a plaque was also unveiled at Thiepval Museum. Hollande had hesitated about coming; he had already played a key role in the Verdun commemoration and many believed that it would be prime minister Manuel Valls who would represent France on this occasion. Ultimately Hollande did attend, and although no speeches were pronounced, this commemorative event was instrumentalised to underline continued Franco-British solidarity despite what had happened the week before.[15] Indeed, French president Emmanuel Macron and British prime minister Theresa May marked the centenary of the end of the First World War by laying a wreath at the Thiepval memorial, further underlining the political significance of this memory site.[16]

A recent journalistic article covering the opening of the new site at Thiepval is positive about the museum but questions whether we have reached a saturation point in remembrance tourism, and asks whether the new museum will be able to sustain an audience.[17] This is a crucial question on the centenary of the First World War and for museums more generally as we see a shift towards museum-going as a leisure activity and an increase in popularity of a more spectacle-oriented museography. As family ties and communicative memory dissolve, will visitors still come to the memorial at Thiepval? Indeed, can the Historial de la Grande Guerre continue to attract visitors without diluting its resolutely intellectual transnational approach to history? In some ways, recent changes there and exhibition development at Thiepval Museum indicate that this is no longer viable in a museum world where visitor numbers and experience are increasingly important. Political instrumentalisation of these historic sites demonstrate that the message of peace and reconciliation is still important to French, German and British politicians. Popular responses appear, however, to differ as the historic event recedes further into the past. Historians, curators and other museum professionals linked to these memory sites have the challenging task of maintaining responsibly a transnational approach which promotes comparison, reflection and self-reflection whilst continuing to attract visitors who may be seeking a different experience from a First World War Museum.

Notes

1 Research on these museums was carried out under the aegis of the Horizon 2020 UNREST (Unsettling Remembering and Social Cohesion in Transnational Europe) project (www.unrest.eu). This project examines memory cultures and practices in war museums and war-related mass grave exhumations in Europe.

2 Jacques Sallois (2008) deplores the lack of history museums in France, although notes the wealth of military history museums. He is positive about the Historial's contribution, stating: 'deux projets dominent au musée de l'armée de l'hôtel des Invalides et à l'Historial de Péronne où une démarche rigoureuse a conduit à la constitution d'une collection présentée dans une architecture de grande qualité.'

3 For correspondence on this subject, see file 'DIVERS COURRIERS' in box marked 'HAIRY,' Historial de la Grande Guerre Documentation Centre.

4 They figure prominently in Hanna and Horne's article tracing the historiography of the centenary: Jean-Jacques Becker was supervised by Pierre Renouvin, a key figure in the first generation of First World War historians. He was a veteran who sought to foreground the 'social psychology' of conflict (Hanna and Horne 2016: 237).

5 For further discussion of multilingualism in museums, see Deganutti, M., N. Parish and E. Rowley. 2018. 'Representing multilingual difficult history: voices of the First World War in the Kobarid Museum (Slovenia) and the Historial de la Grande Guerre (France),' in *JoSTrans: The Journal of Specialised Translation*, 29.

6 Interview with Adeline Rispal.

7 'The Museum of the Great War, in the heart of the Somme battlefields, was duty bound to return the soldiers' collections to the ground' (Studio Adeline Rispal 2017: 152).

8 For further discussion of horizontality and verticality in war museums, see Cercel, C., N. Parish and E. Rowley. 2019. 'War in the museum: the historial of the Great War in Péronne and the Military History Museum in Dresden,' in *Journal of War and Culture Studies*, forthcoming.

9 Interview with Adeline Rispal.

10 Fouquet, V. 'Trop Élitiste, l'Historial?' in *Le Courrier Picard*, 12 February 2017. www.courrier-picard.fr/10330/article/2017-02-11/lhistorial-de-peronne-est-il-trop-elitiste [Accessed 03.01.2019].

11 Historial: Musée de la Grande Guerre, Plan d'action & stratégie 2013–2018 Eté 2012 (supplied by museum director Hervé François).

12 Interview with Emilie Simon.

13 'Les Français retrouvent la Grande Guerre avec un autre regard,' in *Agence France Presse*, 1 November 2004.

14 Lepine, C. 'La Somme exploite le souvenir de la bataille de 1916. Juillet marque le 80e anniversaire de la bataille de la Somme. À Albert, Bapaume et Péronne, le développement local ne pourrait plus se passer des touristes du souvenir,' in *La Croix*, 13 July 1996; 'Tourisme. La culture fait recette,' in *Le Télégramme*, 14 August 2005; 'Le succès du tourisme de la mémoire,' in *Le Figaro*, 7 February 2006.

15 See Flandrin, A. 'Les 100 ans de la bataille de la Somme parasités par le Brexit,' in *Le Monde*, 30 June 2016; Revault d'Allonnes, D. 'Au centenaire de la bataille de la Somme, le Brexit n'empêche pas "l'amitié" franco-britannique,' in *Le Monde*, 7 July 2016.

16 WorldWar One:Theresa May pays respects in France and Belgium. www.bbc.co.uk/news/uk-46145199 [Accessed: 03.01.2019].

17 Trouillard, S. 'Centenary 14–18, Un nouveau musée pour commémorer le centenaire de la Bataille de Somme,' in *France 24*, 12 December 2016. www.france24.com/fr/20160630-grande-guerre-bataille-somme-nouveau-musee-thiepval-centenaire-france-royaume-uni [Accessed 03.01.2019].

References

Albaret, F. 1998. *Historial de Péronne: histoire d'un musée d'histoire*. Unpublished thesis. Ecole du Louvre, Historial de la Grande Guerre Documentation Centre.

Anderson, B. 1983. *Imagined Communities: Reflections on the Origins and Spread of Nationalism*. London:Verso.

Assmann, A. 2008. Canon and archive. In A. Erll and A. Nünning (Eds.), *Cultural Memory Studies: An Interdisciplinary Handbook*. Berlin:Walter de Gruyter, 97–108.

Assmann, A. 2014. European commemorations of the First World War – from national to transnational memory cultures? In E.Wolfrum, O.Triebel, C.Arendes,A. Siebold and J. Borredà (Eds.), *European Commemoration: Locating World War I*. Berlin: IFA Edition Culture and Foreign Policy, 55–66.

Becker, J. J. 2008.The origins of the historial. In C. Fontaine, A. Becker, S. Audoin-Rouzeau, M-P. Prévost-Bault (Eds.), *The Collections of the Historial of the Great War*. Paris: Somogy Éditions d'Art, 30–33.

Cercel, C., N. Parish and E. Rowley. 2019. War in the museum: the historial of the Great War in Péronne and the Military History Museum in Dresden. In *Journal of War and Culture Studies*, forthcoming.

Deganutti, M., N. Parish and E. Rowley. 2018. Representing multilingual difficult history: voices of the First World War in the Kobarid Museum (Slovenia) and the Historial de la Grande Guerre (France). In *JoSTrans:The Journal of Specialised Translation*, 29.

Den Boer, P. 2008. Loci memoriæ – Lieux de mémoire. In A. Erll and A. Nünnning (Eds.), *Cultural Memory Studies: An Interdisciplinary Handbook*. Berlin:Walter de Gruyter, 19–26.

Hanna, M. and J. Horne. 2016. France and the Great War on its centenary. In *French Historical Studies*, 39:2, 233–259.

Historial de la Grande Guerre. 2016. *2 Musées pour découvrir la grande guerre* (promotional brochure).

Jones, H. 2013. As the centenary approaches: the regeneration of First World War historiography. In *The Historical Journal*, 56:3, 857–878.

Kaiser, W. 2012. The transnational turn meets the educational turn: engaging and educating adolescents in history museums in Europe. In *Journal of Educational Media, Memory & Society*, 4:2, 8–22.

Lee, P. 2012. Series introduction. In M. Carretero, M. Asensio and M. Rodriguez-Moneo (Eds.), *History Education and the Construction of National Identities*. Charlotte: Information Age Pub, ix–xvi.

Lévy, M. 1995. *Une visite à l'Historial*. Unpublished manuscript, Historial de la Grande Guerre Documentation Centre.

Mosse, G. L. 1990. *Fallen Soldiers: Reshaping the Memory of the World Wars*. Oxford: Oxford University Press.

Nora, P. (Ed.). 2008. *Lieux de Memoire*,Vol. II. Paris: Gallimard.

Prévost-Bault, M. P. 2008. The collections: past, present and future. In C. Fontaine, A. Becker, S. Audoin-Rouzeau and M. P. Prévost-Bault (Eds.), *The Collections of the Historial of the Great War*. Paris: Somogy Éditions d'Art, 11–15.

Purseigle, P. 2008. A very French debate: the 1914–1918 'war culture.' In *Journal of War and Culture Studies*, 1:1, 9–14.

Ramus, E. 1986. *Le Contenu du Centre Historique et Culturel*. Archives of Studio Adeline Rispal, box marked 'HISTORIAL 1.'

Sallois, J. 2008. *Les musées de France*. Paris: Presses universitaires de France.

Studio Adeline Rispal. 2017. Architectes et scenographes associés. Portfolio.

Wertsch, J. V. and H. L. Roediger. 2008. Collective memory: conceptual foundations and theoretical approaches. In *Memory*, 16:3, 318–326.

Winter, J. 2000. Public history and the historial project. In S. Blowden, M. Demossier and J. Picard (Eds.), *Recollections of France: Memories, Identities and Heritage in Contemporary France*. NewYork:Berghahn, 52–67.

Winter, J. 2006. *Remembering War*. New Haven:Yale University Press.

Winter, J. 2007. Historians and the politics of memory. In *Histoire Politique*, 2:2.

Winter, J. 2011. A century of historical writing. In *The First World War*. Marlborough, UK: Adam Mat-
thew. Available at: www.firstworldwar.amdigital.co.uk/FurtherResources/Essays/HistoricalWriting
[Accessed 03.01.2019].

Winter, J. 2015. The Great War and Jewish memory. In *European Judaism*, 48:1, 3–22.

Winter, J. 2017. *War Beyond Words: Languages of Memory from the Great War to the Present*. Cambridge: Cambridge University Press.

Websites

www.historial.fr

www.culture.gouv.fr/public/mistral/museo_fr?ACTION=CHERCHER&FIELD_1=REF&VALUE_
1=M0816

www.somme-tourisme.com/

Archives consulted

Historial de la Grande Guerre Documentation Centre

Studio Adeline Rispal

Interviews conducted

Marie-Pascale Prévost-Bault (Head Curator at the Historial since 1994) 14.11.2016.

Annette Becker (Historian) 02.02.2017.

Adeline Rispal (Museographer) 03.02.2017.

Jay Winter (Historian) 03.02.2017.

Emilie Simon (Museography Project Manager between 2014 and 2017) 15.03.2017.

18

WAGING THE WAR OF WORDS

Propaganda and the mass media in modern France, 1939–2017

David Lees

The French experience of propaganda has been an exceptional one. France was the only Nazi-occupied country in Western Europe permitted to produce its own cinematographic propaganda in the Second World War, and the French newspaper and television industries have been shaped considerably by the French political landscape. Yet the framework for this control, established initially under the Third Republic and subsequently under the leadership of Charles de Gaulle both at the Liberation and again on his return to power in 1958, was designed in a context of wartime which has long since disappeared. To some extent, the mass media in contemporary French society remain subject to some state intervention and regulation, even if the media landscape has changed significantly since the end of the Gaullist era and contemporary regulators aim as much to protect the media from the state, and the state from the media, than to control media content.

This chapter examines the role played by propaganda in France from the Third Republic to the present day, taking as its corpus the mass media in the form of posters, film propaganda, radio, newspapers and television. The chapter follows a chronological approach to demonstrate that propaganda in the French mass media have been influenced above all by right-wing conservativism, beginning with the increasingly repressive Daladier government in the late 1930s, through to the Vichy regime and Gaullist Resistance, and continuing with the construction of the Gaullist state in the Fifth Republic. State-produced mass media propaganda have tended, the chapter argues, to revolve around familiar themes which enable the projection of these right-wing ideals, most notably traditional family values and French power on the international stage. Indeed, traditional state mass media have historically remained rooted in a reactionary wartime framework which changed only after the end of the Pompidou administration and which today takes the form of retrospective arms-length regulation more than commissioning or actively controlling content. From a historical perspective, even much of the propaganda produced by the BBC French Service during the Occupation was designed to champion the replacement of one form of conservative regime (under Pétain) with another under de Gaulle.

The chapter demonstrates that where there have been significant left-wing influences in the creation of propaganda these have been produced by far left movements in opposition to the status quo, for example movements opposed to both the Gaullist Resistance and the Vichy regime during the Occupation, movements opposed to colonial rule in Algeria and movements opposed to the Gaullist state in May and June 1968. The chapter further argues that major change to the state management of the media did come initially in the form of the government of Valéry Giscard d'Estaing and then with the left-wing governments of François Mitterrand and François Hollande, and that reforms channelled state control through buffer organisations. Finally, the chapter argues that the greatest challenges to the right-wing framework of mass media propaganda in France have come in the form of platforms which allow dissenting or alternative voices to speak directly to the audience, most recently through websites and applications that are not filtered through governmental channels.

Although the definition of propaganda in its broadest form could be extended to include road safety campaigns or the education system (Jowett and O'Donnell 2011: 5) the focus in this chapter is firmly on the mass media – that is to say material with either mass circulation or mass production. The chapter defines propaganda thus as media produced with the intention of persuading or influencing the audience (the French and francophone populations around the world) to act in line with the ideals of the propagandist and their employers, the government of the day (Jowett and O'Donnell 2011: 3; Taylor 2003: 7). By drawing on popular themes like the family and then French international position, chiefly the Empire and then France's standing on the wider world stage, the chapter argues that mass media produced or controlled by successive governments between 1939 and 1974 in particular were designed to influence the audience to identify with and support these broadly right-wing conservative governments and their ideologies.

State mass media propaganda under Daladier

Although the origins of mass media propaganda in France arguably lie in the First World War, when newspapers, the radio and early cinema newsreels were used to encourage patriotic and anti-German sentiment, this period of state control was comparatively short-lived (Williams 2006: 7). Firstly, the First World War witnessed a period of remarkable and rare political coalition driven by anti-German views present in France since the Franco-Prussian War; this political consensus around the Republic ended shortly after and subsequent governments under the Third Republic found themselves with more pressing priorities than the organisation of mass media propaganda (Jackson 2001: 48). Secondly, as Manuela Williams has noted, there was an aversion to propaganda in France caused by the association between the slaughter of the trenches and the politicisation of the mass media (Williams 2006: 7). As a result, the first real Ministry for Information in France was not established until 1939 under Édouard Daladier, who introduced the framework for state control of the media that, as the chapter demonstrates, lasted until the election of Giscard d'Estaing and can be glimpsed in a watered-down, arms-length form, in the present day.

Daladier appointed the writer Jean Giraudoux to the post of minister for information with the remit of both censoring the media to prevent negative coverage of his policies and producing favourable news reports (Bowles 2004a: 351). This framework for propaganda was established in a context of increasing concern over the expansion of Nazi Germany and with a view to competing with France's European neighbours. Daladier had previously made use of the mass media to promote the signing of the Munich accords in 1938, in the doomed hope that this would stave off further war. Yet the failure of the many governments between 1918 and 1938 to formalise state propaganda, and the wider aversion to the term amongst the French population, severely handicapped the efforts of Daladier and Giraudoux. Unlike the Nazis, who had developed a slick propaganda machine under Joseph Goebbels (Garden 2012: 18), and the Italians, whose Ministry for Popular Culture merged mass media propaganda with efforts to shape the leisure activities of the population through the *dopolavoro* programme (Williams 2006: 7), the

French lacked experience of producing mass media propaganda. Even the British could draw on the expertise of the General Post Office Film Unit and the Army Film Unit to develop their mass media propaganda in the face of the Nazi threat (Anthony and Mansell 2011: 5).

As a result, the experience of mass media propaganda under Daladier was mixed. As war appeared increasingly inevitable, Daladier, through Giraudoux, coerced the media into promoting an image of a militarily strong France, while also championing his own ideology, most notably the 1939 Family Code, which drew on traditional Catholic values in an effort to increase the birth-rate (Jackson 2001: 103–104). The Family Code, which was near-universally popular (Delpha and Foucaud 1975: 142) and was taken up by the Vichy authorities as the basis of their own pro-family policies, was the first serious example of a championing of reactionary, traditionalist themes in state propaganda under a formal Ministry for Information in an effort to capitalise on the popularity of the family to improve Daladier's own standing. At the same time, Giraudoux's writings went as far on the subject of a French 'race' as Vichy ever did, while the Empire became increasingly a 'burning issue of national prestige' (Jackson 2001: 101).

To some extent, the ways in which Giraudoux and his team championed both an increasingly patriotic message – as France went to war – and Daladier's conservative programme were innovative. Daladier realised the importance of the cinema for conveying messages to the masses and thus obliged the three French newsreels (Pathé, Gaumont and Éclair-Journal) to incorporate reports from the *Service Cinématographique de l'Armée*, which in turn also produced standalone cinema documentaries intended to raise morale amongst the public (Bowles 2004b: 424). Yet the transition to politicised content for newsreels and documentaries in France was much slower than the experience of France's European neighbours, and as a result this material was not necessarily viewed as propaganda, which led to audiences continuing to see documentary and newsreel film as 'educational' during the Phoney War and beyond (Wharton 2006: 24). This was rather a positive result for Daladier and his successor Paul Reynaud, since it encouraged the audience to engage with the propagandist messages without necessarily believing they were being persuaded to think or act in line with the government's patriotic and conservative ideals.

However, Giraudoux, who was more familiar with the printed press in any case, did little to shift the public's aversion towards other forms of the mass media being used as propaganda. Newspapers became obviously pro-government, while the banning of the Communist *L'Humanité* in 1939 reduced dissenting voices in the press (Jackson 2001: 114). Radio and poster propaganda was also very blunt in conveying the government's message. Whilst this had some of the desired result in making Daladier, who increasingly governed by decree, one of the most popular politicians in the history of the Third Republic (Jackson 2001: 102), part of the message failed to make any impact. For all the efforts of the first Ministry for Information, public morale and appetite for war remained low and the wave of relief that greeted Philippe Pétain's radio broadcast of 17 June 1940 demonstrated the limited impact of state propaganda on reassuring or informing the French people during the Fall of France (Diamond 2007: 156).

The Vichy propaganda machine

The Vichy regime thus inherited a rather mixed track record of previous state mass media propaganda. On the one hand, Daladier and Reynaud had developed an inaugural formal ministry. On the other, though, the mass exodus of May and June 1940 left the Vichy authorities at a considerable disadvantage compared to the Nazis. Not only did the Vichy propaganda ministry – the *Secrétariat Général à l'Information* (SGI) – have to rely on the people it had to hand in the Unoccupied Zone, who were not necessarily the most capable or experienced propagandists, but much of the materials used by the Daladier and Reynaud ministries were left behind in Paris

(Bowles 2004b: 424). The result was a bureaucratic, chaotic ministry under successive ministers, which was often subject to competing interests (Rossignol 1991: 12–25).

There were nonetheless a number of continuities between the final governments of the Third Republic and state mass media propaganda under Vichy. First, the Vichy authorities drew on the pre-existing system of censorship to ensure favourable coverage across the mass media. This was especially the case in newspapers. The majority of established mass-circulation newspapers, upon relocation to the Unoccupied Zone were subject to regular missives from the *Office française de l'Information*, the press agency, which dictated virtually every word that was to appear in the press (Jackson 2001: 253). As a result, unlike the collaborationist newspapers that remained in Paris, national papers in particular, and to a lesser extent local and regional papers, were little more than mouthpieces for the regime. Censorship was extended to other forms of media, but in reality posters, cinema newsreels and documentaries and the radio frequently relied on Vichy funding or approval in order to be produced in the first place, which effectively ensured that they promoted a positive image of the regime (Rossignol 1991). The heads of the radio and poster sections of the SGI, in particular, were appointed for their loyalty to the Vichy leadership (Amaury 1969: 288). The result was a bluntly accurate depiction of Vichy ideology, leading to radio being considered in 1943 to be lagging behind the BBC in its capacity to influence the audience according to an internal SGI memorandum (Archives Nationales 1943: F/41 59). With the broadcasts of Philippe Henriot, however, the medium did become more influential as Henriot sought to attack minorities and the Allies, until his assassination by the Resistance (Chadwick 2011).

Second, the importance placed on the cinema by Daladier continued under Vichy. Although the regime did not have the experience of cinema propaganda of Goebbels and his ministry, the men and women who were responsible for commissioning cinema propaganda nevertheless shared an enthusiasm for the context of the cinema, and its rich history in France, that led to some surprising results. Initially, newsreels and documentary films continued much as they had under Daladier and Reynaud, with a very gradual shift towards the political. This accelerated in newsreels, as content became scarcer and the production team of the Vichy newsreel, *France-Actualités Pathé-Gaumont* (FAPG) – the only such example of a newsreel independent from German influence in any occupied country in Europe – was forced to rely on German footage, with the net result that public sentiments towards these films became negative, a tendency which was acerbated when the Germans took the lead in the successor newsreel, *France-Actualités* (Bowles 2004b: 439). Documentaries, by contrast, promoted the same sorts of traditional and conservative message as other Vichy media, all the while pretending that the war had never happened, with the emphasis on continuity and normality (Lees 2018; Wharton 2006). Although such films failed to acknowledge many of the real hardships experienced under the Occupation, they were nevertheless much less divisive and exclusionary than other media, notably the radio and posters, which consistently presented anti-Semitic, anti-Communist and anti-Masonic messages (Lees 2015). So little has been recorded about the reception of documentary film that it would appear such material, amongst all the other media controlled and produced by the Vichy authorities, had the potential to persuade the audiences that life did indeed continue as normal, even if sometimes the messages conveyed might jar – as with the depiction of food in some documentary films (Lees 2018).

A third continuity between Daladier and Vichy was thus the promotion of traditionalist and conservative themes across all media. Just as Daladier had promoted the Family Code, so, too, Vichy propaganda placed an emphasis on the family, on the Empire (even when the Empire had long since ceased to be beyond Vichy's control) and on traditional methods of work (Lees 2015). There remained, then, a framework for state mass media propaganda during the Occupation that was rooted in a conservative status quo designed to promote conservative interpretations of popular themes with the view of boosting the popularity of a right-wing regime.

The Gaullist model of propaganda

The propaganda developed by the Gaullist Resistance in London during the Second World War laid the foundations for the eventual Gaullist model of state control of the media. The Gaullists drew on the skills and experience of propagandists and broadcasters such as Jean Morin, and Radio Londres (the French Service of the BBC) became easily the most popular radio station in Occupied France, until it gained competition from Henriot on Radio Vichy (Chadwick 2011; Luneau 2010). Under de Gaulle's leadership and awareness of the importance of the mass media, the Gaullists disseminated a message which championed the continuity of the Republic in the form of Free France. Importantly, though, this message was distinct from that promoted by the Communist Resistance; there was no focus on a 'government of the people' as claimed in clandestine editions of *L'Humanité* and other Communist tracts (Turlais 2015). The Gaullists may have sought to undermine the credibility of the Vichy authorities, condemning Pétain and his ministers on all sorts of subjects, including their mismanagement of food supplies (Chadwick 2017), but there were nevertheless similarities in the themes discussed in both Vichy and Gaullist propaganda. The Empire and the family were two such conservative and traditionalist ideals which featured in Gaullist propaganda broadcast to Occupied France (Chadwick 2015: 431).

Such was the desire to avoid any disruption to a conservative status quo under de Gaulle that, upon the Liberation, many of the same personnel who had staffed the Vichy propaganda ministry were retained in post, despite claims of purges. Indeed, de Gaulle built on the pre-established system of state control devised by Daladier and developed by Vichy. The staff of the joint Franco-German newsreel *France-Actualités*, for example, went on to join the rebranded *France-Libre-Actualités* (Archives Nationales 1944: F/42 113). Censorship of all other areas of the media was retained: in the same way as the hardships of the Occupation continued during the Liberation period, so, too, did the pre-existing propaganda framework. The Gaullist myth of the Occupation period played a role in shaping the Gaullist propaganda model. In order to move on from the complexities of collaboration and questions over the legitimacy of de Gaulle and Vichy, the interim Gaullist government repressed any messages that were counter to the simplicity presented by de Gaulle's 25 August 1944 speech (De Gaulle 1944), while continuing to promote many of the same themes that had been present since Daladier's premiership.

Under the Fourth Republic, however, this propaganda framework was diluted by the competing concerns of frequently unstable governments (Pathé-Gaumont archives 2017). It was only on de Gaulle's return to power in 1958 that the Gaullist model was relaunched amid even tighter state control of the mass media. The propaganda framework that de Gaulle inherited in 1944 was one which was firmly associated with wartime; in 1958, de Gaulle was again able to draw on the context of war in order to justify his stringent control of the media. Although it would be unjust to suggest that de Gaulle was alone in realising the importance of addressing the audience directly through state media channels – Pierre Mendès-France had used the radio to try to get closer to the electorate during his premiership (Mendès-France 1954) – de Gaulle drew on the increased powers of the president as laid out in his own 1958 Constitution of the new Fifth Republic to regularly talk to the nation (Fenby 2010: 403). De Gaulle was also quick to understand the powers of the increasingly popular medium of television, which, as the Algerian War dragged on, replaced cinema newsreels as the source of news for most French people. The general's most important intervention on television came during the 1961 Generals' Putsch in Algiers, in which he appeared in full military uniform to demand loyalty, prompting an end to the minor uprising (De Gaulle 1961).

Although the Algerian War had provided the impetus for the Fourth Republic to try to control the media and to develop state propaganda in a more concerted way than at any other point in its brief history, including tight control of cinema newsreels (Pathé-Gaumont archives 2017), in many ways propaganda was not required to convince the French public of the importance of retaining French Algeria when the war first broke out. The Empire – a theme promoted consistently in state mass media propaganda since Daladier – was still hugely popular amongst the French public in 1954 (Kedward 2007: 340). Indeed, the most notable aspects of the propaganda produced during the war, before de Gaulle's return to power in 1958, were posters aimed at the Algerian population, including one which presented an image of French conscripts teaching local children to read and write, in a clear signal of the contribution France was making to Algeria (Textes et documents pour la classe 2010). Yet by the time de Gaulle assumed office, popular opinion in France was turning against the war, in no small part because of the significant human cost of the conflict. As a result, while much of the Radiodiffusion-Télévision Française (RTF), the state television and radio network, was dedicated to continuing to promote French rule in Algeria, de Gaulle's vision of maintaining links with an independent Algeria became an increasing presence in television programmes. Just as Daladier and then the Vichy authorities had realised the importance of the cinema as a medium which could relay nuanced messages, de Gaulle's Ministry for Information permitted the RTF to produce a groundbreaking documentary series, *Cinq colonnes à la Une*, whose coverage of the Algerian War was distinct from other media (Mossman 2013). Led by *Cinq colonnes*, the television was the first medium to gradually shift from promoting French Algeria to rallying support behind de Gaulle's mooted independence referendum – as witnessed by de Gaulle's intervention to end the Generals' Putsch.

Yet as the war came to an end, there was no corresponding signal of an end to the Gaullist control of the media. Indeed, the state media continued to promote the conservative and traditionalist Gaullist ideology that was, in many ways, similar to the ideology of Daladier in the Third Republic and then the programme of National Revolution pursued by Vichy, albeit without the open anti-Semitism. The replacement of the RTF with the new Office de Radiodiffusion Télévision Française (ORTF) led to few real changes in the content of, for example, television news. Staunchly Catholic images of the family were presented on television (family featured on some 500 reports for the Journal-Télévisé, the evening television news bulletin, between 1965 and 1969), while under André Malraux, de Gaulle's Culture Minister, the radio was the preserve of high culture (Ahearne 2003: 130). The Empire was replaced by the loosely defined concept of *la Francophonie* on state media channels. Throughout the Gaullist era, journalists at the ORTF, who produced content for the only two television channels in existence, were briefed directly by the minister for information on the topics to be covered each day. The dual package of censorship of negative coverage and promotion of conservative ideals that had begun under Daladier thus continued to thrive under de Gaulle. Journalists and producers employed by the state were not permitted to cover news which ran counter to de Gaulle's programme and vision of France. As such, during the events of May 1968, the coverage by the state media was patchy. On the one hand, radio and television offered opportunities for protesters and labour movement leaders to debate issues with government spokespeople. On the other hand, they ultimately provided de Gaulle and his government with the means to re-establish Gaullist law and order (Kuhn 1995: 75). It was only when journalists at the ORTF joined the general strike that they covered the events on state television and radio in a more sympathetic manner – and were promptly fired once the events were over (Guidicelli 2009).

A further development in the attempted control of the media under de Gaulle which built on previous regimes was the financial support offered to the ailing newspaper industry. As early as the Liberation, de Gaulle had sought to apply some control over newspapers through requiring discredited titles, such as *Le Figaro*, which had reprinted Vichy directives without question during its relocation to the Unoccupied Zone, to disband and reform, while also creating the new *Le Monde* with a Gaullist founder-editor, Hubert Beuve-Méry (Fenby 2010: 306). Financial support was provided to help newspapers return to mass printing; this system continued upon de Gaulle's return to power and indeed functions today to the extent that virtually every national newspaper is reliant on state subsidies to survive, including *L'Humanité* (Europe 1 2013). While Daladier and the Vichy propaganda authorities had censored the content of newspapers, and, in the case of Vichy, issued instructions over the content of articles, de Gaulle developed a system of state control over the traditional printed press which both sought to ensure positive coverage through censorship – in direct opposition to the apparent stated aims of the Ministry of Information, to ensure a 'free' press (Journal Officiel 1961) – and effectively rendered national newspapers indebted to the state. Longer term, however, such financial subsidies had the impact of enabling far left newspapers, such as *L'Humanité*, to continue printing, and once Giscard d'Estaing ended the framework of active state control of all media in 1974, this ensured the long-term survival of competing voices in the national press.

The Gaullist Ministry for Information reflected the militaristic discipline of the general in many ways. Forged during the Second World War and then developed at the height of the Algerian War, the ministry placed the media in general, and the state television and radio stations in particular, under strict governmental control. State journalists were forced to adhere to the instructions of the Ministry of Information or face disciplinary action, while newspapers became, for all their apparent objectivity and independence, increasingly reliant on the state. The Ministry was also rigorous in its policing of the Constitution of the Fifth Republic, again reflecting de Gaulle's own inclinations. As a result, a rare glimpse of objectivity was seen during the 1965 presidential elections, when de Gaulle was forced to share airtime with competing candidates, including François Mitterrand and one of the men responsible for cinema propaganda under Vichy, Jean-Louis Tixier-Vignancour. For a brief moment, de Gaulle was caught on the hoof as his rivals exploited this coverage on state media, and it was only when the general actively engaged in electioneering, despite his hesitations, that he managed to gain more public support (Fenby 2010: 532). While state media continued to champion conservative and traditionalist ideals for the most part in an effort to persuade the public to continue to support de Gaulle, the strict election coverage guidelines nevertheless provided something of a chink in the armour of the Gaullist propaganda model, which has subsequently been exploited by politicians beyond the traditional status quo.

State intervention in the media from Pompidou to Macron: from control to regulation

Since de Gaulle's resignation in 1969, the state has shifted from a position of proactive control and censorship of the media under Georges Pompidou through to a position of reactive arms-length regulation, which has necessarily ended the state's potential to actively control the content of any of the French mass media. At the same time, the media landscape in France has changed irreversibly, thus ending any government's capacity to manipulate the media in an explicit way to ensure continuing electoral success. Initially, Pompidou's similarities to the general led to a continuity of the Gaullist model of state-sanctioned content on the ORTF and state financial support for ailing newspapers. Formal briefings of ORTF journalists took place regularly as they had under de Gaulle: news items promoted by the state conformed to the same traditionalist and conservative ideals, with the 'high' culture championed by Malraux still an essential component (Guidicelli 2009). Changes took place under Valéry Giscard d'Estaing, including the breaking up of the ORTF into smaller components and the official abolition of the Ministry for Information – which continued on a smaller scale in the form of the Comité interministériel pour l'information – although Giscard did continue to employ the television to speak directly to the audience in an attempt to appear closer to their everyday concerns than his predecessors (Michel 2005). If this was a far cry from de Gaulle's capacity to grind the television schedules to a halt, Giscard nonetheless propagated traditional ideals in his addresses, though his own changes to the framework of control of the media, and the rigour with which the Gaullist constitution was policed during electoral campaigns, failed to help his re-election campaign.

Further change took place under François Mitterrand, and his culture minister Jack Lang, who not only permitted greater competition amongst television channels but whose message, at least during the initial 'Socialist experiment' of his presidency, was altogether more liberal and socialist than any of his predecessors. The clear shift in cultural policy towards a courting of American film stars, such as the bestowing of the *Légion d'honneur* on Sylvester Stallone, was a break with the past but was still championed in state media in a continuity of the Gaullist model. Under Mitterrand, though, as under Giscard, the media reacted to ministerial press releases and presidential addresses, ahead of being directed in an explicit way to feature such policies in their news bulletins. Arguably the greatest change to the state model of propaganda took place under Mitterrand, with the introduction of an organisation which appeared to offer an 'arm's length' approach to state control of the mass media. Initially promised in the 1981 Socialist manifesto, the Haute Autorité de la Communication Audiovisuelle (HCA) was designed to replace the Ministry for Information's functions and to provide a regulatory body for the television and radio. The HCA and its successors, including the current Conseil Supérieur de l'Audiovisuel (CSA), signalled the clear end to the active state commissioning and control of the media that had existed up until Pompidou.

Under Nicolas Sarkozy, though, there was an attempt to reassert state or, more accurately, governmental commissioning of public television in particular, with the 2008 reform enabling the president to name the head of the France-Télévisions network, the successor to the ORTF created during the Mitterrand era of competition. Sarkozy's attempt to control the state television network was manifested as late as 2011 when he chose to address the nation on France 2, the lead state-funded television channel, to announce the intervention of French fighter jets in Libya, grinding the channel's schedule to a halt in an echo of de Gaulle during the Algerian War, and demonstrating a continuity with the focus on the strength of French diplomacy abroad, extending back to the focus on the Empire in the 1930s (Libération 2011). Sarkozy's manipulation of the media also went beyond the official state channels. Before and after his election in 2007, Sarkozy developed a reputation for an ostentatious lifestyle in which he courted wealthy figures from the worlds of business and indeed the media, enjoying a close reputation with Serge Dassault, owner of centre right newspaper *Le Figaro*, which offered very positive coverage of his campaign and presidency (Hewlett 2011: 56). Whilst not altogether surprising given the newspaper's pre-existing political convictions, there was little critical analysis of Sarkozy in the publication at a time when the president's popularity collapsed to a new record low for the Fifth Republic during the height of the 2008 financial crisis. Sarkozy's policies, despite the flurry of promises to break with the status quo upon taking office, in the end simply maintained both the economic and the social status quo. For all of Sarkozy's efforts to draw on the media for positive coverage, he, as with Giscard, could not prevent defeat to Hollande in 2012 and failed to arrest his decline in popularity towards the end of his presidency. For Sarkozy, attempts to control the media and an insistence on near-constant coverage of his every movement, backfired spectacularly, particularly when it came to focus on his private life and high-profile relationship with Carla Bruni. Forced, as with de Gaulle and every president since, to share the platform with Hollande during the 2012 presidential election campaign, Sarkozy could not shake his image of 'président bling-bling' which had been heightened, ironically, through his own curation of his image in state media (Hewlett 2011). François Hollande's major contribution to state intervention in the media was to confer onto the CSA the naming of the head of the France-Télévisions group, reversing Sarkozy's 2008 reform. Although the president was still able to influence the running of state television, since the president retained the right to name the director of the CSA (Libération 2013), Hollande reverted the governmental position back to one of retrospective regulation ahead of Sarkozy's more concerted efforts to regain some control over the media for both president and government.

At this early stage in the presidency of Emmanuel Macron, little appears to have changed from the Hollande administration's approach to media intervention. Indeed, Macron's links with big business and his previous experience as an investment banker led to positive coverage of his election campaign in the French printed press before his election. Although this must be taken in the wider context of the 2017 presidential elections, and the head-to-head between Macron and Marine Le Pen in the second round, which led to negative coverage of Le Pen in the printed press, Macron's neo-liberal economic policies make him favourable to the right-wing press (Kuhn 2019, this volume). Macron's already careful manipulation of his public image is likely to be continued through state media (Jeambar 2017); indeed, much of Macron's rhetoric around his leadership appears to be aping that of de Gaulle, with his claims of 'Jupiter' status above petty politics.

Challenges to historic state control and contemporary regulation of the media: the far left and internet channels

Despite the continuities between Daladier and Pompidou in terms of the framework for state mass media propaganda and the content produced in this material, there have nevertheless been a number of challenges to such state intervention in modern French history. The most significant challenges during de Gaulle's political life (from the Occupation to 1969) came in the form of the far left. Firstly, the content and themes of the propaganda produced by the far left (broadly Communist) Resistance during the Occupation era was radically different from either the material produced by the Gaullists or by Vichy. Tracts and newspapers produced clandestinely called for a government of the people and sought to unite workers against the oppressive militaristic leaders of either Pétain or de Gaulle (Turlais 2015). They also, importantly, acknowledged the discriminatory treatment of minorities and called for an end to such treatment, in direct opposition to either Vichy (which unsurprisingly did not draw attention to round-ups of Jews, but did seek to 'educate' the audience of the necessity of anti-Semitism through radio programmes (Lees 2015)) or indeed the Gaullist Resistance, which was surprisingly slow in condemning the *Rafle du Vel d'hiv*, the single biggest round-up of Jewish men, women and children during the Occupation (Turlais 2015).

Further challenges to the messages of the Gaullist state came from the far left during the Algerian War, particularly in the form of the *Manifeste des 121* intellectuals who campaigned for an end to French control in Algeria – this manifesto was removed by the censor from the pages of *L'Humanité* and *Libération* (Kuhn 1995: 57) – and from the writings of far left authors such as Jean-Paul Sartre and Simone de Beauvoir. Finally, May 1968 was a glorious period for left-wing propaganda against the Gaullist state. Independent radio stations, like Radio Luxembourg, reported directly on the students' demonstrations, the general strikes and the police repression, while posters produced by far left workers' and students' movements railed against de Gaulle. Of these, the most notable were a silhouette of the general, with an exaggerated Gallic nose and the slogan 'La chienlit, c'est lui,' in a direct inversion of the insult aimed by de Gaulle at the student protesters, and an image of de Gaulle placing his hand over the mouth of a student, with the caption 'Sois jeune et tais-toi' – 'Be a good young person and shut up' (Archives Départementales de Landes 2018). During de Gaulle's lifetime, then, the most notable challenges to the conservative status quo in mass media propaganda came from the far left and not from the mainstream opposition in the case of the Algerian War and May 1968.

More recently, challenges to state intervention in the media have come in two forms: the opportunity for politicians and movements to directly address audiences without state interference and, allied to this, the advent of social media, which represent major changes in the French media landscape. Raymond Kuhn (2019, this volume) has argued in Chapter 21 of this handbook that the opportunity for political figures such as François Fillon, Jean-Luc Mélenchon and Marine Le Pen to broadcast speeches online without the need to rely on the state media to convey their views essentially bypasses the controls put in place under de Gaulle and which, in the form of electoral rules, continue to exist to this day. Platforms such as Facebook, Twitter and Snapchat appeal to different audiences to the traditional media. Whereas incumbent presidents have also recently used social media to disseminate their messages, rival candidates have the potential to both make use of their allocated space on state media during election campaigns, generally filtered through the medium of a moderator, and to present an unfiltered version of their views on alternative internet platforms.

Conclusions: propaganda and the French exceptionalism

A clear link can be drawn between the origins of the first minister for information under Daladier and the end of the Ministry for Information under Pompidou, while more recently the history has been one of consistent state regulation, even if Sarkozy sought to reassert some control over the mass media. What was developed as a means of persuading the French population to support Daladier's dual programme of increasing patriotism and, in the repressive climate of the late 1930s, a focus on traditional family values and on retaining the Empire, continued to exist as a framework for promoting the policies of contemporary governments between 1939 and 1974. Each successive government or regime sought to draw on the mass media to increase its popularity through employing themes which have proved enduringly popular. Both France's role on the world stage and family values have continued to feature in the mass media today, although they have been nuanced to reflect the end of the Empire and changing family models. Until the end of the Pompidou government, though, the promotion of these two themes in particular reflected a conservative ideology that could be traced back to Daladier.

Daladier held office in a context of wartime, furthering the pre-existing association between propaganda and slaughter that had prevented the development of a formal ministry before the 1930s. Mass media propaganda has also been associated with other conflicts in French history, including the Algerian War, which provided the opportunity for de Gaulle to place the mass media under very tight control. Yet the two features of mass media propaganda: censorship and insertion of themes which reflected the ideology of the government (frequently conservative in nature) in order to drown out dissenting voices and to increase the popularity of the government continued to exist way beyond such wartime contexts, with historically mixed results. The use of visual media, like the cinema under Daladier, Vichy and the Gaullist Liberation government, and then television since the 1960s, has proved generally effective, drawing on the associations between the cinema and television and escapism and distraction. The cinema and television have thus produced some historically more nuanced portrayals of events and ideals than other media – such as the portrayal of Vichy's ideology in documentary film and the portrayal of the Algerian War in *Cinq colonnes* on the television. By contrast, other media have proved less effective, whether because of over-reliance on the state in the first place or because of a lack of subtlety.

Mass media propaganda has nevertheless faced several limitations and challenges which have on occasions prevented such material from achieving the goal of boosting the popularity of the state. Such media can only ever operate in the context of the time: despite the ongoing usage of themes like the family and France's role in the world, including during the Sarkozy presidency, mass media cannot necessarily prevent the government from becoming unpopular, and the framework of reactive regulation rather than proactive commissioning and censorship since Giscard has failed to prevent defeats at the ballot box for Giscard and Sarkozy. As these presidents of the Fifth Republic have experienced, control of the content of state mass media does not automatically equate to winning elections. In a democratic environment, with clear electioneering rules and increasing opportunities for opposition parties and movements to challenge the status quo in one way or another, through social media or through speaking directly to the people without government filtering, the government can no longer rely as it once did on using the media to seek to ensure popularity through influencing the thoughts and actions of the electorate.

References

Ahearne, J. 2003. Cultural policy in the old Europe: France and Germany. In *International Journal of Cultural Policy*, 9:2, 127–131.

Amaury, P. 1969. *Les Deux Premières Expériences d'un 'Ministère de l'Information' en France*. Paris: Librairie Générale de Droit et de Jurisprudence.

Anthony, S. and J. G. Mansell. 2011. *The Projection of Britain: A History of the GPO Film Unit*. London: Palgrave Macmillan.

Archives Départementales de Landes. 2018. Mai '68: Une révolte en affiches. Available at: www.archives.landes.fr/article.php?larub=135&titre=mai-1968-une-revolte-en-affiches [Accessed: 10.06.2018].

Archives Nationales. 1943. AN F/41 59. Report on the national radio. No precise date (Autumn 1943).

Archives Nationales. 1944: AN F/42 113. Note concernant France-Libre-Actualités. No precise date (probably September 1944).

Bowles, B. 2004a. *La Tragédie de Mers-el-Kébir* and the politics of filmed news in France, 1940–1944. In 'Cultural Practices,' special issue of *The Journal of Modern History*, 76:2, 347–388.

Bowles, B. 2004b. Newsreels, ideology and public opinion under Vichy: the case of *La France en Marche*. In *French Historical Studies*, 27:2, 419–463.

Chadwick, K. 2011. *Philippe Henriot. The Last Act of Vichy: Radio Broadcasts, January–June 1944*. Liverpool: Liverpool University Press.

Chadwick, K. 2015. Our enemy's enemy. In *Media History*, 21:4, 426–442.

Chadwick, K. 2017. An appetite for argument: radio propaganda and food in occupied France. In *French History*, 31:1, 85–106.

De Gaulle, C. 1944. Discours de l'hôtel de ville. 25 August.

De Gaulle, C. 1961. Discours du 23 avril 1961. Available at: www.ina.fr/video/I00012392/charles-de-gaulle-helas-!-helas-!-helas-!-video.html [Accessed: 22.08.2017].

Delpha, F. and J-G. Foucaud. 1975. Les Communistes français et la sexualité, 1932–1938. In *Mouvement Social*, 91.

Diamond, H. 2007. *Fleeing Hitler: France 1940*. Oxford: Oxford University Press.

Europe 1. 2013. Aides publiques à la presse: qui gagne le plus? 13 December. Available at: www.europe1.fr/medias-tele/aides-publiques-a-la-presse-qui-gagne-le-plus-1742229 [Accessed: 22.08.2017].

Evans, M. 2012. *Algeria: France's Undeclared War*. Oxford: Oxford University Press.

Fenby, J. 2010. *The General: Charles de Gaulle and the France He Saved*. London: Simon and Schuster.

Garden, I. 2012. *The Third Reich's Celluloid War: Propaganda in Nazi Feature Films, Documentaries and Television*. Stroud: The History Press.

Guidicelli, J-C. 2009. *Le JT: toute une histoire*. Available at: www.ina.fr/video/CPD09007766/le-jt-toute-une-histoire-video.html [Accessed: 22.08.2017].

Hewlett, N. 2011. *The Sarkozy Phenomenon*. Exeter: Imprint Academic.

Jackson, J. 2001. *France the Dark Years 1940–1944*. Oxford: Oxford University Press.

Jeambar, D. 2017. Rentrée politique: pourquoi Emmanuel Macron doit s'adresser directement aux Français. In *Challenges.fr*, 22 August. Available at: www.challenges.fr/politique/rentree-politique-pourquoi-emmanuel-macron-doit-s-adresser-directement-aux-francais_494203 [Accessed: 22.08.2017].

Journal Officiel. 1961. Procès-verbal de la séance du 7 novembre 1961 – Intervention de Christian de La Malène.

Jowett, G. and V. O'Donnell. 2011. *Propaganda and Persuasion*. London: Sage.

Kedward, R. 2007. *La Vie en bleu: France and the French since 1900*. London: Penguin.

Kuhn, R. 1995. *The Media in France*. London: Routledge.

Kuhn, R. 2019. The media. In M. Demossier, D. Lees, A. Mondon and N. Parish (Eds.), *The Routledge Handbook of French Politics and Culture*. London: Routledge.

Lees, D. 2015. *Vichy on film: the portrayal in documentary propaganda of life under Occupation, 1940–1944*. Unpublished PhD thesis. Coventry: University of Warwick.

Lees, D. 2018. Defining everyday Frenchness under Vichy. In L. Dodd and D. Lees (Eds.), *Vichy France and Everyday Life Confronting the Challenges of Wartime, 1939–1945*. London: Bloomsbury.

Libération. 2011. La coalition internationale est passée à l'action en Libye. 19 March. Available at: www.liberation.fr/planete/2011/03/19/la-coalition-internationale-est-passee-a-l-action-en-libye_722764 [Accessed: 22.08.2017].

Libération. 2013. Filippetti veut raccourcir le CSA pour accroître son indépendance. 6 May. Available at: www.liberation.fr/ecrans/2013/05/06/filippetti-veut-raccourcir-le-csa-pour-accroitre-son-independance_954835 [Accessed: 22.08.2017].

Luneau, A. 2010. *Radio Londres, 1940–1944. Les Voix de la liberté*. Paris: Perrin.

Mendès-France, P. 1954. Mon Intention de m'adresser regulièrement à vous. 26 June. Available through Association Pierre Mendès-France. Available at: www.mendes-france.fr/ [Accessed: 22.08.2017].

Michel, F. 2005. Breaking the Gaullian Mould: Valéry Giscard d'Estaing and the modernisation of French presidential communication. In *Modern and Contemporary France*, 13:3, 291–306.

Mondon, A. 2013. *The Mainstreaming of the Extreme-Right in France and Australia: A Populist Hegemony?* London: Ashgate.

Mossman, I. 2013. Conflicting memories: modernisation, colonialism and the Algerian war appelés in Cinq colonnes a la une. In F. Barclay (Ed.), *France's Colonial Legacies Memory, Identity and Narrative*. Cardiff: University of Wales Press.

Pathé-Gaumont archives. 2017. Introduction aux actualités françaises. Available at: www.gaumontpathearchives.com/index.php?html=4 [Accessed: 22.08.2017].

Rossignol, D. 1991. *Histoire de la propagande en France de 1940 à 1944: l'utopie Pétain*. Paris: Presses Universitaires de France.

Taylor, P. 2003. *Munitions of the Mind: A History of Propaganda from the Ancient World to the Present Day*. Manchester: Manchester University Press.

Textes et documents pour la classe. 2010. In *La Guérre d'Algérie*, 994, April.

Turlais, P. 2015. Tracts et papillons clandestins de la Résistance: papiers d'urgence. Available at: http://resistance.editionsartulis.fr/preface.htm [Accessed: 22.08.2017].

Wharton, S. 2006. *Screening Reality: French Documentary Film during the German Occupation*. Bern: Peter Lang.

Williams, M. 2006. *Mussolini's Propaganda Abroad: Subversion in the Mediterranean and the Middle East, 1936–1940*. London: Routledge.

19

CULTURAL POLICY

A weakened exception? (1959–2016)

Philippe Poirrier

Created in 1959 and entrusted to André Malraux, the Ministry for Cultural Affairs was not the result of a real political agenda, but sought primarily to maintain the novelist's position in government. The Fifth Republic was in fact entering a long-standing legacy. Since its establishment at the end of the nineteenth century, the Third Republic had already been confronted with having to manage a double legacy: one handed down since the seventeenth century by the various monarchical regimes and the other, of equal importance, inherited from the Revolutionary Decade. On the one hand, monarchical legacies – the patron state, academic system and *laïcisation* of censorship – left an enduring mark on the relationship between power and the arts. On the other, 'national heritage,' the revolutionary museum and the belief in the civic and educational virtues of the arts were the indisputable legacies of the revolutionary period. With the Liberation, the Fourth Republic had made the democratic principles of the Popular Front and the Resistance its own, without implementing an independent cultural policy (Poirrier 2006). The Malraux ministry inherited a variety of departments, mainly from the Ministry of Education; but it failed to integrate libraries, radio and television, and France's foreign cultural policy. The decree of 24 July 1959 states:

> The Ministry for Cultural Affairs is responsible for making all major masterpieces, especially those originating from France, accessible to as many French citizens as possible; for ensuring that there is the widest possible audience for our cultural heritage; and for prioritising the creation of works of art and intellectual works which enrich this heritage.

The democratic demand is therefore present in the expectations of this founding decree. The consideration of equality and the desire for cultural democratisation are critical. Malraux's cultural policy was in keeping with the philosophy of the welfare state. The state thus committed to ensuring equal access for everyone to cultural property. Two policies contributed to making this desire a reality: providing everyone with access to cultural works and extending the benefits of social protection to artists. Cultural policy was also promoted in keeping with the philosophy of modernisation supported by the Gaullist Republic. The state had to play a leading role in management, momentum and coordination. The 1970s strengthened central government and ensured the longevity of the ministerial structure (Dubois 1999; Urfalino 1996).

From 1974 onwards, two main themes were prevalent. The introduction of liberal philosophy reinforced the relative withdrawal of state funding. By the end of president Giscard's seven-year term, the cultural state remained weak and gave priority to heritage. Cultural policy was not a government priority. The budget and administrative resources were also weakened. Despite Michel Guy's appointment as secretary of state for culture (1974–1976), seen as a 'cultural spring' by professionals, the prevalence of liberal philosophy contributed to lessening the public service missions of the ministry. Within central government itself, all eyes were on the Parti Socialiste (PS) which was developing a programme that paid particular attention to cultural issues. The true impact of governing institutions is however debatable. In 1978, Augustin Girard caused controversy when he acknowledged that cultural democratisation was undoubtedly occurring mostly through 'cultural industries' rather than state action (Girard 1978). In 1980, the review by Pierre Emmanuel, the poet in charge of the cultural sector within the Gaullist party, condemned the lack of political will and the ministry's difficulty in displaying the meaning of its work (Emmanuel 1980).

When the left came to power in the early 1980s, it caused a threefold break with the past. The most important aspect was the quantitative break with the past, which resulted in a doubling of the ministry of culture's budget from the 1982 policy year. Furthermore, minister Jack Lang, who had the support of president François Mitterrand, knew how to embody this change in scale (Martin 2008). Finally, achieving a synergy between culture and the economy was identified as a priority. The *Grands Travaux* policy also attests to the establishment of a presidential component to cultural policy. All sectors of cultural policy (creativity more than heritage) benefited from these quantitative increases and qualitative breaks with the past.

From the 1990s onwards, the system of reference which determined the direction of public policies for culture took a new, significant turn: the defence of 'cultural exception' – soon renamed 'cultural diversity' – increasingly tempered the references made to democratisation of cultural practices. Democratisation nevertheless continued to be regularly called upon. In 1998, within the framework of the 'Charter of Public Service Missions for the Performing Arts,' the minister Catherine Trautmann reaffirmed the basis of public involvement in cultural matters:

> The commitment of the state to art and culture derives first and foremost from a conception of democracy and the obligations this imposes: to encourage access for all to both works of art and cultural practices; to enrich collective debate and social life through the strong presence of artistic creation, while granting the highest degree of freedom to artists in creation and dissemination; to guarantee each citizen the greatest possible freedom to choose their cultural practices.
>
> *(Ahearne 2002)*

The issue of the globalisation of culture, now a recurring theme, offered the chance to change the scale of justification. Beyond ensuring the survival of the European cinema and audio-visual media sectors, cultural policy was used to preserve European cultural identity. Over the following years, during international trade talks, France stood firm on its philosophy and shaped the approach of the whole European Union. Furthermore, France strove to change the forum of debate from the World Trade Organisation to UNESCO. The Convention on Cultural Diversity, adopted by UNESCO on 20 October 2005, was undoubtedly a victory for this French philosophy. Since the beginning of negotiations with the United States about the Transatlantic Trade and Investment Partnership (TTIP) in 2013, this matter has become topical once again. The European Commission, which negotiates on behalf of the EU, seemed to be opposed to the continuation of this exclusion. France gained support, albeit fluctuating, from 14 EU countries. This was crucial, because the decision to continue or not continue with cultural exception would determine the longevity of a vast support network, which was both regulatory and financial, for production, distribution, cultivation and cultural action in audio-visual sectors, especially cinema. France remained at the cutting-edge of this matter on a national and international scale, with the support of numerous professional organisations and coalitions. This approach confirmed the growing role of cultural industries in public policies for culture.

From guardian-state to partner-state

By creating a Ministry for Cultural Affairs, the Gaullist Republic strengthened the role of the state. In artistic sectors, the state's role was reinforced by an old, mainstream idea which discredited provincial claims to culture. Weak territorialisation of the Ministry for Cultural Affairs remained thus an essential element. The state's cultural policy continued to be fundamentally characterised by the influence of Parisian cultural institutions, even if the Departmental Archives and central lending libraries attested to the presence of the state at local level. The system for decentralising theatres, which was restructured at the start of the 1960s, continued to be perceived as a largely national system (Goetschel 2004). The policy to break with the Fine Arts certainly equipped itself with a 'tool' to do so in the form of the *maisons de la culture*. The stated objective was territorial, but the core aim was to carry out cultural action supported by the ministry. Above all, the *maisons de la culture* created a form of partnership between the state and cities. This method of co-management was beneficial for both parties. With their excellent record and the debates they generated, these few *maisons de la culture* played a significant role in raising awareness of cultural issues in cities.

The Duhamel ministry (1971–1973) instigated the gradual establishment of decentralised services (Regional Directorate of Cultural Affairs). The Cultural Charters, launched by Michel Guy (1974–1975), reflected a desire to develop new kinds of relationships between the state and cities. At the end of the 1970s, the partnership between the state and local authorities was still an uncertain reality. The fragility of state cultural policy, both on a political level and a financial one, contrasted with the increasing power of cultural policies of local authorities.

When the left came to power, there was a repositioning of the principal players in public policies for culture. The combination of a voluntarist state policy with local policies, which had many resources, great overall consistency and were managed by professional services, explains the cultural upturn that characterised the 1980s. Local authorities became fully involved in public policy. From that day forward, public cultural action functioned as a 'system of cooperation.' The state, which could rely on enhanced decentralised services, advocated cooperation between different public actors. The 'Cultural Development Conventions' were the main tool for formalising this contract. The types of contract multiplied over the course of the 1990s. For their part, local authorities understood that cultural policy could be an asset in marketing and economic development policies. They led cooperation strategies, which were different from one authority to another and were adapted to their own territorial project, and they knew how to seize the opportunities provided by the state. The results differed according to the level examined, with regions struggling to adapt more than departments and particularly cities, and they also varied according to cultural sector. This territorialisation was not in fact synonymous with state withdrawal, and cultural sector professionals continued to be in involved in government inspection, assessment and regulatory authorities. Regional cultural life – especially in large cities – no longer came under the label '*hideous provinces*,' once condemned by André Malraux (Poirrier and Rioux 2000; Poirrier and Rizzardo 2009).

This arrangement remained fragile. As regards local authorities, territorial reform (2014–2016), tightening budgets, shifting priorities and declining political ambitions constituted real areas for concern, which were identified by those involved in the worlds of culture. As regards the state, the idea of a 'cultural pact' with local authorities, launched in 2014, was based on a simple principle: the state pledged to continue granting funds from the Ministry of Culture to receiving authorities for three years, provided that the relevant authority also balanced its finances. The Ministry of Culture anticipated around a hundred signatures. The measure remained a far cry from the general contract agreement of the 1990s, it seemed quite insignificant at country level, and did little to hide the substantial decline in funding for territorial authorities.

Mixed reception

Malraux's philosophy only established itself gradually. Campaigners for popular education and locally elected representatives condemned the move away from popular education, the de facto rift with state education, the strictness and complexity of administrative standards imposed by a Jacobin state, and the uneasy collaboration between different ministries. The popularisation of reason and the ethics of commitment and responsibility remained much more central in the approach to cultural policy adopted by popular education associations than in Malraux's strategy, for whom it was of utmost importance to bring about direct contact with works of art and to curb cultural provincialism. The events of May 1968 destabilised the Ministry for Cultural Affairs and revealed the emergence of two criticisms: those on the left attacked Malraux's notion of cultural democratisation; those who supported law and order condemned government support for artists suspected of subversion.

Intellectuals were particularly engaged in these criticisms, which emerged again in the early 1990s. In 1991, Marc Fumaroli's *L'Etat culturel* sparked widespread debate and gained significant media attention (Fumaroli 1991). The debate also highlighted the resistance of people within academic circles who condemned how the inclusive view of national culture had been watered down. It was also a form of nostalgia for a certain kind of cultural mediation deriving from the age of classics and of Enlightenment. Beyond government action alone, the legitimacy of cultural pluralism, which was largely rejected, increasingly characterised French society. Cultural relativism was largely condemned (Poirrier 2014).

Examinations of cultural practices, launched in the 1970s to bolster the strategic goals of the ministry, highlighted the failure of cultural democratisation and the continuation of physical, social and symbolic barriers limiting access to so-called classic culture. They fed the controversy surrounding the adequacy of cultural policy (Donnat and Tolila 2003). The need to have artistic and cultural education within state education had appeared on the political agenda for two decades without ever truly materialising. Any progress made in this regard continued to be undermined by changes of government and a lack of political will in the context of reduced government spending (Wallon 2016).

The voluntarist action of the government did, however, allow artistic life to remain relatively autonomous of market forces and enabled a richer network of cultural institutions to work across the whole country. The French model is characterised by a form of mixed cultural economy which is based on the close interweaving of public and private sectors. The strong mandate for state intervention, enshrined in an emancipatory Republic, the influence of large cultural institutions and the close relationship between arts and culture professionals gives the French model a uniqueness which contrasts with many countries in the European Union and

North America (Poirrier 2011). Direct state intervention, widely accepted by the public, gives a minor role to taxation schemes and private sponsorship. These schemes and sponsorship, certainly facilitated by more favourable legislation from 2003 onwards, mainly benefit large cultural establishments (Rozier 2016).

From the end of the 1990s, there was no longer a sense of purpose, which was based on activism engaged in by the majority of people involved in the world of culture. The ministry increasingly presented itself as a management structure which carried out regulation, guidance, advice and assessment work. The theme of 'radical reform,' commencing in the mid-1990s (Rigaud 1996), continued to be included in a somewhat watered-down capacity, in the form of targeting better governance. As such, the Ministry of Culture was part of the issue of state reform.

The public audio-visual landscape: the Ministry of Culture's defeat

The 1980s had seen a real revolution of the public audio-visual landscape. The creation of Canal + and private stations (La Cinq and TV6), then the privatisation of Channel One in 1986, caused increasing competition between channels. The Ministry of Culture did not manage to assert itself. Arte, a Franco-German cultural channel broadcast on terrestrial televisions since 1992, stood out as an exception in a landscape that was from then on dominated by business philosophy. Some commentators would go on to condemn the creation of a 'cultural ghetto,' which gave a real excuse for the slide towards commercialism on other public channels (Wolton 1989; Cluzel 2002). In 2003, philosopher Catherine Clément, who authored a report for the Ministry of Culture, could only record that business philosophy had simply reinforced the situation over the past two decades. Even though television had become the main cultural practice of French citizens, programmes labelled 'cultural' were only found on the periphery of TV schedules: 'at night and during summertime' (Clément 2003).

Intellectuals – largely from cultural professions – had indeed for a long time enjoyed an ambivalent relationship with audio-visual media, particularly television, divided between those who condemned the spread of mass culture and actions considered harmful to 'legitimate culture,' and those who worried that the media would be used to strengthen cultural democratisation (Eck 2003). On a scientific level, the cultural legitimism of French academics had delayed real consideration of its new issues in social sciences, even though British *Cultural Studies*, established at the fringes of the university system, were at the same time entering this field more proactively.

However, the Lang ministry put all its power into strengthening close coordination between the world of cinema and television. This unique strategy – directly responsible for the idea of cultural exception – had been developed from the start of the 1970s. The Law of 29 July 1982 strengthened television requirements regarding motion pictures by reinforcing the quota system for French films and by precisely defining the arrangements for showing feature films on different channels. Indeed, the creation of the encrypted channel Canal + in 1985 allowed film production to benefit from sound financial footing. In exchange for particularly favourable regulations, Canal + would go on to play a critical role in French film production for over a decade. Television became the film industry's major investor and market. Cinema screenings were now only regarded as a place to showcase and launch films. In 1997, the creation of TPS, satellite television packages, put an end to the monopoly of Canal +. With transnational ambitions and strategies, a third player – communication industries – would go on to threaten this delicate balance (Creton 2002).

A weakened model

For around 15 years, with changes of government, the Ministry of Culture and Communication has shown its desire to modernise its role and how it functions in order to respond to a national and international environment that is undergoing major transformations. At the same time, the meaning, clarity and results of public policies for culture are being debated. However, culture did not receive much attention in public debate during the election campaign of spring 2002, even though the issue of public policy for culture featured in the programmes of all the candidates. With Jean-Marie Le Pen, leader of the Front National, progressing to the second round of the presidential elections, an 'anti-fascist' reflex was triggered within the worlds of art and culture. The issue regarding where cultural democratisation should stop was raised during the discussions about the state of French society that emerged over the following weeks; this involved no contribution to proposing new solutions (Poirrier 2004b). The presidential campaigns that followed, in 2007 and 2012, gave very little attention to the issue of cultural policy.

The state was also challenged by social partners regarding a specific unemployment insurance scheme for workers in the entertainment industry without regular employment. Behind this, the preservation of an important part of cultural activity was at stake. The industrial dispute stalemate, which had a major impact on the schedule and economy of festivals during the summer of 2003, weakened the political position of the minister of culture and communication Jean-Jacques Aillagon. The crisis of those without regular employment at least had some worth: it showed that cultural employment funding was one of the issues missing from cultural policy thinking in France. This crisis was in fact unusual: it affected a rapidly growing sector; those involved defended great flexibility; the alliance between employers and employees of the sector was a real exception; the insurance deficit was distinctive because it grew as employment increased. The same scenario had been ongoing for ten years: those involved had long prioritised the status quo. Over the course of the 1990s, irregular work allowed there to be the illusion of funding for cultural production. The issue had far wider implications because it affected how social protection itself was designed and how the welfare state developed (Menger 2005). Since 2014, this matter has once again been centre stage and the state has acted in conjunction with social partners to try to sustain this status.

France's position on the international scene, at the forefront of defending cultural diversity, contrasted with the approach adopted by the Ministry of Culture, where financial and strategic flexibility seemed to be increasingly reduced. Furthermore, the Ministry of Culture's policy mainly interpreted diversity in its artistic form and tried – as required by the Republican model – to administer policies according to a need for diversity that included places or reflected ethnic or religious backgrounds. The attempts were discernible, but remained relatively remote or fell under other measures, for instance as part of 'urban policy.' Jacques Rigaud pinpointed the difference between cultural policy rhetoric and reality: 'all official speeches on cultural diversity and on France's message would surely gain credibility if our country provided more tangible proof of the place it affords intellectual works, in all their diversity, at home and abroad' (Rigaud 2006). Above all, the increasing power of new technologies and the strategies of cultural industries, conducted on a global scale, call into question the very format of the measures at the heart of the French cultural policy model.

Criticism of cultural policy has once again become topical. Many commentators underline the lack of opportunities, the loss of meaning and the 'cultural policy stalemate' (Esprit 2004). This is the time of disillusionment even though public debate on these issues struggles to go beyond corporate philosophy alone. Within political parties and among locally elected representatives, the issue of cultural policy rarely appears to be a priority, even if some discussions take place. Difficult social conditions and the changes affecting the country's economy have contributed to a shift in the major issues governing the political agenda. Increased decentralisation, very clear over the course of the 1990s, has fuelled this feeling of disillusionment.

With changes of government and a gloomy financial context, the first decade of the new millennium reinforced the philosophy of 'modernisation.' From July 2007, this 'modernisation' became part of the 'General Review of Public Policies' (RGPP). The aim was to 'shift the central government's focus [. . .] back to its more forward-looking responsibilities of leadership and strategy.' It was also necessary to respond to the challenges linked to the 'digital revolution.' The new organisational structure of the ministry, built around a directorate-general responsible for the heritage of France, a directorate-general responsible for supporting creativity and distribution networks, and a directorate-general responsible for the development of the media and economy, was put in place in the context of relative withdrawal of the state; this caused real worry for those involved in the cultural sector. The Council of Artistic Creation, established in 2009 by president Nicolas Sarkozy, was perceived as a reduction in the strategic flexibility of the Ministry of Culture. Generally led over the past few years by technocratic ministers (Jean-Jacques Aillagon, Christine Albanel, Frédéric Mitterrand, Fleur Pellerin, Audrey Azoulay) who could hardly rely on their political standing, the Ministry of Culture and Communication is no longer the driving force of national cultural life; it is rivalled on the one hand by large public institutions, which are increasingly autonomous, and on the other by territorial authorities. However, these duties remain essential in several areas: ensuring equal access to cultural events and practices across regions and strengthening its legislative and regulatory function, which is vital for supporting artistic creation and market regulation during the digital revolution. The most important thing is for the Ministry of Culture to adapt to the new challenges emerging from the 'digital revolution.' There appears to be a mixed record which unites cultural actors and commentators from the major political groupings in a rare consensus: that the ministry has been weakened; that it has been undermined by financial paralysis; that it is not built to respond to the challenges presented by cultural industries and that it is incapable of supporting emerging projects. Ultimately, political will is lacking, which undoubtedly translates into growing disinterest from elites about cultural issues (Le Débat 2015).

Conclusions

The last two decades have seen some significant trends develop, affecting all public policies for culture: the professionalisation of those involved in the worlds of art and culture, the modernisation of management and the autonomy of cultural establishments, the partnership and contract agreements between the state and local authorities, and the endorsed use of private sponsorship. The disillusionment felt by many people involved particularly affected the general aims of cultural policy in a context marked both by the globalisation of challenges on an international scale, growing territorialisation of public policies, French multicultural society which calls the beliefs of the Republican model into question, and a renewed examination of which kinds of art and culture should be backed by the government. These changes, which have been supported to varying extents by the government, weaken the traditional foundations of state intervention in artistic and cultural sectors. Following the attacks of 2015, the ministry reaffirmed the need to make culture a weapon against terrorism and obscurantism (Pellerin 2015). The gap is widening between rhetoric and reality.

Translated by Katy Brown

References

Ahearne, J. 2002. *French Cultural Policy Debates: A Reader*. London: Routledge.

Benhamou, F. 2015. *Politique culturelle, fin de partie ou nouvelle saison?* Paris: La Documentation française.

Clément, C. 2003. *La Nuit et l'été: rapport sur la culture à la télévision*. Paris: Seuil/La Documentation française.

Cluzel, J. 2002. Une ambition justifiée, une réalisation contestable. In *Le Débat*, 4:121, 178–183.

Creton, L. (Ed.). 2002. *Le cinéma à l'épreuve du système télévisuel*. Paris: CNRS Editions.

De Baecque, A. 2008. *Crises dans la culture française*. Paris: Bayard.

De Waresquiel, E. (Ed.). 2001. *Dictionnaire des politiques culturelles de la France depuis 1959*. Paris: Larousse-CNRS.

Donnat, O. and P. Tolila. (Eds.). 2003. *Le(s) public(s) de la culture*, Vol. II. Paris: Presses de Sciences Po.

Dubois, V. 1999. *La politique culturelle: genèse d'une catégorie d'intervention publique*. Paris: Belin.

Eck, H. 2003. Médias audiovisuels et intellectuel. In M. Leymarie and J. F. Sirinelli (Eds.), *L'histoire des intellectuels aujourd'hui*. Paris: PUF, 201–225.

Emmanuel, P. 1980. *Culture, noblesse du monde, histoire d'une politique*. Paris: Stock.

Esprit. 2004. Les impasses de la politique culturelle, May.

Fumaroli, M. 1991. *L'Etat culturel*. Paris: De Fallois.

Girard, A. 1978. Industries culturelles. In *Futuribles*, 17, 598–605.

Goetschel, P. 2004. *Renouveau et décentralisation du théâtre*. Paris: PUF.

Le Brun-Cordier, P. 2005. La crise de la politique culturelle française. In *Contemporary French Civilization*, 29:1, 1–19.

Le Débat. 2015. Que faire du ministère de la Culture? November–December.

Martin, L. 2008. *Jack Lang: Une vie entre culture et politique*. Paris: Editions Complexe.

Menger, P. M. 2005. *Les intermittents du spectacle: sociologie d'une exception*. Paris: Editions de l'Ehess.

Pellerin, F. 2015. On ne va pas au Bataclan pour mourir. In *Le Monde*, 21 November.

Poirrier, P. 1999. *Bibliographie de l'histoire des politiques culturelles. France, XIXe-Xxe siècles*. Paris: La Documentation française-Comité d'histoire du ministère de la Culture.

Poirrier, P. 2003. Heritage and cultural policy in France under the Fifth Republic. In *International Journal of Cultural Policy*, 92, 215–225.

Poirrier, P. 2004a. *Les enjeux de l'histoire culturelle*. Paris: Seuil.

Poirrier, P. 2004b. La culture en campagne: de l'atonie à la mobilisation antifasciste: Politique culturelle et débat public en France lors des élections de 2002. In *French Cultural Studies*, 15:2, 174–189.

Poirrier, P. 2004c. French cultural policy in question, 1981–2003. In J. Bourg (Ed.), *After the Deluge, New Perspectives on Postwar French Intellectual and Cultural History*. Lanham MD: Lexington Books, 301–323.

Poirrier, P. (Ed.). 2006. *Art et pouvoir. De 1848 à nos jours*. Paris: Cndp.

Poirrier, P. 2011. *Pour une histoire des politiques culturelles dans le monde, 1945–2011*. Paris: La Documentation française.

Poirrier, P. 2014. *Quelle politique pour la culture? Florilège des débats 1955–2014*. Paris: La Documentation française.

Poirrier, P. 2016a. *Les politiques de la culture en France*. Paris: La Documentation française.

Poirrier, P. (Ed.). 2016b. *Politiques et pratiques de la culture*. Paris: La Documentation française.

Poirrier, P. and J. P. Rioux. (Eds.). 2000. *Affaires culturelles et territoires*. Paris: La Documentation française.

Poirrier, P. and R. Rizzardo. 2009. *Une ambition partagée? La coopération entre le ministère de la Culture et les collectivités territoriales (1959–2009)*. Paris: La Documentation française-Comité d'histoire du ministère de la Culture.

Rigaud, J. 1996. *Pour une refondation de la politique culturelle*. Paris: La Documentation française.

Rigaud, J. 2006. Libres propos sur la diversité culturelle. In *L'Observatoire*, 30, 23–24.

Rioux, J. P. and J. F. Sirinelli. (Eds.). 1997. *Pour une histoire culturelle*. Paris: Seuil.

Rozier, S. 2016. Les nouveaux visages du mécénat culturel. In P. Poirrier (Ed.), *Politiques et pratiques de la culture*. Paris: La Documentation française.

Saez, G. (Ed.). 2011. *Le Fil de l'esprit. Augustin Girard, Un parcours entre recherche et action*. Paris: La Documentation française.

Schuster, J. M. 2002. *Informing Cultural Policy: The Research and Information Infrastructure*. New Brunswick, NJ: Center for Urban Policy Research.

Urfalino, P. 1996. *L'invention de la politique culturelle*. Paris: Comité d'histoire du ministère de la culture-La Documentation française.

Wallon, E. 2016. L'éducation artistique. In P. Poirrier (Ed.), *Politiques et pratiques de la culture*. Paris: La Documentation française.

Wolton, D. 1989. Télévision culturelle: "l'apartheid" distingué. In *Pouvoirs*, 51, 99–113.

20

POPULAR MUSIC NOSTALGIA IN CONTEMPORARY FRENCH MEDIA DISCOURSE

Chris Tinker

In recent years nostalgia has become a prominent feature of the popular music and media culture of France, particularly following the launch of successful tours such as *Age tendre et têtes de bois* (2006–2015), *RFM Party 80* (2007–2012) and its successor *Stars 80* (2013–). French television has produced several variety shows dedicated to popular music nostalgia, often with a focus on a particular decade, for example, *Si on chantait les années 70* and *La fièvre des années 80* (both broadcast on France 3, 2011). The variety show *Les Années Bonheur* (2006–), hosted by the veteran presenter Patrick Sébastien, has enjoyed a successful run over the last decade in a Saturday prime-time slot, featuring music performances by French, francophone and other international artists; audience participation; roundtable discussion and reminiscence; sketches by comedians; facts and figures on the history of popular music from the resident 'expert' Fabien Lecoeuvre; and 'la petite lettre,' a video sequence voice-overed by Sébastien, which pays tribute to dead French and international popular music artists. In the daytime television schedules the magazine show *C'est au programme* (France 2) includes a regular popular music nostalgia slot presented by the pundit/*chroniqueur* Frédéric Zeitoun. The multichannel television offering in France also includes a niche provider of nostalgia, *Télé Melody* (melody.tv), dedicated to French and international popular music from the 1960s to the 1990s and featuring a team of 'expert' presenters. Its weekly schedule is organised around nightly themes: 'soirée paillettes' (Saturdays), 'soirée Culture chanson' (Sundays), repeats of variety programmes in their entirety (Mondays), popular music and film (Tuesdays), live music (Wednesdays), 'best of Melody' (Thursdays) and 'stars 80–90' (Fridays). As for radio in France, while music-based stations such as Nostalgie and RFM broadcast French and international golden oldies, public and private generalist and thematic talk-based radio stations, such as Europe 1, France Inter, France Culture and RTL, feature discussion of popular music nostalgia in terms of particular decades, genres (particularly *chanson* and hip-hop), artists (French, francophone and other international) and related themes such as exile and homesickness. Where the press is concerned, regional and local newspapers, in contrast with their national newspapers and the magazine press, devote extensive discussion of popular music nostalgia in the areas that they serve via entertainment feature articles, including reviews and interviews, or news-in-brief articles, announcing specific tour dates in a particular location.

Given the relatively significant volume of popular music discourses in the contemporary French media, the aim of this chapter is to situate these in terms of existing studies of nostalgia and its relationship with popular music and the media, and to contribute towards understanding their significance via a case study focusing on recent television coverage of the 1980s nostalgia tour RTL *Party 80* as well as cinematic representations in the spin-off 2012 film *Stars 80* and the press reviews that its release generated.

Approaches to nostalgia, media and popular music

Defined broadly as 'a sentimental longing for one's past' (Sedikides et al. 2008a: 305), the term nostalgia is now widely regarded as a 'common' 'emotion' or 'experience' (Wildschut et al. 2006: 980–981, 2010: 582). As Constantine Sedikides et al. observe, nostalgia was 'regarded throughout centuries as a psychological ailment' (2008a: 307), most notably 'equated with homesickness' (2008a: 304). Moreover, as Barbara Lebrun comments, drawing on David Lowenthal (1985: xi and 13), 'The notion of nostalgia is traditionally defined as the consciousness of a malaise in the present, and as the selective and imaginary mental reconstruction in the present in order to alleviate this unease' (Lebrun 2009a: 42). Several commentators have also viewed nostalgia in ambivalent terms such as 'bittersweet' (Hirsch 1992; Baker and Kennedy 1994; Madrigal and Boerstler 2007), combining 'joy and sadness' (Barrett et al. 2010: 390–402), 'disenchantment' and the 'desire for re-enchantment' (Pickering and Keightley 2006: 936), 'a sense of longing associated with the future' and 'loss associated with the past' (Pickering and Keightley 2006: 936), as well as 'progressive, even utopian impulses' and 'regressive stances and melancholic attitudes' (Pickering and Keightley 2006: 919). More positively however, Sedikides et al. also observe that nostalgia is now 'emerging as a fundamental human strength' and is recognised as fulfilling several 'psychological functions' (2008a: 307).

Several categories or divisions of nostalgia have been highlighted in academic accounts of the phenomenon. Fred Davis (1979) identifies three orders of nostalgia: simple, reflexive and interpreted. As Davis comments, first-order or simple nostalgia 'harbors [*sic*] the largely unexamined belief that things were better (more beautiful) (healthier) (happier) (more civilised) (more exciting) then than now' (1979: 18). In second-order or reflexive nostalgia, the individual raises 'questions concerning the truth, accuracy, completeness or representativeness of the nostalgic claim' (1979: 21). Third-order or interpreted nostalgia 'moves beyond issues of the historical accuracy or felicity of the nostalgic claim on the past and, even as the reaction unfolds, questions and, potentially at least, renders problematic the very reaction itself' (1979: 24). Furthermore, Svetlana Boym (2001) distinguishes between two key forms of nostalgia. The first, restorative nostalgia, 'stresses nostos (home) and attempts a trans-historical reconstruction of the lost home,' 'does not think of itself as nostalgia, but rather as truth and tradition,' and 'is at the core of recent national and religious revivals.' The second form, reflective nostalgia, 'thrives on algia (the longing itself) and delays the homecoming – wistfully, ironically, desperately,' 'dwells on the ambivalences of human longing and belonging and does not shy away from the contradictions of modernity,' and 'calls [the truth] into doubt' (2001: xviii).

Further distinctions have been drawn between nostalgia, which is experienced first-hand ('real' nostalgia) and that which is experienced second-hand via the recollections and reminiscences of other individuals – what may be termed 'simulated' (Baker and Kennedy 1994) or 'vicarious' nostalgia (Goulding 2002), or 'historical nostalgia,' 'in which the past is defined as a time before the audience was born' (Stern 1992). Nostalgia has also been viewed as individually and/or collectively experienced or, to use Jose van Dijck's terms 'individually embodied' and 'culturally embedded' (2006: 359). When nostalgia is experienced individually, concerning 'personally relevant events' (Sedikides et al. 2004: 205), the emotion has been regarded effectively as a 'cushion' (Bose Godbole et al. 2006: 630) – one that 'buffers existential threat' (Juhl et al. 2010) or offers a 'self-protection mechanism against death-related concerns' (Routledge et al.

2008: 137). For certain commentators, nostalgia is also experienced particularly during times of disruption, discontinuity (Davis 1979: 34–35) or instability, particularly when 'societies' are 'in turmoil ... experiencing troubles, turbulence and transformation' (Brown 1999: 368). Nostalgia is identified as a response to the 'uncertainties' (Pickering and Keightley 2006: 920) or 'challenges and threats' of the 'present' (Vess et al. 2010: 9), and, more specifically, to modernity (as well as late modernity) with 'its relentless social uprooting and erosion of time-honoured stabilities' (Pickering and Keightley 2006: 922, 938). More positively, studies have shown that 'nostalgic reverie is a crucial vehicle for maintaining and fostering self-continuity over time and in the face of change' (Sedikides et al. 2008b: 30), countering loneliness and increasing social connectedness and support (Zhou et al. 2008; Wildschut et al. 2010: 582).

While the study of cultural memory within the French context is well established, focusing, for example, on turbulent or traumatic episodes in French history, notably the two world wars, the Holocaust, the Algerian War, the 'events' of May 1968, as well as official forms of remembrance and commemoration (state funerals, monuments, statues, street names, anniversaries, educational practice and legislation; the 'memory laws'), there has been relatively little sustained discussion of nostalgia. Simone Signoret's 1976 volume of memoirs *La nostalgie n'est plus ce qu'elle était* (a title borrowed from the witticism of an unknown New York graffiti artist found on a wall in 1959) demonstrates an interest in the interaction of memory and nostalgia in personal 'histories' (Dauncey and Tinker 2015: 137–138). More recently a 2013 study by the philosopher Barbara Cassin, *La Nostalgie. Quand donc est-on chez soi?*, explores nostalgia based on 'belonging' and relationships between home, exile and (mother-tongue) language (Dauncey and Tinker 2015: 137–138). In French cinema studies Phil Powrie (1997) views the 1980s nostalgia film as an attempt to 'return to a golden age, where all the trappings of high culture, whether it be the adaptation of a classic novel, or the use of classical music and/or painting, or the insistence on the director's credentials ... are shackled to cinematic conservatism' (1997: 23). Moreover, Powrie shows how such films 'attempt to cure loss and failure by embodying them' and create a 'decentred/destabilized masculine subject' (1997: 27). In French popular music studies Barbara Lebrun's work on chanson néo-réaliste, which rose to prominence during the 1990s (e.g. Pigalle, Négresses Vertes and Têtes Raides), highlights the 'incohérences' and 'contradictions' of the genre ('entre nostalgie et conservatisme, contestation et distinction [. . .] réactionnaire et rebelle, vieux-jeu et moderne, élitiste et collectif'), while looking more generally beyond simple binaries such as 'nostalgie de divertissement' and 'nostalgie de contestation' (2009a: 60; see also 2009b: 41–63). Isabelle Marc identifies nostalgia as a recurrent feature of the work of French singer-songwriters: Georges Brassens' persona is viewed as a 'mythe d'une francité foncièrement passéiste, assimilée à une identité universaliste républicaine, située dans un passé fictionnalisé, opposée au multiculturalisme et à la fragmentation problématique de la réalité présente (2012: 226),' while in the case of Charles Aznavour (2014), nostalgia is associated with his dramatic style and is a means by which the music-listening public relates to him.

The relationship between nostalgia and popular music is a developing area of academic enquiry. Existing studies have, for example, explored how nostalgia contributes towards the development and status of particular popular music forms and genres (Lebrun 2009a on 1990s French *chanson néo-réaliste*), identity formation (DeNora 2000: 63; Bennett 2001: 153), the experiences of listeners and consumers (Holbrook and Schindler 2006) and cultural heritage debates (Brandellero et al. 2014; van der Hoeven 2014). Furthermore, a 2014 edited collection of 13 essays on nostalgia published in *Volume! Le revue des musiques populaires*, edited by Hugh Dauncey and myself, has developed further the question of genre and nostalgia with a specific focus on rock and chanson, the role of nostalgia in the construction of space and place, and the temporal dimensions of popular music nostalgia, particularly ersatz and historical forms.

The link between nostalgia and the media has become a further focus of interest. Focusing on the use of analogue nostalgia in digitised environments, the manipulation of nostalgia in areas such as marketing, advertising, corporate alumni networks and the news (2014: 13); 'screened nostalgias' (15) and the 'notion of creative nostalgias' (17), Katharina Niemeyer's (2014) ground-breaking edited volume highlights how the media not only produce nostalgic meaning but also 'are very often nostalgic for themselves, their own past, their structures and contents' (7). More specifically, popular-music-related nostalgia in the media is also a growing area of enquiry. In an article focusing on the media, television and the spin-off CD box set in Québec, Danick Trottier (2014) identifies a process of 'double nostalgia' at work in which nostalgic songs are themselves treated nostalgically. A 2014 study of nostalgia relating to the bands Joy Division and New Order by Alastair Greig and Catherine Strong focuses on mediatised nostalgia books, promotional materials and films; ersatz or imagined nostalgia; nostalgia aimed at staking a claim on the past; the commercialisation of nostalgia for profit as well as a more nuanced view of com-mercialism; and the possibility of actively rejecting, or at least adopting, an ambiguous, reflexive attitude towards nostalgia. In my own work (2012) focusing on the successful French nostalgia tour Âge tendre et têtes de bois concert tours, I show how media coverage emphasises joy rather than the 'bittersweetness' often associated with nostalgia, views the past more positively than the present – what Fred Davis (1979) refers to as 'simple nostalgia,' represents a fantasy return to youth, promotes social and cross-generational cohesion, and identifies the nostalgia tour as a commercial enterprise and in terms of its own problematic status within the wider musical and cultural field; and is, on occasion, also tempered with expressions of ambivalence or reticence. In a 2015 article published in *Modern and Contemporary France*, I also compare the ways in which French and British newspaper discourse has approached nostalgia – as an emotion, social expe-rience and cultural value – in coverage of the 1980s popular music tours *RFM Party 80* and *Here and Now* (2001–2011). Similarities in French and British approaches include an emphasis on joy, the festive, an imagined return to youth, unquestioning nostalgia, social cohesion as well as stereotypical views of 1980s popular music and fashion as kitsch. The study also reveals clear differences between national contexts. British coverage avoids taking life too seriously, but also challenges simple nostalgia, and develops more complex forms. French coverage emphasises the value of emotion, social and intergenerational cohesion as well as national pride. The nostalgia tour is also associated in French coverage with the defence of popular culture, the resistance to perceived Parisian domination and the development of charity and musical creativity.

Developing the case study of *RFM Party 80* further, the remainder of this chapter will con-sider further the nostalgic significance of television coverage of the tour, the spin-off film *Stars 80* (2012) and the press reviews that it generated.

Television coverage of the *RFM Party 80* tour

In 2007 the producers Olivier Kaefer and Hugues Gentelet launched the 1980s nostalgia tour *RFM Party 80* (supported by RFM, the French commercial radio station), which has played a variety of venues across France including the Stade de France and 2012 saw the release of a spin-off film *Stars 80* (Frédéric Forestier and Thomas Langmann). In 2013 *RFM Party 80* was effectively replaced by a new-look 1980s tour, which took its name from the film. The nostalgic significance of the *RFM Party 80* tour is discussed in various programmes (variety shows, maga-zines or a combination of both), which feature individual members of the tour on the road in filmed reports and/or in studio discussion (see list in references).

Television coverage emphasises the joyful experiences of artists and audiences alike. In a 2007 special on nostalgia and popular music in France, the presenter Mireille Dumas describes the atmosphere at the concerts as 'du délire,' while a voice-over report includes terms such as 'paradisiaque' and 'ambiance survoltée et bon enfant' (*Spéciale chansons*); Mario Ramsamy of the group Emile et Images emphasises the 'brin de soleil qu'on met dans chacun chaque soir qu'on est sur scène' (*Vivement Dimanche*).

Programming also reinforces social cohesion and bonding: for the artists taking part in the tours is described in a voice-over report as like being part of a 'grande colonie de vacances' (*Spéciale chansons*). The singer Cookie Dingler describes his participation as a 'belle aventure,' even if it is a little 'cul-cul' to say so, while Jean-Pierre Mader expresses his pleasure at meeting 'copains' again after 20 years apart (*Vivement Dimanche*).

Generational inclusion and cohesion is also highlighted: a voice-over report (*Spéciale chansons*) describes the *RFM Party 80* audience as aged 15 to 65. Different generations of concert-goers are interviewed: an audience member regards *RFM Party 80* simply as his childhood, while another, identified as a 21-year-old, refers to it as 'la génération de mes parents' (*Vie privée vie publique*). Similarly, the host of *RFM Party 80* Laurent Petitguillaume refers to the concerts as a 'boum,' 'sans prétention' for both young people and 'les quinquas' (*Vie privée vie publique*). Cookie Dingler emphasises the interest of younger audiences in their twenties who had not been born in the 1980s, and who would not necessarily listen to 1980s music at home, as they attend the concerts, sing along, and dance in an atmosphere of 'convivialité' (*C'est au programme*). Christophe Willem, part of the current young generation of successful singers in France, describes how 1980s music has become 'cultissime' in Paris and beyond; and observes that such songs have been remixed for his generation (*Chabada*).

'Simple' nostalgia for the 1980s is expressed via social, cultural and musical comparisons with the present. Chantal Lauby views nostalgia as an antidote to the problems of contemporary life 'Tu écoutes Adamo. Dans le monde dans lequel on vit ça fait beaucoup de bien' (*Spéciale chansons*). Moreover, the 1980s are regarded in positive terms as a relatively carefree time when everything seemed possible. Jean-Pierre Mader refers to the attraction of 'une période moins anxiogène'; a time when education led to employment; Michel Wingradoff (of the group le Grand Orchestre du Splendid) describes a time when people had 'beaucoup moins de pression sur les épaules' (*C'est au programme*). In a similar vein, the singer Philippe Lavil considers the 1980s a less competitive time, in terms of his own experience within the music industry (*Chabada*). The singer Julie Pietri describes the 1980s positively in terms of musical innovation, variety, experimentation and pushing boundaries: 'on se permettait un peu tout' (*Chabada*).

On the other hand, the 1980s are viewed as a difficult decade in social terms: 'années SIDA, années chomage, années super dures' (voice-over report, *Spéciale chansons*). On a personal level, Cookie Dingler describes the way he was exploited in the past ('on m'a pressé comme un citron'), refusing to make any concessions today. Similarly Eric Moréna describes how he derives more pleasure from performing today that he did in the 1980s, when he was launched on the market like a new soap powder (*C'est au programme*). In interview, Jean-Luc Lahaye provides a more problematic, ambivalent view of the 1980s in terms of his own biography: while retaining the 'joie' of the period, the development of music afforded by the advent of 'les radios libres,' and his own success as a performer, he regrets not enjoying the success given his own melancholic disposition (regarding himself not as someone 'de léger') and fear of his success ending (*Chabada*).

One particular programme, *Ça va s'Cauet*, presented by Sébastien Cauet, features a clash between 'simple' and 'reflexive' nostalgia. Christine Bravo is particularly critical of today's 'nostalgie jubilatoire'/'joyeux' that the *RFM Party 80* artists represent, even if it can be explained in terms of the current economic crisis and austerity (*Ça va s'Cauet*). Moreover, Bravo argues that socially and politically speaking, the 1980s weren't 'marrant,' but 'merdier,' a difficult period, citing the advent of AIDS; the failed 1981 presidential campaign of the comic and political activist Coluche; the Iran–Iraq and Falklands wars; the sinking of the Greenpeace ship Rainbow Warrior by the French secret service in 1985; several terrorist attacks; the death of the student protester Malik Oussekine, a victim of police brutality in 1986 (the presenter Sébastien Cauet adds the 1986 Chernobyl disaster to the list). Bravo regrets that the *RFM Party 80* artists have idealised the 1980s in a way that is not 'en adéquation avec ce qui se passait.' In response, Cauet claims that the same argument could apply to other periods such as the 1970s, while Bravo counterargues that 'la chanson engagée' (figures such as Georges Brassens, Jacques Brel and Léo Ferré) was still a feature of the French popular music field during the 1970s. Jean-Luc Lahaye adds more positively that the 1980s was a decade of humanitarian action (*Ça va s'Cauet*).

Television coverage contributes to debates regarding the cultural status of popular music nostalgia tours. Artists' initial concerns at taking part for fear of 'ringardisme' are raised (*Spéciale chansons*). The argument is made that nostalgic audiences are drawn to specific songs rather than artists (Frédéric Zeitoun in *C'est au programme*; William Picard of the group Début de Soirée). A patriotic expressions from Michel Jonasz who tells the audience to 'fêter la chanson française' (*Spéciale chansons*). The presenter Danielle Lumbroso regards her programme *Chabada* not only as an opportunity to share collective musical memories songs, but to promote new work (e.g. 'France Culture' by Arnaud Fleurent Didier) (*Chabada*). The production of new material is discussed with reference to Leopold Nord et Eux, the album and the single 'Bruxelles-Toulouse,' recorded in a hotel room during the tour. Jean-Pierre Morgand also describes how taking part in the tour has led to other song-writing enquiries/requests.

Stars 80: cinema spin-off and press reviews

Echoing the experiences of the *RFM Party 80* tour producers, Hugues Gentelet and Olivier Kaefer, *Stars 80*, directed by Frédéric Forestier and Thomas Langmann, was released in October 2012 with Richard Anconina and Patrick Timsit as Antoine and Vincent, old friends and joint owners of a small, failing entertainment company. As a means of generating income, the duo hatch a plan to bring together various popular musicians (playing themselves) who had enjoyed commercial success during the 1980s. The film sees them recruit various artists and organise a concert tour of towns and cities across France, progressing from small audiences in Rouen to a packed concert hall in Reims, larger Zénith arenas in other French cities, and eventually the Stade de France in Paris.

In terms of nostalgia, the film emphasises escapism back to one's youth (the pair listen to old vinyl singles and reminisce over the record covers) to such an extent that the quest to recruit the artists becomes a stereotypical male mid-life crisis: Vincent re-mortgages his home as the pair embark on a road/motorway adventure. In one particular scene Vincent is effectively reminded of his own teenage sexual fantasies in a well-known visual reference to Sabrina's video clip of 'Boys' (1987), in which she rises out of water in slow-motion revealing a see-through swimming costume. Other artists are represented as leaving behind the daily humdrum of their lives in relative obscurity, for example, Peter (Jean-Pierre Savelli) of the duo Peter and Sloane, who runs a café.

The nostalgia tour is represented as an opportunity for social cohesion and togetherness as the various members of the troupe travel (singing on the coach), socialise and live together on the road, sharing after-show meals, performing song medleys together around a piano (including a poignant rendition of Joe Dassin's 'L'Été Indien' as well as the final song in the Stade de France concert by Gilbert Montagné, 'On va s'aimer,' 1984). The closing titles feature a medley of 80s songs around the piano, words appearing on screen in karaoke style (for the benefit of cinema audiences who would like to join in). Although an egalitarian approach is sought by the producers Antoine and Vincent (the latter insists that there is no 'régime de faveur' [...] 'on est un groupe'), an internal hierarchy within the troupe is suggested as certain artists seek to distinguish themselves or demand special treatment, although the representation of stars as divas is admittedly for self-ironising/-mocking comic effect. For example, Jean-Luc Lahaye's character makes Antoine and Vincent read out his autobiography to him and throws them out of his club after they suggest his pay will be limited to the 'tarif syndical.'

The film mobilises a variety of views on cultural legitimacy of popular music nostalgia. While the film recognises the disdain of certain individuals for nostalgia popular music tours (the record company executive who scoffs at the plans of Antoine and Vincent; the sceptical bank manager who describes the artist as 'has beens'; an audience member in Amiens who is tired of hearing the same song by Lio ('Les Brunes Comptent Pas Pour Des Prunes,' 1986) and describes the audience of 500 as 'crétins,' the bank manager and audience member change their minds when they witness the popularity and commercial success of the nostalgia concerts. Antoine and Vincent also emphasise the past achievements of their artists and their potential in this new phase of their careers to attain cult status.

While the concerts are viewed by Antoine as an opportunity to revisit the songs of the 1980s, he stipulates that the artists will adopt a contemporary look. Indeed, the singer Desireless, associated in the 1980s with her distinctive, flat-top hairstyle, decides after trying on several wigs, to retain her simpler 2012 style, a shaved head. In contrast, however, the audience is often seen dressed in colourful party/fancy dress and headwear.

The film also supports the notion that audiences are attached to specific artists. When Antoine and Vincent perform Début de soirée's 'Nuit de folie' instead of the original group as an attempt to demonstrate that audiences are only attached to songs, not artists, they are booed off stage and Début de soirée return to the stage to sing their own song. In another scene the singer Jeanne Mas is reluctant to participate in the tours in the belief that she has been forgotten by the public, but is convinced to join the troupe when Antoine telephones her from on stage: the audience call out for her to participate and sing her song 'Rouge et noir,' while Antoine reassures her, 'Personne ne vous a oublié.' When Jeanne Mas finally appears at the Stade de France concert and is initially unable to sing (so overcome is she with stage fright) the audience sings her song, 'Toute première fois,' which in turn encourages her to join in.

While focusing mainly on French-speaking stars and songs, the international Anglophone dimension of 1980s popular music nostalgia in France is conveyed via the use of illustrative extra-diegetic hit singles such as 'Enola Gay' (Orchestral Manoeuvres in the Dark), 'Sweet Dreams' (Eurythmics), 'Wonderful Life' (Black) and 'Sorry Seems to Be the Hardest Word' (Elton John) (albeit a hit in 1976 rather than in the 1980s) as well as visual references to John Landis' film 'The Blues Brothers' (1980) (Antoine and Vincent wearing dark sunglasses).

Press reviews of the film are, for the most part, divided between mixed and negative reviews. While questioning the quality of the production, storyline and its execution (e.g. Vavasseur 2012; Blondeau 2012; Brejon 2012; Carrière 2012; Ciment 2012; Lacomme 2012; Leherpeur 2012; Leterte 2012; Olivia 2012; Tonton BDM 2012), they view popular music nostalgia in the film as an experience which is emotional, touching, sentimental and empathetic (Lorrain 2012); on occasion as shameful (Cirodde 2012; Tonton BDM 2012) as populist (Ciment 2012; Tonton BDM 2012); as an opportunity for audiences to participate in the festive (Carrière 2012; Tonton BDM 2012); as an escape from the current financial crisis ('anticrise') (Vavasseur 2012); as an opportunity for self-mockery/derision (Blondeau 2012; Carrière 2012; Lacomme 2012; Maille 2012; Odicino 2012; Vavasseur 2012); and as cynical, commercial opportunity (Blondeau 2012; Carrière 2012; Leherpeur 2012; Odicino 2012; Tonton BDM 2012).

Conclusions

In sum, recent press and television coverage of the 1980s *RTL Party 80* nostalgia tour, cinematic representations in the spin-off 2012 film *Stars 80* and associated press reviews identify nostalgia as an intense, emotional, joyous and festive experience; as a combination of 'simple' and more 'reflexive'/complex forms; as an escape from the current financial crisis; as an attempt to reconnect with one's youth; and as a force for social and generational cohesion. Moreover, the popular music nostalgia tour is represented in terms of debates concerning its form and legitimacy; the relative importance of artists and songs to consumers/audiences; its 'restorative,' at times, nationalist function; and its commercial potential. The foregoing case studies have indicated differences in approach and emphasis from one media form to another. For example, both television coverage and the *Stars 80* film express interest in the relative attraction of artists and songs to audiences; while focusing on French popular music, the *Stars 80* film also includes recognition of the influence of Anglophone popular music; press film reviews feature representations of nostalgia based on self-derision, viewed in positive and/or negative terms, as well as shame; and individual television discussion and magazine programmes lend themselves more than newspaper articles towards representing a plurality of voices and viewpoints. Future research could usefully examine further the psychological, cultural, artistic and commercial significance and potential of media discourses of popular music nostalgia in France and how these contribute towards shaping the popular music field as well as social and personal identities.

Acknowledgements

I would like to thank the staff of the Institut National de l'Audiovisuel (INA) in Paris for their assistance in accessing relevant television archive material.

Funding acknowledgement

The television archive research referred to in this chapter was supported by the Carnegie Trust for the Universities of Scotland.

References

Baker, S. M. and P. F. Kennedy. 1994. Death by nostalgia: a diagnosis of context-specific cases. In C. T. Allen and D. Roedder John (Eds.), Advances in Consumer Research, Vol. 21. Provo, UT: Association for Consumer Research, 169–174. Available at: www.acrwebsite.org/volumes/display.asp?id=7580 [Accessed: 01.05.2014].

Barrett, F. S., K. J. Grimm, R. W. Robins, T. Wildschut, C. Sedikides and P. Janata. 2010. Music-evoked nostalgia: affect, memory, and personality. In *Emotion*, 10, 390–403.

Bennett, A. 2001. *Cultures of Popular Music*. Maidenhead: Open University Press.

Bose Godbole, M., O. Shehryar and D. M. Hunt. 2006. Does nostalgia depend on valence of past experience? An empirical analysis of the discontinuity hypothesis. In *Advances in Consumer Research*, 33, 630. Available at: www.acrwebsite.org/volumes/v33/v33_10073.pdf [Accessed: 01.05.2014].

Boym, S. 2001. *The Future of Nostalgia*. New York: Basic Books.

Brandellero, A. et al. 2014. Popular music heritage, cultural memory and cultural identity. In *International Journal of Heritage Studies*, 20:3, 219–223.

Brown, S. 1999. Retro-marketing: yesterday's tomorrows, today! In *Marketing Intelligence and Planning*, 17:7, 363–376.

Cassin, B. 2013. *La Nostalgie: Quand donc est-on chez soi?* Paris: Editions Autrement.

Dauncey, H. and C. Tinker. 2014. Popular music nostalgia. In Volume! La revue des musiques populaires, 11:1, 8–17.

Dauncey, H. and C. Tinker. 2015. Media, memory and nostalgia in contemporary France: between commemoration, memorialisation, reflection and restoration. In *Modern and Contemporary France*, 23:2, 135–145.

Davis, F. 1979. *Yearning for Yesterday: A Sociology of Nostalgia*. New York: Free Press.

DeNora, T. 2000. *Music in Everyday Life*. Cambridge: Cambridge University Press.

Goulding, C. 2002. An exploratory study of age related vicarious nostalgia and aesthetic consumption. In S. M. Broniarczyk and K. Nakamoto (Eds.), *Advances in Consumer Research*, Vol. 29. Valdosta: Association for Consumer Research, 542–546. Available at: http://www.acrwebsite.org/volumes/display.asp?id¼8719 [Accessed: 01.05.2014].

Greig, A. and C. Strong. 2014. 'But we remember when we were young.' Joy Division et les 'ordres nouveaux' de la nostalgie. In *Volume! La Revue des musiques populaires*, 11:1, 191–205.

Hirsch, A. R. 1992. Nostalgia: a neuropsychiatric understanding. In J. F. Sherry Jr. and B. Sternthal (Eds.), *Advances In Consumer Research*, Vol. 19. Provo: Association for Consumer Research, 390–395. Available at: www.acrwebsite.org/volumes/display.asp?id¼7326 [Accessed: 01.05.2014].

Holbrook, M. B. and R. M. Schindler. 2006. Nostalgic bonding: Exploring the role of nostalgia in the consumption experience. In *Journal of Consumer Behaviour*. 3:2, 107–127.

Juhl, J., C. Routledge, J. Arndt, C. Sedikides and T. Wildschut. 2010. Fighting the future with the past: nostalgia buffers existential threat. In *Journal of Research in Personality*, 44, 309–314.

Lebrun, B. 2009a. *Protest Music in France: Production, Identity and Audiences*. Farnham and Burlington, VT: Ashgate.

Lebrun, B. 2009b. René, Ginette, Louise et les autres: nostalgie et authenticité dans la chanson néo-réaliste. In *French Politics, Culture and Society*, 27:2, 47–62.

Lowenthal, D. 1985. *The Past Is a Foreign Country*. Cambridge and New York: Cambridge University Press.

Madrigal, R. and C. Boerstler. 2007. Nostalgia advertisements: a content analysis. In G. Fitzsimons, and V. Morwitz (Eds.), *Advances in Consumer Research*, Vol. 34. Duluth, MN: Association for Consumer Research, 424–426. Available at: www.acrwebsite.org/volumes/v34/acr_v34_139.pdf [Accessed: 01.05.2014].

Marc, I. 2012. Une France passésite? La nostalgie comme leitmotiv thématique et esthétique chez Georges Brassens. In *French Cultural Studies*, 23:3, 225–238.

Marc, I. 2014. Aznavour ou le drame nostalgique populaire. In H. Dauncey and C. Tinker (Eds.), *Souvenirs, Souvenirs: La Nostalgie dans les musiques populaires*, 11:1, 55–67.

Niemeyer, K. 2014. *Media and Nostalgia: Yearning for the Past, Present and Future*. Basingstoke: Palgrave Macmillan.

Pickering, M. and E. Keightley. 2006. The modalities of nostalgia. In *Current Sociology*, 54:6, 919–941.

Powrie, P. 1997. *French Cinema in the 1980s: Nostalgia and the Crisis of Masculinity*. Oxford: Oxford University Press.

Routledge, C., J. Arndt, C. Sedikides and T. Wildschut. 2008. A blast from the past: the terror management function of nostalgia. In *Journal of Experimental Social Psychology*, 44, 132–140.

Sedikides, C., T. Wildschut, J. Arndt and C. Routledge. 2008a. Nostalgia: past, present, and future. In *Current Directions in Psychological Science*, 17, 304–307.

Sedikides, C., T. Wildschut and D. Baden. 2004. Nostalgia: conceptual issues and existential functions. In J. Greenberg, S. L. Koole and T. Pyszczynski (Eds.), *Handbook of Experimental Existential Psychology*. New York: Guilford, 200–214.

Sedikides, C., T. Wildschut, L. Gaertner, C. Routledge and J. Arndt. 2008b. Nostalgia as enabler of self-continuity. In F. Sani (Ed.), *Self-Continuity: Individual and Collective Perspectives*. New York: Psychology Press, 227–239.

Signoret, S. 1976. *La Nostalgie n'est plus ce qu'elle était*. Paris: Points-Seuil.

Stern, B. B. 1992. Abstract – nostalgia in advertising text: romancing the past. In J. F. Sherry Jr. and B. Sternthal (Eds.), *Advances in Consumer Research*, Vol. 19. Provo, UT: Association for Consumer Research, 388–389. Available at: www.acrwebsite.org/search/view-conference-proceedings.aspx?Id=7325 [Accessed: 01.05.2014].

Tinker, C. 2012. Age tendre et têtes de bois: nostalgia, television and popular music in contemporary France. In French Cultural Studies, 23:3, 239–255.

Tinker, C. 2015. The RFM party 80 and here and now tours: 1980s pop nostalgia in the French and British Press. In *Modern and Contemporary France*, 23:2, 163–177.

Trottier, D. 2014. L'Evocation mémorielle des b0îtes à chanson au Québec: Quand le canon se fait complice de la nostalgie. In *Volume! La Revue des musiques populaires*, 11:1, 99–113.

Van der Hoeven, A. 2014. Remembering the popular music of the 1990s: dance music and the cultural meanings of decade-based nostalgia. In *International Journal of Heritage Studies*, 20:3, 316–330.

van Dijck, J. 2006. Record and hold: popular music between personal and collective memory. In Critical Studies in Media Communication, 23:5, 357–374.

Vess, M., J. Arndt, C. Routledge, C. Sedikides and T. Wildschut. 2010. Nostalgia as a resource for the self. In *Self and Identity*, 11:3, 273–284.

Wildschut, T., C. Sedikides, J. Arndt and C. Routledge. 2006. Nostalgia: content, triggers, functions. In *Journal of Personality and Social Psychology*, 91, 975–993.

Wildschut, T., C. Sedikides, C. Routledge, J. Arndt and F. Cordaro. 2010. Nostalgia as a repository of social connectedness: the role of attachment-related avoidance. In *Journal of Personality and Social Psychology*, 98, 573–586.

Zhou, X, C. Sedikides, T. Wildschut and D-G. Gao. 2008. Counteracting loneliness: on the restorative function of nostalgia. In *Psychological Science*, 19, 1023–1029.

Television programmes (consulted at Inathèque, Paris)

Ça va s'Cauet. 2010. TF1, 22 April, 23:36.
C'est au programme. 2009. France 2, 20 June, 09:46.
Chabada. 2010. France 3, 31 January, 16:10.
Spéciale chansons, vive la nostalgie. 2007. France 3, 20 June, 20:53.
Vie privée vie publique l'hebdo. 2010. France 3, 5 February, 23:00.
Vivement dimanche spécial années 80. 2011. France 2, 2 January, 14:36.

Press reviews of Stars 80

Blondeau, R. 2012. 'Stars 80': une comédie lourde et indigeste. In *LesInrocks.com*, 23 October. Available at: www.lesinrocks.com/cinema/films-a-l-affiche/stars-80/ [Accessed: 23.06.2016].

Brejon, D. 2012. Stars 80. In *Abusdecine.com*, 24 October. Available at: www.abusdecine.com/critique/stars-80-frederic-forestier-et-thomas-langmann [Accessed: 23.06.2016].

Carrière, C. 2012. Stars 80. In *LExpress.fr*, 23 October. Available at: www.lexpress.fr/culture/cinema/stars-80_1177721.html [Accessed: 23.06.2016].

Ciment, M. 2012. Stars 80. In *Positif 621*, November, 53.

Cirodde, E. 2012. Back to the 80's! Le plaisir coupable du mois. In *LExpress.fr*, 22 October. Available at: www.lexpress.fr/culture/cinema/stars-80_1175021.html [Accessed: 14.07.2016].

Lacomme, J-P. 2012. Thomas Langmann maître chanteur avec Stars 80. In *Le Journal du dimanche*, 22 October. Available at: www.lejdd.fr/Culture/Cinema/Actualite/Thomas-Langmann-maitre-chanteur-570827 [Accessed: 14.07.2016].

Lamôme, S. 2012. La Critique de Première. In *Première*, October. Available at: www.premiere.fr/film/Stars-80/critiques [Accessed: 14.07.2016].

Leherpeur, X. 2012. Stars 80. In *Le Nouvel Observateur*, 23 October. Available at: http://tempsreel.nouvelobs.com/cinema/20121023.CIN6744/stars-80-de-frederic-forestier-et-thomas-langmann.html [Accessed: 15.07.2016].

Leterte, M. 2012. Sorties ciné: plutôt Werner Herzog ou Début de soirée? In *Metronews.fr*, 24 October. Available at: www.metronews.fr/culture/sorties-cine-plutot-werner-herzog-ou-debut-de-soiree/mljx!dbHPTwETJ2UIY/ [Accessed: 23.06.2016].

Lorrain, F-G. 2012. 'Stars 80': si l'on chantait, si l'on chantait. . . . In *LePoint.fr*, 23 October. Available at: www.lepoint.fr/culture/stars-80-si-l-on-chantait-si-l-on-chantait-23-10-2012-1519960_3.php [Accessed: 23.06.2016].

Maille, N. 2012. Stars 80. In *Critikat.com*, 23 October. Available at: www.critikat.com/actualite-cine/critique/stars-80.html [Accessed: 14.07.016].

Odicino, G. 2012. Stars 80. In *Telerama.fr*, 24 October. Available at: www.telerama.fr/cinema/films/stars-80,435306,critique.php#ifrndnlocgoogle [Accessed: 23.06.2016].

Olivia. 2012. [Critique] Stars 80. In *Leblogducinema*, 3 October. Available at: www.leblogducinema.com/critiques/critique-stars-80-23190/ [Accessed: 23.06.2016].

Sevagamy, J. 2012. Stars 80: Frédéric Forestier et Thomas Langmann surfent sur la nostalgie du public. In *Challenges.fr*. Available at: http://toutlecine.challenges.fr/film/0040/00406190-avis-stars-80.html.

Tonton BDM. 2012. Critique: Stars 80. In *Ecranlarge.com*, 22 October. Available at: www.ecranlarge.com/films/861714-stars-80/critiques [Accessed: 14.07.2016].

Vavasseur, P. 2012. "Stars 80," à pleins tubes (2012). In *Le Parisien*, 24 October. Available at: www.leparisien.fr/cinema/critiques-cinema/stars-80-a-pleins-tubes-24-10-2012-2261171.php [Accessed: 23.06.2016].

Vié, C. 2012. "Stars 80": on connaît les chansons.... In *20 Minutes*, 24 October. Available at: www.20minutes.fr/cinema/1028812-20121024-stars-80-connait-chansons [Accessed: 15.07.2016].

21

THE MEDIA AND PRESIDENTIAL ELECTIONS

Raymond Kuhn

A hybrid media system

From a historical perspective the contemporary French media system consists of a succession of sedimentary strata, resembling a millefeuille, built up over many decades. At the base are the print media. The rise of a mass newspaper industry began in the late nineteenth century, aided by technological improvements in newspaper production, the spread of mass literacy and the implantation of representative democratic institutions. Daily newspaper circulation grew during the first half of the twentieth century, with the peak year occurring at a time of major political renewal in 1946 (Albert and Sonnac 2014: 128). The next stratum is radio, which began to take root in the early 1920s, had a transformative effect on the cultural practices of French society during the interwar period (Scales 2016), played a major role as a means of propaganda during the Second World War and was by far the dominant broadcasting medium throughout the Fourth Republic. Then comes television, which became a mass medium of information and entertainment during the era of Gaullist domination of the Fifth Republic in the 1960s and early 1970s (Bourdon 1990). Starting from a position of limited supply, with a second channel launched in 1964 and a third in 1973, television moved fully to a nationwide multi-channel offer with the roll-out of digital terrestrial transmission during the early years of the twenty-first century. The most recent addition to the media system is the internet, which started to have a public presence in 1994, but whose full social and economic impact began to make itself felt only during the first decade of the twenty-first century, notably through domestic connections in the more densely populated towns and cities. In retrospect it is notable that no pre-existing media stratum was wholly displaced by a subsequent new layer and this remains the case to date: reading newsprint newspapers, listening to live audio output on a radio set and watching free-to-air linear programming on a television screen are practices of media usage that were present in French society in the 1960s and still exist today, particularly among older age groups.

Yet while the notion of sedimentary strata is useful in explaining the historical evolution of the French media landscape, the image of a millefeuille is less helpful, indeed even profoundly misleading, when applied to the contemporary era. This is characterised less by distinct media layers or strands and more by elements of convergence across previously differentiated media sectors to form what one leading writer on political communication has termed a 'hybrid media system' (Chadwick 2013). The main driver of change has been new technology. The transition from analogue to digital and online has radically transformed media production, content, form, distribution and reception, with technological shift fostering the emergence of new outlets, actors and practices at all stages of the value chain. In the early years of this transition it was usual to speak of the emergence of 'new' media, including new means of television transmission such as cable and satellite, in competition with the 'old.' It is now clear that this is a limited and unhelpful bipolar framework, since it presupposes a contrast, at times even an opposition, between two discrete blocks of media that singularly fails to reflect the complexity of their interaction.

Instead, it is more accurate to speak of a hybrid media age, in which 'old' and 'new' media are intertwined and feed off each other, sometimes competing, sometimes complementing, sometimes relating to each other in mutually beneficial ways. A by no means exhaustive list of instances of contemporary media hybridity might include the following: entrepreneurs who take an ownership stake in both long-established ('old') and emerging ('new') communication and media sectors; traditional media outlets, such as the quality daily newspapers *Le Monde* and *Le Figaro*, that have developed a significant online presence (a notable exception to this dual-track approach being the weekly satirical newspaper, *Le Canard enchaîné*, which steadfastly refuses to publish a version online); journalists who contribute to 'old' media outlets but who also blog, tweet and use social media to build up a more personalised following for their work; and citizens who move seamlessly across different media content in an online world where print, audio and video are often embedded in a single media story and where much of that content will be accessed on the move via a smartphone, with some users giving their views and providing comments via different forms of interactive feedback.

This hybrid media system in contemporary France is characterised by six key features: expansion, hypercompetition, segmentation, fragmentation, new patterns of ownership concentration and transnationalisation. Expansion, the most obvious aspect, refers to the huge increase in the supply of media content. There are both more media outlets (radio stations, television channels, internet websites, social media) and more product (print, audio, video, online) than ever before. Indeed, for an internet user there is an almost infinite supply of media content available in real time, much of it freely available. The internet has definitively broken the dam of technologically imposed restriction in the supply of media content, as well as in many cases removing financial constraints on its access by users. It is also popular: 85% of French citizens have access to the internet, 74% use it every day and this figure rises to 95% among the 18 to 24 age group (Chiffres Internet 2017). This expansion of media supply means that among other things there is now a huge amount of political information available to voters. A few may choose to sift through this supply, many will go straight to trusted sources whether in the press or broadcasting, and others will rely on news aggregator sites such as Google *Actualités*. In the age of media hybridity television remains the single most important source of political information for French citizens, while for younger age groups the internet comes second, but still a considerable way behind television (Kantar 2017).

It is important, however, to note two qualifications to this picture of exponential growth in supply. First, not all media sectors have benefited from expansion; indeed the reverse has sometimes been true. Print media in particular have faced huge difficulties in adapting to the online media environment, notably in monetising their content. Newspapers and news magazines face major problems in selling their product in the offline world on the one hand and attracting advertising revenue and securing subscribers willing to pay for their online content on the other. While the difficulties for print media in adapting to the online environment are not a peculiarly French phenomenon, as a litany of recent newspaper closures in the US demonstrates, they are especially challenging in a country where sales of daily newspapers were already low by cross-national comparative standards. Put simply, the French press is in crisis. The second caveat is that more content (quantity) does not necessarily equate with a greater variety of voices (range); nor is more pluralism in terms of media sources and content providers necessarily synonymous with greater diversity of output. Put simply, 'more' may frequently (though clearly not always) translate into 'more of the same.'

The second feature of the contemporary hybrid media system is hypercompetition. Hypercompetition is 'a situation in which there is a lot of very strong competition between companies, markets are changing very quickly, and it is easy to enter a new market, so that it is not possible for one company to keep a competitive advantage for a long time' (*Financial Times* 2017). Competition for users and revenue has long been the norm both within and across different market sectors: national daily newspapers, weekly news magazines, celebrity magazines, radio stations, generalist television networks, specialist television channels and a range of websites. A good example of hypercompetition in the contemporary French media can be found in the field of rolling television news channels, where there are currently no fewer than four main suppliers in the marketplace: BFM TV, LCI, CNews (formerly iTélé) and Franceinfo, all freely accessible via different digital platforms (terrestrial, ADSL, cable and satellite).

This situation of hypercompetition in rolling news channels came about gradually. LCI (part of the TF1 group) was launched in 1994, iTélé (linked to the Canal Plus group) in 1999 and BFM TV (part of the NextRadioTV group) in 2005. After protracted negotiations with the regulatory authority, in April 2016 LCI was finally authorised to change its status from a subscription channel to being freely available on the digital terrestrial platform. This represented a belated recognition by LCI management of its original strategic error that had allowed BFM TV to secure pole position in the supply of rolling television news to domestic audiences. Following LCI's change of status, the degree of competition in rolling news channels further intensified with the launch of the public channel Franceinfo (supported by France Télévisions, Radio France, INA and France 24) in September 2016. It is debatable whether the French market needs or can sustain four national rolling news channels (not to mention the French-based international news channel, France 24, whose output can be received in France via live streaming).

Yet while hypercompetition is now commonplace across the French media system, it is not universal. A notable exception to the rule can be found among regional daily newspapers, which are usually centred on a city or large town and tend to exercise a de facto monopoly in the surrounding geographical area. These regional papers are popular because of their mix of local, regional, national and international news stories, as well as their cover price, which is generally lower than that of the national dailies. The best example of this phenomenon is *Ouest-France*, by far the biggest selling daily newspaper in France, based in Rennes and with a circulation area that covers Brittany, Lower Normandy and the Pays de la Loire. Across this geographical area the newspaper faces limited competition in its particular market sector.

The third feature of hybrid media is segmentation. For the greater part of the second half of the twentieth century one could speak of a system of *mass* media in France, especially in broadcasting where radio stations and television channels targeted a largely undifferentiated nationwide audience. Limited supply in radio and television because of frequency scarcity meant that media outlets usually sought to maximise their audiences with content that had broad appeal. This situation has changed with media expansion. Of course, examples of mass media are still present in contemporary France, notably radio stations such as France Inter (public) and RTL (private) and generalist television channels such as TF1 (private) and France 2 (public). In contrast, however, many media outlets are now niche suppliers, with their content aimed at targeted demographic sectors of the market, differentiated by levels of educational attainment, gender, age, sexual orientation, income, content preferences and so on.

The mirror image of segmentation on the supply side is fragmentation on the demand side. This is the fourth feature of France's contemporary hybrid media system. The mass audience of the twentieth century has given way to many small audiences, which sometimes overlap in terms of their patterns of media consumption. The mass audience still exists, notably in the case of television, for a major sporting event involving the French national football team (the 2016 Euro final against Portugal was watched by an audience of just under 21 million on M6) (L'Équipe 2016) or a political event like the face-to-face debate between the two contenders prior to the second round of the presidential election (the 2017 version between Emmanuel Macron and Marine Le Pen attracted a television audience of 16.5 million) (Le Journal du Dimanche 2017). Yet it is notable that these media occasions assembling a large nationwide audience in real time around a particular event are now remarkable for their relative rarity. For most of the time audiences are much smaller, even those for the main evening news programmes on TF1 and France 2, each of which tends to attract around five million viewers. The popularity of catch-up television and video on demand has accentuated this fragmentation, with television viewers no longer constrained by linear programme schedules.

The fifth feature of the hybrid media system are new patterns of ownership concentration. In principle, concentration of ownership may take place within and/or across the media sectors of press, radio and television, subject to the enforcement of general competition rules and specific media regulations, generally based on market share. In general, cross-media ownership across 'old' media of press and broadcasting has not been particularly pronounced in France, with no equivalent of the significant cross-media holdings of Rupert Murdoch in the UK or Silvio Berlusconi in Italy. Two features of media ownership in the hybrid age are striking. The first, not new, is that in France, major industrial conglomerates frequently have a stake in media/communication companies. Examples include Bouygues, a construction company that has a majority shareholding in the TF1 media group, and Bolloré, a company with holdings in transport and energy that has an ownership stake in the Canal Plus media group. The second feature is the way in which owners of mobile telephone companies have in recent years taken an ownership stake in the media (De Rochegonde and Sénéjoux 2017). Two leading examples of this phenomenon are Patrick Drahi, owner of the Altice group (SFR-Numéricable, *Libération*, the *Express* group) and a shareholder in NextRadioTV (BFM TV and Radio Monte-Carlo) and Xavier Niel, owner of the Free telecommunications group and one of the owners of *Le Monde* and the weekly news magazine *L'Obs*.

The sixth and final feature of France's hybrid media system is transnationalisation. This refers to the increasing porousness of national borders in ownership, production, distribution, content and reception. Until relatively recently the French media system was overwhelmingly dominated by national outlets, much of the content was produced in France and geared for domestic consumption, and the media policymaking community was largely composed of national actors. While to a significant extent this is still the case, the relatively closed and inward-looking French media landscape has also been shaken by transnational developments, including the growing role of non-domestic media and communication players. For instance, the acronym GAFA – Google, Apple, Facebook and Amazon (to which can be added Netflix) – has come to summarise the transnational challenge coming from large US-based multinational companies that have become major players in their particular fields in the French market.

Take the example of Netflix. For more than the past 30 years French audio-visual policy has been constructed to protect and promote the French film industry through among other things a system of cross-subsidy from television, notably Canal Plus. In addition, a system of rules has been applied with regard to when a film can be screened on television so as to protect film production and distribution. As a result of such public policy intervention the French film industry is in relatively good shape when compared to its European neighbours. The spread of Netflix poses a fundamental challenge to these arrangements, since Netflix has no particular interest in the health of the French film industry and is far less open to political pressure than a French-based media company would be. Of course, transnationalisation is not a one-way street, nor is France always on the debit side of the balance sheet. In recent years, for instance, French television series (such as *Engrenages, Marseille* and *Le Bureau des Légendes*) have become big sellers in television export markets. Overall, though, transnationalisation tends to be regarded as a destabilising factor for a media system accustomed to its national way of doing things.

The media and presidential elections

The notion of hybridity can be usefully applied to the way in which the media perform a variety of functions during presidential election campaigns. All three sets of actors involved in the campaign – political candidates and their advisors, journalists, and voters – employ a mix of 'old' and 'new' media to achieve their communication and information objectives. It has long been apparent that the media do not just report on an election campaign that somehow has an existence separate from its media coverage; the media are not simply observers of events. Instead, to a large extent the media are the campaign, in that they have a huge influence on how a campaign is structured and fought. Indeed, many campaign events – so-called pseudo events – would not take place if the media were not present to give them resonance in the public sphere (Boorstin 1961). The media influence the campaigning strategies of candidates, can give greater (or lesser) exposure to a candidate's programme, may focus more (or less) on particular issues and may help to shift voters' partisan preferences. Potentially at least, the media are hugely powerful actors in the electoral process.

The first function performed by the media in election campaigns is to provide factually accurate information to their users about the candidates and their programmes. Since the media are the primary source of information for citizens, as the primary objective of candidates is to be elected rather than to inform and because truth is often the first casualty of the electoral battlefield, the responsibility of the media in the provision of accurate information about the campaign is crucial. This was particularly the case in 2017, when the notions of 'fake news' and 'post-truth politics' from Donald Trump's successful US presidential campaign in 2016 were major subjects of international media coverage, and within France the media were severely criticised by candidates such as Le Pen and Jean-Luc Mélenchon for being too favourable to established economic and political power holders.

What can one say about the performance of this information function by the French media in 2017? Some of the media took their responsibility seriously, even if too much television content focused on the process of the election rather than substantive policy issues. Some media outlets, such as *Le Monde, Libération* and *Mediapart*, subjected candidates' claims to rigorous fact-checking and published the results for their readers. For the politically interested voter, there was a huge amount of campaign information easily available, particularly online. The main issues in France in 2017 were not so much 'fake news,' despite some revelations targeting Emmanuel Macron, as the superficiality of some campaign coverage and the lack of trust displayed by voters in the media. As a result, mainstream media faced daunting challenges in presenting themselves as reliable, informative sources.

A second campaign function for the media is to act as platforms for candidates to communicate their messages to voters. Sometimes this is done without any journalistic filter, as in candidates' official television broadcasts or when a candidate is the author of a newspaper piece. In 2017, at the height of the Penelopegate scandal (more on this follows), the candidate of Les Républicains, François Fillon, held a press conference to announce that despite the beginning of a judicial investigation he was not ending his campaign; since Fillon did not take any questions from journalists at the end of his statement, the live coverage of the event on rolling news effectively provided him with a platform to demonstrate his tenacity (or arrogance).

Sometimes journalists may intervene more actively, though still in a very limited fashion, for instance in posing questions to candidates in a newspaper interview or helping to structure the themes of a television debate, as in March 2017 when TF1 held a live debate featuring the five 'major' candidates: Macron, Le Pen, Fillon, Mélenchon and Benoît Hamon. Finally, the media platform can sometimes morph into a space of contestation, where journalists have more opportunity to question and probe a candidate. For instance, *L'Emission politique* on France 2 broadcast specific two-hour long programmes in which each of the five 'major' candidates was interviewed; the format certainly provided the candidates with a platform, but also subjected their responses to critical journalistic scrutiny and even included a 'mystery guest' who adopted an overtly adversarial stance to the candidate (for instance, the director of the documentary *Merci Patron!*, François Ruffin for Macron and the author Christine Angot for Fillon).

The best media platforms for candidates are those over which they can exercise full control of their message. Social media are excellent in this regard. All of the main candidates in 2017 used social media. For instance, Mélenchon, candidate of La France Insoumise, exploited his YouTube channel to bypass the journalistic filters of the traditional media to get his message across directly to actual and potential supporters. Mélenchon's use of social media reflected his critique of the mainstream media as purveyors of a dominant neo-liberal ideology and the belief among his supporters that they had treated his candidacy unfavourably in the 2012 presidential campaign (Sieffert and Soudais 2012). Marine Le Pen and her supporters also relied significantly on social media for both the propagation of their views and attacks on opponents. In the run-up to the start of the campaign Le Pen went on a mainstream media diet so as not to overexpose herself too soon in the race, but she continued to use social media, such as Twitter, for electoral purposes. In the case of both Mélenchon and Le Pen, their use of social media became stories in the mainstream media as the latter indulged in the metanarrative coverage of candidates' media usage.

Another facet of the way in which the media may act as a platform for a candidate is coverage, largely uncritical and sometimes borderline hagiographic, of their private lives, in particular their relationships with their partners. In French presidential elections the marketing of the private sphere for electoral purposes goes back to Valéry Giscard d'Estaing in the 1974 campaign. More recently, it became particularly associated with Nicolas Sarkozy in the run-up to his victory in 2007. In 2017 it was the turn of Macron. His 'fusional' relationship with his wife, Brigitte, the fascinating background to their life together, and her role as his informal political advisor as well as conjugal partner, were all covered in depth across the mainstream media. While various news weeklies such as *Le Point* and *L'Obs* gave massive coverage to Macron's status as a serious presidential candidate for months prior to the election, other magazines such as *Paris Match* and the celebrity title *VSD* focused on the Macron couple, with several flattering front-page covers. The result is a win–win situation: the candidate raises their profile in an uncritical context with a targeted section of the electorate and gains a secondary media 'buzz' as the original story is covered by other media; the original media outlet benefits commercially from free advertising in other media and a rise in circulation figures. It was hardly surprising that the huge amount of media coverage given to Macron prior to the start of the campaign led some commentators to ask whether Macron was the candidate of the media (Lemaire and Roques 2016; Bénilde 2017; Ortiz 2017).

The most high-profile media platform during the campaign, albeit one reserved only for the two leading candidates from the first round of voting, is the head-to-head televised debate. The debate has become part of the tradition of Fifth Republic presidential campaigns since the inaugural clash between Giscard d'Estaing and François Mitterrand in 1974. The only exception was in 2002 when the incumbent, Jacques Chirac, refused to debate with the Front national candidate, Jean-Marie Le Pen, on the grounds that a debate was impossible 'in the face of intolerance and hatred.' The debates have often been heated, but usually characterised by a formal courtesy between the protagonists. In 2017 Macron clearly considered that he could not repeat Chirac's gambit of 15 years earlier: during the campaign he had already participated in television debates which had included Le Pen, her passage through to the second round was not the surprise that her father's had been and there was no popular mobilisation against Marine Le Pen's qualification for the second round as there had been with her father. Not to have accepted a debate with Marine Le Pen would have been regarded as tantamount to an act of cowardice in the face of the enemy. Macron also probably considered that he could deal with any of the arguments that Le Pen threw at him and in this respect he was absolutely correct. The 2017 debate was a reminder that while a candidate may extract benefit from an appearance on a media platform, in contrast they can also do themselves significant damage.

A third function of at least some of the media during campaigns is to engage overtly and explicitly as partisan advocates in support of a particular candidate. In this regard, the rules vary across different media sectors. The print media are free to be overtly partisan if they so choose. Many daily newspapers, however, are reluctant to display overt partisanship for fear of alienating readers. The broadcasting media are bound by complex rules regarding equity and equality in the coverage of candidates. In 2017 the notion of equity was interpreted to mean reasonably equal coverage for the five 'major' candidates, to the virtual exclusion of the other six. While equality is easier to define, it is difficult to put into practice when there are 11 candidates in contention. One debate programme involving all 11 candidates did take place on BFM TV. However, the problem with this format is that there is no opportunity for a candidate to deepen their argument; the main objective for the 'major' candidates is to escape unscathed and to hope that a sound bite is echoed in other media coverage. While the websites of the broadcast media also enforce impartiality, the internet in general resembles a marketplace of political ideas from which voters can make their own choice – many sites are unashamedly partisan, both positive and negative. In 2017 such partisanship was also evident in the primary contests of both mainstream right and left, with internal party divisions highlighted as supporters of Fillon, Alain Juppé and Sarkozy et al. on the one hand and of Hamon, Manuel Valls and Arnaud Montebourg et al. on the other settled scores in support of their chosen standard bearer.

The fourth function performed by the media lies in the construction of the campaign agenda and the framing of issues. In 2002 the media played a significant role in giving prominence to the issue of insecurity, while in 2007 the cost of living and voters' purchasing power were dominant issues in the campaign. In terms of helping in the construction of the campaign agenda, the French media tend to follow the lead provided by the 'major' candidates, with the result that issues that the candidates do not wish to discuss rarely feature prominently in media coverage.

In 2017 one of the central features of the media in terms of agenda construction and issue framing was the focus on Fillon's involvement in the 'Penelopegate' scandal in which his wife was alleged to have been paid for a non-existent job as his parliamentary assistant over many years. For most media outlets the negative coverage of Fillon – a French version of personalised attack journalism – was not driven by partisan political considerations. Instead, straightforward news values and the highly competitive nature of media markets kept the story going. A financial scandal involving a recent former prime minister and the favourite at the start of January to become the next French president was bound to attract media attention. Added to this was the fact that the story was easily understandable way beyond the ranks of the political cognoscenti. This was not climate change or the Transatlantic Trade and Investment Partnership; instead it was somebody in the public eye, caught with their hand in the cookie jar. For journalists and news editors, so-called Penelopegate was a no brainer as a news story, while for audiences it had many of the elements of a political soap opera. There was no media conspiracy to undermine Fillon; it was simply good commercial sense on the part of the media, illustrated by a significant increase in the circulation of the newspaper that broke the story and kept it simmering, the satirical weekly *Le Canard enchaîné*.

The fifth media function relates to the electoral mobilisation of voters. Opinion poll evidence in the run-up to the first round of voting in 2017 indicated a reluctance on the part of many voters to commit to participating in the election. Despite a strong cultural ethos regarding voting as a civic duty and notwithstanding an extensive range of candidacies on offer, a popular distrust of elite politicians that had built up over many years and had been exacerbated by the perceived failures of the Hollande presidency came to a head in 2017, encouraged by Mélenchon on the far left and Le Pen on the far right. The media are by no means the sole determinant of electoral participation. Voter turnout is influenced by many factors, some related to candidates (programmes and campaigns) and some to voters (sociological variables, level of interest in politics, individual sense of political involvement). Nor is voter mobilisation an act of civil altruism on the part of the media; they have a vested financial self-interest in promoting the campaign or, in the case of public media, an assigned remit to do so. While it is impossible to evaluate the precise impact of the media on voter turnout in 2017, it is clear that many media outlets encouraged citizens to vote. Moreover, prior to the second round in particular much of the French media pushed more or less explicitly for voters to give Macron as large a margin of victory as possible so as to increase the legitimacy of his success.

The sixth and final function relates to the media's influence on voters' partisan preferences. The conventional wisdom of academic research in this area is that the media reinforce but rarely change voter preferences, that is to say that the media are not powerful in influencing a voter's partisan choice. Such a view may be open to dispute in the context of 2017. First, there was evidence that traditional party loyalties were weaker than in previous elections. Second, in the days running up to the first round of voting, no fewer than four candidates (Macron, Le Pen, Mélenchon and Fillon) were in contention for a place in the second round, giving no fewer than six run-off possibilities. In this context, opinion poll evidence as distributed via the media influenced the strategic choices of voters prior to the first round, i.e. voters were voting not necessarily for their first choice candidate but rather to prevent certain second-round scenarios from coming to fruition, such as a Fillon-Le Pen run-off (anathema to voters of the left) or a Mélenchon-Le Pen run-off (anathema to voters across the broad centre of the spectrum). Third, in the primary contests the television debates may have played a role in changing voter preferences in the context of campaigns taking place within the same political family by highlighting differences between the candidates. Finally, Le Pen's disastrous performance in the television debate on 3 May was followed by a drop in her support in the opinion polls and confirmed in the second round: from over 40% in polls just prior to the debate to a final score of under 34%.

Conclusions

In many respects the media system in France is very different from that of 20 or even ten years ago. This is largely due to technological change which has had a strong influence on the practices of the media (production, distribution, content) and of users (reception, interactivity, mobility). At the same time strong elements of continuity are also present, notably the key role of television as a means of political communication and information. New media, including social media, have not replaced mainstream media; nor are they simply another layer in the millefeuille of media strata. Instead, 'old' and 'new' media combine, cooperate and compete in what we have termed a hybrid media environment.

This hybrid media environment conditions the way in which presidential elections are now fought in France. There is now more information available across a diversity of outlets; candidates have to use different media for different electoral purposes, such as television to reach a mass audience and social media for targeted voter groups; media outlets are engaged in hyper-competition to win audiences; voters can gorge on the political content available or choose to dip out almost entirely (but surely no French voter could have remained totally unaware of the Penelopegate affair in 2017).

In presidential election campaigns the media are powerful political communication actors. This was demonstrated in 2017 with the devastating revelations by *Le Canard enchaîné* on Fillon and the television debate prior to the second round. Fillon dropped spectacularly in the polls after the newspaper revelations, while Le Pen's support dipped after the head-to-head debate. Yet the media are not all-powerful; the idea that the French media can make or break a candidate's presidential campaign is hard to substantiate. Fillon, for instance, was the target of virtually non-stop media criticism for three months during the campaign, but still survived, mainly because his party could not agree on a replacement candidate: party politics trumped media character attacks. Moreover, while many voters, including his own supporters, expressed outrage at Fillon's behaviour, levels of voting intentions in opinion polls never fell below 18%. Indeed many Fillon voters blamed the media rather than the candidate for the scandal. In the age of hybrid media, audiences continue to filter messages, often unconsciously; they engage in a selective process of exposure, perception and retention, influenced by pre-existing partisan attitudes.

References

Albert, P. and N. Sonnac. 2014. *La presse française*. Paris: La documentation française.

Bénilde, M. 2017. Le candidat des médias. In *Le Monde diplomatique*. Available at: www.monde-diplomatique.fr/2017/05/BENILDE/57494 [Accessed: 01.06.2017].

Boorstin, D. J. 1961. *The Image: A Guide to Pseudo-Events in America*. New York: Harper.

Bourdon, J. 1990. *Histoire de la télévision sous de Gaulle*. Paris: Anthropos/INA.

Chadwick, A. 2013. *The Hybrid Media System*. Oxford: Oxford University Press.

Chiffres Internet. 2017. Available at: www.blogdumoderateur.com/chiffres-internet/ [Accessed: 23.06.2017].

De Rochegonde, A. and R. Sénéjoux. 2017. *Médias: Les nouveaux empires*. Paris: First.

Financial Times. 2017. Available at: http://lexicon.ft.com/Term?term=hypercompetition [Accessed: 23.06.2017].

Kantar. 2017. Available at: http://fr.kantar.com/m%C3%A9dias/digital/2017/barometre-2017-de-la-confiance-des-francais-dans-les-media/ [Accessed: 14.06.2017].

L'Équipe. 2016. Available at: www.lequipe.fr/Medias/Actualites/M6-ecrase-son-record-d-audience-avec-la-finale-portugal-france/705490 [Accessed: 01.10.2016].

Le Journal du Dimanche. 2017. Available at: www.lejdd.fr/politique/audiences-le-debat-presidentiel-na-jamais-ete-aussi-peu-suivi-3319568 [Accessed: 31.07.2017].

Lemaire, F. and T. Roques. 2016. Emmanuel Macron superstar médiatique. Available at: www.acrimed.org/Emmanuel-Macron-superstar-mediatique [Accessed: 01.06.2017].

Ortiz, V. 2017. Comment les médias ont fabriqué le candidat Macron. Available at: http://lvsl.fr/medias-ont-fabrique-candidat-macron [Accessed: 01.06.2017].

Scales, R. P. 2016. *Radio and the Politics of Sound in Interwar France, 1921–1939*. Cambridge: Cambridge University Press.

Sieffert, D. and M. Soudais. 2012. *Mélenchon et les médias*. Paris: Politis.

22

THE MULTIPLE DEATHS OF
THE INTELLECTUAL
IN FRANCE

Benoît Dillet

What is wrong with the figure of the intellectual?

The romantic figure of the 'intellectual' is a defining feature of twentieth-century France. This figure is usually a white male Parisian who is part of a literary or cultural movement and uses his authority to take sides and give his opinion on current socio-economic affairs. There are different models of intellectuals, for instance sociologist Gisèle Sapiro (2009: 176–177) neatly distinguishes eight forms based on the criteria of autonomy, specialisation and symbolic capital, however something unifies all these: intellectuals all attempt to go beyond their field of expertise to bring about a shift in public discourse. It is a well-entrenched cliché for people outside of France to regret the absence of public intellectuals in their own country and point to France as a model. Another truism is to point the finger at the arrogance of public intellectuals to explain the general misguidedness of the French government and the ideologically drowned French people.

Relationships between the intelligentsia and its decision-making bodies are often assumed to follow some naïve mechanical schema: it is as if intellectuals were paid to come up with great ideas that can be smoothly channelled into policies. This dogmatic image of the intellectual is a relatively recent one yet it is deeply pervasive. It functions as a norm against which public discourse can be measured, evaluated and ultimately challenged. Although there are very few think tanks in France, unlike the US, something that is regretted by many liberal thinkers, journalists, politicians as well as other public actors have increasingly made demands on intellectuals to be relevant and propose specific policies to political parties and representatives. Contrary to this common perspective, I argue in this chapter that the interventions by intellectuals in the public debate and their more or less successful ability to carve out a social space are conditioned by the media and in particular by the hegemonic use of technological apparatus. Oppositions between theory and practice, ideas and institutions, as well as words and technological equipment continue to dominate and thus obscure a lucid analysis of the functions as well as the conditions of possibility of the intellectual voice today in France, and its relations to politics. What is missing or forgotten in this dogmatic image of the intellectual is precisely the material production of ideas. Ideas do not simply appear in a vacuum, floating in the air like clouds, but they have a material basis which forms a core part of the division of labour. Bernard Stiegler rightly notes that 'the figure of the "intellectual" is a regrettable invention, that unquestionably integrates the opposition between "manual workers" and "intellectuals"' (Stiegler 2015a), it reinforces a class-based discourse that divides those who can think and those who cannot.[1] This irreducible process can leave some people feeling marginalised and disparaged.

In this chapter I examine how the end of the French intellectual has been a recurring theme since at least 1980, with the death of Sartre. Newspaper articles and essays that are devoted to the silence or death of intellectuals often point in nostalgia to episodes of French history and the golden age of intellectuals from Zola to Sartre, from Gide to Foucault and Bourdieu. I argue that the question 'where are French intellectuals?' functions as a *refrain* in media discourse; every few years, major newspapers and magazines publish and advertise special reports on the decline of French intelligentsia. It is as if writing about intellectuals in France resembles a kind of necrology: intellectual life now belongs to history and the French intellectual as a universal figure has perished with Sartre. After briefly analysing the 2015 version of the refrain about 'the end of intellectuals,' this chapter will show by returning to the 1983 episode that what is often missing is an assessment of the conditions of possibility of intellectual discourse today in our current technological milieu.

Intellectual history as a criminal investigation: How did the French intellectual die?

The figure of the intellectual is dead, but how did he/she die? It seems more relevant to refer to this disappearance as a 'death' or even an act of 'killing,' rather than in terms of 'dusk,' 'twilight' or 'end.' The criminal investigation of the death of the intellectual has not yet been carried out, and yet this death is an integral part of French politics and discourse. I would like to turn to French philosophers Gilles Deleuze and Michel Foucault for this investigation since they have written and thought extensively about the death of God and the death of man. Deleuze has shown that the way God dies in the work of Nietzsche is significant for understanding not only Nietzsche's philosophy but the repercussions this death has had on Western thought and culture. Indeed, the German philosopher dramatised God's death to emphasise the multiple effects this event has on modern thought and societies. As the first epigraph of this chapter makes clear, a single event can have multiple effects. What if we were to apply this reading of the death of God to the death of French intellectuals? Nietzsche did not point to a single date of death, but read the work of Hegel and Feuerbach as announcing and enacting this death. In our case, we can make the hypothesis for now that the death of the French intellectual occurred with the singular event of Sartre's death but has continued to happen in diverse forms since the 1980s – and as we will see many dates can be pinpointed (1975, 1980, 1983). For Deleuze, Nietzsche dramatised the death of God precisely because this death had become a commonplace in the late nineteenth century: like tales or fables, the older the story, the more variants exist (Deleuze 1986). Deleuze found 12 versions of the death of God in Nietzsche's work, and with every version of this death comes something new.

In an important article, Pierre Grémion recounts the anecdote of a student in the 1990s who regrets the absence of intellectuals as 'semi-Gods' (Grémion 1999). In this nostalgic image, intellectuals are guardians of morality and the sacred. They have a connection to the sphere of the sacred by subtracting things from the domain of humans. They are gifted an exceptional sovereignty that is not shared with the rest of society, thus their ability to act as 'guardians.' We can therefore see the parallel between the intellectual as a universal figure and the sovereignty of God before the Enlightenment and the rationalisation of societies in the West. In the same way that God provided a foundation for individuals, intellectuals appeared as secularised versions of priests (and it is worth noting that both Julien Benda and Paul Nizan in the 1920s and

1930s used the term *clerc* to refer to intellectuals, a usage that was probably very common at that time). To put it perhaps too bluntly, intellectuals in France moved from the status of semi-Gods to tame pets; the process of secularisation has also been a process of domestication (Surya 2000). By occupying the media space, there has been a de-valorisation of intellectual charisma and discourse. Michel Surya notes that the media are not responsible for the domestication of intellectual speech but the real culprits are '*some* intellectuals' who used the media to domesticate thought and resign from thinking of alternatives (Surya 2000: 25–27). I disagree with his analysis on this point. First, we cannot reflect on the domestication of intellectuals without developing a media analysis of intellectuals. Second, this domestication of intellectual discourse has coincided and converged with the commodification of information and ideas as well as the rise of so-called knowledge economies from the 1970s.

The explosion of real-time media and the accompanying deluge of information have reshaped public discourse by neutralising intellectual discourse and levelling its value. A symptom of this is found in Pierre Bourdieu's 1996 *On Television*, in which he critiqued the format of talk shows for not allowing rational arguments to be developed, partly due to time constraints imposed by the programmes (Bourdieu 2011). However, as Bernard Stiegler has argued, Bourdieu's *On Television* was a missed opportunity from one of the leading intellectuals at that time to analyse the technical dimension of television (Stiegler 2011).[2] The shifts to television and then to blogs and social media have transformed the intellectual space in radical ways. The arrival of new technologies often creates shocks and disruptions to existing social systems, which in turn take years to readjust.

Today, the socio-technical space shaped by social media and enriched content, for instance by responding to the imperative of creating 'viral' content, has meant that there is a becoming-hysterical of the symbolic that is taking place. Increasingly, with the use of social media such as Twitter and Facebook, blogs and online newspapers tend to 'tabloidise' their headlines to receive sufficient attention to reach a viral status. To give an example of viral content: how have we come to the point when an academic or journalist can write an article entitled 'How French Intellectuals Ruined the West?' (Pluckrose 2017). How can it sound right to any editor? Why is there such resentment to a class or a cast (the intellectuals) that is supposed to write for the common good? We know that Perry Anderson famously wrote in 1983 that Paris had become the 'capital of intellectual reaction' (Anderson 1983),[3] but what have French intellectuals done to receive such bad press? After infecting academia, the next victim is 'Western society,' according to Helen Pluckrose. Paradoxically, the author uses a very traditional and idealist conception of the intellectual as the guardian of the universal, sheltered from external influences. Not only does she not analyse the socio-technical context of the intellectuals she is writing about, but she does not even distinguish different models of intellectuals and conflates all of them into a single category. Her conception of the intellectual corresponds to Julien Benda's own 'authentic intellectual' in *La Trahison des clercs*, first published in 1927; for Benda intellectuals work for the love of ideals and need to be autonomous from socio-economic obligations. Benda argues that intellectuals should not be corrupted by earthly passions, like politics: 'My Kingdom is not from this world' (Benda 2009: 43).

Today, media intellectuals such as Alain Finkelkraut, Michel Onfray and Éric Zemmour are all either in charge of a radio or television programme, not to mention Bernard Henri-Lévy who has recently become a film-maker. Some like Onfray have opened their own YouTube channel in order to broadcast their own television programme. YouTube allows the possibility to be at the same time cameraman, producer, writer, journalist and guest speaker (Brouze 2016). Intellectuals and philosophers have cultivated intimate relationships with the media (newspapers, radio and television), from Jean-Paul Sartre's radio shows on *La tribune des temps modernes* from October to December 1947 to Alain Badiou's interviews with philosophers in the 1960s and his recent programme *Contre-courant* with journalist Aude Lancelin which began in February 2014 on *Mediapart*.[4] Badiou has reflected on the role television can have on philosophical speech, not only in terms of reaching out to other audiences but in terms of representation and incorporation of speech. The general rule of a good televised allocation for Badiou is to make sure that 'speech does not end up being devoured by the image' (Badiou in Tho and Bianco 2013: 159–160). For him, a good televised philosophy programme needs to show tensions rather than obvious facts and simplicity: 'The reticence of a body with regard to the speech that had just been pronounced, a tension between the existence that manifests in the body, of the body of the philosopher, and the order of thought that is in the process of developing' (Badiou in Tho and Bianco 2013: 160).

In sum, the death of the intellectual is not due to the engagement with television or new media in general but by being fully integrated to the sensational and profit-making logic of television (Fassin 1996: 32–33). The transformation of the socio-technical milieu requires writers, philosophers and intellectuals to develop creative ways of intervening. The modes of intervention in new media have been influenced by two general trends: segmentation and professionalisation. First, the actions of intellectuals today divide society while, before 1980, these actions had the capacity to project the image of a unified society (Grémion 1999: 96). Second, French intellectuals used to mainly be writers, especially novelists and essayists, until the 1960s with the advent of *sciences humaines* and the sudden popularity of psychoanalysis, linguistics, literary criticism, sociology and anthropology (Fassin 1996).

The end of intellectuals (2015 extended remix)

The theme of the disappearance of intellectual life in France partly mirrors the booming declinist industry, with Michel Houellebecq, Éric Zemmour and Alain Finkielkraut as the leading products (Donado 2017). The obsession with decline in France has been felt particularly since the 2008 financial crisis but continued throughout François Hollande's presidency (Waters 2013). The term *déclinisme* was added to the Larousse dictionary in 2016. Much like with the reboots of the biggest Hollywood franchises, in recent years, the theme of the death of the French intellectual has dominated the press both nationally and internationally in unprecedented ways.[5] This is a vicious circle: the discourse that laments the end of intellectuals gives even more media space to the 'declinologues' and their pessimism about the present and the future.

The Israeli intellectual Shlomo Sand (2016) has published an insightful study explaining the metamorphoses of French intelligentsia. Sand has a large readership and once it is published in English, this book will certainly be the subject of a larger debate than in literary magazines. It is worth noting that the title in French reads *La Fin de l'intellectuel français?* while in English it reads *The End of French Intellectuals*. The absence of the question mark and the plural in the English translation somewhat shift the overall objective of the book. The end of 'French intellectuals' denotes that there are no longer intellectuals in France, perhaps even regretting the golden age of intellectual debates in twentieth-century France. The title in French is more precise; the singular denotes the figure or the ideal-type of the intellectual, implying that perhaps there are famous fiction and non-fiction writers in France but they no longer conform to the model that was once followed by generations of French intellectuals.

If the theme of the silence of intellectuals dominated the media in 2015, it is partly due to the terrorist attacks on the offices of *Charlie Hebdo* and on the Bataclan.[6] Intellectuals were not only targeted by the press, following their for-profit logic, but also by the social democrat government. Prime minister Manuel Valls had difficult relations with intellectuals and academics when he claimed two days after the *Charlie Hebdo* terrorist attacks that 'to explain Jihadism is to start forgiving' ('*expliquer le jihadisme, c'est déjà vouloir un peu excuser*'). This comment was highly mediatised and Valls referred to this 'culture of forgiveness' repeatedly in the weeks and months following the attacks. Sociologists felt particularly targeted and responded to the prime minister's attacks by referring to Wilhelm Dilthey's epistemological distinction between explaining (in science) and understanding (in social sciences).[7] Valls' statement was symptomatic of the distant and difficult relations that the social democrat government had with academics, intellectuals and sociologists in particular. This overt discrediting of sociological work was received with contempt and surprise, but it was inextricable from the previous governments' own relationships with intellectuals and academics.

In an assault on the 'culture of forgiveness,' Valls had in fact used one of the dominant features of the new reactionary thinkers in the 1990s and early 2000s (Lindenberg 2016: 25). To hear Valls refer to this tradition of thought confirmed the mainstreaming of reactionary ideas. For instance, the 'new philosopher' and writer of the controversial *The Tears of the White Man* (1983), Pascal Bruckner had already condemned this 'culture of forgiveness' two weeks after the 9/11 terrorist attacks by arguing that the US and Europe should not feel guilty or responsible for the attacks (Lagarde 2005: 95). Bruckner is notorious for writing against the self-flagellants of the West and arguing that Islamophobia is an ideology. In regretting the absence of intellectuals and the approaches taken by sociologists, Valls borrowed the framework used by reactionary thinkers, ignoring erudite debates that are often relayed in the press. Valls' belligerent rhetoric repeated that France was at 'war' in line with his previous comments in 2012 about terrorism as the 'enemy within,' and clearly adopting an 'Islam versus the West' perspective (Mondon 2017: 41–43). The then-prime minister was using the 'silence of intellectuals' refrain to strengthen his rhetoric and his 'analysis.' French politicians, especially presidents and prime ministers, always dream of being intellectuals as Deleuze and Félix Guattari wrote.

Interestingly, after 2015, academics working on the Middle-East, Islam and terrorism have received a lot of media attention in order to understand these terrorist attacks. I am thinking here of the debate between François Burgat, Olivier Roy and Gilles Kepel on Jihadism and terrorism, which was largely commented on in the press.[8] Kepel refers to religious factors to explain the radicalisation of terrorists and the Paris attacks, Roy insists in contrast that the motivations are not religious but that the perpetrators are in fact nihilists and committed their acts for political reasons. This fascinating debate is what is missing in blanket accusations of the absence of committed intellectuals or simply eclipsed by the omnipresence of the same few individuals occupying the media space. As Sapiro rightly notes:

> Even though newspapers frequently invite the enlightened opinions of researchers and academics on specific questions, their analyses are often drowned in the flood made by the discourse of the same few individuals, who are white and male, in their fifties or over, and who pretend to speak in the name of community, the 'nation,' the 'people,' or 'Europe.'
>
> *(Sapiro 2016: 132)*

On the same line, Jean-Luc Nancy intervened in the debate to remind readers as well as journalists that the silence of intellectuals contains a lot more, and that we should listen to the silence of intellectuals and look at what is not shown (Nancy 2015).

What is also striking in Valls' interpellation is the reference to other moments in France's intellectual and social history. In furthering this polemic about the 'culture of forgiveness,' in March 2015, Valls denounced the silence of intellectuals, imitating Max Gallo's call to intellectuals in July 1983 to get involved in debating France's economic policies (Le Monde 2015). Gallo, who was at that time the spokesperson of the Mauroy government, wrote:

> Has the left abandoned the battle of ideas? [...] Where are the Gide, the Malraux, the Alain, the Langevin today? [...] Who does not see that our society suffers from a deficit of modernity? [...] Will the country carry out the mutation that is required, both at the economic level as well as at the social one? [...] France does not need big names on opinion columns but concrete commitments.
>
> *(Gallo 1983)*

In this text, Gallo called for the neo-liberalisation of French society and for intellectuals to provide ideas on how to carry this forward. 1983 is indeed a crucial date in the socio-economic history of France but also for intellectuals, one of the deaths of the French intellectual as a figure. Valls' interventions in 2015 and 2016 against intellectuals and academics can therefore be considered a continuation of this period, a crude caricature of the debate about the end of intellectuals analysed at length by Michel Foucault, Jean-François Lyotard, Pierre Nora and Max Gallo.

The multiple crime scenes: Pierre Nora's experts (1980) and Max Gallo's deficit of modernity (1983)

In the 1960s and 1970s when Foucault argued violently against Sartre, he mainly did this to position himself against the previous generation of philosophers. Foucault claimed that with the rise of social sciences or *sciences humaines*, in particular sociology and psychology, but also with the democratisation of the university and the success of cheaper paperback books, the intellectual as a universal figure was no longer operative in the 1960s. Humanism as a doctrine was challenged and Foucault famously coined the term *intellectuel spécifique* to denote the mutation of the intellectual as a figure: from being the 'spokesman of the universal' and the 'master of truth and justice' (Foucault, 'Truth and Power' 1977/1979), he or she had become an expert who worked within his or her specific field and intervened in local struggles (Dartigues 2014). This passion for singular problems in philosophical research shaped Foucault's own thinking about the role of the intellectual; for instance, in 1968, he writes:

> A theoretical text had to tell you what is life, death, sexuality, if God existed . . . and how to intervene in politics, how to behave towards the other and so on. It seems that today we can no longer have recourse to this kind of philosophy and that, if you wish, philosophy has perhaps not entirely vanished into thin air, but it appears as dispersed, and that there is a theoretical work that comes in its plural form.
>
> *(Foucault 2001a)*

In its periodisation, the 'end of intellectuals' as a refrain comes therefore as the point of contestation of the specific intellectual that was recognised for most of the 1970s. This new figure of the intellectual suits Foucault's own work particularly well as it focused on micro-analyses of archival material together with the nominalist delineation of larger historical periods (between the classical period and the modern period for relations between reason and unreason, for instance). Although Foucault did not expand on the model of this new intellectual figure (Foucault 2001a, 2001b, 2001c), the founder of the influential interdisciplinary journal *Le Débat*, Pierre Nora seemed to have largely integrated this contestation and published in the first issue of the journal an important article on the transformation of French intellectuals and the new discursive regime. Nora justifies the creation of this new journal as a necessity and a response to this mutation:

> It is the end of the leisure class. The intellectual is no longer idle, a rentier, he has become a civil servant, an expert, an administrative potentate, free to not use his power. [. . .] The intellectual is now a secular figure, with a different kind of prophetism. Scientific investment has submerged him in a large network of teams and grants. [. . .] In this vast transfer from the literary to the scientific, the magic dimension of intellectuals has disappeared.
>
> *(Nora 1980: 3)*

Foucault's 'specific intellectual' and Nora's experts are not so distant but the most insightful development of Foucault's analysis is found in Jean-François Lyotard's 1983 text 'Tomb of the Intellectual' written in response to Gallo's rallying cry for intellectuals to support the neo-liberal turn of the social democrat government.

The perspective taken by Lyotard in this response develops some of the points from his 1979 *The Postmodern Condition*, particularly about the end of Enlightenment ideals and universals as well as the rise of the information society and the commodification of knowledge. He set out the new conditions of possibility and impossibility for intellectuals to exert an influence on society. Given the changes in the modes of production and the arrival of what he calls the 'techno-sciences of language' in all administrative, economic and political offices, the capacities sought after and the responsibilities have changed:

> These new cadres are not intellectuals as such. The professional exercise of their intelligence is not directed toward the fullest possible embodiment of the universal subject in the domain of their competence, but to the achievement of the best possible performance in that domain.
>
> *(Lyotard 1993b: 4)*

Lyotard refused to come on side of the government mainly because he believed the tasks of writers, painters, artists and philosophers are specific to each and cannot be subsumed or conditioned by criteria of 'better performativity' and economic growth. He argues that they do not know their 'addressee' and have the duty to ignore any objection to their own work (Lyotard 1993b). Yet, for him, artists will not retreat but will continue to work and face the responsibilities of this new age: 'Max Gallo will not find what he is looking for. What he is looking for belongs to another age' (Lyotard 1993b: 7). Lyotard acknowledges the death of the intellectual as a figure, and to him this death is related to the socio-technological changes in society as well as the adoption by most sectors of new imperatives in terms of performativity. For instance, the goals of university have changed: from training young minds to delivering professional qualifications and ever-more quantifiable skills. 'There ought no longer to be "intellectuals," and if there are any, it is because they are blind to this new fact in Western history' (Lyotard 1993b: 6). While Lyotard's analysis is luminous, especially since this transformation was taking place right under his eyes with no distance to make sense of it all, his position remains ambiguous and defeatist. He does not envisage other practices of these new technologies that could serve a different type of politics from the social democrat government which had furthered the imperatives of performativity and the contamination of language by capitalism.[9]

Conclusions: the death of the intellectual-form

At the beginning of this chapter, we drew a parallel between gods and intellectuals to show that there is a pervasive belief to conceive of intellectuals as moral legislators. This is probably what Lyotard had in mind when he wrote about the tomb of the intellectual, that the intellectual as god had disappeared with the secularisation of society and the end of eschatological thinking. The death of the intellectual was thus a consequence of the death of two other conceptual functions in French thought, namely god and man. Indeed when Deleuze reads Foucault's controversial work in the 1960s on the death of man as a concept, he draws a direct parallel with Nietzsche's dramatisation of the death of God. I want to suggest in conclusion that the death of the French intellectual-form can be read in continuation with the deaths of these two previous forms: the 'God-form' and the 'Man-form' (Deleuze 1988: 124–130). Following this line of thought, the intellectual-form is only an avatar – though an important one – of the Man-form. Thus, Foucault's texts on the intellectual-form follow his earlier theses on the death of man.

Much like the death of man in Foucault, 'there is no point in crying over the death of man [or the intellectual]' but to accompany 'the advent of a new form that is neither God nor man and which, it is hoped, will not prove worse than its two previous forms' (Deleuze 1988: 130–132). If the figure of the intellectual is disappearing, the question worth exploring should be about what comes after this figure. The new forms to emerge need not be unified around centre points but follow a distributed agency of floating points and transductive relations. If we want to adopt an absolutely non-nostalgic perspective on intellectuals, expectations will also change, and what will produce sense and symbolic texture are no longer the new Sartre or Foucault, but entirely new forms of distributed agency that will not be reduced to 'content providers.' They will not be domesticated intellectuals that are passively integrated in op-eds, TV talk-shows and radio programmes, nor would they be reactive forces that absolutely reject the media. When writing virulently about the new philosophers as pure products of television, Deleuze insisted that intellectuals need to develop new creative uses of technologies, to become producers instead of authors, to refuse to be simply assigned to the role of content-provider but to engage with the creations of technical forms of thought:

> Given the new power relations between journalists and intellectuals, and the situation of intellectuals regarding the media, I would like to propose a charter: refuse, make more demands, become producers, instead of authors who now display only the insolence of domestics or the brilliance of a hired clown.
>
> *(Deleuze 2007a: 147)*

This text was written 40 years ago, and Onfray made good use of this quotation to justify his own dubious agenda.[10] What forms will the new intellectuals take, after the death of the intellectual? We can think of two new antagonist forms of intellectual power that have emerged, one is barely recognisable since it is constituted using distributed agency, computer programmes, large data-sets and building new infrastructures. Whistleblowing is in its nascent state but something particularly new is taking place at this level. It is less the persona (as whistleblower) than the practice (whistleblowing) that matters, hence the role of anonymous groups and identities. The practices developed by whistleblowers establishing new relationships with journalists (especially with the International Consortium of Investigative Journalists [ICIJ]) are perhaps some of the most creative developments that have taken place in developing a new public discourse and counter-power. The second form of intellectual power that has developed very recently is the rise of thought-leaders against public intellectuals; thought-leaders are the intellectuals for the

1% as David Sessions (2017) has brilliantly called them. These two new forms of intellectual powers come positively and negatively after the end of intellectual-form, but they are mainly US-based, it will be interesting to see if these two new forms also actualise in the French context.

Notes

1 This text (Stiegler's article in *L'Humanité*) was published in response to Edouard Louis and Geoffroy de Lagasnerie's 'Manifeste pour une contre-offensive intellectuelle et politique,' in *Le Monde*, 27–28 September 2015. I discuss this manifesto later.

2 A first study of the impact of new technologies on intellectuals can be found in Debray, R. 1979. *Le Pouvoir intellectuel en France*. Paris: Ramsay.

3 'The veritable *débandade* of so many leading French thinkers of the Left since 1976 missing some of this sentence? Its consequences have been drastic. Paris today is the capital of European intellectual reaction, in much the same way that London was thirty years ago.' Anderson, P. 1983. *In the Tracks of Historical Materialism*. London: Verso, 32.

4 Tho, T. and G. Bianco. (Eds.). 2013. *Badiou and the Philosophers: Interrogating 1960s French Philosophy*. London: Bloomsbury; Chaplin, T. 2007. *Turning on the Mind: French Philosophers on Television*. Chicago: University of Chicago Press; Dillet, B. 2017. Radiographing philosophy. In B. Dillet and B. Stiegler (Eds.), *Philosophising by Accident: Interview with Élie During*. Translated by B. Dillet. Edinburgh: Edinburgh University Press, 2–10.

5 Traverso, E. 2013. *Où sont passés les intellectuels? Conversation avec Régis Meyran*. Paris: Éditions Textuel; Zarka, Y. C. 2015. *La Destitution des intellectuels*. Paris: PUF; Sand, S. 2016. *La Fin de l'intellectuel français: De Zola à Houellebecq?* Translated by M. Billis. Paris: Le Seuil; Truong, N. (Ed.). 2016. *Le crépuscule des intellectuels français?* La Tour d'Aigues: Editions de l'aube.

6 A good overview of the debate of media intellectuals in France can be found in two volumes: the first compiles a series of columns published in *Le Monde* in 2015; the second from *FigaroVox* is much more polemical since it contains articles by some far right thinkers. Truong, N. (Ed.). 2016. *Le Crépuscule des intellectuels français?* Paris: Le Monde/l'aube; Trémolet de Villers, V. (Ed.). 2016. *Conversations françaises: École, islam, Europe, laïcité . . . débats en toute liberté*. Paris: FigaroVox/Cerf éditions.

7 Montvalon, J-B. '"Expliquer, c'est déjà vouloir un peu excuser": la cinglante réponse des chercheurs à Manuel Valls,' in *Le Monde*, 3 March 2016. www.lemonde.fr/societe/article/2016/03/03/terrorisme-la-cinglante-reponse-des-sciences-sociales-a-manuel-valls_4875959_3224.html [Accessed: 01.12.2017]; Faure, S., C. Daumas and A. Vécrin. '"Culture de l'excuse": les sociologues répondent à Valls,' in *Libé-ration*, 12 January 2016. www.liberation.fr/debats/2016/01/12/culture-de-l-excuse-les-sociologues-repondent-a-valls_1425855 [Accessed: 01.12.2017]; Lahire, B. 2016. *Pour la sociologie: Et pour en finir avec une prétendue « culture de l'excuse »*. Paris: La Découverte.

8 Nossiter, A. '"That igonaramus": 2 French scholars of radical Islam turn bitter rivals,' in *The New York Times*, 12 July 2016. www.nytimes.com/2016/07/13/world/europe/france-radical-islam.html [Accessed: 01.12.2017]; Burgat, F. 'Djihadisme: Kepel et Roy oublient l'essentiel. Une troisième voie est nécessaire,' in *L'Obs*, 7 July 2016. http://leplus.nouvelobs.com/contribution/1536258-djihadisme-kepel-et-roy-oublient-l-essentiel-une-troisieme-voie-est-necessaire.html [Accessed: 01.12.2017]; Daumas, C, O. Roy and G. Kepel. 'Querelle française sur le jihadisme,' in *Libération*, 14 April 2016. www.liberation.fr/debats/2016/04/14/olivier-roy-et-gilles-kepel-querelle-francaise-sur-le-jihadisme_1446226 [Accessed: 01.12.2017].

9 Lyotard, J-F. 1993a. A Svelte appendix to the postmodern question (1982). In J-F. Lyotard (Ed.), *Political Writings*. Minneapolis: University of Minnesota Press, 27. See also Stiegler, B. 2015. *States of Shock: Stupidity and Knowledge in the Twenty-First Century*. Translated by D. Ross. Cambridge: Polity Press, 94–96.

10 See Brouze, E. 2016. Michel Onfray lance sa webTV. This quotation by Deleuze motivated a large part of the argument of this chapter, hence my surprise to find Onfray when he read it out during his first video presenting his YouTube channel in September 2016.

References

Anderson, P. 1983. *In the Tracks of Historical Materialism*. London: Verso.
Badiou, A. 2013. The critical value of images. In T. Tho and G. Bianco (Eds.), *Badiou and the Philosophers Interrogating 1960s French Philosophy*. London: Bloomsbury, 159–160.

Benda, J. 2009. *The Treason of the Intellectuals*. Translated by R. Aldington. Piscataway, NJ: Transactions Publishers.

Bourdieu, P. 2011. *On Television*. Translated by P. Parkhurst Ferguson. Cambridge: Polity Press.

Brouze, E. 2016. Michel Onfray lance sa webTV. In *L'Obs*, 6 September. Available at: http://tempsreel.nouvelobs.com/rue89/rue89-medias/20160906.RUE3766/michel-onfray-lance-sa-webtv.html [Accessed: 01.12.2017].

Burgat, F. 2016. Djihadisme: Kepel et Roy oublient l'essentiel. Une troisième voie est nécessaire. In *L'Obs*, 7 July. Available at: http://leplus.nouvelobs.com/contribution/1536258-djihadisme-kepel-et-roy-oublient-l-essentiel-une-troisieme-voie-est-necessaire.html [Accessed: 01.12.2017].

Chaplin, T. 2007. *Turning on the Mind: French Philosophers on Television*. Chicago: University of Chicago Press.

Dartigues, L. 2014. Une Généalogie de l'intellectuel spécifique. In *Astérion*, 12. Available at: https://asterion.revues.org/2560 [Accessed: 01.12.2017].

Daumas, C., O. Roy and G. Kepel. 2016. Querelle française sur le jihadisme. In *Libération*, 14 April. Available at: www.liberation.fr/debats/2016/04/14/olivier-roy-et-gilles-kepel-querelle-francaise-sur-le-jihadisme_1446226 [Accessed: 01.12.2017].

de Montvalon, J-B. 2016. 'Expliquer, c'est déjà vouloir un peu excuser': la cinglante réponse des chercheurs à Manuel Valls. In *Le Monde*, 3 March. Available at: www.lemonde.fr/societe/article/2016/03/03/terrorisme-la-cinglante-reponse-des-sciences-sociales-a-manuel-valls_4875959_3224.html [Accessed: 01.12.2017].

Debray, R. 1979. *Le Pouvoir Intellectuel en France*. Paris: Ramsay.

Deleuze, G. 1986. Cours de Gilles Deleuze à l'Université Paris VIII: Foucault 1985–1986. 18 March. Available at: http://www2.univ-paris8.fr/deleuze/article.php3?id_article=472 [Accessed: 01.12.2017].

Deleuze, G. 1988. *Foucault*. Translated and edited by S. Hand. Minnesota: University of Minnesota Press.

Deleuze, G. 2007a. Intellectuals and power (1972). In G. Deleuze (Ed.), *Two Regimes of Madness: Text and Interviews 1975–1995*. Edited by D. Lapoujade, translated by A. Hodges and M. Taormina. Cambridge, MA: MIT Press.

Deleuze, G. 2007b. On the new philosophers (plus a more general problem). In G. Deleuze (Ed.), *Two Regimes of Madness: Text and Interviews 1975–1995*. Edited by D. Lapoujade, translated by A. Hodges and M. Taormina. Cambridge, MA: MIT Press.

Dillet, B. and B. Stiegler. 2017. *Philosophising by Accident: Interview with Élie During*. Translated by B. Dillet. Edinburgh: Edinburgh University Press.

Donado, R. 2017. France's obsession with decline is a booming industry. In *The New York Times*, 3 February. Available at: www.nytimes.com/2017/02/03/books/france-michel-onfray-decadence.html [Accessed: 01.12.2017].

Fassin, E. 1996. Why French intellectual history should repeat itself as a farce? In *London Review of Books*, 18:21, 32–33.

Faure, S., C. Daumas and A. Vécrin. 2016. 'Culture de l'excuse': les sociologues répondent à Valls. In *Libération*, 12 January. Available at: www.liberation.fr/debats/2016/01/12/culture-de-l-excuse-les-sociologues-repondent-a-valls_1425855 [Accessed: 01.12.2017].

Foucault, M. 2001a. Foucault répond à Sartre. In M. Foucault (Ed.), *Dits et écrits 1 (1954–1975)*. Paris: Gallimard.

Foucault, M. 2001b. La fonction politique de l'intellectuel. In M. Foucault (Ed.), *Dits et écrits 1 (1954–1975)*. Paris: Gallimard.

Foucault, M. 2001c. Truth and power. In M. Foucault (Ed.), *Dits et écrits 1 (1954–1975)*. Paris: Gallimard.

Gallo, M. 1983. Les Intellectuels, la politique et la modernité. In *Le Monde*, 26 July.

Grémion, P. 1999. Écrivains et intellectuels à Paris: Une esquisse. In *Le Débat*, 103, 74–99.

Lagarde, F. 2005. Penser l'impensable: le 11 septembre des penseurs français. In *French Politics, Culture and Society*, 23:2, 91–100.

Lahire, B. 2016. *Pour la sociologie: Et pour en finir avec une prétendue "culture de l'excuse."* Paris: La Découverte.

Le Monde. 2015. Départementales: Valls dénonce un 'endormissement généralisé' face au 'danger' du FN. 5 March. Available at: www.lemonde.fr/politique/article/2015/03/05/departementales-valls-denonce-un-endormissement-generalise-face-au-danger-du-fn_4588426_823448.html [Accessed: 01.12.2017].

Lindenberg, D. 2016. *Le Rappel à l'ordre: Enquête sur les nouveaux réactionnaires*. Paris: Le Seuil.

Louis, E. and G. Lagasnerie. 2015. Manifeste pour une contre-offensive intellectuelle et politique. In *Le Monde*, 27–28 September.

Lyotard, J-F. 1993a. A svelte appendix to the postmodern question (1982). In J-F. Lyotard (Ed.), *Political Writings*. Translated by B. Readings and K. P. Geiman. Minneapolis: University of Minnesota Press.

Lyotard, J-F. 1993b. Tomb of the intellectual (1983). In J-F. Lyotard (Ed.), *Political Writings*. Translated by B. Readings and K. P. Geiman. Minneapolis: University of Minnesota Press.

Mondon, A. 2017. *Charlie Hebdo*, republican secularism, Islamophobia. In G. Titley, D. Freedman, G. Khiabany and A. Mondon (Eds.), *After Charlie Hebdo: Terror, Racism and Free Speech*. London: Zed Books, 41–43.

Nancy, J-L. 2015. Savoir écouter le silence des intelletuels. In *Libération*, 22 September. Available at: www.liberation.fr/debats/2015/09/22/savoir-ecouter-le-silence-des-intellectuels_1388232 [Accessed: 01.12.2017].

Nossiter, A. 2016. 'That ignoramus': 2 French scholars of radical Islam turn bitter rivals. In *The New York Times*, 12 July. Available at: www.nytimes.com/2016/07/13/world/europe/france-radical-islam.html [Accessed: 01.12.2017].

Pluckrose, H. 2017. How French 'intellectuals' ruined the west: postmodernism and its impact, explained. In *Areo*, 27 March. Available at: https://areomagazine.com/2017/03/27/how-french-intellectuals-ruined-the-west-postmodernism-and-its-impact-explained/ [Accessed: 01.12.2017].

Sand, S. 2016. *La Fin de l'intellectuel français: De Zola à Houellebecq?* Translated by M. Billis. Paris: Le Seuil.

Sapiro, G. 2009. Modèles d'intervention politique des intellectuels: Le cas français. In *Actes de la recherche en sciences sociales*, 176–177, 8–31.

Sapiro, G. 2016. L'inquiétante dérive des intellectuels médiatiques. In N. Truong (Ed.), *Le Crépuscule des intellectuels?* La Tour d'Aigues: Editions de l'aube, 127–133.

Sessions, D. 2017. The rise of the thought leader: how the superrich have funded a new class of intellectual. In *New Republic*, 28 June. Available at: http://newrepublic.com/article/143004/rise-thought-leader-how-superrich-funded-new-class-intellectual [Accessed: 01.12.2017].

Stiegler, B. 2011. *Technics and Time*, Vol. 3: Cinematic Time and the Question of Malaise. Translated by Stephen Barker. Stanford: Stanford University Press.

Stiegler, B. 2015a. *States of Shock: Stupidity and Knowledge in the Twenty-First Century*. Translated by D. Ross. Cambridge: Polity Press.

Stiegler, B. 2015b. Puissance, impuissance, pensée et avenir. In *L'Humanité*, 15 October. Available at: www.humanite.fr/puissance-impuissance-pensee-et-avenir-586852 [Accessed: 01.12.2017].

Surya, M. 2000. *Portrait de l'intellectuel en animal de compagnie: De la domination*, Vol. 3. Tours: Farrago.

Tho, T. and G. Bianco. (Eds.). 2013. *Badiou and the Philosophers: Interrogating 1960s French Philosophy*. London: Bloomsbury.

Traverso, E. 2013. *Où sont passés les intellectuels? Conversation avec Régis Meyran*. Paris: Éditions Textuel.

Trémolet de Villers, V. (Ed.). 2016. *Conversations françaises: École, islam, Europe, laïcité . . . débats en toute liberté*. Paris: FigaroVox/Cerf éditions.

Truong, N. (Ed.). 2016. *Le crépuscule des intellectuels français?* La Tour d'Aigues: Editions de l'aube.

Waters, S. 2013. The 2008 Economic Crisis and the French Narrative of National Decline: Une causalité diabolique. In *Modern and Contemporary France*, 21:3, 335–354.

Winock, M. 1997. *Le Siècle des intellectuels*. Paris: Le Seuil.

Zarka, Y. C. 2015. *La Destitution des intellectuels*. Paris: PUF.

23

JEWISH CULTURE IN TWENTY-FIRST-CENTURY FRANCE

Rebecca Infield and Rebekah Vince

Contemporary Jewish culture in France is inherently transcultural, transnational and transcontinental (Europe, North America, Africa, Middle East), crossing and challenging national and cultural borders. French Jews share a dark past with the rest of European Jews with whom they commemorate the Nazi Holocaust, specifically remembering the round-up by French police at the Vélodrome d'Hiver in 1942. They find themselves implicated in the Israeli–Palestinian conflict, many against their will, not least of all because Israeli prime minister Benjamin Netanyahu claims to speak on behalf of all Jews, and has been particularly strategic in encouraging French Jewish emigration to Israel following anti-Semitic attacks in France. Finally, they contribute to French culture in a variety of ways, including through literature, cinema and comedy.

France currently houses Europe's largest Jewish population of around 600,000 Jews, although this number is approximate given that it is illegal to collect information based on an individual's religion in France.[1] France is also home to Europe's largest Muslim population, which is estimated to be around one million, again an approximation. It is therefore important to take into account Jewish–Muslim tensions (connected to the Israeli–Palestinian conflict), and specifically anti-Semitism and Islamophobia within and outside of the Jewish and Muslim communities of France, while recognising the potential for solidarity between Jews and Muslims in combating all forms of racism. In contemporary France there reside two main groups of Jews: Ashkenazim and Sephardim. Ashkenazi Jews originally hail from Eastern Europe, and were often the target of pogroms in areas of Russia and what is now modern Ukraine during the eighteenth and nineteenth centuries and so found refuge in France. Many of these Jews were naturalised in 1860 when they were able to gain French nationality, although this was taken away under the Vichy regime which oversaw mass deportations to Nazi concentration and extermination camps, via French detention centres. Meanwhile, Sephardim originally refers to Jews who were driven out of Southern Spain by King Ferdinand and Queen Isabella during the Spanish Inquisition in 1492. The majority of these Jews fled to the Ottoman Empire, notably North Africa, later to be displaced a second time following the foundation of the state of Israel and decolonisation of France's department (Algeria) and protectorates (Morocco, Tunisia), at which point they left for France and, in fewer cases, to Israel or Canada. It is often forgotten that there were Jews living in North Africa before the inquisitions; some had been there since the destruction of the Second Temple in Jerusalem, others came with the Muslim conquest as merchants and scribes. Today, the majority of Jews in France are considered to be Sephardi Jews, itself not a monolithic group, although most Sephardi Jews in France are of North African heritage, which they embrace or reject to varying degrees (see Benbassa 2002). Nevertheless, in France, Sephardi has come to encompass all Jews whose descendants are not from Europe, including those who have origins in Turkey as well as North Africa (see Attias and Benbassa [2001] 2002: 15, 93–94, 120). Suffice to say that the majority of Jews in France have not lived in the hexagon for generations,[2] but rather originate from elsewhere, contributing to the multicultural societal reality of France in spite of its assimilationist policies.

Despite having achieved French nationality (including in colonial Algeria), French Jews encountered problems in twentieth-century assimilationist France with the introduction of the *état laïque* (secular state) in 1905. The centenary of French secularism was celebrated by the introduction of the 'Loi sur le port des signes réligieux ostensibles dans les établissements d'enseignement publics'; 'The Law on the wearing of ostentatious religious symbols in public education establishments.' The law was officially implemented in March 2004 in preparation for the beginning of the new school year, known as *la rentrée*, and forbids the wearing of religious symbols or clothing in government-run establishments, schools in particular. The law has been widely criticised for the difficulty it poses to female Muslim students no longer able to wear the veil to school but also affects male Jewish students as it prevents them from wearing the traditional 'kippa' or skullcap. Further to this, there have been several cases of girls, both Muslim and Orthodox Jewish, being sent home for wearing skirts and dresses that were deemed 'too long' for school, again creating difficulty for those who wish to cover their legs for religious purposes.

This chapter begins by examining the ongoing question of anti-Semitism in France, with a particular focus on how events such as the Toulouse school violence (2012) and Hypercacher shootings (2015) have impacted upon the community. It then attempts to discern the situation of Jews in modern France, whether there exists a specific French anti-Semitism or if the ever-present Israeli–Palestinian conflict and Jewish–Muslim tensions are the reason for the thousands of French Jews moving to Israel each year. The chapter concludes with an exploration of more positive representations of Jewish identity and contributions to cultural life in France as well as examples of Jewish–Muslim collaboration in artistic projects.

Anti-Semitism

Unfortunately, a major aspect of contemporary Jewish life remains anti-Semitism, which manifests itself in various ways, and has three main motivations: radical Islam, the Israeli–Palestinian conflict and old stereotypes about Jews such as their wealth or success in society being an inevitability. This section will explore some of the most recent anti-Semitic acts, how they have impacted upon the French community, the motives that drove individuals to commit such atrocities, and what the French government is doing to prevent further violence. In 2004, the then Israeli prime minister Ariel Sharon called France 'the most anti-Semitic country in Europe' following violent attacks on synagogues, Jewish businesses and cemeteries in the early 2000s.[3] These attacks are seen as being a reaction to the events taking place in the Middle East at the time which came to be known as the Second Intifada. Sharon continued with a call for French Jews to migrate to Israel (or 'make Aliyah' as it is known within the Jewish community), declaring that Israel would welcome them with open arms. A feeling of insecurity seems to have continued in France, particularly following events such as the shooting at a Jewish school in Toulouse in 2012, which will be explored later. This may explain why over 7,000 Jews migrated to Israel in 2014, more than double compared to the preceding year, meaning that, for the first time ever, France was the country from which the biggest number of Jews made Aliyah, beating both the US (which saw 3,870 leave in 2014) and Russia (4,830).[4] This would suggest that French Jews no longer feel safe in France and prefer to seek refuge in the Holy Land instead.

However, anti-Semitism is certainly not new to French Jews. The Dreyfus Affair, which began in 1894, is often seen as the first example of public French anti-Semitism which received international media attention, and followed the publication of the popular anti-Semitic tract *La france juive* by Édouard Drumont (1886).[5] It was the Dreyfus Affair which led the Swiss journalist Theodore Herzl, who was horrified by calls of 'death to the Jews' in the streets of Paris, to begin the Zionist movement. Nevertheless, the majority of Jews preferred to stay in France. Things improved for French Jews during the First World War as many gained respect for fighting in the French army. By the 1920s and 30s, with the rise of fascism, anti-Semitism returned with well-known and respected French writers such as Louis-Ferdinand Céline openly expressing their dislike for the Jewish population.[6] Under the Nazi Occupation of France and the collaborating Vichy regime, especially between 1942 and 1944, many French Jews met the same fate as those in other European countries occupied by Nazi troops. It was not until 1995 that then-president Jacques Chirac acknowledged the French government's role in the Holocaust, notably in the *Vel' d'hiv* round-up suggesting a difficulty of coming to terms with France's underlying anti-Semitism prior to, during and after Vichy.

Despite the French government's attempts to acknowledge (if not apologise for) the past, several political and intellectual figures in the public eye have made this more difficult. The far right Front National (FN) was founded in 1972 by Jean-Marie Le Pen, an outspoken Holocaust denier who referred to the gas chambers as being a 'un point de détail de l'histoire de la Seconde Guerre mondiale' (Jean-Marie Le Pen quoted in Deleersnijde 2001: 126). In 2011, Jean-Marie Le Pen was replaced by his daughter, Marine Le Pen, as leader of the party. Marine, as she is popularly known, has launched a process of *dédiabolisation* into the party in an attempt to improve its image and make it more widely appealing.[7] As a result of this, the party was very careful when addressing the Jewish population until the 2017 presidential elections during which Marine Le Pen denied French responsibility for the *Vel' d'hiv* round-ups. Le Pen later argued she was simply reflecting general Charles de Gaulle's belief that the Vichy regime was not the one true France (The Guardian 2017). Despite these views, Marine Le Pen still gained 10.6 million votes in the second round of the 2017 elections. It would therefore seem that the Le Pen family are not alone in their beliefs about the Holocaust, and their approach to minorities in France (including Jews and Muslims).

Ilan Halimi, or the affair of the Gang of Barbarians

Holocaust denial is not the only manifestation of anti-Semitism in modern France. Physical violence against Jews still occurs regularly, contributing to the fear experienced by many French Jewish communities. The kidnapping and eventual murder of Ilan Halimi in January 2006 is an extreme example of this violence and caused a great deal of distress for French Jews. Halimi was a 23-year-old shop assistant from a Moroccan Jewish family living in Paris' 12th arrondissement who was targeted by a gang known as the Gang of Barbarians and lured by a girl who called herself Yalda to an apartment block in the suburbs of Paris. There he was overpowered by several gang members and held captive for 24 days. Halimi was beaten and tortured whilst the gang demanded €450,000 as ransom from his family. When the family, who were of humble means, did not provide the money, the gang are said to have contacted a rabbi, local to Halimi's family, in order to collect money together within the community. Nevertheless, paying ransoms is forbidden under French law and so the police did not allow any kind of a deal to be made. Halimi was released by his captors and found by a member of the public but had been tortured so badly that he died on the way to the hospital. After the gang members had been arrested, they admitted that their motive for capturing Halimi was the fact that he came from a Jewish family. They assumed that Halimi would have money based on him being Jewish, believing the old anti-Semitic stereotype that all Jews are rich (Willsher 2006). The horrific events received a great deal of attention in French media and a film recounting Halimi's ordeal was released in 2014, based on the book written by his mother Ruth Halimi and Emilie Frèche, namely *24 jours: La vérité sur la mort d'Ilan Halimi*, published in 2009 (Halimi and Frèche 2009). Contrary to the following two examples of anti-Semitism explored in this chapter, this crime seems to have been motivated by old clichés and stereotypes about Jews that have existed for centuries, as opposed to radical Islam or the Israeli–Palestinian conflict. However, these stereotypes could also originate from the colonial Maghreb, particularly in Algeria, where Jews were given French nationality in 1870 and assimilated into French-speaking schools, whereas Algerian Muslims were not given the same status.

Toulouse shootings

In 2012, Mohammed Merah, a French citizen of Algerian origin, attacked the Ozar Hatorah school in Toulouse after having set upon several French paratroopers a number of days before. A rabbi and three children were killed in the shootings and many others were injured. The police tracked down Merah and after a battle at his apartment, he was killed. Significantly, before his death, Merah admitted to the police that his motivation for the attack was anti-Semitic. The media and public response to the shootings was one of shock, and the then-president Nicolas Sarkozy mentioned the inexcusable anti-Semitic nature of the attack. Nevertheless, numerous calls were made to take into account the difficult psychiatric history of Merah as a contributing factor to his actions. However, on a wider scale, it seemed as if many were in agreement with Merah's actions, as the French Jewish community documented 90 anti-Semitic incidents in the ten days following Merah's attack. The Service de Protection de la Communauté Juive (SPCJ) recorded 148 anti-Semitic incidents in the two months following the attacks, and the police recorded a further 105 instances of anti-Semitic intimidation such as the vandalism of Jewish graves in Nice. These events, being so violent and random in nature, frightened the Jewish population and could explain the increase in Jews moving to Israel in the years that followed (notably in 2013 and 2014). Moreover, despite claims about the mental health of the attacker, the domino effect of attacks that followed the Toulouse shooting highlight a sense of agreement with the violence within certain sections of French society. When Merah's neighbours were asked about the violence, many acknowledged that they felt frustrated with their own financial and social situations (Vincour 2013). This would suggest that anti-Semitism acted as a means of expressing their anger towards the French government and the society in which they live. These events appear to have been the start of a new kind of violence targeting French Jews for being Jewish.

Hypercacher

The events that occurred at the start of January 2015 were broadcast around the world. The attacks on the *Charlie Hebdo* magazine by the Kouachi brothers sparked the 'Je suis Charlie' movement and reinforced the message to protect freedom of expression wherever possible. Two days later, on 9 January 2015, Amedy Coulibaly entered the Hypercacher (a kosher supermarket) in the twentieth arrondissement in Paris armed with guns and grenades. Several shoppers were killed outright, hostages were taken, and a number of customers were hidden in the fridge by Muslim shop assistant Lassana Bathily. Police surprised Coulibaly after Bathily had warned them about the situation. Although these events were widely reported in the French media and four of the victims were posthumously awarded the Légion d'Honneur (France's most respected award), voices in the Jewish community felt that the situation had not been dealt with in the same way as the Charlie Hebdo attack.[8] Sefy Hendler from the Israeli newspaper Haaretz claimed that 'French president François Hollande and prime minister Manuel Valls said the right words, as they have been doing for a long time,' as did the police, however 'the vast majority of "the children of the fatherland," as the "Marseillaise" calls them, remained at home' (2015).

Thus it would seem that the French government is doing everything in its power to acknowledge and prevent anti-Semitism, but certain Jewish communities do not feel that this message is shared by the general public. So why is this the case? Is it because the French public feel overloaded by information and laws concerning the French Jewish community? Recent changes in law such as the controversial 'Loi Gayssot' have created a great deal of debate as they are viewed as an infringement on freedom of speech, which the 'Je suis Charlie' movement seeks to uphold at all costs. The Gayssot law, established in 1990, made it illegal to deny the existence of crimes against humanity, with a particular emphasis on the Holocaust. Many leading French historians, such as Pierre Nora, Pierre Vidal-Naquet and Claude Liauzu, highlighted the dangers of the Gayssot law, citing that it was dangerous to prevent freedom of research and preferable to face Holocaust deniers (*négationnistes*) in a battle of ideas.[9] Even Simone Veil, herself a Holocaust survivor, opposed the law with a number of other leading politicians, such as Jacques Chirac and François Fillon. The law has been put into practice with individuals such as comedian Dieudonné M'bala M'bala who, in 2017, was sentenced to two months of prison and a fine of 9,000 euros for inciting hatred and anti-Semitic remarks in one of his shows from 2012. Critics of the Gayssot law argue that these convictions have only served to increase Dieudonné's following, giving him more media coverage.

Following the shootings which took place on 7 and 9 January, a 'Marche pour les victimes' was organised on 11 January in Paris.[10] The event was intended to be a non-political memorial for all of those who had died during the attacks. For this reason, then-president François Hollande did not invite Israeli prime minister Benjamin Netanyahu to the event in order to avoid conflict and also perhaps to differentiate between the Jews of France and the state of Israel. Nevertheless, Netanyahu insisted on attending the ceremony despite Hollande's wishes. As a result, Hollande invited Palestinian leader Mahmoud Abbas to ensure that the memorial was as politically equal as possible. Contrary to Hollande, the newly elected president Emmanuel Macron seems to be taking a different approach. Macron appears to be less careful to differentiate between the Jews of France and the 'Jewish state.' At the 2017 memorial for the victims of the *Vel' d'hiv* deportations, commemorating the 75th anniversary, Macron invited Netanyahu to stand by his side and addressed him as 'mon cher Bibi,' an affectionate name used by Israeli supporters for their leader. This was the first time ever that an Israeli prime minister was invited to commemorate the events of July 1942 in France. It will therefore be interesting to see how the French Jewish community reacts to this friendly alliance.

Contrary to previous periods of anti-Semitism, such as the Vichy regime, modern anti-Semitism takes several forms. Further to this, again differing to Vichy, the French government appears to be doing as much as possible to protect its Jewish population. However, is the prioritisation of protecting Jews worsening the situation? Islamophobia is also on the rise in France and receives significantly less media and government attention, which could lead to feelings of resentment towards the Jewish community. Therefore, it is not just behaviour towards Jews but public opinion that must be changed. All of the measures taken by the French government would seem to suggest that they are doing their utmost to prevent anti-Semitism and violence towards Jews. Nevertheless, anti-Semitism persists, suggesting that laws and campaigns alone cannot solve anti-Semitism in France. It is the attitudes of the public which need to be worked on as French Jews seem to once again become a scapegoat for the difficulties encountered by those on the edges of society, such as unemployment, poverty, and social exclusion. Benbassa notes that:

> [one] explanation for this anti-Semitism currently spreading among Arab-Moslem [*sic*] milieus could be found in the absence of a real integration policy and a social and professional mobility still in its embryonic stages. [. . .] Anti-Semitism [was] worsened with the two Intifadas [as there was a focus] on the enemy but in fact served to obscure prevailing social and economic problems.
>
> *(2007a: 191–192)*

Thus it would seem as though anti-Semitism is the go-to explanation for many of the difficulties facing poorer or marginalised individuals in France. In order to remedy this, France needs to address issues such as unemployment, poverty and the integration of all communities, in particular Muslims, so as to avoid creating pockets of anti-Semitic feeling. These examples of modern anti-Semitism on French soil suggest that there are several different motives behind modern anti-Semitic sentiment and behaviour. The conflict in the Middle East presents itself as one of the major reasons for violence in France, and Merah acknowledged that he had carried out the Toulouse shootings in order to avenge his 'brothers and sisters,' or Palestinians, killed fighting against the State of Israel. This is after the Gaza–Israel clashes of March 2012, referred to by Israel as Operation Returning Echo. The Hypercacher murders had strong links to Islamic state and Coulibaly is said to have been an accomplice to the Kouachi brothers. Nevertheless, despite these modern motivations for anti-Semitism, it would seem that in cases such as the murder of Ilan Halimi, old stereotypes such as the notion that Jews are wealthy simply because they are Jews, are still at play. But do the representations of Jews in the French media and within cinema and literature also have a role to play in fighting anti-Semitism?

Cultural representations

Although fears for safety and even existential paranoia in the face of past and present anti-Semitism persist, there is a rich cultural heritage and continuation of creative output by French Jews through literature, film, music and comedy. Jewish culture in France notably represents and responds to memory of the Holocaust and nostalgia over exile from North Africa in sensitive, thought-provoking and creative ways. Moreover, collaborative projects which create links with other minorities in France form bridges between communities, challenging stereotypes and offering spaces for dialogue.

In his book *In Lieu of Memory: Contemporary Jewish Writing in France* (2006), Thomas Nolden writes that contemporary French Jewish writing in particular is marked by the repercussions of 'both the Vichy experience and the Jewish exodus from the Maghreb [. . .] during decolonization' (2006: xi–xii). Hubert Haddad is a contemporary 'Franco-Maghrebi' writer who sits at the intersection between Holocaust memory, the Israeli–Palestinian conflict and North Africa as a French Jew.[11] He was born in Tunisia the year before Israel was founded as a nation-state in 1948, to an Algerian-Jewish mother with French citizenship and a Tunisian father of Judeo-Berber heritage. The family immigrated to Paris a few years later, in the aftermath of the Shoah. Haddad is best known for his prize-winning novel *Palestine* (2007), which explores Arab–Jewish identity and the Israeli–Palestinian conflict. He has also played a key role in reviving the short story genre in France. His collection of short stories *Vent printanier* (2010) is particularly striking. In an interview, Haddad speaks of his motivation for writing the title short story:

> Près de l'ex-camp de Drancy, [. . .] il y a une petite gare, l'ancienne gare de Bobigny, d'où partaient les trains pour Auschwitz. Chaque année les officiels y font une commémoration en mémoire des déportés [. . .]. Il y avait un campement de Roms près de la gare, sur les terrains vagues. La police est venue détruire tout ce camp et chasser les bohémiens, parce que ça faisait vilain dans le décor. Comment peut-on commémorer la déportation des Juifs, aussi des Roms, en chassant brutalement ces derniers? Ce petit fait-divers tout à fait absurde m'a inspiré la nouvelle-titre ('Vent printanier' était le nom de code de la rafle du Vel d'hiv, en 1942).
>
> *(Haddad quoted in Vince 2017: 7)*

In this way, the title short story 'Vent printanier' can be seen as a commemorative, inclusive and corrective gesture of cultural memory. In 'Vent printanier' Haddad narrates a fictional encounter between a Jewish Holocaust survivor called Michaï and a Roma child called Nicolaï, whose camp has been destroyed to make way for the commemorations of the *Vel' d'hiv* round-up of French Jews. Michaï himself escaped the infamous round-up in 1942, only to be later denounced by a French 'bigote pesteuse' (27), leading to his internment at Drancy, followed by the infamous journey from Bobigny train station to the gates of Auschwitz-Birkenau. It is thanks to a group of Roma children that Michaï escapes an almost certain death, as an SS guard finds him in the wrong queue to the gas chambers. Wearing the Jewish star of David as opposed to the brown triangle worn by Roma victims of Nazi persecution, Michaï is sent back to join the other Jewish children who are to meet the same fate, but manages to flee the camp with other fugitives (29–31). In the modern-day encounter between Michaï, a Jewish Holocaust survivor, and Nicolaï, a contemporary victim of expulsion, a connection is made not only through common albeit distinct suffering in the past and present but also through redemptive joint creativity, as they combine Yiddish and tzigane music to bring life to 'la Cité de la Muette' with the fiddle and accordion (34). Through this short story, Haddad demonstrates the potential for 'differentiating solidarity' between diverse victims of persecution in France, both in terms of 'multidirectional memory' and present-day reality (see Rothberg 2009: 309, 2011: 525), challenging the view that French Jews are inward-looking or obsessed with the past. Fictional texts of (Jewish) cultural memory like this one are all the more significant in the light of Marine Le Pen's denial of French involvement in the Holocaust, and Macron's controversial decision to invite Israeli prime minister Benjamin Netanyahu to the 75th anniversary of the *Vel' d'hiv* round-ups in Paris.

Psychoanalyst Philippe Grimbert is among the second generation of French Jews who survived the Holocaust. His autobiographical novel *Un Secret* (2004), which won the Prix Goncourt des Lycéens, narrates the tale of Philippe, whose half-brother Simon died in the Holocaust before he was born (see Hand 2012). *Un Secret* can be seen as a work of postmemory, and indeed is identified as such by Marianne Hirsch who coined the term (see 2012: 272). 'Postmemory,' by Hirsch's definition, refers to that which 'characterises the experience of those who grow up dominated by narratives that preceded their birth, whose own belated stories are evacuated by the stories of the previous generation shaped by traumatic events that can be neither understood nor recreated' (1997: 22). Thus, Philippe Grimbert can be seen as an 'agent of postmemory' in that he gives 'narrative shape to the surviving fragments of an irretrievable past' (Hirsch 1996: 666). Mathieu Almaric, himself a French Jew of Polish descent, plays the lead role in the film adaptation, *Un Secret* (2007), directed by French Jewish film director Claude Miller. Interestingly, French Sephardi singer and actor Patrick Bruel, born Patrick Benguigui in Algeria to parents of Judeo-Berber origins, plays the role of Philippe Grimbert's father, a French Ashkenazi Jew of Polish origins.

While referring in the first instance to the Shoah, and the children of Holocaust survivors in particular, the postmemory framework can be extended to other traumatic memories transmitted across generations. Indeed, Esther Benbassa speaks of the 'trauma' of the departure of Jews from North Africa to France, which she argues is interpreted today as 'expulsion' and projected onto the Israeli–Palestinian conflict by the second generation of Maghrebi Jews in France, who live with the postmemory of exile from North Africa (2007a: 190). Benbassa was born in Turkey in 1950, grew up in Israel, and later immigrated to France. She founded the Centre Alberto-Benveniste d'études sépharades et d'histoire socioculturelle des Juifs in 2002, and received the Seligmann Prize against racism, intolerance and injustice in 2007. Benbassa has written extensively on Jewish history, culture and identity (with a particularly focus on Sephardi Jews), as well as on the Israeli–Palestinian conflict and Jewish–Muslim relations in France. In her controversial book *La Souffrance comme identité* (2008), she argues that Jewish identity is too often defined by suffering, which she claims has become 'une religion civile' amongst Jews (this is particularly ironic in the context of *laïcité* in France) and carries the risk of exclusive victimhood as collective self-definition (see Attias and Benbassa [2001] 2002: 275). Throughout her work, Benbassa advocates an ethical alternative by which French Jews see themselves as part of a larger 'travail de mémoire' (as opposed to 'devoir de mémoire') in which 'nos mémoires singulières s'entrelacent dans notre commune histoire d'hommes et de femmes' (2007b: 252). She argues that 'le devoir de mémoire n'aide pas à se projeter dans l'avenir, il est plutôt fermeture sur le passé' (2007b: 250). Instead, she calls for political engagement in the present, through combating discrimination in France as it appears in various forms (anti-Semitism, Islamophobia, racism, sexism, homophobia), in an act of differentiating solidarity. In this way, she follows in the footsteps of the recently deceased (in 2017) French political icon Simone Veil, a Jewish Holocaust survivor and the first elected female president of the European Parliament, who fought against anti-Semitism and racism, and promoted women's rights in general and those of Algerian female prisoners and rape victims in particular. Veil served as the founding president of the Fondation pour la Mémoire de la Shoah from 2000 to 2007, and was elected to the Académie française in 2008. She was voted by the French to be the most admired woman in the world in 2015, and was buried in Paris' Panthéon mausoleum by popular demand following her death in 2017.

Benbassa writes that the cultural identity of the Sephardi Jew entered national consciousness through the comedy film trilogy *La Vérité si je mens!* (1997, 2001, 2012).[12] The first film, which sets the scene for the following two, narrates the story of an unemployed French non-Jew who is mistaken for a Jew and welcomed into a Sephardi community, entering the world of Shabbat dinners, bar mitzvahs, ketubahs and overall chutzpah of the Mediterranean variety. Ironically, the lead role is played by Richard Anconina, who is in fact a French Jew of Moroccan origin, and Bruno Solo, who plays one of his Sephardi Jewish friends is himself not Jewish. This did not prevent Solo from being the victim of anti-Semitic aggression in 2014 after having appeared in all three films in a Jewish role and having openly declared his disapproval of French comedian Dieudonné's anti-Semitic rhetoric.[13] The second film in the trilogy sees French-Moroccan comedian Gad Elmaleh, perhaps the best-known Sephardi Jew in France, take on the role of the notorious sleaze Dov, played by Vincent Elbaz (also of Moroccan descent) in the other two films. Taking inspiration from American Jewish comedian Jerry Seinfeld,[14] and following in the footsteps of French Sephardi comedians Michel Boujenah, Patrick Timsit, Élie Semoun and Eli Kakou, Gad Elmaleh is at the forefront of stand-up comedy in France and has appeared in dozens of films. Although Sephardi, he played the role of real-life Ashkenazi Jew Schmuel Weismann, the father of a Polish Jewish family, in *La Rafle* (2010), which deals with the *Vel' d'hiv* round-ups of 1942.[15] Elmaleh has also taken on several non-Jewish roles, including that of a gypsy in the tragicomedy *Train de vie* (1998), which includes a scene combining gypsy folk with klezmer music, finding its echo in the aforementioned short story by Hubert Haddad. Born to a Jewish family in Morocco, Elmaleh moved to Canada to study in the late 1980s before immigrating to France, where he established himself as an actor and comedian. Gad Elmaleh was awarded the Chevalier dans l'ordre des arts et des lettres in 2006, and was voted the 'funniest man of the year' by TF1 viewers in 2007. He often features alongside French-Moroccan Muslim Jamal Debbouze, in a way reminiscent of the comedy double-act Élie et Dieudonné in the 1990s before the latter took an anti-Semitic turn, subsequently losing the respect of Elmaleh and Debbouze among other French comedians. A new duo has emerged in recent years, performing at Marrakech des Rires and Jamel Comedy Club[16] which goes under the name Younes et Bambi, and performs a set entitled 'un Juif et un Arabe,' demonstrating the power of comedy to build bridges between different minority groups in France by addressing taboos and taking apart stereotypes.

Conclusions

To conclude, contrary to how they may be viewed in French society or in the media, French Jews are not inward-looking and homogeneous but outward-looking and diverse. Moreover, whether being Jewish in France means tradition, religion, culture, memory or any combination of these, it is not in contradiction with French nationality. Problems ensue when French citizens *de confession israélite* to use a now archaic phrase, are confused with Zionists or even Israelis, who are wrongly perceived to be made up of Jews only, when in reality these include both Muslim and Christian Arabs alongside Druze and Armenians (see Attias and Benbassa [2001] 2002: 189, 193). It is not enough that Jews are protected by the state in France; indeed the French government can at times be dangerously interventionist or even instrumentalist. Rather it is necessary to acknowledge and encourage the continuation of on-the-ground and bottom-up initiatives, including interfaith dialogue, collaborative cultural activities, joint anti-racism and anti-Semitism organisations like Licra and SOS Racisme, academic research resulting in accessible resources like *Juifs et musulmans: retissons les liens!* from the Centre national de recherche scientifique (CNRS) and the like. Moreover, it is important for cultural activity initiated by French Jews, whether this take the form of film, comedy, music or literature, to have a wide-reaching audience of viewers, listeners and readers. Collaboration on cultural projects between Jews and other minority groups in France serves to debunk myths and challenge stereotypes, leading to greater understanding and opportunities for dialogue. Esther Benbassa and Jean-Christophe Attias ask the provocative question: 'les Juifs ont-ils un avenir?' ('Do the Jews have a future?') ([2001] 2002: 248). With regard to French Jews, it is first important to note that they have a past, overshadowed certainly but also varied and rich, from emancipation to the present day. Then it must be acknowledged that they continue to contribute to French society on a political, societal, and (trans)cultural level in the present, in spite of continued anti-Semitism manifested in various ways. And, finally, it is important to remain optimistic. Yes, French Jews have a future. Whether they choose to spend it in France, Israel, or elsewhere is for each individual to decide.

Notes

1 The 14th October 1991 saw the introduction of decree number 91–1051 which added to the Loi informatique et libertés (1978), stating that the collection of information on political activities, philosophical, religious or union beliefs was prohibited by the French state.
2 Here we must also remember the Eastern European Jews, who were the primary targets of the Nazi Holocaust as it unravelled in France during the Vichy regime.

3 Between 1 January and 30 June 2004, 135 anti-Semitic acts were listed, as opposed to 127 in 2003. Dominique de Villepin, the then-minister of internal affairs, confirmed 160 aggressions or degradations for the first seven months of the year 2004, as opposed to 75 over the same period in 2003. The anti-Semitic acts dropped by 48% in the first part of 2005, in comparison with the same period one year before: 290 in 2005 against 561 in 2004, which is probably partly an effect of the government's policy against anti-Semitism. It is important to note that nobody is able to register the number of acts of violence against Arabs and black populations in the country. See Benbassa (2007a: 191–192).

4 See 'Le départ des juifs de France vers l'Israel a doublé en 2014,' in *L'Express*, 2 January 2015. www. lexpress.fr/actualite/societe/le-depart-des-juifs-de-france-vers-israel-a-double-en-2014_1636938. html [Accessed: 01.12.2017].

5 The Dreyfus Affair was a series of events surrounding the Jewish captain Alfred Dreyfus who was falsely convicted of passing military secrets to the Germans. The events sparked a great deal of public interest and inspired Émile Zola to write his famous 'J'accuse' article. For more information on the Dreyfus Affair, see Malinovich (2008: 22, 26–29, 35).

6 In *Bagatelles pour un massacre*, an anti-Jewish pamphlet published by Louis-Ferdinand Céline in 1937, Céline asks his readers, 'avez-vous idée du rythme de l'invasion juive à Paris?' and then cites the figures of how many Jews had entered France in recent years (141).

7 See for example the chapter by Aurélien Mondon in the present volume (Chapter 1).

8 It is interesting to note that Lassana Bathily, despite being awarded French citizenship after his brave actions at the Hypercacher, was not awarded the Legion d'honneur. It is also worth noting that all the victims of the attacks mentioned in this chapter (including Ilan Halimi) were buried in Israel in the Givat Shaul cemetery.

9 A call to reject the law was published in the newspaper *Libération* on 13 December 2005.

10 See for example the chapter by Chris Reynolds in the present volume (Chapter 11).

11 A Jew born in Algeria with French citizenship (excluding the Vichy period), before later immigrating to France, philosopher Jacques Derrida famously spoke of himself as a 'Franco-Maghrébin' revealing 'un trouble de l'identité' (1996: 32).

12 See Attias and Benbassa ([2001] 2002: 120). Attias reminds us that '[l]es Juifs de *La vérité si je mens* sont des Juifs, pas tous les Juifs.' The male-dominated *Vérité si je mens* trilogy found its female counterpart in *Comme t'y es belle* (2006), which depicts four Sephardi Jewish female friends in Paris who negotiate relationships, motherhood and what it means to be Jewish in twenty-first-century France.

13 See 'Bruno Solo agressé suite à ses propos sur Dieudonné,' in *Le Figaro*, 22 July 2014. www.lefigaro. fr/culture/2014/07/22/03004-20140722ARTFIG00047-bruno-solo-agresse-suite-a-ses-propos-sur-dieudonne.php [Accessed: 14.08.2017].

14 In July 2017, the two comedians featured alongside one another at a one-night-only show in Montreal.

15 The film was heralded by Simone Veil and Jacques Chirac, who in 1995 had acknowledged French collaboration with the Nazis for the first time in an official statement regarding the *Vel' d'hiv* round-ups.

16 Founded in 2011 by Jamel Debbouze, this annual comedy festival is screened on French television station M6. Jamel Comedy Club is a comedy show, featuring established and emerging stand-up comedians, produced by Jamel Debbouze which began in 2006 and is screened on French television station Canal +. In 2008, Debbouze founded the Parisian theatre Comedy Club.

References

Attias, J-C. and E. Benbassa. (2001) 2002. *Les Juifs ont-ils un avenir?* Paris: Hachette.

Benbassa, E. 2002. *Histoire des Juifs sépharades*. Paris: Seuil.

Benbassa, E. 2007a. Jewish-Moslem relations in contemporary France. In *Contemporary French and Francophone Studies*, 11:2, 189–194. doi: 10.1080/17409290701248849.

Benbassa, E. 2007b. *La Souffrance comme identité*. Paris: Fayard.

Céline, L-F. 1937. *Bagatelles Pour un Massacre*. Paris: Editions Denoël.

Deleersnijder, H. 2001. *L'Affaire du point de détail: effet médiatique et enjeux de mémoire*. Liège: Editions de l'Université de Liege.

Derrida, J. 1996. *Le Monolinguisme de l'autre ou la prothèse d'origine*. Paris: Galilée.

The Guardian. 2017. Marine Le Pen denies French role in wartime roundup of Paris Jews. 9 April. Available at: www.theguardian.com/world/2017/apr/09/marine-le-pen-denies-french-role-wartime-roundup-paris-jews [Accessed: 01.12.2017].

Halimi, R. and E. Frèche. 2009. *24 Jours: La vérité sur la mort d'Ilan Halimi*. Paris: Broché.

Hand, S. 2012. Never tell: dynamics of secrecy in Philippe Grimbert's *Un secret*. In *French Studies*, 66, 208–221. doi: 10.1093/fs/knr268.

Hendler, S. 2015. Who in France will shout 'I am a Jew? In *Haaretz*, 11 January. Available at: www.haaretz.com/opinion/.premium-1.636386 [Accessed: 01.12.2017].

Hirsch, M. 1996. Past lives: postmemories in exile. In *Poetics Today*, 17, 659–686. doi: 10.2307/1773218.

Hirsch, M. 1997. *Family Frames: Photography, Narrative, and Postmemory*. Cambridge, MA: Harvard University Press.

Hirsch, M. 2012. *Generation of Postmemory: Writing and Visual Culture after the Holocaust*. Columbia: Columbia University Press.

L'Express and Agence France-Press. 2015. Le départ des juifs de France vers l'Israel a doublé en 2014. In *L'Express*, 2 January. Available at: www.lexpress.fr/actulalite/societe/le-depart-des-juifs-de-france-vers-israel-a-double-en-2014_1636938.html [Accessed: 01.12.2017].

Le Figaro. 2014. Bruno Solo agressé suite à ses propos sur Dieudonné. In *Le Figaro*, 22 July. Available at: www.lefigaro.fr/culture/2014/07/22/03004-20140722ARTFIG00047-bruno-solo-agresse-suite-a-ses-propos-sur-dieudonne.php [Accessed: 01.12.2017].

Malinovich, N. 2008. *French and Jewish: Culture and the Politics of Identity in Early Twentieth-Century France*. Oxford and Portland, OR: Littman Library of Jewish Civilization.

Nolden, T. 2006. *In Lieu of Memory: Contemporary Jewish Writing in France*. Syracuse: Syracuse University Press.

Rothberg, M. 2009. *Multidirectional Memory: Remembering the Holocaust in the Age of Decolonization*. Stanford: Stanford University Press.

Rothberg, M. 2011. From Gaza to Warsaw: mapping multidirectional memory. In *Criticism*, 53, 523–548. doi: 10.1353/crt.2011.0032.

Vince, R. 2017. 'L'humain n'a pas de frontière': an interview with Hubert Haddad. In *Bulletin of the Society for Francophone Postcolonial Studies*, 8.1, 2–11.

Vincour, N. 2013. In Toulouse suburb, 'scooter killer' is 'one of us.' In *Reuters*, 20 March. Available at: www.reuters.com/article/us-france-shootings-neighbourhood-idUSBRE82T14X20120330 [Accessed: 01.12.2017].

Willsher, K. 2006. Brutal murder was anti-Semitic crime says Sarkozy. In *The Guardian*, 22 February. Available at: www.theguardian.com/world/2006/feb/22/france.mainsection [Accessed: 01.12.2017].

SELECT BIBLIOGRAPHY

On modern and contemporary France in general

Drake, H. 2011. *Contemporary France*. Basingstoke: Palgrave Macmillan.
Howarth, D., D. Lees, C. Reynolds and G.Varouxakis. 2019. *Contemporary France*. London: Routledge.
Kedward, R. 2007. *La Vie en bleu: France and the French since 1900*. London: Penguin.
Sowerwine, C. 2018. *France since 1870: Culture, Politics and Society*. London: Palgrave Macmillan.

On recent French elections, recent French presidents, the political system in France and political parties in modern and contemporary France

Bell, D. and J. Gaffney. (Eds.). 2013. *The Presidents of the French Fifth Republic*. Basingstoke: Palgrave Macmillan.
Cautrés, B. and A. Muxel. (Eds.). 2011. *The New Voter in Western Europe: France and Beyond*. New York: Palgrave Macmillan.
Cole, A. 2005. *French Politics and Society*. Harlow: Pearson Longman.
Cole, A. 2013. Sarkozy's political leadership and the institutions of the Fifth Republic. In G. Raymond (Ed.), *The Sarkozy Presidency: Breaking the Mould?* Basingstoke: Palgrave Macmillan, 56–78.
Evans, J. and G. Ivaldi. 2013. *The 2012 French Presidential Elections: The Inevitable Alternation*. Basingstoke: Palgrave Macmillan.
Evans, J. and G. Ivaldi. 2017. An atypical 'honeymoon' election? Contextual and strategic opportunities in the 2017 French legislative race. In *French Politics*, 15:3, 322–339.
Evans, J. and G. Ivaldi. 2018. *The 2017 French Presidential Elections. A Political Reformation?* London: Palgrave Macmillan.
Gaffney, J. 2010. *Political Leadership in France. From Charles de Gaulle to Nicolas Sarkozy*. London: Palgrave Macmillan.
Hewlett, N. 2011. *The Sarkozy Phenomenon*. Exeter: Imprint Academic.
Kuhn, R. (Ed.). 2017. Special Issue on the 2017 French presidential and legislative elections. In *Modern and Contemporary France*, 25:4.
Pasquier, R. 2015. *Regional Governance and Power in France: The Dynamics of Political Space*. London: Palgrave Macmillan.
Raymond, G. (Ed.). 2013. *The Sarkozy Presidency: Breaking the Mould?* Basingstoke: Palgrave Macmillan.

On the far right in France

Alduy, C. and S. Wahnich. 2015. *Marine Le Pen prise aux mots: Décryptage du nouveau discours frontiste*. Paris: Seuil.
Girard, V. 2017. *Le vote FN au village. Trajectoires de ménages populaires du périurbain*. Bellecombe-en-Bauges: Le Croquant.

Mayer, N. 2013. From Jean-Marie to Marine Le Pen: Electoral Change on the Far Right. In *Parliamentary Affairs*, 66:1, 160–178.

Mondon, A. 2013. *A Populist Hegemony? The Mainstreaming of the Extreme Right in France and Australia*. London: Ashgate.

Mondon, A. 2015. Populism, the people and the illusion of democracy – the Front National and UKIP in a comparative context. In *French Politics*, 13:2, 141–156.

Mondon, A. 2017. Limiting democratic horizons to a nationalist reaction: populism, the radical right and the working class. In *Javnost/The Public: Journal of the European Institute for Communication and Culture*, 24:3, 355–374.

Perrineau, P. 2014. *La France au Front: Essai sur l'avenir du FN*. Paris: Fayard.

Shields, J. G. 2007. *The Extreme Right in France: From Pétain to Le Pen*. London: Routledge.

On the left and far left in France

Bell, D. and B. Criddle. 1989. The decline of the French communist party. In *British Journal of Political Science*, 19:4, 515–536.

Bell, D. and B. Criddle. 2014. *Exceptional Socialists: The Case of the French Socialist Party*. London: Palgrave Macmillan.

Gaffney, J. 2015. *France in the Hollande Presidency: The Unhappy Republic*. London: Palgrave Macmillan.

Hanley, D. 2017. Left and Centre-Left in France – endgame or renewal? In *Parliamentary Affairs*. doi: 10.1093/pa/gsx042.

On French foreign policy

Chafer, T. 2014. Hollande and Africa policy. In *Modern and Contemporary France*, 22:4, 513–531.

Chafer, T. 2016a. France in Mali: towards a new Africa strategy? In *International Journal of Francophone Studies*, 19:2, 119–141.

Chafer, T. 2016b. The French military in Africa: successes, challenges ahead? In *Rethinking Francophone Africa* blog. Available at: http://francophone.port.ac.uk/?p=1051 [Accessed: 21.04.2016].

Chafer, T. and A. Keese. (Eds.). 2013. *Francophone Africa at Fifty*. Manchester and New York: Manchester University Press.

Charbonneau, B. 2008. *France and the New Imperialism: Security Policy in Sub-Saharan Africa*. Aldershot: Ashgate.

Conklin, A. L., S. Fishman and R. Zaretsky. 2015. *France and its Empire since 1870*, 2nd edition. New York: Oxford University Press.

Smith, S. 2010. *Voyage en postcolonie: Le Nouveau Monde franco-africain*. Paris: Grasset.

On gender in modern and contemporary France

Allwood, G. and K. Wadia. 2009. *Gender and Policy in France*. Basingstoke: Palgrave Macmillan.

Allwood, G. and K. Wadia. 2010. *Refugee Women in Britain and France*. Manchester: Manchester University Press.

Amara, F. and S. Zappi. 2003. *Ni Putes Ni Soumises*. Paris: La Découverte.

Bantegni, G., Y. Benahmed Daho, J. Sorman, S. Vincent. 2007. *14 femmes: Pour un féminisme pragmatique*. Paris: Gallimard.

Bousquet, D., R. Sénac, M-P. Badre and M. Berthy. 2017. *Quel partage du pouvoir entre les femmes et les hommes élu.e.s au niveau local?* Paris: Haut Conseil à l'Egalité entre les Femmes et les Hommes.

Edwards, N. 2016. *Voicing Voluntary Childlessness: Narratives of Non-Mothering in French*. Oxford: Peter Lang, Coll. "Studies in Contemporary Women's Writing, Vol. 3."

Fayard, N. 2013. Bodies matter: the materiality of rape in twenty-first century France. In M. Allison and I. Long (Eds.), *Women Matter/Femmes Matière*. Oxford: Peter Lang, 35–51.

Joly, D. and K. Wadia. 2017. *Muslim Women and Power: Political and Civic Engagement in West European Societies*. London: Palgrave Macmillan. doi: 10.1057/978-1-137-48062-0.

Jordan, S. 2018. *Private Lives, Public Display: Intimacy and Excess in French Women's Self-Narrative Experiment*. Liverpool: Liverpool University Press.

Lépinard, E. 2013. For women only? Gender quotas and intersectionality in France. In *Politics and Gender*, 9, 276–298.

Murray, R. 2016. The political representation of ethnic minority women in France. In *Parliamentary Affairs*, 69, 586–602. doi: 10.1093/pa/gsv064.

On protest movements, on 'la rue' and on the responses to the Charlie Hebdo attacks

Ancelovici, M. 2011. In search of lost radicalism: the hot autumn of 2010 and the transformation of labor contention in France. In *French Politics, Culture and Society*, 29:3, 121–139.

Artières, P. and M. Zancarini-Fournel. (Eds.). 2008. *68, une histoire collective (1962–1981)*. Paris: La Découverte.

Chabal, E. 2015. *A Divided Republic: Nations, State and Citizenship in Contemporary France*. Cambridge: Cambridge University Press.

Damamme, D., B. Gobille, F. Matonti and B. Pudal. (Eds.). 2013. *Mai-Juin 68*. Ivry: Éditions de l'Atelier.

Davis, O. (Ed.). 2018. Special issue: the anti-police of May '68 fifty years on. In *Modern and Contemporary France*, 26:2.

Gobille, B. 2009. *Mai 68*. Paris: La Découverte.

Gordon, D. 2012. *Immigrants and Intellectuals: May '68 and The Rise of Anti-Racism in France*. London: Merlin Press.

Jackson, J., A-L. Milne and J. Williams. (Eds.). 2011. *May '68: Rethinking France's Last Revolution*. Basingstoke: Palgrave Macmillan.

Lindvall, J. 2011. The political foundations of trust and distrust: reforms and protests in France. In *West European Politics*, 34:2, 296–316.

Mathieu, L. 2011. *La démocratie protestataire*. Paris: Presses de Sciences Po.

Reynolds, C. 2011. *Memories of May '68: France's Convenient Consensus*. Cardiff: University of Wales Press.

Reynolds, C. 2014. *Sous les pavés .... The Troubles: Northern Ireland, France and the European Collective Memory of 1968*. Bern: Peter Lang.

Reynolds, C. 2018. From mai-juin '68 to Nuit Debout: shifting perspectives on France's anti-police. In *Modern and Contemporary France*, 26:2, 145–163.

Titley, G., D. Freedman, G. Khiabany and A. Mondon. (Eds.). 2017. *After Charlie Hebdo: Terror, Racism and Free Speech*. London: Zed Books.

Todd, E. 2015. *Qui est Charlie? Sociologie d'une crise religieuse*. Paris: Seuil.

Zagato, A. (Ed.). 2015. *The event of Charlie Hebdo*. New York: Berghahn.

On racism and anti-racism in France

Badinter, E. et al. 2009. *Le retour de la race: contre les 'statistiques ethniques.'* Paris: Éditions de l'Aube.

Khiari, S. 2006. *Pour une politique de la racaille*. Paris: Textuel.

Lentin, A. 2004. *Racism & Anti-racism in Europe*. London: Pluto Press.

Martin, T. 2015. SOS Racisme and the legacies of colonialism 2005–2009: an ambivalent relationship. In *Modern and Contemporary France*, 25:1, 65–80.

On immigration and integration, on life in the banlieues, on representations of the banlieues and of immigrants

About, I. and V. Denis. 2010. *Histoire de l'identification des personnes*. Paris: La Découverte.

Chaumont, F. 2009. *Homo-Ghetto: Gays et Lesbiennes Dans Les Cités: Les Clandestins de La République*. Paris: Le Cherche Midi.

Hajjat, A. 2012. *Les frontières de l' "identité nationale."* Paris: La Découverte.

Hajjat, A. 2013. *La Marche pour l'égalité et contre le racisme*. Paris: Éditions Amsterdam.

Higbee, W. 2007. Re-presenting the urban periphery: Maghreb-French filmmaking and the *banlieue* film. In *Cinéaste*, Winter, 38–43.

Horvath, C. 2016. Écrire la banlieue dans les années 2000–2015. In B. Wallon (Ed.), *Banlieues vues d'ailleurs*. *Les Essentiels d'Hermès*. Paris: CNRS Editions, 47–68.

Marlière, E. 2011. *Les Jeunes et la discothèque: Entre fêtes urbaines et violences ritualisées*. Paris: Editions du Cygne.
Obertone, L. 2013. *La France Orange Mécanique*. Paris: Ring.
Shepard, T. 2017. *Sex, France, and Arab Men, 1962–1979*. Chicago and London: University of Chicago Press.
Tarr, C. 2005. *Reframing Difference: Beur and banlieue filmmaking in France*. Manchester: Manchester University Press.
Tissot, S. 2007. *L'État et les quartiers*. Paris: Seuil.
Truong, F. 2013. *Des capuches et des hommes: Trajectoires de 'jeunes de banlieues.'* Paris: Buchet-Chastel.
Truong, F. 2015. *Jeunesses françaises: Bac+ 5 made in banlieue*. Paris: La Découverte.
Turpin, B. 2012. *Discours et sémiotisation de l'espace: Les représentations de la banlieue et de sa jeunesse*. Paris: L'Harmattan.
Weil, P. 2005. *La France et ses étrangers*. Paris: Gallimard.
Weil, P. 2008. *How to be French? Nationality in the Making since 1789*. Durham, NC: Duke University Press.

On Islam and Islamophobia in France

Ali, Z. 2012. *Féminismes islamiques*. Paris: La Fabrique Éditions.
Dakhlia, J. and B. Vincent. (Eds.). 2011. *Les Musulmans dans l'histoire de l'Europe*. Paris: Albin Michel.
Göle, N. 2015. *Musulmans au quotidien. Une enquête européenne sur les controverses autour de l'islam*. Paris: La Découverte.
Hajjat, A. and M. Mohammed. 2013. *Islamophobie*. Paris: La Découverte.
Liogier, R. 2012. *Le mythe de l'islamisation: essai sur une obsession collective*. Paris: Seuil.
Mondon, A. and A. Winter. 2017. Articulations of Islamophobia: from the extreme to the mainstream? In *Ethnic and Racial Studies*, 40:13, 2151–2179.
Tévanian, P. 2013. *La haine de la religion*. Paris: La Découverte.

On gypsies and travelling communities

Demossier, M. 2014. Sarkozy and Roma: performing securitization. In C. Frois, M. Maguire and N. Zurawski (Eds.), *The Anthropology of Security: Perspectives from the Frontline of Policing Counter-Terrorism and Border Control*. London: Pluto Press.
Liégeois, J-P. 2009. *Roms et Tsiganes*. Paris: La Découverte, Coll. "Repères Sociologie."
Nacu, A. 2012. From silent marginality to spotlight scapegoating? A brief case study of French policy towards the Roma. In *Journal of Ethnic and Migration Studies*, 38:8, 1323–1328.

On Judaism, Jewish culture and anti-Semitism in France

Attias, J-C. and E. Benbassa. (2001) 2002. *Les Juifs ont-ils un avenir?* Paris: Hachette.
Benbassa, E. 2002. *Histoire des Juifs sépharades*. Paris: Seuil.
Benbassa, E. 2007. Jewish-Moslem relations in contemporary France. In *Contemporary French and Francophone Studies*, 11:2, 189–194. doi: 10.1080/17409290701248849.
Nolden, T. 2006. *In Lieu of Memory: Contemporary Jewish Writing in France*. Syracuse: Syracuse University Press.

On youth movements and youth experiences in France, including rural France

Bessière, C., I. Bruneau and G. Laferté. 2014. Les agriculteurs dans la France contemporaine. In *Sociétés Contemporaines*, 96, 5–25.
Bruneau, I., G. Laferté, J. Mischi and N. Renahy. (Eds.). 2018. *Mondes ruraux et classes sociales*. Paris: EHESS, 'En temps & lieux.'
Chamboredon, J. 2015. *Jeunesse et classes sociales*. Paris: Editions Rue d'Ulm/Presses de l'ENS.
Renahy, N. 2005. *Les gars du coin. Enquête sur une jeunesse rurale*. Paris: La Découverte.

On French cultural policy

Ahearne, J. 2002. *French Cultural Policy Debates: A Reader*. London: Routledge.
Ahearne, J. 2014. *Government through Culture and the Contemporary French Right*. London: Palgrave Macmillan.
Benhamou, F. 2015. *Politique culturelle, fin de partie ou nouvelle saison?* Paris: La Documentation française.
Clement, C. 2003. *La Nuit et l'été: rapport sur la culture à la télévision*. Paris: Seuil/La Documentation française.
De Baecque, A. 2008. *Crises dans la culture française*. Paris: Bayard.
Poirrier, P. (Ed.). 2006. *Art et pouvoir. De 1848 à nos jours*. Paris: Cndp.
Poirrier, P. 2016a. *Les politiques de la culture en France*. Paris: La Documentation française.
Poirrier, P. (Ed.). 2016b. *Politiques et pratiques de la culture*. Paris: La Documentation française.

On the French media (including television and popular music)

Albert, P. and N. Sonnac. 2014. *La presse française*. Paris: La documentation française.
Dauncey, H. and C. Tinker. 2014. Popular music nostalgia. In Volume! La revue des musiques populaires, 11:1, 8–17.
De Rochegonde, A. and R. Sénéjoux. 2017. *Médias: Les nouveaux empires*. Paris: First.
Eck, H. 2003. Médias audiovisuels et intellectuel. In M. Leymarie and J. F. Sirinelli (Eds.), *L'histoire des intellectuels aujourd'hui*. Paris: PUF, 201–225.
Kuhn, R. 2011. *The Media in Contemporary France*. London: Open University Press.
Lebrun, B. 2009. *Protest Music in France: Production, Identity and Audiences*. Farnham and Burlington, VT: Ashgate.
Scales, R. P. 2016. *Radio and the Politics of Sound in Interwar France, 1921–1939*. Cambridge: Cambridge University Press.
Sieffert, D. and M. Soudais. 2012. *Mélenchon et les médias*. Paris: Politis.
Tinker, C. 2015. The RFM party 80 and here and now tours: 1980s pop nostalgia in the French and British Press. In *Modern and Contemporary France*, 23:2, 163–177.

On memory and commemoration in France

Cassin, B. 2013. *La Nostalgie. Quand donc est-on chez soi?* Paris: Editions Autrement.
Nora, P. (Ed.). 2008. *Lieux de Memoire*. Paris, Gallimard.
Purseigle, P. 2008. A very French debate: the 1914–1918 'war culture.' In *Journal of War and Culture Studies*, 1:1, 9–14.
Rousso, H. 1987. *Le Syndrome de Vichy*. Paris: Seuil.
Sallois, J. 2008. *Les musées de France*. Paris: Presses universitaires de France.

On intellectuals in France

Ahearne, J. 2010. *Intellectuals, Culture and Public Policy in France: Approaches from the Left*. Liverpool: Liverpool University Press.
Benda, J. 2009. *The Treason of the Intellectuals*. Translated by R. Aldington. Piscataway, NJ: Transactions publishers.
Hazareesingh, S. 2015. *How the French Think: An Affectionate Portrait of an Intellectual People*. London: Penguin.
Tho, T. and G. Bianco. (Eds.). 2013. *Badiou and the Philosophers: Interrogating 1960s French Philosophy*. London: Bloomsbury.
Traverso, E. 2013. *Où sont passés les intellectuels? Conversation avec Régis Meyran*. Paris: Éditions Textuel.
Zarka, Y. C. 2015. *La Destitution des intellectuels*. Paris: PUF.

INDEX

Printed in the United States
by Baker & Taylor Publisher Services